Military Space-A Air Basic Training

& Reader Trip Reports

by

William "Roy" Crawford, Sr., Ph.D.
President, Military Marketing Services, Inc.
and Military Living Publications

and

L. Ann Crawford, Executive Vice-President,
Military Marketing Services, Inc.
and Publisher, Military Living Publications

Executive Vice-President - Marketing
R.J. Crawford

Vice-President - Editorial - J.J. Caddell

Editor - J.J. Caddell

Project Editor - Deborah K. Harder

Cover Design - Lynn Olinger

Military Living Publications
P.O. Box 2347
Falls Church, Virginia 22042-0347
TEL: (703) 237-0203
FAX: (703) 237-2233
E-mail: militaryliving@aol.com
Website: www.militaryliving.com

Printed in Canada

◁ S0-DVD-674

Library of Congress Cataloging-in-Publication Data

Crawford, William Roy, 1932-
    Military space-A air basic training and reader trip reports / by William Roy Crawford
and L. Ann Crawford.
        p. cm.
    Rev. ed of: Military living's military Space-A air basic training and reader trip reports /
L. Ann Crawford, William Roy Crawford.
    Includes index.
    ISBN 0-914862-89-8
    1. United States--Armed Forces--Transportation. 2. Air travel. 3. Soldiers--United
States--Recreation. 4. Military dependents--United States--Recreation. I. Crawford, Ann
Caddell. II. Crawford, Ann Caddell. Military living's military Space-A air basic training
and reader trip reports. III. Title.

UC333 .C7253 2000
358.4'4--dc21

                                                                            00-031891

Contents

Section II: An Imaginary Space-A Air Trip by CONUS Medical Evacuation (MEDEVAC) Flight

Section III: National Guard and Reserve Personnel Eligible for Space-A Air Travel

APPENDICES

Space-A Helpers

In addition to *Military Living Space-A Air Basic Training*, the following Military Living publications can help make your Space-A air travel more successful!

Military Space-A Air Opportunities Around the World

An advanced book on military Space-A air travel. It provides information on the military air terminals of all services, phone, fax and e-mail addresses, where available. Tentative schedules give you the routings of the military flights. This book can save you thousands of dollars on your next trip.

Military Space-A Air Opportunities Air Route Map

A new and unique planning guide for Space-A air travel with a graphic presentation of all worldwide Air Mobility Command routes.

This new map employs Military Living's Multi-Route Graphic Techniques.™

It includes international station locations, as well as important addresses, phone, fax and e-mail info, where available.

New, easier-to-use size - a hip-pocket guide to Space-A air travel.

You can save thousands of dollars using this powerful Space-A air travel planning tool!

INTRODUCTION

If you have never flown Space-A or if you have not flown Space-A recently, *Military Space-A Air Basic Training and Reader Trip Reports* has important information to help make your next trip successful. The new Space-A rules are entirely different from previous years.

The privilege of flying Space-A on U.S. military aircraft has saved literally millions of military and their family members a great deal of money. More importantly, however, is that this unique privilege has enabled military and their families to take morale-boosting trips that they could not have afforded otherwise.

Have you and your family joined in on the fun? *Military Space-A Air Basic Training and Reader Trip Reports* will give you the information you need to get started "traveling on less per day . . . the military way!™"

In surveys, military ID card holders (active, guard/reserve and retired) have responded that Space-A air travel is one of the privileges that they value most because it gives the military member and his/her family an immediate cash-saving benefit in addition to the immeasurable value of being a part of the military family.

Space-A air travel is also important to retirees, giving them a continued sense of camaraderie and recognition for their service to their country.

HOW SPACE-A AIR TRAVEL HAS CHANGED IN RECENT YEARS

The Space-A travel booking ($10.00) fee has been eliminated, thanks to General Colin Powell USA, (Ret.) and General Ronald R. Fogleman, USAF, (Ret.) and their staff. General Fogleman, while commander of AMC, did everything possible to help uniformed service personnel have a simpler and easier Space-A system. His staff diligently worked on new initiatives which are now a huge success. Subsequent AMC commanders have continued to improve Space-A air opportunities.

Space-A regulations have changed dramatically in the last few years for the better; many of the bureaucratic procedures have been eliminated. Here are just a few of the changes that you will learn about in *Military Space-A Air Basic Training and Reader Trip Reports*:

In the early years of Space-A travel, potential passengers had to show up at every flight call or be removed from the list. Later, passengers did not have to show up for every flight, but they had to revalidate their records every 15 days (in person) to indicate they still wanted to fly Space-A.

Sponsors from one place in the country had to make their way to a military air passenger terminal (sometimes across the

USA) to sign up for a flight from a given location. Sometimes, the passenger would go back to his/her home base and wait while their names made their way up the list and then travel back to the air terminal again hoping they would get a flight. Often, the cost involved in this procedure obliterated any savings on the actual flight. All of that has now changed so that a greatly improved system of sign-up is now in place.

Those wishing to fly Space-A no longer have to appear at the departure terminal to sign up; they can now do this by fax, e-mail or letter. The new fax numbers and some e-mail, as available, are included in this book. This remote sign-up capability levels the Space-A playing field so that Space-A passengers are treated more fairly in having an opportunity to fly.

For those who still prefer to sign up for a military Space-A trip in person, a self-service sign-up procedure, which is easy to access, is still available in most cases.

A one-time sign-up prcedure allows Space-A passengers to keep their original date of being added to the Space-A passenger roster at the originating terminal. If one mission terminates, the Space-A passenger may sign up for a new flight using the original date. Details on this one-time sign-up are in this book.

All of the previous Military Airlift Command (MAC) and the major portions of the Strategic Air Command (SAC) have merged into a highly efficient Air Mobility Command (AMC). Especially good news for Space-A passengers is that the AMC now has a wide variety of aircraft, including tankers. While the former MAC was very user-friendly to Space-A passengers, SAC was not as well organized to serve them. Now, AMC has applied Space-A regulations on a uniform basis. Many tanker locations have moved to other Air Force bases (many in the heartland of the country) bringing Space-A air travel to new places not previously served by such aircraft. Tankers remain a favorite with Space-A passengers because of the opportunity to observe actual refueling of other aircraft. There is a special and unique excitement to tanker missions.

Attitudes have improved toward Space-A passengers. While many terminal staff members and aircraft crews have been helpful in the past, it appears that there is a new emphasis on courtesy and helpfulness from the very "top" to the "bottom."

Luggage allowances have been increased to 140 pounds per passenger with two bags not weighing more than 70 pounds each. Even so, remember there are no porters in the middle of an airfield where passengers often debark! Smart Space-A ravelers travel as light as possible. Golf clubs or other sporting gear can travel as checked baggage.

Another reason to travel light is that by doing so, if an opportunity arises for you to get Space-A on an "executive" aircraft, the luggage allowed is only 30 pounds.

On AMC flights returning from overseas, Space-A passengers who are eligible family members may now fly with their sponsor to the final destination of a military flight within the United States; they no longer have to deplane at the first stop. Conversely, family members may take flights with their sponsor which make an interim stop within the United States on a mission which continues overseas. Also, active duty families which are Command Sponsored Overseas may now fly to CONUS and in overseas theaters without their sponsors.

In-flight meals have been changed to a healthy heart variety and breakfast menus have been added. The meals are very reasonable in cost, and we have heard many good comments about them from Space-A passengers.

The wearing of the military uniform by active duty when traveling on a Space-A basis has been eliminated. All service members and their accompanying family members must be in clean clothes. No open-toed sandals or t-shirts with slogans or vulgar language are allowed.

Eligible passengers who are handicapped will now find AMC to be a lot more helpful than in previous years.

Passengers will find many improved terminals due to extensive ongoing renovation projects. Many terminals are now brighter and much more comfortable. "No smoking" rules now apply to all DoD and DoT aircraft missions.

Now that AMC has made all of these improvements, those who have a desire to fly Space-A should learn the rules and customs of flying Space-A in order to be knowledgeable about how this wonderful system operates. Most importantly this knowledge will aid in eliminating any "fear of flying." This book, *Military Space-A Air Basic Training and Reader Trip Reports*, will give you the information you need to have successful Space-A air travel flights on U.S. military aircraft.

Once you have familiarized yourself with the basic information, you may want to delve into our other publications to truly become a "Space-A Expert." Military Living currently has three other publications to help you do just that. Our worldwide, all ranks military travel newsletter, Military Living's *R&R Travel News®,* will keep you informed on the latest rules, improvements, locations of new opportunities and more. The reader trip reports in the *R&R Travel News®* (worldwide military travel newsletter) are invaluable and form the nucleus of a powerful reader clearinghouse of information.

Military Living also publishes an advanced book on Space-A air travel which gives locations of Space-A opportunities and schedules: *Military Space-A Air Opportunities Around the World*. In addition, Military Living has its popular map, *Military Space-A Air Opportunities Air Route Map*. Check at your military exchange to purchase these helpful publications. Not only will you save money by doing so, exchange profits are recycled back into the military community for their recreation programs. If not available, you may, of course, order them directly from Military Living. Phone orders are accepted with Visa, MasterCard, American Express or Discover. Please call **703-237-0203** or see our website **www.militaryliving.com** for information on how to order directly from your online Exchange at substantial savings. An order form also appears in the back of the book.

On behalf of military families all over the world, Military Living would like to thank the Air Mobility Command (AMC) for all they have done to improve the life of military ID card holders. Thanks guys and gals for letting uniformed services personnel and their families tag along on your missions.

You'll never really know how many hearts have been healed by a visit home, how many elderly parents and other family members have given thanks that their loved one could come home for a visit by Space-A, especially emergency leave travel, how many marriages may have been saved when military members serving apart have had reunions by AMC and other service organizations' Space-A flights or even how military families have become better educated by being able to travel to far-off lands and view countries first-hand. Families flying together form unique bonds and have a favorable impression of military life.

AMC's service to those who have also served is a part of military life which makes the bad days be evened out by the good days. **We know how important AMC personnel are because our readers have told us.** AMC would like to hear from you directly. You may pick up AMC form #253, Air Passenger Comments, at any AMC air passenger terminal or write to: **HQ AMC DOJP, 402 Scott Drive, Unit 3A1, Scott AFB, IL 62225-5302.** Thanks again! Happy Travels!

Ann, Roy Sr & RJ Crawford

NOTICE

Contrary to rumor, unaccompanied family members living in the U.S. or another location CANNOT fly Space-A to join or visit their sponsors in another location. If this rule changes, we will publish the info in Military Living's *R&R Travel News®*. See our Appendix N for info on EML travel for those stationed/assigned overseas on an accompanied tour.

BACKGROUND

The air cargo and passenger capabilities of all the Military Services were greatly expanded during World War II. These capabilities have been maintained since that time to support our worldwide peacekeeping military forces, diplomatic missions, unilateral, multinational and international obligations and commitments. A uniform policy for the administration of this much sought-after air travel benefit was established by the newly created Department of Defense (DoD) in 1947, and communicated through Department of Defense Directive (DoDD): Chapters 1 (portions) and 6, DoD Directive 4515.13-R, Air Transportation Eligibility, November 1994, as amended.

This directive ensures that Space-A air travel priorities and procedures are equitably administered for all of the seven Uniformed Services (U.S. Army, U.S. Navy, U.S. Marine Corps, U.S. Air Force (in DoD), U.S. Coast Guard (Department of Transportation), U.S. Public Health Service (Department of Health and Human Resources) and the National Oceanic and Atmospheric Administration (Department of Commerce)).

WHAT IS SPACE-AVAILABLE (SPACE-A) AIR TRAVEL?

SPACE-A: The term Space-A is used in the military community to mean many things. Space-A is used to describe the use of or access to facilities and transportation of the military services, after all known, required and authorized use and access has been satisfied. The term Space-A is primarily used to describe the availability of air passenger travel to Uniformed Services members (active, Cadets of the Service Academies, Reservist, ROTC, NUPOC, CEC and retired), active and retired dependents and eligible DoD and other civilian employees when they are stationed overseas. (See Eligible Passengers, DoDD 4515.13-R, Paragraphs 2-B, 6-C and Table 6-1: Eligible Space-A travelers, priorities, and approved geographical travel segments.)

Space-A is also used to describe travel on military trains (discontinued in Germany in 1991), buses, temporary military lodging or use of military recreational facilities which are available after all required official duty and other authorized uses have been satisfied. Space-A on military ships was discontinued during the Vietnam era.

The DoD has described Space-A air travel as a "by-product" of the DoD's primary mission, which is the movement of space-required military cargo and passengers. This means that space not required for the movement of official cargo and passengers can be used for the worldwide travel of Uniformed Services members and their dependents on flights with overseas destinations. (Dependents are not allowed to travel point-to-point in the 48 contiguous United States (CONUS), exceptions for dependents traveling with their sponsor on emergency leave and house-hunting trips.)

SPACE-A AIR TRAVEL STUDY AND TRAINING

SPACE-A AIR BASIC TRAINING: Members of all of the seven Uniformed Services undergo elementary or basic training. If you hope to save thousands of dollars on air fares, you too will need some basic training or at least a refresher course because policies, procedures and techniques of Space-A air travel are constantly changing. If you have never availed yourself of this highly sought-after benefit of Space-A air travel or if you have several Space-A trips under your belt, you can learn a great deal from this **"primer"/book.** This book can save you a great deal of money in your air travels.

This *Military Space-A Air Basic Training and Reader Trip Reports* book will be kept simple. We are using a "step-by-step" approach which will cover, by example, all of the essential elements of Space-A air travel. We will also repeat key points to reinforce your training. This basic training will give you all the information that you will need to plan and successfully complete a typical Space-A air trip. We recommend that you, as the sponsor, study *Military Space-A Air Basic Training and Reader Trip Reports* and that each dependent family member traveling with you study along in order to sweep away some of the mystery and unknown about Space-A air travel. The information in this book will instill confidence in military members and their families while traveling Space-A.

SECTION I

AN IMAGINARY OVERSEAS (FOREIGN COUNTRY) MILITARY SPACE-A AIR TRIP WITH THE FAMILY

TRIP PLANNING

A TYPICAL OVERSEAS SPACE-A AIR TRIP: For the purpose of *Military Space-A Air Basic Training and Reader Trip Reports,* this typical Space-A air trip is made by a sponsor (active or retired), his/her dependent spouse, and two dependent children up to 21 years of age (or 23 years of age if a full-time college student with a valid military dependent ID card (DD Form - 1173 or 2765). NOTE: The sponsor may take some or all of his/her eligible family members (dependents).

Some readers may prefer the term "family members" to "dependents" (we will discuss the documents required for Space-A travel later), but "dependents" is a necessary legal term in regard to the Space-A air travel regulation which must be met for Space-A air travel. (The DoD Office of General Counsel has ruled that the use of "dependent" may be avoided, except to the extent necessary to satisfy explicit statutory requirements regarding entitlement to benefits and/or privileges.)

The typical trip begins on the East Coast of the Continental United States (CONUS) and continues to Western Europe and returns to CONUS; or it begins on the West Coast of CONUS and continues to the Western Pacific and returns to CONUS. A full description of worldwide major scheduled Space-A air routes is in Appendix V.

There are other typical variations, such as trips to the Middle East, Africa, the Caribbean, Central and South America, the South Pacific (Australia/New Zealand), Alaska and Hawaii, Japan, Korea and other stations in the Far East. We cannot cover all possible alternatives in the limited space of this book. We have covered all of the major Space-A air routes. The most popular Space-A air trip is from East Coast CONUS to Western Europe and return. This is largely because Western Europe remains the number one foreign-country travel destination for United States overseas travelers. We have selected this trip but with slight adjustments. You can adapt this same scenario to your own travel needs.

Hang on—here we go on an imaginary Space-A air adventure from the East Coast of CONUS to Western Europe and return.

PLANNING YOUR SPACE-A TRIP: Your most important task to ensure success of your voyage is **Pre-Trip Planning.** Most Space-A travelers have selected a destination or destinations for a variety of reasons which are clear, logical and rational for the travelers. Based on our scenario, we are going to Western Europe. Let's get more specific: What is our prime and most desired destination in Western Europe? We want to make the central Rhein River area of Germany our base of operation.

First we should consult Military Living's *Military Space-A Air Opportunities Air Route Map* (Military Living's SPA Map), which, along with its many other essential information features, is a prime route planning guide. This Space-A map is indispensable to both the basic and advanced Space-A air traveler. It shows you, in graphic multi-color design, the scheduled air routes around the world. Because most air flights originate in the CONUS, this world map is centered on the continents of North and South America. From this air route map we can see that the best destinations in the Central German Rhein River area are Ramstein AB (RMS/ETAR), Germany, and Rhein-Main AB (FRF/EDAF), Germany. (Rhein-Main AB is scheduled to close by 2005.)

These three and four character letters/symbols are the Federal Aviation Administration (FAA) Location Identifiers (LI) (three letter) and the International Civil Aviation Organization (ICAO) location identifiers (four letters), which are fully explained in Appendix E. The popular FAA three character location identifiers are being replaced or supplemented more frequently by the ICAO four letter identifier for international stations (airports) in order to improve the positive identification of all stations worldwide. Many cities now have more than one airport and some have multiple international airports. Also, military airports are located in and near major cites worldwide and thus easily confused with other airports. We will list these identifiers after each location/destination when it is first mentioned in order to reinforce the identifiers in your mind. You will find that these identifiers are indispensable to your understanding of basic Space-A air travel.

We also note that we can depart from a variety of East Coast stations (north to south): McGuire AFB (WRI/KWRI), NJ, Baltimore/Washington IAP (BWI/KBWI), MD, Dover AFB (DOV/KDOV), DE, Andrews AFB (ADW/KADW), MD, Norfolk NAS (NGU/KNGU), VA and Charleston AFB/IAP (CHS/KCHS), SC. With accompanying dependents, we are required to depart from a station which will provide our dependents air travel on the same mission and aircraft to a destination outside of CONUS. There are some stations which have this capability but to keep this initial work simple, we will concentrate on stations which have departures from the East Coast area and flights going outside of CONUS en route to their next station.

The key question at this point in our trip planning is from which CONUS East Coast locations can we depart in order to reach our desired destination in Germany? The Location Identifiers and Cross-Reference Index, in the back (page-183) of Military Living's *Military Space-A Air Opportunities Around the World* book, also gives departure locations (other than the East Coast) for reaching the central German Rhein River area. As you can see from Military Living's *Military Space-A Air Opportunities Air Route Map* and *Military Space-A Air Opportunities Around the World* book, there are more opportunities in terms of the number of flights to our destination from Dover AFB, DE, or from McGuire AFB, NJ, than the other departure locations.

Do not rule out these other departure locations because they all have potential for flights to our selected destination. In fact, as you will see later, armed with a Space-A tip from Military Living Publications, we are going to register or apply for Space-A travel from at least three of the above listed departure locations/stations in order to increase our chances of selection for a Space-A flight. The Dover AFB, DE, departure location is feasible for us since we live in the Mid-Atlantic states area (Falls Church, VA, only seven miles from Washington, D.C.). *Please note: The Location Identifiers and Cross-Reference Index, (near the back of the book, in *Military Space-A Air Opportunities Around the World*) gives other departure locations for reaching the Central German Rhein River area.

BACKUP PLANS: If making this trip is very important to you, you will want to have backup plans to ensure that you reach your goal or destination and return within your desired time frame. You cannot rely on DoD for this assurance. As the DoD Space-A directive says: "DoD cannot guarantee seats to Space-A passengers and is not obligated to continue travel or return Space-A passengers to the original point of travel" (DoD 4515.13R, Chapter 6, Par A-9).

If you must return by a specific date, you may want to purchase backup commercial tickets. The commercial tickets will assure that you will be able to return within your desired time frame. If you do not use the tickets, there is a cancellation fee of $50-$300 or even up to a $100% penalty (at the time we went to press.) For example, if you purchase tickets to fly from Washington, D.C. to Germany and return and you do not use the tickets, a cancellation fee would be charged. The terms and conditions of commercial air travel tickets change frequently as marketplace supply and demand, among other factors, change. Even with this cancellation fee, the savings of flying Space-A is far more than the cost of flying round trip commercially. If you are a gambler, you can wait and buy a ticket from a discount consolidator one way back to the U.S. for about 25 percent less than a round trip tourist class ticket from the East Coast to Germany and return. If you wait until one-two hours before flight time these tickets are much cheaper, sometimes as cheap as $100 one way.

Unlike military Space-A travel, dependents/family members using commercial airlines may fly without their sponsor accompanying them. Another advantage of making commercial back-up plans is that you do have a reserved seat on a flight heading for a definite location. If you have left your car at a particular base or airport, or if you need to return to CONUS by a certain date, you can rest easy. Commercial backup assures you that you can return to your point of departure in a timely fashion. Also, should you fall in love with a place and want to stay an extra day, week, month or even up to a year of the date of purchase of the tickets, you can do so with commercial backup tickets. You will need to call the airline involved and see if a seat is available on the day you wish to travel.

Military air fares may be available (situation changes with market conditions) from most major cities throughout the United States to Germany. The tickets are usually good for one year from the date of purchase. Be sure and ask about this, travel "blackout" days or days that you cannot travel with your particular restricted ticket and other restrictions when buying a ticket. Rules are subject to change and may vary from airline to airline.

In Military Living's *R&R Travel News®,* we often have one or more travel agency sponsors who are knowledgeable in locating a military fare in their computers, and who will work with you in the event you need a backup ticket. Some agents do not want to work with anyone attempting to fly Space-A part or all of the way. Armed Services Vacations, a sponsor of Military Living

Publications, has agreed to work with our military readers to help them utilize a combination of military Space-A and commercial travel. The matter of using backup tickets can be complicated. We advise you to talk this out with the travel agent listed below to make sure you know the pluses and minuses. For information on backup tickets, please call Godfrey Crowe, Colonel USA (Ret) at (703) 836-1100 or toll free 1-800-833-4382. Godfrey may also be reached by mail at Armed Services Vacations, a Division of MacNair Travel Management, 1703 Duke Street, Alexandria, VA 22314. We hope that you will reward our sponsor with any other travel business you may have, as there is not a substantial profit in issuing backup tickets which may well be canceled! NOTE: These tickets are not available for some destinations.

In addition, if in attempting to return home by Space-A you find yourself in a tight spot overseas, you can check with the base travel office provided by various contractors who have ticket facilities on many U.S. military installations overseas. Some of our readers have reported that they were able to buy discounted one-way tickets from other commercial ticket agents located in or near the military air passenger terminals. We have heard that the closer you get to departure time the cheaper the remaining tickets become!

This backup travel arrangement does not use your Space-A air travel benefit, but it may save you untold money if you cannot for some reason use your Space-A privilege to meet your travel needs.

PRE-FLIGHT

REGISTRATION/SIGN-IN AT TERMINAL (STATION/ AERIAL PORT): As the sponsor or lead traveler of a group, you must register at the Space-A passenger departure or service center at each station from which you seek to depart on your Space-A trip. Registration can be made via fax, e-mail, mail/courier or in person. Registration times may be limited at some terminals/stations due to manpower limitations and demonstrated need. Please check Military Living's *Military Space-A Air Opportunities Around the World* book and reconfirm registration times with the terminals from which you plan to register for Space-A air travel. NOTE: In most cases faxes and e-mail may be transmitted 24 hours daily. If a fax or e-mail means of communication is not available to you, try your local service center, i.e., Kinko's. (**Save the proof of fax and carry it with you when you report for travel, just in case your fax has been lost. Most terminal personnel will accept this proof of sign-up.**)

SPONSOR or LEAD TRAVELER REGISTRATION: The sponsor or lead traveler of a group may register for dependents and other persons who are traveling with them by sending a fax, e-mail, letter/courier application or by presenting all required documents when registering in person. If registering for Space-A travel via fax, e-mail, letter or military/commercial courier, the sponsor must provide the following: Active Duty - application and service leave or pass form, a statement that border clearance documents are current and a list of five countries (or four countries plus all/any country), overseas destinations or CONUS. **See AMC, SPACE AVAILABLE TRAVEL REQUEST, Form 140, Feb. 95, Appendix D** (We also have this form as a pull-out in the back of the book). We recommend that you take all documents of each traveler in your party when registering in person including each traveler's Uniformed Services ID card. There may be some inconvenience, but play it safe. Take the ID cards because one terminal may sign up your dependents without your showing their cards, but the other terminals may not!

DOCUMENTS: For our trip the following documents will be required: DD Form 2 (green) U.S. Armed Forces Identification Card (active), or Form 2 NOAA (green) Uniform Services Identification and Privilege Card (active), or PHS Form 1866-3 (green) United States Public Health Service Identification Card (active) for the active duty sponsor or DD Form 2 (gray or blue) Armed Forces Identification Card (retired) for the retired sponsor; Uniformed Services Identification & Privilege Card, DD Form 1173 for all dependents accompanying active duty & retired Uniformed Services members; passports for accompanying dependents and retired sponsors (active duty for some destinations); and immunization records (recommended but not normally required). **NOTE: Reservist (DD Form 2 (red)) cannot currently fly to foreign countries but only to CONUS and U.S. Possessions overseas. Reservists may fly to foreign countries when they are retired at age 60 and receiving retired pay.** Watch *R&R Travel News®* for any change in this policy.

Visas must be obtained when required by the DoD Foreign Clearance Guides. See Appendix S, Visa and Personnel Entrance Requirements, or check with the Space-A desk at any DoD international departure location/station or Military Personnel Offices which issue international travel orders. Please note that these personnel entrance requirements to foreign countries may be different (usually more restrictive) if entering the foreign country via a U.S. military owned or contract aircraft. Visas are not required for Western European countries but most Eastern European countries require them. See Appendix S: Visa Information and Personnel Entrance Requirements.

Also, if you are active duty, you must have valid leave or pass orders in writing and be in a leave or pass status throughout the registration, waiting and travel periods. The DoD Space-A directive no longer requires that active duty personnel travel in the class A or B uniform of their service. At press time, the uniform is not required for active duty personnel.

APPLICATION FOR SPACE-A AIR TRAVEL: As an active or retired member of one of the seven Uniformed Services (U.S. Army, U.S. Navy, U.S. Marine Corps, U.S. Coast Guard, U.S. Public Health Service, U.S. Air Force, and National Oceanic and Atmospheric Administration), you can be the sponsor or lead traveler of a group as shown in our imaginary trip. You may apply for Space-A travel via fax, e-mail, letter/courier or in person to the Dover AFB, DE 19902-5501, Space-A desk/counter at Bldg 150, Passenger Terminal (new in 1998), 24 hours daily; telephone: Commercial (C) 302-677-4088, Defense Switched Network (D) 312-445-4088, Fax: C-302-677-2953, (D) 312-445-2953, E-mail: <spacea@dover.af.mil>, Recording: (updated 2000 hrs daily) C-302-677-2854, D-312-445-2854. From North Gate on US-13: follow Atlantic Avenue approximately 1.5 miles to Eagle Way. Make a left on Eagle Way then first right on Purple Heart Avenue. The Passenger Terminal and USO are located on left in building 150. Directions to almost 300 other terminals are listed in Military Living's *Military Space-A Air Opportunities Around the World* book.

Present your documentation and request an application for Space-A air travel. You will be given a **SPACE-AVAILABLE TRAVEL REQUEST,** also known as the **SPACE-A PASSENGER BOOKING CARD,** Air Mobility Command (AMC) Form 140, Feb 95, to complete. Please see a copy in Appendix D*. You will be allowed to specify a maximum of five countries as destinations. The fifth designation may be "ALL" to take advantage of airlift opportunities to other countries that may fit your plans. All destinations within a country are included in this definition, i.e., Germany, would include all destinations/stations in Germany. You will be assigned a category for your travel (based on the Space-A DoD directive). In our example, active duty (ordinary leave and pass) is Category III, retired is Category VI. Complete Categories, Travelers Status and Situation, approved geographic travel segments and important restrictions/limitations are presented in table format in Appendix A: Space-A Passenger Regulations.

Editors Note: Public law (14CFR Part 243) requires emergency next of kin information for all international airline passengers. As such, AMC is modifying their procedures for passenger process on AMC aircraft to comply with this law. All AMC passengers must provide their names, SSAN of all passengers including dependents. The SSAN will be used as a link to Defense Eligibility Enrollment Report System (DEERS) to positively identify the travelers and obtain next of kin notification information in the event of an emergency. (Other military departments must adopt similar procedures for international passengers.)

The DoD directive states, "The numerical order of Space-Available categories indicates the precedence of movement between categories, e.g., travelers in Category III move before travelers in Category IV. The order in which travelers are listed in a particular category within table 6-1, Appendix A, does not indicate priority of movement in each category. In each category, transportation is furnished on a "first-in, first-out basis" to all passengers in that category. This policy is implemented by establishing, at each station, a Space-A roster of categories of travelers arranged higher priority (category) for movement to lower priority (category) for movement by their registration/sign-in times/dates. The registration times/dates form the basis for movement of passengers within each category. There is a Space-A roster for each category, or in effect, a total of six Space-A rosters (maintained as one combined roster on the station computer systems). These times are recorded in Julian date and time format which is explained in Appendix F. This system allows registered Space-A persons to compete for seats within categories based on their date and time of registration.

The Space-A processing personnel will verify the information contained in your application, examine your identification and travel documents for validity, completeness and accuracy. If you are an active duty sponsor, you must be on leave when you apply for Space-A travel and your leave or pass orders will be stamped on the back with the terminal name and the Julian date and time at which you applied for Space-A air travel. This category of traveler (active duty on ordinary leave) must have a validated copy of the leave or pass document when he/she is processed for the Space-A trip. If the application for Space-A is made by fax or mail/courier, the leave or pass must be transmitted with the fax and will be effective no later than the date of the fax or receipt of the mail or courier Space-A Travel Request.

Your application for Space-A travel will be entered into a computer-based waiting list by priority category, Name and Social Security Account Number (SSAN), Julian date and time, and destination. Our application is entered for Colonel (0-6) Francis O. Hardknuckle, USA (Ret), SSAN-000-00-0000 and family for four seats, Category VI for the following maximum five countries which we have specified: Germany, Italy, Spain, United Kingdom and "ALL."

If you are active duty, your application is entered for four seats, Category III and for the same five countries. Whether or not you report for Space-A calls, your application will remain current in the computer for a maximum of 60 days or until the end of your leave or pass, whichever comes first. If you are retired, your application will remain current in the computer for a maximum of 60 days whether or not you report for Space-A calls.

You will compete for seats within your category based on the Julian date and time of your registration. Reservations for Space-A air travel will not be accepted as there is no guaranteed space for passengers in any category. If applying in person, as evidence of our application, we will be given a Space-A Travel Information slip (developed locally) which will contain, among other things, the five locations we have selected, our category, Julian date and time (accepted), leave expiration date (active duty only), sponsor's name, rank/grade, SSAN, number of seats required and the names and SSAN of each dependent traveler. The three dependents accompanying Colonel Hardknuckle are Elizabeth Ann Hardknuckle, spouse, SSAN 000-00-0000; Linda Sue Hardknuckle, daughter, SSAN 000-00-0000, age 22, full-time graduate student; and Loren A. Hardknuckle, daughter, SSAN-000-00-0000, age 20, full-time college student. We will need this information anytime we inquire about our application for Space-A air travel.

As we indicated earlier, in order to maximize our chances for obtaining Space-A air travel to our destination, we are also going to apply for Space-A air travel at several other convenient Space-A departure locations. Why take this action? Space-A seats are always a function of the number of perspective passengers waiting for a specific destination, the number of aircraft missions, the carrying capacity (available seats) on each mission and the time at which all of these variables converge. Sound complicated? Yes, but with so many unknown variables, your chances are improved if you apply for air travel in the Space-A system at four terminals/stations rather than one.

Through careful study of this text, you can better understand and use the Military Space-A air travel system. We suggest that you also apply for Space-A air travel at Andrews AFB (ADW/KADW), MD, Baltimore/ Washington IAP (BWI/KBWI), MD and McGuire AFB (WRI/KWRI), NJ. NOTE: Application at Baltimore/Washington IAP or McGuire AFB provides automatic application at both. You can send Space-A air travel request via faxes, e-mail or letters to these locations, apply in person, or there are several limo (micro-bus) transportation companies that service all of these stations for about $30-$35 for each leg of the journey. Please see Military Living's *Military Space-A Air Opportunities Around the World* book for complete information on ground transportation at each terminal/station. For the strong at heart, you could also apply at Norfolk NAS (NGU/KNGU), VA, to further improve your chances of obtaining a Space-A air trip to Western Europe.

REGISTRATION FOR RETURN TRAVEL: We are very optimistic that we will get our Space-A trip to Europe. In order to obtain an advance/early position on the Germany Space-A rosters for return travel, we fax our Space-A Travel Request, AMC Form 140, Feb 95 to both Ramstein AB (RMS/ETAR), DE, (C-011-49-6371-47-2364) and Rhein-Main AB (FRF/EDAF), DE, (C-011-49-69-699-6309).

TRAVEL DATES: In our planning we should establish approximate desired dates for departure. In addition to when active duty sponsors can obtain ordinary leave, we can establish an approximate departure date by examining several other pieces of information. First, check the Space-A backlog for the desired destinations at the departure terminals through the recording numbers or by telephoning the terminal personnel (for these numbers consult your copy of *Military Living's Military Space-A Air Opportunities Around the World* book or *Military Living's Military Space-A Air Opportunities Air Route Map*). The Dover AFB (DOV/KDOV), DE, passenger information numbers are C-302-677-4088, D-312-445-4088, Fax: C-302-677-2953, D-312-445-2953, Rec: C-302-677-2854, D-312-445-2854 (updated 2000 daily); e-mail: spacea@dover.af.mil. Also check the number and frequency of flights by consulting the above documents. You must decide how much of your leave time you want to use while waiting for your Space-A flight; if retired, your time is also valuable and waiting can cost you money which you could spend on your trip overseas.

TRAVEL READY: Note carefully! If you are in or near the passenger terminal and you report for each scheduled and non-scheduled flight departure, your chances of obtaining a Space-A flight to your desired destination are greatly improved. You have the right to "stand-by" for (wait and report yourself available for air travel) any flight that you believe you may have a reasonable opportunity on which to travel. In fact, you may stand-by for any flight regardless of your chances or circumstances.

Many prospective Space-A travelers call the various terminals through the recording number, if available, or speak with the passenger terminal personnel to determine their numerical position on the waiting list for their registered destination. They also check their travel category and traveler's status and situation on the waiting list as well as the waiting list of higher category personnel. They do not go to the terminal to wait for a flight until their names are near the top of the Space-A waiting list and there are one or more flights scheduled in the immediate future. This is a useful technique, but don't forget that there are flights of opportunity. If you are not in the passenger terminal and "travel ready" (discussed later), you won't fly. Also many people on the waiting list may not show up at all.

The passenger terminal will not call you or notify you of a flight. In fact, they are prohibited from doing so by regulations. As a personal note, Ann, our author/publisher, and Roy, Sr. were in the Travis AFB (SUU/KSUU), CA, passenger terminal recently. There were 600 plus Space-A applications for Hickam AFB (HIK/PHIK), HI, and after repeated announcements in the terminal there were only nine passengers who reported for the Space-A call and took the C-005B flight with 73 available Space-A seats to Hawaii. This Space-A air opportunity is repeated many times every day around the world. To wait or not to wait in the terminal, or nearby, to keep your finger on the pulse of activity should be your informed choice.

SPACE-A FLIGHT CALL/SELECTION PROCESS: If you make the decision to wait in the terminal, or at any time you report to the terminal for the purpose of standing-by for a prospective flight, you should be "travel ready." Travel ready simply means that you are ready and prepared to travel with very short notice. You have all of your required documentation, baggage, funds, and you are ready to report for a Space-A flight call/selection process and subsequent boarding. We have heard from many of our *R&R Travel News*® readers that they have missed a flight opportunity because they did not have enough time to return a rental car, move their baggage to the terminal or other essential chores. You must be travel ready in order to maximize your chances for flying as you have planned.

Whether you have been waiting in the terminal for a long time, or you have reported for a flight call based on information that a flight is scheduled for departure to your desired destination, the processing procedure is the same. Many Space-A passengers enter their selected departure terminal and are processed and boarded for their desired destination within an hour, if and only if, they are travel ready!

Space-A seats are normally identified as early as two to three hours or as late as 30 minutes prior to departure. The standard notice time (Space-A call) for International/Overseas Space-A flights is two hours. Due to security requirements the notice-time can be as much as three hours for some international/overseas flights. This is the same standard for international flights on commercial airlines. In fact, many commercial international flights now require up to three hours for processing. Always check with the passenger service center for the Space-A show time for the flight on which you expect to travel. Show time is the time that the Space-A Call/Selection begins and subsequent flight processing and boarding. Show time is important for the Space-A traveler because it not only means the time at which selection of registered Space-A prospective passengers begins, but you must now be present to answer when your (sponsor's) name (family/travel group) is called in your travel category (I-VI).

This Space-A traveler is "travel-ready!"

You will hear the announcement familiar to the seasoned Space-A traveler. The Space-A flight call: "Anyone desiring Space-A air transportation to a series of stations (e.g., Ramstein AB (RMS/ETAR), DE) please assemble at the Space-A desk" or other location in the terminal. This is a roll call of prospective Space-A travelers. The Space-A terminal flight pro-

Ready to make the Space-A roll call

cessing team will be armed with the latest printout of the station Space-A roster. (In fact, there is a Space-A roster for all categories by date/time of sign-up for ease in processing.) They will first call all the names of Category I: Emergency Leave Unfunded Travel, and process these travelers first. Next they will proceed to call travelers in each travel category (from highest priority to lowest priority) by earliest Julian date and time until they have filled all of the available seats for this flight.

The flight processing team knows the number of seats available and will select a sign-up Julian date and time near the middle of the register. They will ask if anyone has that date and time, or an earlier date and time, then work forward or move back to the top of the list as appropriate. It is important to remember that the number of seats your party requires is a factor in your selection. There must be sufficient seats for your party or the processors will move on and select someone with a later sign-up date who requires fewer seats. As you can see, single and couple travelers may have a better chance of selection for Space-A air travel.

FLIGHT PROCESSING

Let us assume that your party has been selected for Space-A air travel, and you are told to proceed immediately to flight processing (this may particularly be the case when the flight is non-scheduled). You must be travel ready when you report for the Space-A call. It is not uncommon to proceed immediately to flight processing after the end of the Space-A call. Also, you can be told to report back for flight processing at a later time. In our case, we are told to report immediately to the Space-A desk for processing.

SPACE-A PROCESSING FEE: You may have heard that Space-A is "free." This is true. The Space-A $10 processing fee was eliminated in early 1993 by the then Chairman of the Joint Chiefs of Staff, General Colin Powell, USA (Ret).

Please note that all passengers departing CONUS, Alaska and Hawaii on contract commercial aircraft must pay a $6 airport departure tax that goes toward airport improvements. Also, all Space-A passengers **departing on contract commercial missions (aircraft) from overseas to the United States** must pay a $12.40 Head Tax and an $11.00 Federal Inspection Fee, for a total of $23.40. Please note that all commercial airline passengers pay these taxes and fees in the price of their airline tickets.

PAYMENT OF FEES AND DOCUMENTS REVIEW: You must pay these fees in United States dollars or via your personal U.S. dollar check drawn on a U.S. Bank. No credit/debit cards, travelers checks or other payment instruments are accepted. These charges may be collected at the beginning or at other times in the flight processing.

IDENTIFICATION AND DOCUMENTS CHECK: The next action/step is an identification and travel documents check. The processing team will ensure that you have the following documents: appropriate ID cards for all travelers and that they are current; passports (signed) with required visas for active/retired service members and all dependents and that they are current and valid; leave or pass orders for active duty personnel which were effective at the time of initial registration by the terminal and will be in force until at least the end of the flight for which you have been selected.

We have not been asked to show our International Certificates of Vaccination and our Personal Health History, both as approved by the World Health Organization, Form: PHS-731 or similar (see Appendix L) for each passenger, but we have them as recommended for use as needed. At some point, the processing team will want to observe each passenger directly and verify their identity against their travel documents.

BAGGAGE PROCESSING: You will of course need to pack prudently, sparingly, lightly and appropriately for your planned activities and for the climate of Western Europe during the season in which you will be traveling. Northern Europe has approximately the same climate as U.S. New England except a bit cooler (average about 10 degrees Fahrenheit) with more moisture. Each person is authorized two pieces of checked baggage, and each piece must not exceed 62 linear inches (length + height + width = 62 inches) and not more than 70 pounds for a total of 140 pounds for both pieces (DoD 4515.13-R, Chapter 1, paragraph D, 2a through f). Family members and travel groups may pool their baggage allowances. A Baggage Identification Tag (DD Form 1839 or AMC Form 20) is available for use on your hand-carried bags/items. Baggage claim tag USAF Form 94 (or similar) will be attached to each bag checked and you will receive a stub copy. Sample copies are at Appendix J.

Active duty members on a PCS may take pets on commercial contract Patriot Flights. Space-A passengers, however, may NOT take pets by Space-A air travel. Sorry, Fido.

Space-A passengers may check oversized baggage (golf clubs, snow skis, folding bicycles, etc.) if it is the only piece to be checked (per person) and meets the weight requirement of 140 pounds total. Hand-carried baggage cannot exceed 45 linear inches (length + height + width = 45 inches) and must fit under the seat or in the overhead compartment if available. Space-A passengers cannot pay for baggage in excess of the allowed weight limit.

A few precautions: You cannot pack or carry weapons of any type (including cutting instruments), ammunition, explosive devices, chemicals, aerosol cans, matches or other incendiary devices. NOTE: There are amnesty containers at the entrance to most terminals or boarding areas where you may discard any prohibited items anonymously and without penalty. Also, you must remove the batteries from all electronic equipment in your checked baggage. You may keep the batteries in your checked baggage. At boarding time, you may be required to undergo an inspection of your hand-carried baggage or all of your baggage in some cases.

DRESS: Although the wearing of uniforms by active duty and Reservists is no longer required, every Space-A passenger must be appropriately dressed. For your comfort and safety you will want to dress with layers of clothes that can be added or removed as needed. Prohibited clothing items are open-toed sandals and shoes (on military aircraft), T-shirts and tanktops as outer garments, shorts and revealing clothing. Strictly prohibited as an outer garment are clothing with profane language and any attire depicting the desecration of the U.S. Flag. If in doubt, call your air terminal for specific information. You must use good conservative taste in your dress.

The Amnesty Box- where you can dispose of prohibited items before boarding.

IN-FLIGHT MEALS: Since the spring of 1988, AMC has developed and implemented a series of healthy heart menus for their flights. These meals are prepared in their own in-flight kitchens. Snack menus cost $1.90 and include sandwich, salad or vegetable, fruit, milk or soft drink. Breakfast menus cost $1.50 and include cereal or bagel, fruit, danish and milk or juice. Sandwich menus cost $3.00 and include sandwich, fruit, vegetable or salad, snack or dessert, milk, juice or soft drink. Expect in-flight meal prices to change each 1 October. Also, prices are not standard worldwide. We reserve the sandwich and breakfast menus since we will be departing in the early evening, 1930 hours local time and arriving approximately 0930 hours local time the next day in Germany. If you reserve one or more meals, the reserve meals will be entered on your **AMC BOARDING PASS/TICKET/RECEIPT, AMC FORM 148/2** (see Appendix I) or similar form, and your payment will be collected (cash or personal check). You may bring your own snacks aboard; however, you should check with the Air Passenger Terminal representative regarding any restrictions that may be in place due to Department of Agriculture regulations. Whole fruit is a good snack choice if there are no restrictions. No alcoholic beverages for consumption on military aircraft are allowed. Meals are free only on AMC commercial contract flights. Wine and beer are for sale only on AMC commercial contract flights. Specialized meals are made available for duty passengers only. You can request special food, and passenger service personnel will help if they can. If you need special food, we suggest that you bring your own in order to maintain flexibility. (See remarks above regarding snacks.)

Snacks and meals are available on most Space-A flights.

BOARDING PASS/TICKET RECEIPT: At this point, we have successfully passed the flight call/selection process. All of our travel documents have been reviewed and accepted for travel, we have registered for in-flight meals and paid the charge, we have checked our baggage and received our claim checks, we have not selected a smoking section, since smoking on all military aircraft flights (including both military and contract civilian flights) has been eliminated and lastly, we have been issued our Boarding Pass/Ticket Receipt which assigns our seats, verifies and documents the above items and **shows our one-time sign-up Julian date.**

Now we wait for our flight number and destination to be called for boarding. They are listed on our Boarding Pass and the Terminal Departure board as follows:

ROUTE	EQUIPMENT	DEPARTURE
A2R3D	C-005B	160/00/1830L (2330GMT)

ROUTING	ARRIVAL
KDOV-EGUN-ETAR-EGUN-KDOV	160/00/0930L (0830GMT)

Due to space limitations, we will not decipher the route numbers in this elementary text. The equipment is a C-005B, which is described in Appendix M. The departure date of 160 is Thursday, 08 June 2000, 1830 local time which is also 2330, in Greenwich Mean Time (GMT) (Greenwich, United Kingdom). See Appendices F and G for a detailed explanation of GMT. The routing is Dover AFB (DOV/KDOV), DE, from which we are departing, to RAF Mildenhall (MHZ/EGUN), GB, to Ramstein AB (RMS/ETAR), DE, where the mission turns around, and returns to RAF Mildenhall, GB and terminates at Dover AFB, DE. See Appendix E for explanation of location identifiers. Our arrival is 09 June 2000 at 0930 local time at Ramstein AB, DE, which is also 0830 GMT.

BUMPING: All Space-A travelers share a common fear that they will be "bumped." The bumping action means that after being manifested (accepted) at a departure location for transportation on a flight or at any station en route to your final destination, you are removed from the flight in order to have the mission essential accommodations for space required cargo and passengers.

NOTE: You cannot be bumped by another Space-A passenger except Category I, Emergency Leave Unfunded Travel personnel and then only with the direction of local authority. The good news is that if you are bumped, you are placed on the Space-A list at the location where you are bumped with the sign-up time, date and category that you received at your originating station. (This information is included on the manifest.) As a practical matter, bumping occurs infrequently because passenger service personnel take every action possible (reorganize cargo or move cargo to other flights), within appropriate regulations, to preclude bumping one or more Space-A passengers.

PARKING: Since we will be about three weeks on our trip, we will want to park our car in the long-term parking lots at Dover

AFB, DE. Long-term parking is in long term lots 1, 2, and 3, which are marked. Please ask the Space-A desk for directions or a map and procedures. The location is a short distance away (very near the passenger terminal) and the parking fee is approximately $5 per week. There is an honor system for payment: Lock the vehicle and keep the keys. Security police will patrol the parking lot often thereby providing security for your vehicle. This is another example of how wonderful it is to be a member of the Military Family. NOTE: Do not leave your car parked in the short-term lot. It will be impounded after 12 hours, and you will pay a towing fee and a fine to get your car back.

PASSENGER SECURITY SCREENING: Boarding has been announced as 1730 hours local time on Thursday. We will be flying directly/non-stop from Dover AFB, DE, to RAF Mildenhall, GB on a C005B Galaxy. Our scheduled departure time will be 1830 hours local time, and we are scheduled to arrive at RAF Mildenhall, GB at 0530 hours local time (also 0530 hours GMT) on Friday morning. A two hour ground time is scheduled at RAF Mildenhall with a departure of 0730 local time, one hour flying time to Ramstein AB, DE arriving at 0930 hours local time on Friday morning. Similar to commercial airlines, passengers are screened through electronic gates. Body searches may also be required. All carry-on baggage, briefcases, purses, packages, etc., are screened before you are allowed to enter the secure boarding area. This security is for everyone's protection.

BOARDING/GATES: Space-A boarding processes are similar to commercial airlines. There is only one passenger class, and with the exception of some sensible and conventional practices, all passengers are boarded alike. Families with infants and small children are boarded first, passengers requiring assistance are boarded next, then Distinguished Visitor/Very Important Persons (DV/VIP) passengers (Colonel USA, USMC, USAF; Captain USN, USCG, NOAA; Director USPHS) in pay grade O6+ and Senior Enlisted Personnel (Pay grade E-9) of the Military Services are boarded. Colonel (O6) Francis O. Hardknuckle, USA (Ret), is the ranking officer on today's flight, so our party will be boarded next. Our boarding is followed by a

Passengers line up to go through security screening and then to the aircraft.

general boarding of the remaining passengers. (NOTE: Some terminals may not follow the DV/VIP ranking officer boarding and deplaning procedures.)

GATES: There may be a few conventional and some not-so-conventional obstacles to overcome. Today we are flying a C-005B Galaxy aircraft. We leave the boarding gate and enter a "blue" Air Force bus for a short ride to the aircraft parked on the ramp near the terminal. Today, courtesy truck stairs are not available. These stairs, when available, will allow easy access to the

Passengers board a Navy C-009B.

second deck passenger compartment of the C-005B Galaxy aircraft. We are instructed to walk through the forward cargo door of the aircraft and up a cargo ramp to a point near the rear of the cargo compartment. There we will climb (not walk) up an almost vertical (approximately 18 feet), metal ladder with hand rails on both sides to the C-005B passenger flight deck. Female passengers should preferably wear slacks (more about travel dress later).

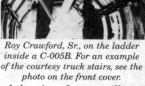

Roy Crawford, Sr., on the ladder inside a C-005B. For an example of the courtesy truck stairs, see the photo on the front cover.

The passenger processing team and the aircraft crew will provide you with assistance. Elderly people, mothers with infants in arms and people with physical handicaps may have difficulty in climbing the passenger ladder. Space-A regulations require, for safety considerations, however, that you must be capable of boarding and exiting the aircraft with limited assistance in boarding and deplaning by the AMC staff.

If you have a nonapparent handicap such as a hearing impairment, asthma, heart pacemaker, etc., please advise the passenger processing team at time of check-in. Frequently, the C-005B and similar aircraft will have mobile stairways (stair truck) for direct access to the passenger deck, but as indicated earlier, no stairs are available for today's flight departure. This is probably the most challenging boarding encounter that you will find in your Space-A travel experiences.

IN-FLIGHT

SEATING: The seats in these aircraft are conventional commercial airline seats; however, we immediately note that the seats face to the rear of the aircraft. This configuration is for safety purposes. The only difference you will notice from commercial airline seating, which faces forward, is a different sensation during takeoff and landing of the aircraft. Pillows, blankets, and other comfort items are available. We hope you have brought along your own reading or other amusement materials (games, non electronic) as there are no reading materials, inflight movies or music on military aircraft.

Inside the 2nd deck, passenger seating of a C005B is similar to commercial airline seating (shown above and right).

CLOTHING: Your clothing should be loose fitting and in layers. Wear comfortable walking shoes. Women should preferably wear slacks and a blouse or sweater. Take along a light jacket or coat depending upon the climate. Remember that western Europe is always a bit cooler with more moisture than the corresponding latitudes in North America. The layers of clothes will come in handy if you return, as a passenger not a patient, on a Medical Evacuation (MEDEVAC) flight where the temperatures are kept quite warm for the comfort of the patients.

RESTROOMS: The restrooms on the C-005B are adequate in number and are similar to commercial airlines. They are unisex and you are expected to keep them clean after your use.

CLIMATE CONTROL: As mentioned, the climate in the cabin is similar to that of commercial airlines. The temperature can vary and you have been given blankets to make your travel comfortable. If it gets too cold or warm, you may ask the cabin personnel to adjust the temperature. Like all large heavy lift aircraft there can be cold and hot spots on this aircraft. Whether or not your wishes are complied with may depend on the capabilities of the aircraft, the crew and other passengers' needs.

NOISE: This is not a noisy aircraft in the passenger cabin. You may experience some higher than normal levels of noise during takeoff, landing and special maneuvers and turns. At other times you should be most comfortable. There is no need for ear plugs on this flight (this is not true of some other flights, such as those aboard the C-130E aircraft). If you travel often on noisy aircraft, you should obtain form fitting ear plugs at your medical facility ear clinic. These plugs will improve your comfort and conserve your hearing. The crew may have wax, self-forming ear plugs. Ask for a set if you would be more comfortable.

SAFETY: You will be required to use your safety belts as instructed by the aircraft commander and/or cabin crew. Only walk about the aircraft when allowed to do so. Never tamper with controls, doors or equipment within the aircraft. Listen very carefully to the in-flight safety lecture given by the cabin crew members prior to takeoff. Pay particular attention to the location of exits and identify the exit which is most convenient to your seating. Become familiar with the location of your emergency oxygen supply and life preserver since most of this flight will be over water.

ELECTRONIC DEVICES: The playing and usage of radios, recorders, TVs, computers, etc., which may interfere with aircraft navigation, radar and radio systems is prohibited. As noted earlier, these items in your checked baggage must have the batteries removed.

SMOKING: Smoking is not allowed on United States military aircraft or military contract flights.

REFRESHMENTS: There is always self service fresh water, coffee and tea available in the galley. The meals we ordered will be served at the appropriate times given flight conditions. Our dinner sandwich meal will be served about an hour-and-a-half after departure and our breakfast meal will be served approximately one hour before our arrival.

Our flight departed as scheduled and all travel en route has been flawless. Further, we are told that we will be arriving at RAF Mildenhall, GB, as scheduled at 0530 Friday morning. While the aircraft is serviced, we deplane the aircraft and wait in the Special Category lounge (06+) which has lockers, TV, telephones (Commercial and DSN), restrooms, and over-stuffed seats. After about one and one half hours we re-board the aircraft to continue our journey to Germany. After about one hour of flying time, we arrive at Ramstein AB, DE. Wow! All this flying for "free."

POST-FLIGHT

ARRIVAL OF AIRCRAFT/CLEARANCE: We are notified that our flight will arrive on time. We are given immigration and customs forms to be completed for each passport and/or ID card holder. The flight attendants spray fumigation/insect repellent throughout the cabin as required by international health rule. After landing, our manifest and declaration of the health of the crew and passengers will be handed over to German immigration authorities or the United States authorities acting on their behalf. This is necessary to obtain clearance for the crew and passengers of our aircraft to disembark. Once clearance has been obtained, deplaning will begin as instructed.

DEPLANING: Prior to deplaning, we will be given instructions regarding post-flight processing such as immigration, baggage claim and Customs. We're fortunate today in that we'll be deplaning through passenger level doors onto a stair truck and a short 50-yard walk into the air passenger terminal at Ramstein AB, DE. Colonel (O6) Hardknuckle USA (Ret) is the ranking officer on our flight. He and his family will depart the aircraft first followed by a priority for deplaning designated by the flight cabin crew. In most cases, those families with children and other people in need of assistance during deplaning will be the last to exit. (NOTE: Some terminals may no longer follow the DV/VIP ranking officer boarding and deplaning procedures.)

The passenger services terminal at Ramstein AB, Germany

IMMIGRATION: Next we must report to the immigration processing station/desk, and present to the German/U.S. authorities our immigration/customs form and other travel documents. Sponsors will need their ID cards. Retired sponsors will also require a passport. Dependent family members will need their ID cards and passports. All passengers must be present for this processing to verify their identities. The authorities will examine your travel documents carefully. As part of the processing, they may also check for persons barred entry and other wanted persons. Passengers may be questioned about previous visits to Germany, the purpose of their visit, places to be visited and accommodations (place of residence) in the country.

We are delighted to find that all is in order for our family; our immigration forms and passports are stamped, and we are instructed to claim our baggage and report for customs clearance. We are lucky; our four bags are waiting for us on the carrousel. Colonel Hardknuckle has allowed us only one bag, that can be rolled or carried, per person. We move with ease to Customs Inspection.

CUSTOMS: The customs inspection is a breeze. We are not bringing any dutiable or prohibited items such as tobacco, coffee, tea, or alcoholic beverages into the country. Our customs documents are stamped, and we are now cleared to leave the terminal. Before we leave for our vacation, a very important task regarding our return Space-A trip should have our top attention.

REGISTRATION FOR RETURN SPACE-A AIR OPPORTUNITIES: We should verify our fax application for departure back to CONUS from Ramstein AB (RMS/ETAR), DE, if this is our planned return departure terminal (it is a good idea for the sponsor, with everyone's travel documents, to verify our application for return air transportation while other members fetch taxis or attend to other arrival chores). We can also apply at Rhein-Main AB, DE, or at any other terminal in Europe.

A special caution! If you apply to return to CONUS from any European terminal (i.e., Ramstein AB, DE), and subsequently take a local flight from Ramstein AB, DE, (for example, a visit to Aviano AB (AVB/LIPA), IT, your application for CONUS and any other applications from Ramstein AB, DE, will be deleted from the computer-based Space-A list. NOTE: Under the remote sign-up procedures Colonel Hardknuckle has signed up in advance by fax for his party's return air travel prior to arriving at Ramstein AB. This rule is in the Space-A DoDD and applies at any station worldwide. Once you depart on any flight from a station, all of your other applications for flights from that station are deleted from that station's Space-A roster system.

RETURN FLIGHT TO CONUS

As told by Linda Sue Hardknuckle, daughter: We took a local taxi at the terminal to the temporary lodging facility. We enjoyed dinner in the Officers' Club and a comfortable night in two adjacent rooms in the temporary military lodging (TML) facility, Bldg 305 Washington Avenue, C-011-49-6371-47-4920. We had signed up immediately upon arrival at Ramstein AB, DE, for flights to Italy and Spain in order to retain our Dover AFB, DE, initial registration time and travel priority. The priority can be retained and is effective for a trip which continues in the same general direction from CONUS. In this case, we are continuing southeast to Spain/Italy. The countries must be on our CONUS sign-up and if active duty, we must be on leave.

SIDE TRIPS: We took the early morning, 0535 hrs MARKL "White Swan" Shuttle Bus Service to Rhein-Main AB AMC Pax Term arrival at 0730 hrs. The cost is $20 each or 35 DM. The Ramstein AB passenger personnel told us that there was a flight to Rota NS (RTA/LERT), ES, with many open seats. We were fortunate to get this flight to Cadiz, Spain. On arrival we were careful to obtain a "Letter of Entrada and a Base Pass" from passenger service personnel before leaving the base to ensure our easy reentry. This is a Spanish NB where the USN is a tenant under our Status of Forces Agreement (SOFA) with Spain. We also signed up for a flight to Capodichino Airport (NAP/LIRN) in Naples, Italy, which we took after our four-day visit to the Cadiz area.

The passenger terminal at Rhein-Main AB, Germany.

The flight to Naples was aboard a C-130E aircraft with bucket seats along the side and cargo in the middle of the aircraft. The aircraft was very noisy, particularly on takeoff and landing/braking. The crew chief passed out shapeable wax ear plugs to decrease the noise. The ride was short, and it was a new and interesting experience. After two days of shopping in Naples, we departed Naples for Ramstein AB, DE, on a C-009E Nightingale aircraft, MEDEVAC flight, which was a special experience for my sister, Loren, who is studying nursing.

At Ramstein AB, DE, we checked our progress on the waiting list for CONUS. Our names had only moved up the Category VI waiting list from number 404 when signing up to number 314; however, our plan was to leave in approximately one more week's time, so we continued with our travel plans.

After a week visiting the Rhein and Mosel River areas via a major company rental car (Ramstein has Avis, Budget, Hertz, Powell's Auto, and Raule on base and in the village of Ramstein), we returned to Ramstein AB, DE, to discover that we were number 273 on the waiting list for CONUS. No category VI applicants had flown in the past three days.

There were two flights scheduled for the next day. The first was a flight to RAF Mildenhall (MHZ/EGUN), GB, and then on to Charleston AFB, (CHS/KCHS) SC. The second scheduled flight was to go directly to Dover AFB, (DOV/KDOV) DE, where we had left our car, and was exactly where we wanted to go. We stood by for the Space-A call for both flights, but there were a lot of emergency leave people in Category I, Emergency Leave Unfunded Travel, some active duty leave people in Category III, a few military personnel on permissive no/cost TDY in Category III, 20 or more Dependents with children traveling in category V without their sponsors who were on deployment for more than 120 days in Eastern Europe on Peacekeeping Missions and only 10 retirees in Category VI who were ahead of us on the Space-A list. Some of these retirees obtained Space-A transportation. We did not!

CIRCUITOUS ROUTING: After this failure and armed with tips from Military Living Publications, we discovered a flight scheduled for the next morning which was routed from Ramstein AB, DE, to Incirlik Airport (Adana) (ADA/LTAG), TR. The flight was scheduled to depart Ramstein AB, DE, at 1015 hours local time and arrive at Incirlik Airport (Adana), TR, at 1315 hours local time and remain at Adana for a 15-hour crew rest after arrival. The schedule for this mission was to fly the next day from Incirlik Airport, TR, back to Ramstein AB, DE, where the aircraft would remain three hours on the ground and then continue on to our desired destination, Dover AFB, DE. If we can be manifested, we will be flying our favorite C-005B Galaxy aircraft. (We are manifested, with a new sign-up date because TR was not on our original sign-up at Dover AFB, DE. There are a few active duty Space-A passengers on leave who are returning to duty at Incirlik Airport, TR.) There is also a C-005B departing at about the same time for Aviano AB (AVB/LIPA), IT then to RAF Mildenhall (MHZ/EGUN), GB (15-hour crew rest) then terminating at Dover AFB, DE but this flight from Aviano AB, IT has only 3 available seats and we require four seats, so this shorter route will not work for us.

We have learned another principle of Space-A Basic Training: a straight route may not be the best route for Space-A Air Opportunity travel. Circuitous routing is often used to get to your destination on Space-A. We are eager, risk-taking, Space-A travelers, so we go for it! Please recall that our registration for CONUS from Ramstein AB, DE, will automatically be deleted from the system when we take the flight to Incirlik Airport, Adana, TR.

Once we arrived at Incirlik Airport, TR, and signed up for our return flight to Dover AFB, DE, we lost our original Ramstein AB, DE, date/time sign-up and picked up a new date/time at Incirlik since we would be changing direction completely and heading back west to CONUS. We remembered to list Dover AFB, DE, as our final destination. Incirlik Airport was able to manifest us all the way to Dover AFB, DE, thereby allowing us to bypass having to terminate our flight at Ramstein AB, DE, and reapply for Dover AFB. Otherwise, we would have been back where we started before going to Incirlik Airport, TR.

Gosh! The first leg of the trip worked as planned. After about four hours flying time, we arrived at Incirlik Airport at 1315 hours local time. We departed the aircraft first. After showing our travel documents to Turkish and U.S. Officials, (we were required to purchase a sticker visa for our passports at a cost of $45.00 each), we moved smoothly through immigration, claimed our bags and clearing customs. Colonel Hardknuckle, USA (Ret), applied for air travel for our group for the return to CONUS. We were 20-23 on the Category VI list for CONUS. We concluded that we had a very good chance of obtaining travel on this flight, which was scheduled to depart at 0445 hours the next day. This flight had an early show time of 0245 hours.

We had called from Ramstein AB, DE, after we were manifested to reserve our temporary military lodging so all was set. We took a taxi to our temporary lodging facility, Bldg 1081, 7th Street at Incirlik Airport, C-011-90-322-316-6786 (billeting office). Again, we found Incirlik Airport (the USAF is a tenant on a Turkish AB) to be a well-appointed facility with a splendid consolidated club complex for drinks and dinner and a very comfortable temporary military lodging facility.

The next morning we called the Space-A desk about one hour before show time to discover that our flight would not be departing until 1700 hours due to changes in cargo and other space-required needs. There were no other flights to Ramstein AB, DE, or CONUS prior to this time. So on the bright side, we had most of the day to spend as we pleased. The new show time was 1500 hours, but my dad, Colonel Hardknuckle, wanted to maximize our chances for travel; he set our personal show time at the terminal for 1400 hours.

In order to spend the day wisely and have some fun, different members of our family group planned the day's activities. Dad set up a day of tennis. Other family members arranged tours with the USAF Ticket and Tour Office of archaeological ruins and museums in the local area. A relaxing travel day was had by all.

We arrived at the passenger terminal promptly at 1400 hours. Our flight was posted as follows: Leave LTAG/ADA, 180/00/1700, arrive ETAR/RMS, 180/00/2210. We knew from our Space-A Air Basic Training that we were scheduled to leave from Incirlik Airport (Adana), TR, at 1700 hours local time on Wednesday, 28 June 2000.

RETURN FLIGHT: Luck and good planning were with us. The Space-A flight call was made and we were on the flight to Ramstein AB, DE. We had paid the $3.00 per person fee for the sandwich menus we ordered for this leg of the trip to Ramstein AB. Aware that we would have about seven-and-a-half hours' ground time at Ramstein AB, DE, before our flight continued on to Dover AFB, DE, we attempted to obtain billeting at Ramstein AB, DE, but nothing was available.

Our lodging reservation at Ramstein AB, DE had expired but we were very fortunate to obtain temporary military lodging (TML) space at the Kaiserslautern East Community (Vogelweh) Tel: C-011-49-6371-47-7345/7864/2445/2614. Our best transportation option was a taxi, which we took straight to the Vogelweh lodging office. We rushed to bed because we had to be back at the airport for an 0400 Space-A call. We were smart travelers; we brought our toilet articles, sleeping attire and a clean shirt/blouse in our carry-on luggage, so we were prepared for the overnight in Vogelweh, DE, as our luggage was checked through to Dover AFB, DE.

Being cautious types, we made arrangements with the desk clerk for a wake-up call. All went well, and we met our early morning Space-A call. Since we were continuing on the same flight on which we arrived, we checked in with Passenger Service, signed up and paid for the in-flight meals, and received our boarding passes. We recognized some of the faces of Category VI people who were still waiting for transportation to CONUS at Ramstein AB when we departed for Adana, TR. They met the Space-A call but were not boarded on our flight to CONUS due to lack of available seating. We enjoyed our trip to Turkey and were now on our way home. If we had been unable to obtain military lodging, we would have had to use, if available, a pension (small hotel) in the local Ramstein/Landstuhl area.

ARRIVAL AND CLEARING: The flight to Dover AFB, DE, was uneventful. Before landing we were given immigration and customs forms to complete as a family group. We completed the immigration forms for our passports and ID cards as a family group. Likewise, we completed the customs declaration as returning residents and we made an oral declaration since the value of goods which we brought into the country did not exceed $400 per person. We were not bringing in tobacco, tea, liquor or any other exempted items. Also, we were not bringing in items for other persons. We arrived on time at 181/00/1505L (also known as Thursday, 29 June 2000, 1505). We checked through immigration, claimed our four bags and cleared customs.

In a stroke of good luck, my dad, Colonel Hardknuckle, obtained a local ride to claim our station wagon located in the long-term overflow parking facility. He met a Space-A passenger who wanted to hear of his Space-A experiences and who still had his car at the main terminal.

We met one of our friends, LtCol Zachary Sadbag, USAF (Ret), whose bag did not arrive with his flight. As a matter of interest, we inquired as to how this loss is handled. He told us that the Dover AFB, DE, Passenger Service personnel were most helpful. The procedure was similar to passengers who have lost baggage on commercial airlines. He was requested to fill out an **AMC Form 134, BAGGAGE IRREGULARITY REPORT.** A copy of his baggage claim check (USAF Form 94) was secured to this form. He was also requested to fill out an **AMC Form 70, RUSH BAGGAGE MANIFEST,** specifying whether he wanted them to hold the bag for pickup when it came in or forward it to his home in the Washington, D.C. area at his expense. LtCol Sadbag elected to wait for his bag which was scheduled to arrive on the very next flight from Germany in about two hours.

POST SPACE-A TRIP REPORT

We departed the terminal for a short, 2-and-3/4-hour trip via car to our home in Falls Church, VA. On the way home we compared notes on our trip which are to be submitted the next day to our dad, who will be preparing an After Trip Report. It will emphasize the Space-A lessons we have learned and will be circulated among our friends. We will also send it to Military Living's *R&R Travel News*® for possible publication in their reader report sharing section. This information will be very useful to us and others on future trips.

Linda Sue Hardknuckle

LESSONS LEARNED: The following key lessons were learned from the above overseas Space-A air trip with the family:

A. Plan your flight ahead of time to include information about desired departure location/station, destination/countries, routes of Space-A travel, schedules including overnight stops and flight conditions.

B. If you have a definite/required return date, a commercial backup ticket is essential.

C. Applications for Space-A air travel can be made for four countries plus "all" 60 days before travel is desired and at multiple departure stations in CONUS and overseas for both departure and return travel.

D. If you are in the station terminal and "travel ready" your chances of obtaining Space-A air transportation are considerably improved over reporting to the terminal only when flights are scheduled.

E. Travel light; each person should be able to carry his or her bags for at least 1/2 mile. Bags should have built-in wheels or strap on wheels. There are limited-to-no porters in the terminal area.

F. Buy in-flight meals or bring your own snacks. They keep you busy and help pass the time.

G. Wear loose fitting clothes in layers and ear plugs for comfort.

H. Verify your return registration at your destination station before departing for your travels.

I. Circuitous routing may be required to get to your desired destination on Space-A.

SECTION II

AN IMAGINARY SPACE-A AIR TRIP BY CONUS MEDICAL EVACUATION (MEDEVAC) FLIGHT

BACKGROUND

MEDICAL EVACUATION (MEDEVAC) FLIGHTS: These flights are flown all over the world in support of the medical programs of the Uniformed Services. The vital United States Air Force, Air Mobility Command (AMC) aeromedical airlift mission is implemented by highly trained medical technicians, flight nurses and aircraft crews which moved nearly 70,000 DoD patients on some 4,500 C-009A/E, C-141A/B and C-130A-H missions during 1996. Medical evacuation missions include both litter and ambulatory patients. In addition to these patients, thousands of Space-A air opportunity passengers were also served by the MEDEVAC system worldwide.

THE MEDEVAC SYSTEM: There are several elements of the worldwide MEDEVAC system which operate in CONUS. Next, each major overseas theater of operations, i.e., Europe and Pacific, has its own internal and intra-theater MEDEVAC system. Lastly, there is a MEDEVAC system which operates between CONUS and overseas theaters. We have discussed Space-A travel between CONUS and overseas with return and travel in the European theater. In this section we will only discuss Space-A air opportunities in CONUS via MEDEVAC missions. As our example, we will use an active duty Uniformed Service Member, First Lieutenant John A. Hardcharger, USAF, stationed in Northern California.

CONUS MEDEVAC FLIGHT EQUIPMENT: The major aircraft used in CONUS MEDEVAC is appropriately named the C-009A/E NIGHTINGALE. This aircraft has been derived from the DC-9, Series 30 commercial airliner. The C-009A/E has been configured as an aeromedical airlift transport. This aircraft in this configuration has been in service in the USAF since August 1968. The aircraft accommodates a crew of three, medical staff of five, 40 litter patients or 40 ambulatory patients or a combination of both. More details regarding the specifications and performance of this aircraft are in Appendix M. Two other aircraft, the C-130A-H Hercules and the C-141A/B Starlifter, have also been configured for aeromedical airlift and are used for long distance Theater and Intra-Theater aeromedical airlift missions. Specifications, Configuration and Performance of these aircraft are also at Appendix M.

WHAT IS DIFFERENT ABOUT SPACE-A ON MEDEVAC FLIGHTS?: We will answer this general question by taking another round-trip on the Space-A system. With the help of 1Lt Hardcharger, we will take another one of those favorite Space-A air opportunity trips. First, let's examine the special aspects of Space-A travel on aeromedical airlift (commonly known as MEDEVAC) flights. The seating for Space-A passengers on the C-009A/E Nightingale MEDEVAC flights is commercial airline-type reclining chairs facing the rear of the aircraft. The C-009A/E is a very smooth-riding aircraft; however, for patient comfort, the temperature is kept at approximately 75 degrees and may be kept even higher for patient needs. Caution: wear clothes in layers that you can take off or add as needed. The temperature will only be adjusted for the comfort of patients.

The Space-A seating is away from the litter patients, frequently in the front part of the passenger cabin. Litter patients are boarded first followed by ambulatory patients, Space-required (if any) and Space-A passengers. A key item to remember is that at any time MEDEVAC flights can be diverted, without prior notice, from their planned flight schedule to pick up or discharge MEDEVAC patients.

PLANNING YOUR CONUS MEDEVAC FLIGHT

The CONUS MEDEVAC system is based on a revolving weekly (up to six months) proforma schedule which includes many stations. These stations are visited on different days of the week depending upon station need for MEDEVAC (Aeromedical) Services. For specific details, please see *Military Space-A Air Opportunities Around The World Air Route Map* (Military Living's Space-A map) and *Military Space-A Air Opportunities Around the World* (Military Living's Space-A book). With these valuable tools in hand, 1Lt Hardcharger is ready to take his Space-A air trip.

As told by 1Lt Hardcharger: My plan is to travel from Northern California (San Francisco, CA) area, where I am stationed, to Florida (Orlando, FL, area) and return to the West Coast (San Francisco, CA). I examine the MEDEVAC schedules carefully and determine that my Space-A MEDEVAC travel plan is indeed feasible.

I note from Military Living's Space-A book and Space-A map that I can take a flight from Travis AFB (SUU/KSUU), CA, on Monday or Tuesday to Scott AFB (BLV/KBLV), IL. The purpose of my leave travel is to visit relatives, see some fun places and be introduced by cousins to their friends. I have my Air Force leave form signed by Colonel Michael Q. Topmissile, USAF, my project manager, and it is valid for 20 days. I register for only CONUS destinations at Travis AFB, CA, by fax the day that my leave is effective. This means that I am eligible for any flight that departs from Travis AFB, CA, to a CONUS destination. It is reassuring to know that I can travel on any mission on any Services' aircraft.

REGISTRATION AND DEPARTURE: I have registered for Space-A travel on Tuesday, my first day of leave, at Travis AFB, CA, for CONUS. I have a registration for one person, Category III (ordinary leave), CONUS destination with my Julian date and time of registration from my fax transmission receipt (see Appendix B for an explanation). To improve my chances for a Space-A flight out of Scott AFB, IL, I also fax a Space-A Travel Request to Scott AFB, IL. I report on Tuesday (0530 hrs) for a Space-A call for Scott AFB, IL. Fortunately, I am selected for the flight. Wow! I am on my way and it is free. I reserve the snack menu (healthy heart menus) for $1.90 which includes a deli sandwich, salad or vegetable, fruit and milk or a soft drink.

ROUTING AND REMAINING OVERNIGHT (LODGING): I had called ahead to check on temporary military lodging (TML) at Scott AFB, IL, using Military Living's *Temporary Military Lodging Around The World* book. Since I have called 24 hours in advance, I am given a confirmed reservation (Scott Inn, Bldg 1510 F Street, C-1-888-AFLODGE) using my credit card. The flight to Scott AFB, IL, is smooth, over a long northwest loop but uneventful. Immediately upon arrival, I verify my fax Space-A Travel Request for Space-A air to CONUS. Next, I claim my bag in the passenger terminal, Bldg P-8, 801 Hangar Road, Tel: 618-256-2014/3017/4042. (NOTE: AMC is making an effort to use the same line number (extension 1854) as the air passenger terminal information or recording number at all AMC bases. This may take some time to accomplish.)

Due to the late hour of arrival, the shuttle bus is not operating. I have two ways to reach the billets: walk the approximately one mile (four blocks) or call for a commercial taxi to come on base. In the interest of saving money and since I have only one small bag, I decide to walk. The directions are given on the Scott AFB map in my Military Living Military Space-A Air Opportunities ATW book. It pays to travel light. You will find more flying options when traveling in CONUS if you keep your baggage under 30 pounds. The baggage limit on the smaller executive aircraft is 30 pounds.

I arrive at the TML and check in at Bldg 1510 F Street, which is a 24-hour per day operation. I have a late dinner at the Officers' Club C-618-256-5501, which is a short walk, less than one block from the TML.

I leave on Wednesday from Scott AFB, IL, for MacDill AFB (MCF/KMCF), FL. The flight to McDill is diverted from our scheduled route to pick up an emergency MEDEVAC patient at Homestead ARB (HST/KHST), FL and this makes it a very long day for everyone on board.

On arrival at MacDill AFB passenger terminal, hangar 4, I claim my baggage and register in person for CONUS so that when I am ready to return, I will be much higher on the Space-A waiting list.

I reserved a rental car by calling ahead to C-813-840-2613, located at Bldg 17, Dayton Avenue, on base. My rental car is ready and I depart to spend a few wonderful days visiting relatives and enjoying Florida sights.

After a week in Florida, I am ready to head home to California. I take the Wednesday flight from MacDill AFB, FL, to Scott AFB, IL, where I remain overnight. On Thursday I discover that there are no MEDEVAC flights to Travis AFB, CA until Sunday. Nevertheless, I sign up for CONUS and hope for the best. I check back at the terminal all day Thursday while visiting the Bowling Center and the tennis courts on base. I go to the Community Center where I book an overnight bus tour of St. Louis, returning Saturday afternoon. We see the Gateway Arch, take a Mississippi River Tour, Fox Theater and Soulard Market area. I had a wonderful time.

I check with the passenger terminal at Scott AFB on Saturday night after returning from St Louis and my name is on the top of the list for the Sunday flight to Travis AFB, CA. I am up early on Sunday for the 0530 hours Space-A Flight Call. The trip to Travis AFB is long again because we are flying from the beginning of the route to the end of the route.

THE SCHEDULED MEDEVAC SYSTEM: Careful planning and coordination was required to reach my desired locations. The MEDEVAC system has been very reliable and has met my needs. The requirement to stop overnight several times was a different experience for me but very enjoyable. This is a wonderful system for the unaccompanied individual Service member, active or retired, to move about CONUS.

Given a short period of time you can go to almost any area in CONUS and return to your station with minimum waiting time. Please also note that while you are registered for CONUS at a departure location, you can take any flight regardless of the type mission to any location in CONUS. If you are patient, relaxed and flexible, any Space-A trip is easy. If I had missed a leg on my flight schedule, I would have checked to see about other Space-A flight opportunities. Space-A air travel is not always a series of flights in a direct line. It was a comfort to know that if all my Space-A plans fell through, I could use my active duty military ID card to get a discount on a commercial flight. Most military bases have travel offices, known as Scheduled Airline Ticket Offices (SATO), or you can call the airline direct.

1Lt John A. Hardcharger

LESSONS LEARNED: The following key lessons were learned from an imaginary Space-A trip by CONUS Medical Evacuation (MEDEVAC) flight:

A. The CONUS MEDEVAC system is comprehensive and reliable for Space-A travel and is ideal for sponsors flying in CONUS.

B. MEDEVAC flights are comfortable and smooth but tend to be warmer in the cabin than other flights. Wear clothes in layers.

C. These flights frequently require overnight stops to reach your (long distance) desired destination.

D. You can intermix MEDEVAC flights with other types of flights in order to reach your destination.

SECTION III

NATIONAL GUARD AND RESERVE PERSONNEL ELIGIBLE FOR SPACE-A AIR TRAVEL

NATIONAL GUARD AND RESERVE PERSONNEL: All National Guard and Reserve personnel are eligible for Space-A air transportation with the exception of those who are not receiving pay or have not completed their requirements for retirement. First, let us look at the seven Uniformed Services to see which Services have National Guard and Reserve components. There are Army and Air Force National Guard components; but there are no National Guard components in the other five Uniformed Services. There are active Reserve components in the Army, Navy, Marine Corps, Coast Guard and Air Force. There are no active Reserve components in the USPHS or NOAA.

ACTIVE DUTY STATUS RESERVE COMPONENT MEMBERS: In order to be classified as an active duty status Reserve component member, you must be a full-time member of a National Guard or Reserve Unit or drill independently and receive National Guard/Reserve pay. This means that you drill or train with your National Guard or Reserve unit on a regular basis, you are in active status and you receive pay for your attendance at drills or training sessions. You may be an officer, warrant officer or enlisted grade. This describes the active duty status Reservist of all the Uniformed Services (Armed Services).

RETIRED RESERVISTS (GRAY AREA): National Guard and Reserve members of the Armed Services cannot receive full retirement status until they attain age 60. When Reserve component personnel, who have not attained age 60, receive their official notification of retirement eligibility, they may continue to travel by Space-A air as Reservists. The date that Reservists receive official notice of retirement eligibility until they reach the age of 60 and are officially retired and begin to receive retired pay, is known as the "Gray Area." When the retired Reservist reaches age 60, he or she is fully retired and receives the DD Form 2, Blue ID card and begins to receive retired pay. At this point the retired Reservist has all the benefits of any retired member of the Uniformed Services. Family members (Dependents) of active duty status Reserve component members and retired Reservist (Gray Area) are not eligible to fly Space-A until their sponsors are fully retired at age 60 and receiving retired pay.

DOCUMENTATION REQUIRED FOR NATIONAL GUARD AND RESERVE COMPONENT PERSONNEL TO FLY SPACE-A: First, Reserve component personnel must have their DD Form 2, Red ID. Second, they must have a copy of DD Form 1853, **AUTHENTICATION OF RESERVE STATUS FOR TRAVEL ELIGIBILITY,** signed by their unit commander within the past 180 days (Appendix H is a copy of DD Form 1853). Gray Area retirees must have their DD Form 2, Red ID card and a copy of their official notification (letter) of retirement eligibility. (If the Gray Area retiree has received the new DD Form 2765 ID card, in lieu of the DD Form 1173 ID card, the letter of retirement eligibility is not required.) Also, a copy of DD Form 1853 is not required for Gray Area retirees.

NATIONAL GUARD AND RESERVE TRAVEL-GEO- GRAPHIC AREAS AND DEPENDENTS: National Guard and Reserve component members may travel in CONUS and between Alaska, Hawaii, Puerto Rico, the U.S. Virgin Islands, American Samoa and Guam (Guam and American Samoa travelers may fly via Hawaii). Except for National Guard and Reserve retirees aged 60 and above and receiving retired pay from a Service Department, National Guard and Reserve personnel may not travel Space-A to a foreign country. The above geographic restrictions on Reserve component personnel travel also apply to the Gray Area Reserve component retiree.

National Guard and Reserve component personnel cannot be accompanied by dependents, as a minor exception, when Reserve component personnel are on active duty for training for 30 days or more overseas, which is a regular active duty status, their dependents may accompany them on Space-A air travel within the overseas area. Gray Area retirees cannot be accompanied by their dependents prior to attaining age 60 and receiving full retirement and their DD Form 2, Blue ID card. At this point their dependents will also be eligible for the DD Form 1173 Uniform Service Identification and Privilege Card reflecting the retired status of the sponsor.

THE SCOPE OF NATIONAL GUARD AND RESERVE SPACE-A TRAVEL: Although there is a restriction against National Guard and Reserve personnel traveling to foreign countries, there are many exciting places to visit. Also, from these overseas (OCONUS) points, you can continue your travels to many foreign countries at a minimum expense. For example, American Samoa is 3/4 of the way to Australia/New Zealand. Likewise, Puerto Rico and the U.S. Virgin Islands open up to you the entire Caribbean area. Guam is on the doorstep of Asia; Japan, the Philippines, Taiwan, the Pacific Islands and Indonesia are nearby. A Space-A flight to Alaska places the traveler near to Japan and Korea in the northern Pacific. Of course, there are also the foreign countries bordering CONUS which you can easily visit.

AN IMAGINARY SPACE-A AIR TRIP BY NATIONAL GUARD AND RESERVE PERSONNEL

TRIP PLANNING

This Space-A trip will be taken by Sergeant (SSgt), E-5, Roy L. Straitlaced, USAF Reserve, (who lives in Dayton, OH) and Staff Sergeant (SSgt), E-5, Kathleen L. Truelove, USAF Reserve, Pope AFB, NC (who lives in Fayetteville, NC). They met during Operation Desert Storm at a United Services Organization (USO) canteen and have stayed in close contact since that time. Now they have planned a Space-A air trip to Puerto Rico where they will have a joint vacation and hopefully get to know each other better under more normal conditions.

ROUTING: SGT Straitlaced checks Military Living's *Military Space-A Air Opportunities Air Route Map* and *Military Space-A Air Opportunities Around the World* book and finds that there are several flights monthly from Wright-Patterson AFB, (FFO/KFFO), OH to Andrews AFB (ADW/KADW), MD or Norfolk NAS (NGU/KNGU), VA and on to their target destination of Roosevelt Roads NS (NRR/TJNR), PR. His review of Space-A air opportunities reveals that there are also numerous flights from Norfolk NAS, VA, to Roosevelt Roads NAS, PR. Knowing the value of prior planning, SGT Straitlaced also checks return flights because he must return within 10 days to his civilian job as a Bank Security Guard in Dayton, OH. He notes that there are numerous flights from Roosevelt Roads NAS, PR, to Norfolk NAS, VA.

Using Military Living's Space-A book and map, Staff Sergeant Truelove finds that there are many flights each month from Pope AFB (POB/KPOB), NC, to Norfolk NAS, VA which continue on to Roosevelt Roads NAS, PR. Most of these flights are via C-130E mixed passenger/cargo missions. As the result of her active duty in the Persian Gulf area, SSgt Truelove has her own form-fitted ear plugs and also has some experience flying the C-130E aircraft. At SGT Straitlaced's insistence, she checks the return flights because she, too, must be back in 10 days to report for a new job that she has obtained as a medical technician at an area hospital. Luck is with everyone, and there are many return flights from Roosevelt Roads NAS, PR to Pope AFB, NC through Norfolk NAS, VA.

APPLICATION FOR SPACE-A TRAVEL: The two sergeants apply for air travel at their respective locations. SGT Straitlaced applies in person for air travel at Wright-Patterson AFB, OH, Bldg 206, Tel: C-937-257-7741. SSgt Straitlaced has learned from Military Living's Space-A book that in order to cover any destinations that he may need, he should apply for travel to CONUS, Puerto Rico and the U.S. Virgin Islands. He also lists "ALL" as one of his five possible destinations as protection to provide for any circuitous routing which will get him to his desired destination.

Following SSgt Straitlaced's lead, SSgt Truelove applies in person for air travel at Pope AFB, NC, Bldg 704, C-910-394-6527/8. She applies for travel to CONUS, Puerto Rico, the U.S. Virgin Islands and "ALL."

Both sergeants also send a fax of their Space-A Travel Request (AMC Form 140, Feb 95) with a copy of their authenticated DD Form 1853, Authentication of Reserve Status for Travel Eligibility, to air passenger terminal Roosevelt Roads NAS (NRR/TJNR), PR, for registration for return travel to CONUS. This will give them a higher position on the Space-A register than if they wait until they are in Puerto Rico to apply for return Space-A air travel to CONUS.

THE OUTBOUND TRIP

Our sergeants are all set to go. It looks like Thursday is the best day for SSgt Truelove to travel and Friday is the best day for SSgt Straitlaced to travel. The sergeants agree to meet in Norfolk and continue on to Roosevelt Roads on Friday if they can get a flight together. Both sergeants have sent Space-A Travel Request via fax to Norfolk NAS, VA for transportation to Roosevelt Roads NS, PR.

SSgt Truelove has made a reservation at the Norfolk Navy Lodge for Thursday night and uses the base shuttle bus to travel from the terminal to the Navy Lodge. This is the largest Navy Lodge in the system and a single room with kitchenette is just $46. She has a wonderful dinner at Norfolk Live, a trendy restaurant a short walk from the Navy Lodge.

MEETING: SSgt Truelove takes the base shuttle bus back to the passenger terminal in time to meet SSgt Straitlaced's flight from Wright-Patterson AFB. All went well and after a big long hug they check on their flight to Roosevelt Roads, PR.

They are in luck; their names are high on the list for the same C-141C from Wright-Patterson AFB, OH which SSgt Straitlaced came in on and will be departing in about one hour for Guantanamo Bay NAS, CU and then on to Roosevelt Roads NS, PR. They are on the flight with an unexpected stop in Guantanamo Bay NAS, CU.

The sergeants have checked on the schedule for the commercial bus to San Juan (about 50 miles northwest). Before leaving the airport, they both confirm that the passenger terminal has received their fax application for return flights to CONUS and that their requests have been entered into the Space-A register.

VACATION: They have reserved adjoining rooms for the first three nights in a San Juan hotel, which grants special military rates. After they become oriented to the island, they plan several trips to the interior rain forest and beautiful beaches. They have an enjoyable vacation and discover a greater than expected renewal of their friendship. In that vein, they also plan their engagement announcement.

RETURN FLIGHT

The two sergeants keep checking back with the Space-A desk at the Roosevelt Roads NAS and find that there is a flight one week from the following Friday. When they report to the passenger terminal travel ready, they find that their names are near the top of the waiting list. They are both selected for the flight, which is a C130-E. The flight is routed from Roosevelt Roads NAS to Norfolk NAS, VA, and on to Pope AFB, NC. SSgt Straitlaced departs the flight at Norfolk NAS, VA. He registers for a flight which departs the next day to CONUS and remains overnight at the Naval Base BEQ. The next morning, Saturday, SSgt Straitlaced catches a C-21 flight to the Washington NAF, DC. After arrival, SSgt Straitlaced takes the base shuttle bus to the Air Force Terminal on the west side of the runway structure. He is just in time to catch a C-20B Gulfstream direct to Wright-Patterson AFB, OH and home. He was able to take the flights on a small executive aircraft because his luggage did not weigh more than 30 pounds.

REFLECTIONS: National Guard and Reserve members and their dependents are (as of press time) **not** allowed to fly Space-A to foreign counties until they reach age 60 and are retired; however, they can have lots of fun flying by Space-A in CONUS and to and from United States Possessions overseas, such as Puerto Rico, "the star of the Caribbean."

Ed's Note: The following legislation has been introduced in the U.S. House of Representatives. Hopefully, a similar bill will be introduced in the U.S. Senate and passed by both houses, submitted to Joint Conference, approved and sent to the president and approved for this legislation to become law. Subscribe to Military Living's *R&R Travel News*® to track the progress of this legislation.

H.R. 3267, FAIRNESS FOR THE MILITARY RESERVE ACT OF 1999.

Congressman Tom Campbell of California, Tel: C-202-225-2631 or Fax: C-202-225-6788 has introduced the referenced bill which among other things, would extend Space-A Air travel to selected Reservists (which includes National Guard as well) to areas outside of the United States and its possessions, to foreign countries—-the same as retired military, and would give reservists the same priority as active duty personnel when traveling for their monthly drills. This bill differs from the bill unsuccessfully introduced in 1998 which would have moved Reservists up in priority to Category III with active duty personnel. This bill, H. R. 3267 retains the Reservist in category VI. The bill also grants "grey area retirees" the right to travel Space-A under the same conditions as the retired military receiving retired pay. Also, a key feature of the bill would provide selected Reservists, when traveling to attend monthly military drills, the same billeting privileges as active duty personnel. We will keep you posted on the status of this proposed legislation.

LESSONS LEARNED: The following key lessons were learned from an imaginary Space-A air trip by National Guard and Reserve personnel:

A. In addition to ID cards, Reservists require DD Form 1853, Authentication of Reserve Status for Travel Eligibility or Letter of Retirement Eligibility if in the "Grey Area" and have not been issued the new ID, DD Form 2765.

B. Reservists cannot travel to a foreign country until they are age 60 and receiving retired pay.

C. Reservists can fly to U.S. Possessions which position them near foreign countries at considerably reduced cost.

D. A law is pending to allow Reservists to travel on Space-A under the same terms and conditions as active duty.

E. If there is a flight going in the direction of your destination - TAKE IT!

SECTION IV

AN IMAGINARY SPACE-A AIR TRIP TO AUSTRALIA AND NEW ZEALAND

TRIP PLANNING

The trip from CONUS or Hawaii to Australia and New Zealand has become a highly valued and sought-after travel experience by an ever increasing number of Uniformed Services members and their eligible family members. When one thinks about the Australia and New Zealand travel destination it brings to mind time-consuming travel and long distances between modern cities; however, it also brings to mind English speaking countries with unique customs and culture, exotic plants and animals, vast deserts and alpine mountains, 20th to 21st century modern infrastructure, industry, commerce and capitalism and best of all, democratic republics based on the rule of law. Does this sound like a place you would want to visit? There is much more to come. Let me mention up front, the airfare via Space-A air opportunities is free. We will discuss specific exciting travel sites and activities as we move along in this imaginary (near true) Space-A journey.

The routes on the Australia and New Zealand routing (stations visited) are stable and change infrequently. This route is flown to Australia in support of U.S. Air Force satellite tracking and related missions and to New Zealand in support of U.S. Navy and National Science Foundation Antarctica research and related matters. All of the stations along this route are small in size, remote (except RAAF Richmond) and have very limited support facilities. Travelers on this route should take special note of the above point and not expect extensive local military logistical and related support.

This trip is being made by Sergeant First Class (SFC) John Q. O'Neary, U.S. Army (USA) (Ret) and his new bride of one year Donna Lasagna-O'Neary. When SFC O'Neary was on active duty, he traveled extensively in CONUS, Europe, Hawaii, Japan, Korea and Vietnam. Donna has never traveled outside the CONUS. They are both looking forward to a new adventure together to celebrate their first wedding anniversary. The following is the O'Nearys' account of their trip to Australia/New Zealand:

We both study carefully the *Military Space-A Air Opportunities Around The World* book, primarily using the Location Identifiers and Cross-Reference Index, and the *Military Space-A Air Opportunities Air Route Map.* Our study disclosed that the best departure locations/stations in CONUS for Australia and New Zealand are McChord AFB

(TCM/KTCM), WA, and Travis AFB (SUU/KSUU), CA, in terms of favorable routing and frequency of flights. The distance of this trip, cargo requirements and other considerations make the C-141B the best aircraft in the AMC fleet to perform this mission. The aircraft is configured approximately 1/2 cargo and 1/2 passenger (approximately 100 airline type seats) to meet the mission needs.

We discover that there are three distinct routes from the West Coast of CONUS to Australia and New Zealand. The flights that depart McChord AFB (TCM/KTCM), WA, each Sunday fly the following route: McChord AFB, WA, to Travis AFB (SUU/KSUU), CA, to Hickam AFB (HIK/PHIK), HI, to Andersen AFB (UAM/PGUA), GU to RAAFB Richmond (RCM/YSRI), AU, (mission turn around point), to Andersen AFB, GU, to Hickam AFB, HI and terminating at the starting station McChord AFB, WA, over a seven day period. For identification purposes we will call this route #1.

The second route departs McChord AFB, WA, 1st and 3rd Friday and flies the following route: McChord AFB to Travis AFB, to Hickam AFB to Pago Pago IAP (PPG/NSTU), AS to RAAFB Richmond to Alice Springs Airport (ASP/YBAS), AU (mission turnaround point), to RAAFB Richmond to Pago Pago IAP to Hickam AFB to Travis AFB, to the terminal station at McChord AFB. The entire mission is accomplished over a seven day period. For identification purposes we will call this route #2.

The third route departs McChord AFB, WA 1st and 3rd Sunday and flies the following route: McChord AFB to Travis AFB to Hickam AFB to Andersen AFB to RAAFB Richmond (mission turnaround point) to Christchurch IAP (CHC/NZCH), NZ to Pago Pago IAP to Hickam AFB to terminal station at McChord AFB. The entire mission is accomplished over a seven day period. For identification purposes we will call this route #3.

We have been advised by previous travelers to Australia/New Zealand to travel first to Australia then to New Zealand as part of the return to the United States; therefore, we elect to pick up our flight on route #2 at Travis AFB, CA. We note that trips to Australia/New Zealand originate at Travis AFB on 1st and 3rd Fridays (route #2) and Sundays come through Travis AFB (route #1 and #3), another reason for selecting Travis AFB as a starting point. This departure location will give us three chances at a Space-A departure for our desired travel destination within a three day period.

We note that Appendix S, Visa Information and Personnel Entrance Requirements, shows that a passport and Australian Electronic Travel Authority (ETA) or visa is required for Australia and a passport without visa is required for New Zealand (if staying less than 90 days). The ETA is obtained by calling the immigration section, Australian Embassy C-202-797-3145 and giving the information from the title pages of your U.S. passports. The address is: Embassy of Australia, 1601 Massachusetts Avenue NW, Washington, D.C. 20036.

We live in San Clemente, CA, which is midway between Los Angeles and San Diego. Since dependents cannot fly point-to-point in the CONUS (except with the active duty sponsor when on emergency leave or house hunting incidental to a PCS), we are required to utilize a flight which will transport our dependents outside of CONUS. We check the Space-A Air Opportunities book and find that there is a flight which departs March Air Reserve Base (RIV/KRIV), CA (near Riverside, CA), each Tuesday and flies to Travis AFB, CA, and the same aircraft and mission continues on to Hickam AFB, HI, en route to other Pacific area stations. Also there are infrequent flights to Hawaii from North Island NAS (NZY/KNZY), CA (near San Diego, CA). These flights meet the requirement to transport our dependents outside of CONUS. Once outside of CONUS, dependents may move around in the overseas theaters freely with their sponsors.

If we can get a flight from Southern California to Hawaii, we can join the Australia/New Zealand flight at Hickam AFB, HI. We will also need to get a flight from Hawaii to Southern California on our return to CONUS. We learn from Military Living Publications that it is more difficult to join the Australia/New Zealand flight at Hickam AFB, HI, than Travis AFB, CA, or McChord AFB, WA. In order to reduce the risk of not obtaining a flight to our target destination and also have more flexibility at the departure location, we decide to drive from San Clemente, CA, to Travis AFB, CA, with an overnight stop in San Francisco, CA. We have not been to San Francisco in many years and look forward to a renewed visit. It is 61 miles from San Clemente north to Los Angeles and 379 miles from Los Angeles north to San Francisco, or a first-day drive of 440 miles or about 8.5 hours including brief rest stops and changing drivers. Travis AFB in Fairfield, CA, is 50 miles northeast of San Francisco.

We fax our Space-A Travel Request, AMC Form 140, to McChord AFB, Fax: C-253-512-3815; Travis AFB, Fax: C-707-424-4021 and Hickam AFB, Fax: C-808-448-1503. We list the five countries (and overseas locations) in order of priority: Hawaii, Guam, Australia, New Zealand and "ALL" (we will take any flight going in our direction). This action is taken about 55 days before we plan to fly. We also send our Space-A Travel Request to the above countries for our return to CONUS. The faxes to the overseas return countries and areas (Australia, New Zealand, American Samoa, Guam and Hawaii) go out about 50 days before our desired return from overseas. The fax numbers are in the *Military Space-A Air Opportunities Around The World* book.

In order to become more familiar with the Australia/New Zealand area, we have, on the recommendation of Military

Living Publications editorial staff, purchased the two Maverick Guides to Australia and New Zealand, by Robert W. Bone, and published by Pelican (we could have also obtained these on library loan, but we wanted them for our trip). Roy Sr., an editor at Military Living Publications, evaluated the Maverick titles on a trip to our target area in 1989 (more recent editions are available). He found them to have extensive coverage of key travel locations and to be almost flawless in accuracy. We find that Australia and New Zealand are in the southern hemisphere and have reverse seasons to North America. We have planned our travel for late October which will be spring in our destination area.

For the map enthusiast, RAAFB Richmond, AU, is 45 miles northwest of Sydney, AU, and the coordinates are 151 degrees and 30 minutes east longitude and 33 degrees and 48 minutes south latitude. Christchurch, NZ (located on the eastern shore of the South Island) is at coordinates 172 degrees and 30 minutes east longitude and 43 degrees and 35 minutes south latitude. The corresponding location in the northern hemisphere to RAAFB Richmond, AU, is located in the North Pacific Ocean, 750 miles east of Tokyo, JP. The corresponding location in the northern hemisphere to Christchurch, NZ, is located in the Northern Pacific Ocean 500 miles south of the Aleutian Rat Islands, AK, and 1000 miles southeast of the port city of Petropavlovsk in Siberia, Russia.

We depart San Clemente very early on Tuesday in late October and arrive in San Francisco at the Marines' Memorial Club, 609 Sutter Street, where we have advance reservations. (We are the guest of a friend who has a life membership at the club.) Room prices are low here compared with other hotels in the area. There is a great rooftop restaurant and bar, theater, museum, library, athletic center with indoor pool, one block to the Powell Street Cable Car, Union Square and much more. After registering and obtaining a car pass, we park our car in a garage a half a block away on Sutter where the club has a discount. Our queen-size room on the 7th floor is newly decorated and very comfortable.

We take a cab to Tadisch Grill, on California Street in the financial district-the "Wall Street of the West," our favorite seafood restaurant in San Francisco. Service is efficient and friendly with old world waiters. The fish main course is large portions of natural charcoaled West Coast fish varieties—delicious beyond words and prepared just right. After dinner, we take a cable car (California Street line in front of the restaurant and transfer to the Powell Street line) to Fisherman's Wharf. We walk around a bit on the wharf to loosen up and listen to the street music. We end up at the Buena Vista on Bay Street overlooking the Bay for a few late night Irish coffees, which are reputed to be the very best in the world—after two it's the fog, big crowd of happy people that makes your head swim. The cable car turns around in front of the Buena Vista, so we queue up and are on the first car back to the corner of Powell and Sutter. It is a very short hike one block up the hill to the Marines' Memorial Club and to bed.

PRE-FLIGHT

After a great night's rest (Wednesday) and a good breakfast in the Restaurant on the 12th floor of the club, we check out, pick up our car, store our bags and head north over the Oakland-San Francisco Bay Bridge for Travis AFB. After entering the base, where we pick up a base map at the gate, we head for the Westwind Inn Lodging Office, Bldg 404 Sevedge Drive, C-707-424-4779. We called on Monday and obtained a reservation starting today, Wednesday, through Friday. We will try to renew if needed. After check-in, we head for the Passenger Terminal, Bldg 3, open 24 hours daily, to check the status of our Space-A Travel Request and the flight to Australia.

We learn that the flight to Hickam AFB, HI (continuing on to Australia) on Friday is on schedule. In Category VI (retirees and others) we are number 3 and 4 with only one couple ahead of us in this category. There are no emergency leave passengers in Category I, no EML leave in Category II, 20 active duty on ordinary leave, two on house hunting to Hawaii and one Medal Of Honor holder for a total of 23 in Category III. There are no Unaccompanied Dependents on EML in Category IV; there is one passenger on Permissive TDY in Category V. In our Category VI there are a total of 14 passengers. This means a total of 38 passengers. The Space-A desk clerk tells us that the terminal expects to receive about 48 to 54 seats. As indicated, our flight is a C-141B Starlifter, cargo mission (primary), which will be mixed passenger and cargo. We know that flights fill up as the departure time approaches, but we feel good about our chances for making the flight.

We decide to travel (about 20 miles) to the Napa Valley area. Our car seems to know its own way to the Robert Mondavi winery just north of the town of Napa. We arrive in time to visit the cellar tours, taste some wine and visit the wine shop where we buy a bottle of Coastal Chardonnay for our TML room. On the way back to Travis AFB, we stop on CA-29 two miles south of the winery and north of Napa at Mustard's, a trendy restaurant with delightful American and European food (mostly grilled). There is an extensive wine menu and the service is good and prompt. Try the garlic mashed potatoes. The char-coaled quail with mustard sauce in season is terrific. Home to bed after a great day.

We have breakfast at Burger King, Bldg 685 (Thursday) and then go to the passenger terminal to check on events of the night and our status. There are now two Emergency Leave passengers in Category I, but they may get transportation on other flights bound for Hawaii. There are now over 50 passengers in Category III, but two flights have been added for an early departure on Friday to Hawaii. Things are now getting more complicated, but we have faith in the system and hope for the best. Along with many others, we spend the afternoon doing laundry and writing letters to friends. We have a light dinner at the Enlisted Club and see an old movie on the VCR in our room. Early to bed for an early start tomorrow.

We are up early on Friday. I drop Donna off at the terminal, and I drive to long-term parking at the MWR Bldg 741, Ellis Avenue; the fee is $5 per week. I am fortunate to get a ride back to the terminal with a passenger picking up his car after arriving Space-A from Alaska. Donna has completed her breakfast at the terminal cafeteria and tells me that she has learned the good news that many of the Category III active duty passengers have moved during the night or early morning. The Space-A call for our flight is expected around 1000 local time. We visit the comfortable USO which is across the hall from the cafeteria in the passenger terminal building. The coffee and donuts are good, and we leave the USO a generous donation.

FLIGHT PROCESSING

Before we know it, the Space-A call is announced to begin in waiting area II promptly at 1000 hours. We have learned that there are 60 seats to Hickam AFB, HI. Of course we want to be booked all the way to RAAFB Richmond, AU, if possible. The call moves right along. When it gets to Category VI, there are only eight seats left, and we are luckily booked to RAAFB Richmond. We order and pay for our meals, our travel documents are carefully checked (passports must be good for at least six months) and we have Electronic Travel Authority (ETA) for Australia. Our weight is recorded and our bags (with wheels) are weighed (tight cargo limits on this flight). We are released to report back in 30 minutes for boarding at 1120 hours local time.

IN-FLIGHT

We board a blue bus for the trip to the aircraft which is parked down the ramp about a mile. Colonel Stanford B. Leavenworth, USA (Ret) (descendent of the Military Hero and the Leavenworth that the Fort is named for) is the ranking officer on today's flight. Families are boarded first and then Colonel Leavenworth followed by everyone else. We are seated near the pallets of cargo in seats facing the rear of the aircraft (for safety considerations). We hit our block time (when the aircraft starts its taxi for takeoff) of 1155 hours, and the aircraft is rolling down the taxiway. We are airborne precisely at 1215 hours as scheduled. The aircraft is very comfortable, and we are served lunch after about one hour of flying. Today's flight leg to Hickam AFB, HI, is scheduled for about five hours flying time.

We arrive in Hawaii on time and are told that we will have a longer than usual ground time of 33 1/2 hours. We will depart at

0110 Local Standard Time (LST) which is days out +2 or Sunday. We are fortunate to get a room at the Hale Koa Hotel (we spent our honeymoon here). It is now greatly expanded (the new Maui tower has 500 rooms for a total of 817 guest rooms and suites) and as wonderful as we remember. The beautiful beach is a great place to spend a layover in travel to our destination.

We get airborne on time for a scheduled five-hour and 50-minute flight to Pago Pago IAP (PPG/NSTU), AS. We arrive a few minutes late due to head winds and are met by the AMC ground service commercial contractor (GCA International, Inc.), who gives us bus service to the Rainmaker Hotel (largest hotel on the island) for our estimated two hours and 15 minutes of ground time. We depart Pago Pago at 0915 local time for a six hour and 35 minute flight to RAAFB Richmond, AU. When we arrive in Australia, we will have logged over 17 hours of flying time, days out +3 or the fourth day, and it will be 1210 hours on Monday (we have gained one day by traveling west across the International Date Line). Of course, we will lose this day when we return across the date line to Pago Pago, AS.

POST-FLIGHT

We clear immigration and customs at RAAFB Richmond with little effort. Later in our trip, we will be leaving from here to fly over (east 1,000 miles) to Christchurch IAP (CHC/NZCH), NZ. This is a Royal Australian Air Force Base where the USAF is a tenant. Everyone is very friendly and eager to be of assistance. We pick up a cab at the terminal for Windsor train station (about two miles), cost $8.00 AU. The train station is open from 0500-2400 hours daily with several trains into Sydney. We are in luck and get a train within the hour.

OUR VISIT TO AUSTRALIA

We check the hotel board in the Sydney train station and pick a medium-priced hotel (The Russell) near the Rocks Area (old town Sydney) and waterfront which is also near the renowned Opera House. After a short taxi ride, we check in the hotel and select a nice room at $80 AU or about $55 US ($1.00 US=$1.45 AU). After we freshen up, we dress for a walk to the Rocks Area and dine at one of the excellent seafood restaurants in that area.

Australia is a very large country. In fact, Australia is almost as large geographically as the USA. It is clear that we cannot see the entire country in one visit. We decide on visiting the Great Barrier Reef near the northern tropical city of Cairns. I have been an avid diver since my first tour in Vietnam. We will also be visiting Alice Springs and Ayers Rock, which are Donna's view of the real Australia. We book our airline travel to start on Friday with the popular domestic airline, Ansett Airlines of Australia to Sydney-Cairns-Alice Springs-Sydney. We could have flown to Alice Springs by Space-A Air but there is no Space-A to Cairns and the round trip Cairns-Sydney fare would

In Australia, John O'Neary checks out a kangaroo up close.

have been only slightly cheaper than the ticket we bought through Alice Springs. Also, we have much more flexibility.

A short walk from our hotel in Cairns we found the **Returned Services League of Australia** club. We were welcomed as allied service members and asked to sign in their guest book. We were given free use of the club, which had a large bar and lounge with service, a large dining room, reading/writing rooms, television rooms, game rooms and live music entertainment on Friday and Saturday evenings. The prices are moderate for bar, food and other services. There are similar clubs in New Zealand, **The New Zealand Returned Services Association, Inc.**

We enjoyed the QUICKSILVER catamaran on the Outer Barrier Reef Cruise from Port Douglas. The trip on the Kuranda Rail up to the 2,000-foot-high Atherton Tableland (home of fruit and vegetable farms) was also exciting and colorful. We were surprised to find a Returned Services League of Australia club in Atherton where we had lunch on sandwiches and beer at the bar. The drive through the rich sugar cane fields on the way back to Cairns was very interesting. It is now Monday and the flight from Cairns out west to the center of the continent at Alice Springs is over a very sparsely populated area of Australia. Among other things, we visit the Royal Flying Doctor's Service headquarters in Alice Springs and a Camel Station on the bus (coach) ride to Ayers Rock, which is as big and all-imposing as we had imagined. As we head (fly) back to Sydney, it is Friday.

We call RAAFB Richmond (as we have learned from the Space-A Air Opportunities book that we can telephone in for seats, Tel: C-011-61-245-87-1651) for seats to Christchurch IAP, NZ and learn that the flight will be departing on Thursday and that we are near the top of the Category VI list. There is time for a side trip to the Blue Mountains, about 60 miles west of Sydney. We book this as a bus tour including lodging. The mountains were beautiful and the trip was easy. We take the train up to Windsor on Wednesday and spend the night as our flight is due to depart at 0845 hours on Thursday. We make the flight which is three hours flying time. Immigration and customs clearance is a snap, and we are on our way within the hour.

OUR VISIT TO NEW ZEALAND

We plan an overnight in Christchurch and have reserved a hotel there before leaving Sydney. This is the most English city outside of England, and it is true to its reputation. Again we realize that we can't see everything on this, our first trip, so we plan to stay on the South Island of New Zealand and concentrate our fun there, which is still a large place. We plan to tour the Queenstown area, Milford Sound, Mount Cook and the Farley sheep farm country.

We map out a bus (coach) itinerary, which will allow us to see more of the countryside, and visit a travel agent. When we leave the agent, we are equipped with an exciting tour which will put us back in Christchurch a week from Thursday to catch the Friday flight to Pago Pago IAP, AS.

The all day coach run from Christchurch to Queenstown costs about $50 NZ (1.00 US=1.65 NZ so our bus ticket is $30.30 US) and is about 25% of the airfare. The coaches are very comfortable with restrooms and music. Take your own reading materials and games. There are rest stops about every two-and-a-half hours. The scenery is wonderful. Our lodging was in a neat small motel right on Lake Wakatipu, a large S-shaped lake scooped out by glaciers millions of years ago. We got in town in time to take the cable lift to the Skyline Restaurant on Bob's Peak (great view, wonderful live music for dancing and good buffet food).

We took one of the first buses to Milford Sound, a memorable 75-mile trip to New Zealand's most famous natural feature. Milford Sound is an awesome fiord that resulted from prehistoric glaciers which melted and let in the sea to form the sound. We took one of the two-hour narrated boat tours with lunch for about $25 NZ. The boat goes all the way out to the mouth of the fiord and turns around in the Tasman Sea on the west coast of New Zealand. On the trip back to Queenstown we saw helicopters with nets catching wild deer in the area and placing them with sling loads in waiting 18 wheelers for movement to ranch paddocks and domestic ranching. We are reminded that Queenstown is a major snow skiing area during the winter months of June, July and August. It is Saturday night, and we leave tomorrow for Mount Cook.

We are now traveling up the backbone of the South Island. There are many hydroelectric dams on lakes and rivers in this area which is the Alps of New Zealand. EnZed's peak in the Mount Cook National Park is over 12,400 feet above sea level.

From the hotel at the base of Mount Cook, 5000 feet, we saw helicopters ferrying people to the summit for a day of skiing down the mountain. We journey on to the town of Farley where our host for the Sheep Farm Stay meets us.

The sheep ranch is wonderful, and we go trout fishing in a lake for a big trout to cook in the smoker for lunch the next day. We help with chores such as checking the paddocks for strays, fallen sheep, etc. The rancher sometimes makes his rounds from paddock to paddock in a Volvo with an electric control to open gates. Dogs play a big part in working the sheep. The rancher's wife is a great cook. All meals are served family style and very informal. The rancher's wife takes us on a shopping trip at a delightful ski sweater shop. One is impressed with the clean and pristine nature of the country. The lifestyle here is simple, uncomplicated, peaceful and very straightforward. Great country.

RETURN FLIGHT TO CONUS

We make it back to Christchurch on Thursday night. We check on our Friday flight and find that all is A-OK; we are on the flight all the way to Hickam AFB, HI. The flight goes directly from Hickam AFB to McChord AFB, WA. Our car is at Travis AFB, CA, and we have a request in at Hickam AFB for Travis AFB, CA. The flight to Pago Pago IAP, AS, is five hours and 35 minutes with two-and-a-half hours of ground time and then on to Hickam AFB with a flying time of five hours and 50 minutes. We spend the next two nights in the Hickam AFB, BEQ and get a C-005B flight out to Travis, AFB.

We pick up our car from long-term parking and head home. Wow! What a trip and the price was right. The destination and return airfares were free. We would do it again. See you in the terminals!

LESSONS LEARNED: The following key lessons were learned from an imaginary Space-A air trip to Australia and New Zealand:

A. Pre-flight planning to include research on the countries to be visited and attractions is indispensable to a good visit. Knowing where you are going, how to get there, what it costs and what to expect, are all important to travel planning.

B. Pre-position your return request for Space-A travel at several locations in order to increase your chances of returning to your desired location.

Trivia Note: There are more sheep than people in New Zealand!

SECTION V

AN IMAGINARY SPACE-A AIR TRIP TO
SOUTH AMERICA (CHILE AND ARGENTINA)

TRIP PLANNING

The trip from CONUS to South America and return is a very popular and unusual trip as you will see. This military airlift route has been established to support United States Embassies and political and economic interests in the region. Spanish is the official language in all of the South American countries, with the exception of Brazil, where the national language is Portuguese; however, English is a popular second language in the South American region. Flights are less frequent on this route than, for example, the Central European and Middle Pacific routes. The routing (stations visited) on the South American trip is stable and changes very infrequently.

This trip is being made by Hans Maltsmittle, Master Warrant Officer (MW-5), USA (Ret) and his lovely bride of over forty years, Gretchen Maltsmittle. They have traveled extensively in Western Europe and the United States. Neither of them has ever traveled to the Caribbean, Central or South America. Both of them are very fluent in German and Polish. They both read and speak very limited Spanish. Their general health and physical mobility are good for their 70 years. The following is the Maltsmittles' account of their trip to South America:

The major personal objective of this trip is to locate relatives and friends who immigrated from Germany to the Lake Districts of Chile and Argentina during the 1920s, 1930s and 1940s. The broader overall travel objective is to visit and learn firsthand about a new area of the Americas.

We carefully study the *Military Space-A Air Opportunities Around the World* book primarily using the Location Identifiers and Cross-Reference Index and the Space-A Air Route Map. Our study discloses that the best departure location/station in CONUS for Caribbean, Central and South American flights is Charleston AFB (CHS/KCHS), SC, in terms of favorable routing and frequency of flights among other things. The second-best CONUS departure location to reach our destination of Santiago, CL is Jackson IAP/Allen C. Thompson Field (JAN/KJAN), MS.

Our primary destination is the Lake Districts of Chile and Argentina. The major towns on the Chile side (west) of the lakes are Puerto Varas and Puerto Montt; on the Argentina side (east) of the lakes are San Carlos and Nahuel Huapi. This lake area is approximately 580 statute miles south of Santiago, CL, and 875 statute miles southwest of Buenos Aires, AG. For the map enthusiast, the coordinates for Puerto Montt are 41 degrees and 50 minutes south latitude and 73 degrees and 5 minutes west longitude. For a reference, the corresponding coordinate in the northern latitude and longitude, is Torrington, CT, which is located in northwest Connecticut near the Massachusetts border. With this essential geographic information in mind, we are prepared to select the best routing.

We can access the Lake Districts by flights which originate at Jackson IAP/Allen C. Thompson Field (JAN/KJAN), MS and fly to Charleston AFB (CHS/KCHS), SC, to Juan Santamaria IAP (SJO/MROC), CR to Arturo Merino Benitez IAP (SCL/SCEL), Santiago, Chile (CL). This approach will take us south from Santiago to Puerto Montt and then east through the Lake Districts to Argentina. We also have the option of starting our trip via flights which originate at Memphis IAP/ANGB (MEM/KMEM), TN to Charleston AFB (CHS/KCHS), SC, to Alexander Hamilton Apt (St Croix), VI to Brasilia Airport (BSB/SBBR), BR, to Carrasco IAP (MVD/SUMU), UY to Ezeiza Airport (BUE/SAEZ), Buenos Aires, AR. We could then proceed southwest to San Carlos. Since we want to spend more time on the Chile side of the Andes mountains, we have selected Charleston AFB, SC, as our point of departure for Santiago, CH, because there are more Space-A Air Opportunities from this station which is the staging area/station for the Caribbean, Central and South America. As residents and natives of Lancaster, PA, this trip will require an approximate 625-mile automobile drive of about 14 hours, including brief rest stops.

We note that our entry and exit point in Chile is Arturo Merino Benitez Airport (SCL/SCEL) (Santiago), CH, and in Argentina is Ezeiza Airport (BUE/SAEZ) (Buenos Aires), AR.

We fax our Space-A Travel Request, AMC Form 140 to Charleston AFB, SC, C-843-963-3060. We list the following five countries in order of priority: Chile, Argentina, Peru, Uruguay and Brazil. This action is taken about 55 days before we plan to fly. We also send our Space-A Travel Request to the above countries for our return to CONUS. The faxes to the overseas return countries go out about 50 to 55 days before our desired return from overseas. The overseas fax numbers are in the *Military Space-A Air Opportunities Around The World* book.

We have reviewed carefully Appendix S, Visa Information and Personnel Entrance Requirements. We discover the following Personnel Entrance Requirements for the countries which we will be visiting: Argentina: ID cards, passport, no visa up to 3 months; Brazil: ID cards, passport and visa (required prior to arrival); Chile: ID cards, passport, onward/return ticket; Peru: ID card, passport, onward/return ticket. If we are flying through a country and not leaving the airport then entrance requirements do not apply. Visa information is contained in Appendix S. To be on the safe side, we send our passports to the Brazilian embassy along with passport pictures, $45.00 ea fee and SASE for return of passports. We also comply with the notification requirements to USDAO of travel plans.

We begin our car trip to Charleston AFB early on the fourth Sunday in October in order to provide time for any unforeseen delays in road travel. We have planned our trip for late October/November because the seasons in the Southern Hemisphere, where we will be traveling, are the opposite of those in the U.S.; therefore it will be spring in November. Several calls ahead to the Charleston AFB passenger terminal information office at C-843-963-3083 have indicated that the flight originating on the first Wednesday from Jackson IAP/Allen C. Thompson Field, MS is on schedule and will depart Charleston AFB on days out +0 or the first Wednesday. The terminal has our Space-A application and reports to us that we are numbers four and five in Category VI. We trade off the driving assignment and arrive at the temporary military lodging (TML), The Inns of Charleston, 102 North Davis Drive, Charleston AFB, SC, 29404-4825, C-843-963-3806, Fax: C-843-963-3394, reservation hours 0800-1700, where we have reserved accommodations for three nights. Our reservations are confirmed with a credit card for a late (after 1800 hours) arrival on Sunday.

We are early risers on Monday and head for the terminal to confirm our Space-A application because among other things, we want to see what the overall waiting list looks like. Again we confirm that we are near the top of the Category VI list. There are no emergency leave passengers, seven active duty Marines returning to duty at various stations on our scheduled route, three foreign officers and their families (for a total of 12 seats), three retirees ahead of us in Category VI and four retirees below us in category VI. We calculate a total passenger load (manifest) of 28 seats. There may be some Space-A passengers from Jackson IAP/Allen C. Thompson Field, MS continuing on to South America. Looks like there will be a lot of room as our aircraft is scheduled to be a C-141B Starlifter cargo mission which is to be configured at Jackson IAP/Allen C. Thompson Field, MS with airline passenger type seats, up front and facing to the rear plus many wrapped pallets of cargo.

We have a quick breakfast at Burger King and attend Mass at the Catholic Chapel on base. After Church we head for the golf course where I rent clubs and shoes and play a round of golf while Gretchen reads the Monday Atlanta Constitution, "which covers Dixie like the dew," or something like that! After nine holes of golf, we have delicious hamburgers and beer for lunch at the club. We take a quick orientation drive around the base using the map which we picked up from the security guard on entering the base on Sunday night. We find the long-term parking, where we will be leaving our car, at Scott Street and Davis Drive across from the Child Care Center. The long-term parking is four blocks from the passenger terminal. We decide on a light dinner at a local restaurant, which was recommended by the golf pro, and afterwards head for our room to watch TV then early to bed.

On Tuesday morning we check the passenger information and our status at the terminal. There are no material changes. Confident that we have a good chance of making this trip, we leave the base to tour old town Charleston and lunch in one of the many seafood restaurants. After a super seafood luncheon, we take one of the walking tours outlined in a brochure which we picked up in the passenger terminal. This is real inexpensive sightseeing and healthful fun. We return to the base passenger terminal to check our status. The clerk tells us that all is the same except that eight government civilian employees with a lot of strange looking equipment signed in and will be accommodated as Space-Required passengers on our flight. The passenger load is growing, and we are told that we should expect the passenger list to increase as we near the departure time.

The early afternoon is spent in a laundromat doing our laundry and picking up some last minute supplies at the base exchange. About 1430 hours we go back to the terminal to see if our C-141B from Jackson IAP/Allen C. Thompson Field, MS has arrived. The flight arrived at 1100 hours local time, and the aircraft crew will have a minimum 15 hour rest here before beginning our flight to Central and South America. We learn that the show time is 0015 hours (Wednesday) which is three hours before the scheduled departure time of 0315 hours. We are told that three hours rather than the customary two hours of show time (reporting time before departure) is due to increased security for the flight; so we are early to bed at 1530 hours to make our show time of 0015 hours, Wednesday.

On Tuesday night we are awakened at 2300 hours by the 24-hour desk. We had packed before going to bed; our toilet articles are added to our carry-on bags, we grab a cup of coffee in the billeting lounge, check out and drive to the passenger terminal where I drop off Gretchen and the bags. I drive to long-term parking, find a spot under a light, lock the car and see a security guard car which I hail. He can't give me a lift due to police regulations, but he does point out the shortest route to the passenger terminal.

PRE-FLIGHT

I get to the passenger terminal by 2400, and we have time for a cup of coffee. We learn that there are 48 seats on this flight. The Space-A call begins promptly at 0015 (Wednesday) with the familiar Space-A refrain, "Anyone desiring transportation to San Jose, CR, Santiago, CL, etc., please assemble at the Space-A desk in the main passenger terminal." The NCOIC of passenger services, SMSgt Gomez, is managing the call. The Space-Required passengers, eight government civilian employees are processed first and given their boarding passes. Next there were four passengers from Jackson IAP/Allen C. Thompson Field, MS who are processed, turning in their old boarding passes for new passes. There are no emergency leave passengers, Category I, no EML passengers in Category II, seven active duty passengers, Category III, no unaccompanied EML passengers, Category IV, 12 foreign officer passengers, Category V and the passengers who were ahead of us in Category VI did not show; we are processed next. Also there are six more passengers in Category VI who are processed for a total passenger load of 39. As you can see there are six Space-A lists, one for each of the six categories of travel.

During the in-processing, we have checked our two pieces of luggage with wheels, each weighing less than the maximum 70 pounds each. Also, we paid $1.50 each for breakfast meals and $1.90 each for lunch meals en route to Santiago, CL, or a total of $6.80. The paid meals information is recorded on our boarding passes along with our Julian sign-up date (retain all boarding passes until your trip is over). The flying time to San Jose, CR is approximately three hours and thirty minutes. We go through a pre-boarding security check of both our checked bags and our carry-on bag; all is well. We have about 40 minutes to wait before boarding. Families with children are boarded first followed by an LTC from the Bolivian Army who is the ranking passenger on today's flight. There is a short walk from the passenger terminal to the waiting C-141B aircraft. About 15 minutes after boarding, we depart the ramp (block time) and move to the taxi-way and wait behind two other aircraft for our turn to enter the runway and depart. We are airborne at about 0315 as planned.

IN-FLIGHT

Our breakfast meal is served at 0415 U.S. EST. The aircraft has fresh coffee and water in the galley. The restrooms are unisex and more than adequate. There are also blankets and pillows for our comfort. We have brought along our own reading materials and games (non-electronic), Gretchen has movie magazines and I have crossword puzzles. We arrive at Juan Santamaria IAP, San Jose, CR and deplane and remain in the secure lounge until our aircraft is serviced and ready for departure. The servicing takes about two hours, we re-board for the approximately six-hour flight to Santiago, CL. At 1000 hours we are served our lunch meal. The ride to Santiago, CL is smooth and relatively uneventful. We arrive at 1445 hours local time (GMT-4, same as AST) at Arturo Merino Benitez IAP, Santiago, CL. We show our ID cards to the U.S. personnel processing the aircraft and our passports to immigration, and we are required to buy a tourist card for a fee of $20.00 each in U.S. dollars. The Customs process is a breeze as we are not carrying any prohibited or dutiable items.

We expect less jet lag since we are traveling north to south rather than east to west or west to east. In fact, from Charleston AFB, SC, to Santiago, CL we have remained in the same time zone, GMT-5 until we reached southern Peru where we crossed into the GMT-4 time zone.

We checked our bags at Charleston AFB for Santiago, CL. In case of an unexpected stopover, our carry-on bags contained toilet articles, medications, night-shirts and clean shirts and underwear for the next day. Checking bags through is advisable anytime that you have an overnight en route to your destination.

POST-FLIGHT

We line up for a taxi into the city. Santiago is located in the center of the country and set between the Pacific Ocean and the Andes Mountains. The city has evolved as the country's political, commercial and cultural capital. The city's history and heritage goes back to the 16th century. Our hotel is small and near the 18th century cathedral and the main square.

After settling in our hotel, we take a walk through the city central, select a seafood restaurant from several recommended by the hotel. The shellfish cocktails (shrimp/lobster) are wonderful and cheap by US standards. The grilled game fish (probably tuna) is outstanding, and the chocolate pie is also wonderful with very dark coffee. The premium Chilean chardonnay with a medium oak cast is cheap and wonderful. The TV in the hotel lounge is in Spanish, so we retire for a long night's sleep.

OUR VISIT TO CHILE AND ARGENTINA

After a very restful sleep, (Wednesday night) we have recovered from our mild jet lag, if any, and we go in search of a recommended English-speaking travel agent. We learn of a tour through the Lake Districts of Chile and Argentina which terminates in Buenos Aires, AR - just what we want. The best part is that we can interrupt the tour at several points in the Lake Districts then continue on with a later tour. We buy the tour which departs the next day (Friday) for Puerto Montt via air.

After a night in Puerto Montt, (Friday) we bus to Puerto Varas where we leave the tour to contact those relatives. Through leads we have, we are fortunate to contact two cousins, and they in turn know several other cousins and two uncles. A party is arranged for the next day (Sunday), and we are very excited. The party is a type of German festival with zither and accordion players (some dancing) and loads of German wurst, strudel, great Chilean wines and oh yes, beer. It is wonderful to establish contact with our distant relatives and best of all to be able to speak freely in our native German. We have invited our German cousins and uncles to visit us in the U.S., and we hope to host them there soon.

After three days (Tuesday), from our hotel along the festive rosebush-lined streets in the lakeside resort of Puerto Varas, we rejoin a new tour via motor coach which travels along the southern shore of Lago Llanquihue. We take pictures of the thundering Petrohue Rapids. We check the soaring Osorno Volcano as we cross Lago Todos los Santos by ferry. We continue by motor coach through an area of pristine wilderness adorned by emerald lakes, thick pine forests and snow-capped peaks. We stay overnight in the quaint village of Peulia which is on the Chilean side of the border on a lake at about 3,000 meters or 10,000 feet above sea level.

The next day (Wednesday) we continue our motor coach tour. We capture the splendid vistas of the surrounding lakes and mountains. This is a leisurely drive to Lopez Bay, Lago Moreno and the Llao Peninsula. There was a brief stop at the border. Inspectors came on board the motor coach for a look around; the driver and tour guide had our passports and took care of the immigration and customs details. We arrived at the chic alpine resort of Bariloche on the shores of fjord-like Lago Nahuel Huapi where we took an exciting chair-lift ride up to one of the lookout points at Gerro Campanario. This is the heart of Argentina's beautiful Lake District. We finish up the day's activities by admiring the famous chocolate factories - each built like a Swiss Chalet.

After a great night in the cabarets of Bariloche with a few great glasses of wine and some sleep, we are up and ready for our flight from San Carlos to Buenos Aires (Thursday). We arrive by noon and immediately go on a leather shopping tour to seek out the best buys. After a night here in the hotel, our formal tour is over (Friday). Now we are on our own for more travel and the return trip home.

Our return trip back to Charleston AFB, SC, is scheduled for departure the next Wednesday. On Friday afternoon we call the AMC contact at the USMILGP, C-011-54-1-777-1207. We are assured that they have our fax and that it looks like there will be no problem in our making the flight. There is very little for us to do now except check the status of our flight again on next Tuesday and enjoy our visit.

We arrange a tour in our hotel to the pampas where we experience the atmosphere of Argentine country life as we visit an estancia (cattle ranch). We get acquainted with the lifestyle, folklore and traditions of the gauchos. An excellent barbecue lunch is served with the warm hospitality of the host before we return to the city.

For Saturday we have arranged a tour which starts at the Plaza de Mayo for a visit to the President's Pink House and the Metropolitan Cathedral. Also on the agenda is the historic San Telmo, the oldest neighborhood of Buenos Aires, the ornate Colon Opera House, the Recoleta district and the cemetery where Eva Peron is buried. The evening portion of the tour includes a typical Argentine steak dinner and a great performance of the latin tango.

Sunday is a day to attend church and rest. Argentina is a predominately Catholic country, the large cathedrals are crowded. Our hotel recommends a smaller church which is a short walk. We enjoy the Mass and singing in Spanish. In the afternoon we window-shop along the broad city boulevards.

We spend Monday and Tuesday searching for just the right presents for family members at home. The leather shops are plentiful, and the assortment of handcrafted leather goods is vast.

RETURN FLIGHT TO CONUS

After enjoying several days of sightseeing, we are ready to go home. A call to the USMILGP in Buenos Aires confirms that all is well and that we will be on the flight departing on Wednesday for Alexander Hamilton Apt (St Croix), VI terminating in Charleston AFB, SC. The flight to Alexander Hamilton Apt, VI is long. Our scheduled flight duration is for about six hours. We have reserved a dinner meal at $3.00 each. We are processed and join a passenger group of about 40 people. We depart on time at 1845 hours and arrive at Alexander Hamilton, VI at 0145 hours local time (Thursday). There is a two-hour ground time scheduled for Alexander Hamilton. We wait in the secure area while the aircraft is serviced for our flight to Charleston AFB, SC.

We drop off a few passengers and pick up new passengers at Alexander Hamilton Apt (St Croix), VI as we fly north back to the U.S. The longest leg of our flight is from Ezeiza APT (BUE/SAEZ), Buenos Aires, AR to Alexander Hamilton APT (STX/TISX), VI six hours.

We arrive back at Charleston AFB, SC, at 0630 hours on Friday. We go through immigration and customs. We have a few leather items to declare, far less than our $400 per person duty free exemption.

I walk to long-term parking to claim our car. Gretchen waits at the terminal with the luggage. It is Friday. We will be home tomorrow, Saturday, just three weeks since we departed. Wow, what a trip! The price was right; most of the airfares were free.

LESSONS LEARNED: The following key lessons were learned from an imaginary Space-A air trip to South America (Chile and Argentina):

A. The most important step in successful Space-A air travel is to plan ahead.

B. Check frequently on the Space-A roster/waiting list. New people with higher priorities can and do join the waiting list. Know your chance of obtaining a particular flight; this gives you the flexibility to stay or not stay in the terminal and to join other flights at this or nearby stations.

C. Learn the local ground rules regarding registration via telephone, reporting times, Space-A calls, processing, block and departure times.

SECTION VI

AN IMAGINARY SPACE-A TRIP TO SOUTHEAST ASIA (JAPAN, KOREA, THAILAND AND SINGAPORE)

BACKGROUND: Like the veterans of World War II, the veterans of the Korean Conflict (referred to as "a war" by those who were directly involved) and the Vietnam War want to return to the area and revisit, if possible, where they were in combat and relive other aspects of the country. They want to again smell the pungent smells, see the skies, the morning calm, monsoon rains, and hear the languages spoken again. They want to see the people going about their daily lives, embracing their customs and culture. The veterans need to know that they lived through an experience which was real and not only a faint dream from their imagination. There are other reasons for wanting to visit Northeast and Southeast Asia. The countries of this region are each unique in their own ways. A visit to this area is always a different and pleasurable experience for most people of the western world.

TRIP PLANNING

We have selected Japan because it has been a gateway to the Northeast and Southeast Asia region, particularly after World War II. During both the Korean and Vietnam wars many United States military units and individual service members went through Japan as "a staging area" en route to the combat zones in Korea and Vietnam. Many wounded were also evacuated from the battle areas to Japan before being evacuated on to the CONUS for treatment. Japan continues as the logistical base for many of our forces deployed throughout Northeast and Southeast Asia. In view of this fact, many of our airlift missions originate in the CONUS and fly to Japan before flying on to other stations in the region.

Our trip is taken by MGySgt Alfred Rockertime, USMC (Ret) and his wife Brenda Rockertime who live in Portland, OR. MGySgt Rockertime has recently retired from his second career as a high school physical education (gymnastics) teacher. Brenda is also a retired teacher from the Portland, OR school system where she taught English (and sometimes morale philosophy) for over 30 years. The Rockertimes do not have children, but they do have two loving dogs, a bull terrier for the MGySgt (named Gunnie) and a toy Fox Terrier for Brenda (named Tootie). The dogs will be left with friends as dogs are not permitted on Space-A flights. Duty passengers can take their pets (country restrictions allowing) and pay for their transportation.

Since MGySgt Rockertime served in both Korea and Vietnam, we plan to visit Japan (Tokyo area), Kadena, (Okinawa) Japan, Seoul, DMZ area, Korea, Bangkok, Thailand, and Singapore. There is no Space-A Air travel at this time to Vietnam. We could take a commercial air trip from Bangkok, to Ho Chi Minh City (Saigon), Vietnam and return to Bangkok, but this would make our trip too long and there are many other things that we want to see during the three to four weeks which we have planned for this trip.

We both review the *Military Space-A Air Opportunities Around The World* book and the *Military Space-A Air Route Map* and find that there are three major departure areas on the West Coast that will get us to Yokota Air Base (OKO/RJTY), JP which is our target destination. In southern California there are flights to Yokota AB from Los Angeles IAP (LAX/KLAX) CA. These flights go through Seattle/Tacoma IAP, WA before going to Yokota AB. In northern California, Travis AFB (SUU/KSUU), CA has numerous flights to Yokota AB. Most flights travel the central Pacific route through Hawaii, Guam and Okinawa to Yokota AB. In the Seattle/Tacoma, WA area there are flights from McChord AFB (TCM/KTCM), WA and Seattle/Tacoma IAP (SEA/KSEA), WA which fly to Yokota AB through Hawaii or Alaska. Given this information, we decide that the best departure locations for us are in the Seattle/Tacoma area.

We fax our Space-A Travel Request, AMC Form 140, to McChord AFB, WA C-253-512-3815 This will also record our request at Seattle/Tacoma IAP, WA as there is dual sign-up for these two stations. We list Singapore as our final destination and also list Japan, Korea, Hawaii and "all" as our five countries. This is about 55 days before our planned departure during the first week of October. The weather is ideal this time of year in our destination area. The weather in central Japan and south Korea is similar to the weather found in the northeastern United States. The weather in Bangkok and Singapore is always hot but October is a bit cooler and dryer than other times of the year.

PRE-FLIGHT

We decide to drive from our home in Portland, OR to the Seattle/Tacoma area, a distance of 170 miles. We decide to seek lodging at McChord AFB, WA which is one of our departure points. McChord AFB (TCM/KTCM), WA is located 8 miles south of Tacoma, WA. Our second planned departure station, Seattle/Tacoma IAP (SEA/KSEA), WA is 15 miles south of Seattle, WA. We call the Evergreen Inn, Bldg 166, Tel: C-888-235-6343, and reserve a double room in the VAQ for $15.50 per night for three nights beginning Sunday, 1 October 2000.

We take I-5 north, which is an easy ride, and we stop at the Lewis and Clark State Park off I-5 to eat our picnic lunch which Brenda has packed for our trip. We arrive at McChord AFB at 1500 hrs and go directly to the Passenger Terminal at Bldg 1179 which operates 24 hours daily. We check the status board and find that there are no flights until Friday which will get us to Yokota AB. The Friday flight is a C017A with the following routing: KTCM to SUU to PHIK to RJTY to {turnaround}PHIK to KSUU to KTCM. From a study of ICAOs we translate this into: McChord AFB, WA (originating station) to Travis AFB, CA to Hickam AFB, HI to Yokota AB, JP, mission turnaround point, to Hickam AFB, HI to Travis AFB, CA to McChord AFB, WA (terminating station).

The board does not show the AMC contract or "Patriot Flights" departing Seattle/Tacoma IAP (SEA/KSEA), WA but the Air Force Sergeant tells us that there are Patriot Flights on Tuesday and Friday and both are direct flights to Yokota AB, JP. The show time is 0030hrs Wednesday morning. The flight originates at Los Angeles IAP on Tuesday. We call the Seattle/Tacoma IAP Space-A desk and discover that they have our Space-A Travel Request and that we are numbers 3 and 4 on the Category VI waiting list. The Sergeant also tells us that the Patriot Flight coming in from Los Angles IAP on Tuesday is an L1011 wide-body jet with 150 seats allocated to Seattle/Tacoma IAP. At the moment there are only about 80 Active Duty Passengers expected for this flight. This is an ideal opportunity from many points of view; first it is a direct flight, second it is a commercial passenger aircraft with all the comforts (hot meals, drinks, movies, etc.) and last, it is the first flight to our destination. We decide to check in at our Temporary Military Lodging (TML), have dinner at the combined club and watch a movie on TV.

Monday we are up early, go to the gym for a quick work-out, shower and eat breakfast at McDonald's. The MGySgt takes the car to the on post gas station for an oil change, lubrication and fill-up with gas. I spend my time in the Exchange shopping for toilet items, snacks, and magazines for the trip. I also pick up a new copy of *Temporary Military Lodging Around The World* and *Military Space-A Air Opportunities Around The World* to replace our well-worn and outdated copies. After watching a movie on TV we get to bed early for an early rise and a move north to Seattle/Tacoma IAP on Wednesday.

We have breakfast at the NCO club and decide to leave our car in long-term parking at McChord AFB. The long-term lot is an easy walk from/to the Passenger Terminal. Alfred drops Brenda and the bags at the PaxTerm and walks back after parking in the long-term lot. This is a lock-up with a 60-day maximum period. We learn from our *Military Living Military Space-A Air Opportunities* book that we can take the SEA-TAC Airporter (bus), Tel: C-1-800-562-7948, a service that operates daily, 0520-2250 (two hour intervals), reservations required, $10 one way. We reserve an early afternoon shuttle-run to Seattle/Tacoma IAP. The bus is prompt and comfortable.

The AMC desk is located on the south side of the main terminal between American West and Asiana Airlines. Hours: 0800-1600 daily. The desk is also manned when flights are departing or arriving. As a safety precaution, we check with the desk on our place on the category VI Space-A roster and find that we are still No. 3 and 4 on the waiting list. We put our bags in a commercial locker and take a cab to an early dinner near the airport. After dinner we attend a war movie "Saving Private Ryan." Alfred enjoys the movie very much.

We have lunch and bowl a few lanes at the Bowling Center. Alfred meets a service mate, John P. Sneary, 1stSgt, USMC, (Ret) at the gas station who is also trying to get to Japan. 1stSgt Sneary goes to Japan often as he has family living there. He is meeting us at a great pizza restaurant he frequents, outside the gate at 1900 hours.

We get back to the airport in plenty of time for our 0330 hours Space-A call. The categories I through V are called and processed for boarding. There are over 20 seats remaining for category VI, so we make the flight with ease. In the processing we each pay a $6.00 airport departure tax. The meals are paid for in the contract for the aircraft by the Air Force. We will be able to see free movies and may order a beer or wine with our meals on board the aircraft. Security is tight and it takes a long time to process and board the aircraft. However, all is well and we depart at 0300 hours local Pacific Time or GMT-8. It is 2000 hours on Thursday (we will be crossing the international date line) in Tokyo as we depart the West Coast.

IN-FLIGHT

The flight will be cruising above 30,000 feet to take advantage of the jet streams and we will be flying the sub-polar route northwest over Alaska, then southwest over the Bering Sea staying east of the Russian territories over which we do not have permission for overflight, a bit east of the Japanese north island of Hokkaido, to over the Japanese main island of Honshu to the Tokyo area and Yokota AB, JP. Our total flying distance is approximately 3,750 miles or 6 hours and 20 minutes flying time. It will be 0230 hours, Friday, local time in Japan when we arrive.

The cabin service is wonderful. We get a hot breakfast after about two hours of flight and a hot lunch/dinner is served about one hour before arrival. The free movies are wonderful and up-to-date. Beer is $2.00 and wine is $3.00, both are good quality. The seating is typical. Airline spacing is a bit tight because the MGySgt is a solid 6' 1", 240 lbs. We lift the arm rest between our seats and Brenda who is 5' 8", 140 lbs shares some of her room in the seats. We have asked for one aisle seat in order to avoid disturbing others when moving to restrooms. We eat and drink lightly and consume a lot of water as the cabin air is very dry.

OUR VISIT TO JAPAN

We land at Yokota AB, JP on time and taxi to our gate. Deplaning is prompt with families and those needing assistance last. The Japanese immigration and customs processing is easy and we exit the terminal with our bags. We called ahead for lodging but were unable to make a reservation, so we are going to try a walk-in at the Kanto Lodge, Bldg 10, Airlift Avenue and 1st Street. The lodging facility is a short one block away. We are fortunate to get one of the last rooms, book it for two days at $24 per night. We promptly go to bed to get some much needed sleep.

After resting for one day we check out and take the Government Shuttle bus, 0930 hrs, from PaxTerm, Bldg 80, free to the New Sanno hotel in Tokyo. We book a double for 3 nights at $77 per night. We pick up some travel brochures at the Information and Tours desk and study them during lunch in the hotel. Lunch was wonderful. We pick an afternoon tour of the city because it goes to some of the areas which Alfred visited when he was stationed at Iwakuni MCAS, on the south island of Honshu, 750 kilometers southwest of Tokyo. The tour was wonderful with a very good English-speaking guide. We decide to eat Mongolian barbecue in the hotel, one of Alfred's favorites. Brenda has bought Alfred a Japanese style kimono bathrobe in silk with black outside and red inside, an ideal combination of colors for a man of the corps. Happy birthday-Alfred's 68th. After purchasing some Japanese Yen at the hotel cashier, we are not sleepy, so we take an expensive taxi ride to the Ginza District where we wander about admiring the nightlife. We stop in a bar which we find out later is a cross-dressing place. This is too much for Brenda, so we leave immediately.

OUR VISIT TO SINGAPORE

We enjoy our re-visit to Tokyo and are ready to continue our travels. We call Yokota AB Pax Term at C-011-81-3117-55-9540/5661 and discover that there is a C-017A flight to RSAF Paya Lebar (QPG/WSAP), Singapore at 1600 hours today. Show time is 1400 hours. The information desk informs us that we can get a shuttle bus to Yokota AB leaving at 1130 hours with a 1300 hours arrival. We go for it and are "travel ready" in the terminal by 1330 hours. "Travel ready" means that our entire party is present in the terminal, we have our checked baggage ready to check, our carry-on baggage in hand, our documentation is on our person and correct, i.e., ID cards, passports and immunization records and we have funds (currency and travelers checks).

We make the flight and find ourselves airborne to RSAF Paya Lebar, SG direct. The new C-017A is a very smooth ride but the plastic-formed seats are as uncomfortable as we had heard. However, the price is right, "free" except for the in-flight meal which we ordered at $3.00 each. Prior to landing, the load master tells us that an Air Force bus is meeting the flight to take the crew and 10 airmen on board to the combined Air Force/Navy Headquarters at Sembawang. This complex (a previous United Kingdom Naval Base) is located in the north central section of the island of Singapore on the Straits of Johore. It is 19 kilometers north of the city (central) of Singapore. They confirm that there is lodging at the Sling Inn, 247 Bermuda Road, FPO AP 96534-5000, Tel: C-011-65-257-0256. Space-A is $40.00 per room.

The next day, we have breakfast at the Eagle Club, in walking distance. We check out, take a taxi to the Orchard Road district and to a small but nice hotel, economy rate ($50.00 per night). After checking in we tour Chinatown and stay there for dinner; the food is absolutely wonderful.The next day we spend shopping for Christmas presents for friends and relatives. By four o'clock (1600 hours) we are tired and head for the Raffles Hotel and have of course, a "Singapore Sling" at the bar overlooking the pool. The room rates here start at about $250.00 per room per night.

The MGySgt had always wanted to take the overnight train between Singapore and Bangkok, so Brenda checks it out and finds that they can get a first-class reserved roomette for two on a special express train which leaves the next night at 1900 hours and arrives the next day at 1100 hours in Bangkok. The fare is not cheap; in addition to the first-class tickets there is a 50 baht each surcharge for the special express train and 250 baht for the sleeping cabin. These surcharges are about $9.50. Fortunately the dollar is strong against the baht at $1.00=37.00 baht. These are first-class tickets with the roomette sleeper, dining car, and club car with entertainment. They may not travel this way again so they go for it.

OUR VISIT TO THAILAND

Bangkok is north and slightly west of Singapore. The train northbound, crosses over the Straits of Johore into mainland Malaysia and continues north along the peninsula to Thailand. Then north up the Thailand peninsula along the Gulf of Thailand to an eastern direction into Bangkok. We enjoy a wonderful dinner with white glove service and a few drinks in the club car while enjoying singers and piano players. We turn in for an early rise to see the sights. Traveling at night we can't see very much. The room porter brings our coffee and tea early and after dressing, we have breakfast and then return to a made-up fresh compartment where we can see the sights from our window. This train does not make many stops. The train is powered by twin diesel locomotives and the route speed is up to 120 kilometers per hour in some sections. The total distance is 1,050 miles in 16 hours or an average speed of 66 kilometers per hour. We arrive on time like we departed on time at the Bangkok's Hua Lamphong Railway Station on Rama IV Road.

This has been a terrific trip and we enjoyed every moment of the trip from boarding to departure.

We went through immigration and customs when we crossed into Thailand on the train. So we grab a cab and head for our hotel, the Siam Inter-Continental at 967 Rama I Road, a three-night package, $55.00 per night, reserved based on a friend's recommendation. This is a beautiful hotel and a bargin at our package rates. We have lunch at the hotel and then retire to our room for an afternoon nap. We wake in time for dinner and go to the Three Vikens for dinner, a favorite of Alfred's who was here in 1968 on R & R from Vietnam. The food is mainly smorgasbord and very good.

The next day we go on a motor launch tour on the Chao Phraya River. We visit the vegetable and flower markets along the river and also go through the royal barge sheds on the river where some of the royal barges are hundreds of years old and still in serviceable condition. We lunch at the Oriental Hotel on the Chao Phraya River. In the afternoon we visit the Wat Traimit "Temple of the Golden Buddha." It is solid gold, three meters high and weighs 5.5 tons. It was at one time covered with plaster to conceal it from enemies. It is treasured for its cultural value and the value of the gold.

That evening we attend Mui-Thi boxing where they use elbows, knees, bare feet, as well as gloved fists. The MGySgt loves every minute and it reminds him of his basic training.

We had called the CHJUSMAGTHAI when we arrived to check on our application for Space-A travel. We discover that we are near the top of the category VI list and that there is a flight to Yokota AB, JP in two days. The flight is scheduled to stop in Kadena AB, JP en route. We report on Monday at 1200 hours show time at CHJUSMAGTHAI, Bldg D, Room 114, 7 Sathorntal Road. After reporting, we transfer by Thai Airways bus directly to the Military Terminal at the Royal Thai Air Force Base, Don Muang. All Space-A passengers cannot report directly to the terminal but must take the transfer bus. Security is very tight on this base.

OUR VISIT TO KOREA

We get airborne quickly on the C-130E aircraft. The noise level is high. Alfred has personalized earplugs from his service in Vietnam and has flown this aircraft many times. Brenda gets earplugs from the crew chief. We are soon at Kadena AB, JP. We discover that there is a flight with plenty of seats leaving for Osan AB, RK near Seoul, RK where we want to go. We persuade the Space-A desk to off load our bags. We meet the Space-A call, get on the manifest and we are off to our last oriental city visit. This is a mixed passenger/cargo flight via a commercial L100. The ride is smooth and effortless. Korean Immigration and customs is easy and we catch the Air Force bus to Yongsan South

Post in Seoul and the Dragon Hill Lodge where we called from Kadena AB, JP for a reservation. We check into a double room for $65.00 per night. This is a beautiful new facility which is part of the Army's operated Armed Forces Recreation facilities. A 14 million dollar expansion will be completed in 2000 which will add 95 rooms and a 233-space parking garage. This is plush military living at a fair price.

The next day we visit south post, get a temporary ration card which allows us to purchase items in the exchange and the commissary. We spend the afternoon loosening up in the bowling alley. Also, we have one of their famous hamburgers for lunch.

The next day we hire a rental car with driver to try to find the area where Alfred was wounded during the Korean war as a 18-year-old rifleman. Alfred's memory is a bit foggy but he remembers the direction from Seoul, so equipped with some old maps and some new maps we set out on our journey. We find the rail crossing which now has an overhead bridge but is recognizable as the place the USMC company level fight with the North Korean Regiment took place. We take some pictures; it is obviously painful for Alfred, so we do not stay too long but head back to Yongsan and the Dragon Lodge.

We have booked the special tour to the DMZ. We leave from Yongsan Post on a special bus with a tour guide. It is a 2 and 1/2-hour drive to the DMZ area where we pick up a military guide to the conference facility. From the Red Cross house on the south side we are able to see North Korean guards in the DMZ. Frankly they look short, small and weak in stature. We look through binoculars into the north area and the propaganda village which is spouting music and propaganda messages aimed at South Korea. The tunneling activity under the DMZ seems to have stopped, but we see one of the previous tunnels which we intercepted that could pass through an infantry division in a few hours.

We have lunch and a drink at the DMZ detachment club. The club is noted for its food quality and we are not disappointed with the quality and presentation of our lunch. We climb back on the bus for the long ride back to Yongsan. We have dinner at the NCO club and stayed to play the slots for an hour or so. We don't win much—a few quarters.

The next day we head for Itaewan, a discount shopping area outside the gate from South Post Yongsan. They are famous for such items as men's and ladies' tailored clothing, luggage, brass items, sports shoes and clothing, sweaters, shirts and other soft goods manufactured in Korea. Most items have designer brand labels but also most of the merchandise is seconds. The prime quality goods have been shipped to the U.S. and around the world. We find a few sweaters that are a good buy. We have been warned that the cheap running shoes will damage your feet, so we look but do not buy. There is a haggling system on price and no one buys at the first offered price. After you hear the first price, make a large frown and say with a coarse guttural sound as if you are in great pain, "Pie sie ou," which means roughly "It costs too much."

We decide on dinner at a Korean restaurant with local dishes. On recommendation, we take a taxi to the Woo Lae Oak. We order the special marinated beef steak (bul-go-gi) and beef marinated ribs (Kalbi) which the server or yourself can cook over a very hot charcoal burner which is brought to the table. The dishes are served with pickled root vegetables and kimchi (a pickled hot cabbage with lots of garlic) and rice and more rice. The marinade is very heavy with garlic, onions and salt. Hot peppers are served to Koreans and to Americans on request. This is great food but we could not handle it every day.

RETURN FLIGHT TO CONUS

We have checked with the Osan AB PaxTerm to find that our names are near the top of the category VI Space-A list. We also learn that the Patriot Flight for Seattle/Tacoma will be leaving from Osan AB, RK on Thursday which is the next day. Show time is 0900 hours; we are there and "Travel Ready." We make the Space-A call and this is a long but direct flight. This time we pay a $23.40 fee each for processing in the U.S. There is a $12.40 Head Tax and an $11.00 Federal Inspection fee. These fees are in included in the cost of commercial tickets. The fees for duty passengers are paid by the government. These meager fees are reasonable as the only fee for a comfortable flight with good service.

We are both happy to be back in the U.S. and the welcome home greeting from the immigration agent is a happy sound. We have shipped less than our $400.00 each allowance including gifts that we have in our bags. We make a family oral declaration and are passed quickly through customs. We take our bags to the bus pick-up where we wait less than 30 minutes for our trip to McChord AFB, WA. We pick up our car and head home to Portland, OR. We talk all the way home about our trip which will always be an important memory.

TEN ESSENTIAL STEPS
FOR TRAVELING BY SPACE-A AIR

We have listed below the ten essential steps or functions which are required for all Space-A Air Opportunity travel. These ten steps must be executed or performed for each and every Space-A Air Opportunity travel or trip. Due to space limitations, we have not included here all of the details about each step. However, the details are contained in other text or appendices of *Military Space-A Air Basic Training and Reader Trip Reports*.

Step 1. Destination Planning and Selection: What is your destination? In your Space Available Travel Request (AMC Form 140 or equivalent) you can designate (in order of priority) five foreign countries (including CONUS and U.S. Possessions overseas), or four countries, U.S. Possessions overseas and "all" to take advantage of opportune airlift. The "all" designation means that you will accept transportation to CONUS, U.S. Possessions or any foreign country. This system gives you a wide range of destinations.

Step 2. Travel Identification and Documentation:
A. All Space-A travelers must have been issued a Uniformed Services Identification Card (from one of the seven Uniformed Services).
B. All Active Duty personnel must have a Leave or Pass Authorization (approved by their Service).
C. Depending upon your category of travel (I-VI) and Personnel Entrance Requirements to Foreign Countries and Areas, the following identification and authorization documentation are required: 1. Passports; 2. Visas; 3. International Certificates of Vaccination and Personal Health History, PHS Form 1839; 4. Authentication of Reserve Status For Travel Eligibility, DD Form 1853; 5. Medal of Honor Award Certificate; 6. Active Duty Environmental & Morale Leave (EML) Orders; 7. House Hunting Orders; 8. Permissive TDY/TAD Orders; 9. Students and Unaccompanied Dependents Orders/Letters and; 10. Special Entry Authorization Letters. All documentation will be reviewed by Passenger Service Personnel at the "Show Time" of your flight.

Step 3. Space Available Travel Request (AMC Form 140 or Equivalent): You can apply for Space-A travel one of four ways:
A. Report to any terminal, complete AMC Form 140 and present your identification/documentation as in 2 above.
B. Apply to any terminal for Space-A Travel by mail/package service with completed AMC Form 140 and statement that all Personnel Entrance Requirements as appropriate for your travel have been met.
C. Fax to any terminal a completed AMC Form 140 and statement that all Personnel Entrance Requirements as appropriate for your travel have been met.
D. E-mail any terminal with the information required in the AMC Form 140 and statement that all Personnel Entrance Requirements as appropriate for your travel have been met. Carry with you copies of all correspondence with the terminals. A few days after you make your application, it is prudent to confirm/verify your application with the terminals and obtain the "Julian Date" which has been assigned to your application. You may apply at more than one terminal for Space-A Air Travel (some areas, i.e., Mid-Atlantic have terminals which are located in the same or nearby areas). Applications are deleted when you fly or at the end of 60 days or the end of your leave,

whichever is earlier. Note: All terminals may not have fax and/or e-mail sign-up capability.

Step 4. Space Available Travel Request for Return Trip: You may also apply for return transportation at one or more overseas terminals via mail/package service, fax and e-mail at anytime. The timing of this application should fit with your expected departure, duration overseas and expected return. Caution: If you have your return application positioned at a terminal for return to CONUS from that terminal, and you fly from that terminal to other locations, your application for CONUS travel will be deleted from the system. Pick another terminal for local travel or you will lose your priority return to CONUS.

Step 5. Reporting To The Terminal and "Travel Ready": When to report to the terminal is an important decision that may well determine the success of your trip. Determine via telephone, fax or e-mail that your application is at the departure terminal. Verify that flights are departing for your desired destinations and your category and priority status on the Space-A waiting list. These factors: Your priority category for travel, position on the Space-A waiting list, available flights/seats to your destinations and other Space-A travelers competing for these seats, will determine your chances for travel. You should be "Travel Ready" which means that you (and all your party) have all required documentation, baggage and essential funds (including emergency commercial backup travel ticket or funds. Also if over 65 years old, you need medical insurance, as MEDICARE is not valid in foreign countries. Rental cars should be turned in. Personal cars should be parked in long-term parking. You should be checked out of hotels. Frequently there is not enough time to accomplish these essential items before "Show Time" and you may miss a flight.

Step 6. Space-A Flight Call/Selection Process: A. Space-A seats are normally identified as early as two or three hours or as late as 30 minutes prior to flight departure. The standard Space-A Show Time (Space-A Flight Call) for international/overseas flights is two hours. Due to increased security this time could be three hours. This is the same standard for international flights on commercial airlines. Always check with the passenger service center for the Space-A Show Time. It may be posted on monitors or status boards in the passenger terminal waiting and processing areas.
B. Space-A "Show Time" is important because it is the time at which selection of registered Space-A prospective passengers begins and you must be present to answer when your (sponsor's) name (family/travel group) is called in your travel category (I-VI).
C. The Space-A Flight Call---example, "Anyone desiring Space-A air transportation to a series of stations i.e., Ramstein, DE please assemble at the Space-A desk or other location."

D. All registered Space-A passengers will be offered air transportation on a "first-in, first-out" basis (regardless of rank or service), based on established Space-A categories. The flight processing team knows the number of seats available and will select a sign up or Julian Date near the middle of the register. They will ask if anyone has that date and time, or an earlier date and time, then work forward or move back on the list as appropriate. Each category is processed separately, starting with Category I and moving through to Category VI (there is a roster for each category which is combined into one roster at each terminal). It is important to remember that the number of seats your party requires is a factor in your selection. There must be sufficient seats for your party or the processor will move on and select someone with a later sign-up date. Space-A passengers arriving at the flight information counter after a specific Space-A call has begun must wait until all other Space-A passengers at the Space-A Call have been afforded an opportunity for available seats.

Step 7. Flight Processing: After selection for a flight the following processing is required.

A. Payment of Fees and Document Review: There are no fees for departure or arrival at U.S. Military Airports on U.S. military aircraft. The following fees apply to each passenger departing or arriving at U.S. Commercial airports on Category B, "Patriot" flights. These fees are as follows: 1. U.S. Airport Departure tax-$6; 2. Arrivals Fees: Immigration Inspection fee $, Customs Inspection fee $, Agriculture Inspection fee $, total fees $ Please note that all commercial airline passengers pay these taxes and fees in the price of their airline tickets. Payment for these fees must be in United States Dollar Currency or via personal check in U.S. dollars.

B. Documents Processing: All documents are inspected for authenticity, dates, and compliance with regulations. Active Duty leave/pass orders must cover sign-up to end of flight. At some point the processing team will want to observe each passenger directly and verify their identity against their travel documents.

C. Baggage Processing: Each person is authorized two pieces of checked baggage, and each piece must not exceed 62 linear inches (length + height + width =62 inches) and not more than 70 pounds for a total of 140 pounds for both pieces. Groups/families may pool their baggage allowances. All hand carried items must fit under the seat or in the overhead bins or other approved storage areas and may not exceed 45 linear inches. There is a 30 pound, one piece limit on small executive aircraft and a 45 pound, one piece limit on C-9 MEDEVAC aircraft. Space-A passengers may not pay for baggage in excess of the allowed weight limit.

D. Ordering and Payment for In-Flight Meals: Current meal cost are as follows: Breakfast=$1.50; Snack Meal=$1.90; Dinner=$3.00. Meals include milk or a soft drink of your choice. Meal prices change are made on 1 October. Each Space-A passenger orders and pays for the meals of their choice. Food and soft drinks are free on AMC "Patriot Flights" (Commercial Contract). You may purchase wine or beer on these flights. No specialized meals are available for Space-A passengers. If you require special food, suggest that you bring your own. No alcoholic beverages for consumption on military aircraft are allowed.

E. Boarding Pass/Ticket Receipt, AMC Form 148/2 or similar: This document assigns seats, verifies and documents payment of fees, if appropriate, payment for meals and most importantly shows your one-time sign-up Julian Date. You now wait for your flight number and destination to be called for boarding.

F. Passenger Security Screening and Boarding Gates: Passengers and carry on items are screened through electronic gates into a secure boarding area. Some passenger terminals perform this screening for everyone entering the passenger terminal. Body searches may also be required. Boarding is as instructed, often in this order: families with small children, passengers needing assistance, DV/VIP and others. The boarding will be through a bus to the aircraft and then up a courtesy/mobile stairs, cargo ramp, or passenger stairs. Some terminals may have the conventional commercial boarding ramp direct from the terminal to the aircraft.

Step 8. In-Flight: A. Seating: Most seats will be comfortable padded commercial airline seats mounted facing to the rear of the aircraft for safety. Some aircraft will have plastic formed seating or even web seating along the sides of the aircraft. There will be pillows and blankets and other comfort items. Bring your own reading materials and non-electronic games, as these items along with in-flight movies and music are not available on military aircraft.

B. Clothing: Your clothing should be loose fitting and in layers. Wear comfortable walking shoes. Women should wear slacks and a blouse or sweater. Take a light jacket depending upon the climate. The layers of clothing will be handy on MEDEVAC flights, which are keep warm for patient comfort.

C. Rest Rooms: Restrooms are similar to commercial airlines—plentiful and unisex. Passengers are expected to keep the restrooms clean.

D. Climate Control: The climate is maintained at a comfortable temperature. However there are cold and hot spots on some aircraft. The cabin personnel may be able to adjust the temperature.

E. Noise: You may experience some higher than normal levels of noise during takeoff, landings, special maneuvers and turns. There is no need for earplugs on most aircraft. You will most definitely want earplugs on flights on the C-130 aircraft. Bring your own or ask the cabin crew for wax self-forming earplugs.

F. Safety: Use safety belts when instructed to do so. Only walk about the aircraft when allowed to do so. Never tamper with controls, doors or equipment within the aircraft. Listen very carefully to the in-flight safety lecture given by the cabin crew. Locate the exit nearest to your seating. Know where the emergency oxygen and your life preserver are located.

G. Electronic Devices: The use of computers, electronic games, radios, recorders, TVs, and other devices which may interfere with the aircraft navigation, radar and communication systems is prohibited.

H. Refreshments: There is always fresh water, coffee and tea available in the galley. Meals which were ordered will be served at the appropriate time given, flight conditions.

Step 9. Post-Flight: A. Arrival and Aircraft Clearance: After landing, the flight attendants will spray fumigation/insect repellent throughout the cabin as required by international health rules. The manifest and declaration of the health of the crew and passengers will be handed over to local authorities or United States authorities acting on their behalf. After clearance is obtained from the local authority, deplaning of passengers and crew can begin.

B. Deplaning. Passengers are required to complete immigration and customs forms prior to deplaning. The crew will give instructions regarding post-flight processing such as deplaning, immigration, baggage claims and customs. Physical deplaning will be through a passenger chute, stairs or ramp into the terminal or to a bus which will take passengers to the terminal.

C. Immigration: All passengers must report to the immigration processing station with their documentation (Service ID Cards, Passports, Visas, and others as required). Documents are examined carefully and may be checked against persons barred entry to that country.

D. Baggage Claim and Customs: After you have all of your baggage, report to the customs inspection with your customs form and baggage. If you do not have items on which duties are due, entry will quick and easy.

Step 10. Return Flight to CONUS: Registration and Return Space-A Air Opportunities: A. Pre-Registration: We recommend that you apply for Space-A travel from one or more overseas departure stations back to CONUS before arriving overseas. This can be done via mail/package delivery, fax or e-mail up to 60 days before you plan to return to CONUS. Note: All travel applications from a station are deleted at that location when you fly or travel from that location to another location overseas. If you have not applied for return travel prior to arriving overseas, the application for return travel should be an item of urgency.

B. Circuitous Routing: You may not find an immediate direct return to your home station when you plan to return to CONUS. You may want to consider taking a less than direct route to CONUS depending upon the availability of flights, i.e., you may want to travel farther east, turn around at some point and go back CONUS.

C. Return Flight: Same general process as flight from CONUS. With luck- "welcome home."

APPROACHES TO THE STUDY OF SPACE-A AIR OPPORTUNITIES

Space-A Air Opportunities appear on the surface to be very complicated and difficult to use. A brief study of the Space-A Air Opportunity systems using one or more approaches will significantly improve your success with and understanding of the Space-A systems. The knowledge possessed by users of the Space-A systems range from first-time users to seasoned Space-A users. Many persons have experience in two or more priority of use categories, i.e., Active Duty and Retired or Active Reservist/Gray Area Retirees and Retired.

There are four basic approaches to the study and understanding of Space-A Air Opportunities. The Space-A user can use one, two, three or all four of these basic approaches to gain knowledge, and therefore better understand and use the Space-A Air Opportunity Systems. These four basic approaches are

I. Space-A, DoD 4515.13R Air Transportation Eligibility, and Service Department Implementing Instructions. **"WHAT ARE THE SPACE-A RULES AND PROCEDURES?"**

II. Routes, Scheduling, Type Missions and Aircraft Equipment. **"WHERE DO THE AIRCRAFT GO, WHEN, WHY AND HOW?"**

III. Organizations/Commands-Stations (Airports/Bases) of Assignment of Aircraft, Air Crews and Support Facilities in CONUS, OCONUS and Foreign Countries. **"WHERE ARE THE AIRCRAFT?"**

IV. Aircraft type, Number, Performance, Passenger Capability Owned or Operated (Leased) by the Military Department (U.S. Army, U.S. Navy, U.S. Marine Corps, U.S. Coast Guard and U.S. Air Force) which are Passenger Capable Aircraft. **"WHO HAS THE AIRCRAFT (MEANS OF TRANSPORTATION)?"**

The Space-A student can start the study of Space-A Air Opportunities at any level, I through IV, or from the top down or bottom up, IV through I. Most people start where they have the most expertise, experience or knowledge of the Space-A systems. This arrangement of study levels or areas can be viewed conceptually as: **"THE PYRAMID OF SPACE-A KNOWLEDGE."** A graphic of the pyramid is shown on page 77.

The books ***Military Space-A Air Basic Training and Reader Trip Reports*** and ***Military Space-A Air Opportunities Around the World*** provide the information needed to study the Space-A systems.

I: Both titles contain the complete Space-A regulations with all approved changes. The detailed information on how the system works or Services implementing instructions are contained in the sample Space-A trip and trip reports contained in the text portion of *Military Space-A Air Basic Training and Reader Trip Reports.* Thorough and in-depth knowledge of the Space-A rules and implementing procedures are essential to successful Space-A travel.

II. The Military Space-A Air Opportunities book contains detailed routes, scheduling, mission and equipment information for AMC scheduled international flights and domestic (CONUS) MEDEVAC flights around the world. Also, the *Military Space-A Air Opportunities Air Route Map* shows the details of worldwide Space-A routes and is a wonderful planning tool. These scheduled flights move the predominance of the Space-A flights (trips) made by authorized persons each year. These along with the Location Identifier and Cross Reference Index are indispensable tools for planning Space-A trips. Routes, scheduling, mission and equipment are the centerpieces of successful Space-A air travel.

III. The Military Space-A Air Opportunities book shows where each type of aircraft is stationed in CONUS, OCONUS and Foreign Country by station or location. Also, the crews and essential support for these aircraft are in most cases located with the aircraft at each station. Good Space-A Air Opportunities include the use of aircraft which are capable of executing missions to your desired destinations.

IV. The Military Space-A Air Opportunities book at each station lists the types of aircraft stationed at that location, also Appendix H lists the stationing of aircraft by each military department around the world. Appendix C lists a description and performance characteristics of aircraft on which most Space-A travel occurs and the recent inventory of each type of aircraft by military departments.

This approach can be used on a top down basis as described above or on a bottom up basis to obtain a clearer understanding of Space-A systems. In addition to the above, the *Military Space-A Air Opportunities Air Route Map* clearly shows the major overseas/international routes and the CONUS MEDEVAC routes. Traveling to your desired Space-A destination may not always be in a straight line. In fact, sometimes it is beneficial to travel east in order to eventually go west to your desired destination, i.e., you may want to go east from Germany to stations in the Near East in order to turn around and return through Germany to CONUS. This and many other useful tips are contained in the Military Space-A Air Basic Training book.

APPROACHES TO THE STUDY OF SPACE-A AIR OPPORTUNITIES
(TOP DOWN OR BOTTOM UP)

I   "WHAT ARE THE SPACE-A RULES AND PROCEDURES?"
DoD Directive 4515.13R AIR TRANSPORTATION ELIGIBILITY with changes and Military Departments Implementing Instructions

II   "WHERE DO THE AIRCRAFT GO, WHEN, WHY AND HOW?"
Space-A Routes, Schedules, Missions and Equipment

III   "WHERE ARE THE AIRCRAFT?"
Organizations/Commands, Stations of Assignment in CONUS, OCONUS and Foreign Countries

IV   "WHO HAS THE AIRCRAFT (MEANS OF TRANSPORTATION)?"
Aircraft Type, Number(Inventory), Performance, Passenger Capability; Military Department Passenger Capable Aircraft U.S. Army; U.S. Navy; U.S. Marine Corps; U.S. Coast Guard and U.S. Air Force

IV   "WHO HAS THE AIRCRAFT (MEANS OF TRANSPORTATION)?"
Aircraft Type, Number(Inventory), Performance, Passenger Capability; Military Department Passenger Capable Aircraft U.S. Army; U.S. Navy; U.S. Marine Corps; U.S. Coast Guard and U.S. Air Force

III   "WHERE ARE THE AIRCRAFT?"
Organizations/Commands, Stations of Assignment in CONUS, OCONUS and Foreign Countries

II   "WHERE DO THE AIRCRAFT GO, WHEN, WHY AND HOW?"
Space-A Routes, Schedules, Missions and Equipment

I   "WHAT ARE THE SPACE-A RULES AND PROCEDURES?"
DoD Directive 4515.13R AIR TRANSPORTATION ELIGIBILITY with changes and Military Departments Implementing Instructions

R&R Travel News™

By subscription. Published six times yearly. Subscription rate, shipped by business standard mail*:

| 1 year $18.00 | 2 years $28.00 |
| 3 years $38.00 | 5 years $57.00 |

*For first class delivery, mailed in an envelope, add $1 per issue ($6 per year extra)

To subscribe
using Visa, Mastercard, American Express or Discover
call 703-237-0203
or visit our secure web order online at
www.MilitaryLiving.com.

To keep costs down, billing is not available–pre-payment is required.

Military Living's *R&R Travel News* covers all facets of military leisure travel, including Space-A air travel, Temporary Military Lodging and RV Camping and outdoor recreation worldwide. We also include reader trip reports so that you can get the info "first-hand." **If you would like to receive 2 previous issues for $5, call 703-237-0203 and request 2 R&R samples for $5 (charged to your credit card) as mentioned in Military Living's *Space-A Air Basic Training and Reader Trip Reports***

This special offer expires 1 December 2001. Please note: We are not able to provide specific back issues covering specific locations / topics.

R&R Travel News™
keeps you up-to-date on all facets of
military leisure travel, including
Space-A air travel, Temporary
Military Lodging and RV Camping
and outdoor recreation worldwide.

SECTION VII

READER TRIP REPORTS

Space-A Travel– A is for Adventure
by Helen Keough Sears

We leave our home in Knoxville, Tennessee, on Sunday with all the right information. Even though it is our first experience traveling Space-Available, my husband, Colonel Ray Sears, USMC (Retired), has read everything he can get his hands on about Space-A travel through the Air Mobility Command. We are feeling confident during our drive to Dover, Delaware, where our adventure will begin. We know the rules: (1) Register for travel by e-mail, fax or mail before leaving home, or in person when you arrive at the terminal. We registered by e-mail and have an early Julian date which will be good for 60 days. (2) Two pieces of baggage per passenger. We know the baggage allowances: 70 pounds each and up to 62 linear inches in size. We are within the guidelines. (3) Be flexible; be prepared to pay for lodging or commercial travel if your personal deadlines cannot be met; and, if possible, travel at off-peak periods (not July-August or December-January.) Two out of three is not bad. We have to travel during the summer months because we have a wedding to attend in England on August 2. We leave home early so we can tour Ireland prior to the wedding. As retirees, being flexible will be easy. (4) Be prepared to consider an alternate destination. We are prepared. We have Plan A: RAF Mildenhall, UK, and Plan B: Ramstein, Germany.

Helen and Ray Sears at Cavan, Ireland,
Halcyon B&B.

We arrive at Dover's Passenger Terminal at 0830 Monday morning, June 30. The Departures Schedule has no flights listed for RAF Mildenhall, but there is one for Ramstein, Germany, with 73 seats available. Show time is 2000. Great! We'll go straight to Plan B - we'll get on that plane, tour Germany and then go to England. How lucky can we get - our first day in Dover and we'll leave that very evening! Since it's early in the day, we leave the terminal and spend the day in Dover. We ride out to the beaches along the Atlantic, do a little shopping, and have an early supper before returning to the terminal at 1800. What are all these men, women and children doing milling around the outside of the terminal? And, inside are hundreds of people with luggage: couples with two, three, and four children, students, retirees with and without spouses! Where do they all want to go? Ramstein, Germany.

Six categories of military personnel are eligible to travel Space-A and the first five belong to active duty personnel and their families. To summarize briefly: Category I is emergency travel; Category II is morale leave; Category III is active duty members with or without families; Category IV is unaccompanied family members; Category V is students; Category VI is retirees and their spouses (if traveling abroad - no Space-A CONUS travel for spouses). Filling available seats on the various flights is a two-step procedure. First, all the categories are called, beginning with the Category I and continuing through Category VI. Within the categories the earliest Julian dates take precedence. Sounds simple enough.

It is now 2000 and time for the procedure to begin for filling the 73 available seats on the flight to Ramstein, Germany. The call comes over the loud speaker for persons in Category I to come to the passenger counter. A few people get in line and get accepted. Nobody answers the call for Category II. When the call for Category III comes, at least a hundred and fifty people congregate. The flight is filled even before all the Category III travelers can be accommodated. Still no planes leaving for RAF Mildenhall, but thirty minutes later another plane is going to Ramstein with ten seats available. This time we don't even bother to stand in the lobby. As suspected, the seats are grabbed up immediately.

The Departures Schedule shows another plane for Ramstein will have a show time of 0110 Tuesday morning with another ten seats available. We'll try for that one; nobody will come back for a 1:00 a.m. showing. Fifty people show up for that flight and in one day's time, we've seen three planes leave for Ramstein without us. No sightseeing for us on Tuesday. We spend all day in the passenger terminal and watch five planes leave for Ramstein - all filled with people from Categories I, II, and III. There are no more planes scheduled for Ramstein or RAF Mildenhall this week. Forget Plan A and Plan B. We create Plan C: We'll get across the ocean and then we'll go to England. We'll consider anything! Another look at the Departures Schedule. A plane with 53 seats available will be leaving Wednesday for Rota, Spain. The show time is 0400. We'll give it a try. Yes! We'll go to Rota, Spain.

Even though the early show time doesn't discourage the crowd from arriving, we are hopeful. For the first time, we see the call reach Category VI and Ray turns in our paperwork. We aren't accepted; others have earlier Julian dates. Everybody must be preregistered from home. Before we did. I wonder what the commercial airlines have available.

Wednesday afternoon a new Departures Schedule is posted: an 1800 show time for another plane to Rota, Spain (a C-5 Galaxy with 73 seats.) Plus, a plane will leave on Thursday for RAF Mildenhall. We decide to try for the Rota plane. It's a "bird in the hand" - who knows what tomorrow will bring? Again, the passenger terminal is crowded with people and luggage at show time; and again it looks as if we have no hope. The call gets all the way through Categories I, II, III, IV, and V. Finally Category VI is called, and all the Julians are checked. Ray's name is called. Did I hear that right? Yeah! We're going to Rota. It's across the ocean; we'll go to England from Spain. We're on Plan C. We get our boarding passes, purchase two in-flight meals; our luggage is taken to the plane, our carry-ons are checked and we sit (all 73 of us) waiting for the buses to take us out to the plane. I pull out the Atlas and locate Rota. We can go see the Rock of Gibraltar. Maybe I can use some of the Spanish phrases I studied in school. Si, Senor, queremos ir a Espana! A flight clerk comes into the waiting room and announces the mission of the plane has changed. It is now going to Aviano, Italy. Huh? Italy, the country shaped like a boot, was never even considered, but it is across the ocean. Cross out Plan C. We're going to Aviano, Italy, on Plan D! From Italy we'll go to Germany and then to England.

We board the bus which will take us out to the plane. We're getting all settled and the bus driver is preparing to leave the terminal when we receive another announcement: The mission of the plane has changed. It is now going to Naples, Italy. I wonder what the commercial airlines have available. . . .

Ray must be reading my mind, "Have you ever been to Naples?" Considering alternate destinations has left me completely speechless so I simply shake my head, "No." "Neither have I," he says. "We only live once."

Helen Sears in Naples, Italy.

It is Wednesday, July 2, at 2345 and we are actually on a C-5 Galaxy (the largest plane in the free world) in our first Space-A flight. We're on our way to Naples. It is Plan E. Four days in Napoli! Ahh, Mama-Mia! In a little pizzeria, we have the Margherita Pizza, the first pizza ever made, which originates in Naples. And, the best lasagna we've ever eaten, delicious Italian wine, every man on every street corner looks like Dean Martin. I think I hear him singing, "That's Amore" to me. Ahh. But, that's another story. We need to continue our trip north to England.

When we arrive at the Naples Passenger Terminal, it is Monday morning, July 7, my birthday. Three departures are scheduled: two to Rota, Spain, and one to Ramstein, Germany. By afternoon we are flying over the spectacular Swiss Alps on our way to Ramstein. This time we're in a seven passenger C-21 Lear Jet. How did Ray arrange such a wonderful birthday present for me? Four days ago we were on the largest plane in the free world - and, now we're in a small, sleek Lear Jet. Hmm. Can't travel like this on commercial airlines!

For about four weeks we tour Germany, Belgium, France, and Ireland before we finally end up in England for the August 2 wedding. But, these are other stories. Now it is time to go home. Late Monday afternoon, August 4, we arrive at RAF Mildenhall with one goal: Catch a plane to Dover, Delaware, USA, where our car is waiting for us. A quick look at the Departures Schedule tells us the next show time for a plane leaving for Dover is 0500 Tuesday. Fine with us. We'll get a good supper, a good night's sleep and we will be ready to travel home tomorrow.

Tuesday. Two flights are scheduled for Dover. One has five seats available and the other is postponed for 24 hours. But, there is a flight scheduled for Wright-Patterson in Ohio. Hmm. Ohio is only two states north of Tennessee - but our car is waiting for us in Dover. We stand at the window and watch as the plane leaves for the USA without us. Wednesday. Two flights are scheduled for Dover. One is postponed and the other is canceled. Nothing listed for Thursday. Early Thursday morning, August 7, we change our goal: We'll get across the ocean and then we'll go to Dover. Anything east of the Mississippi River in the United States of America will be considered. Another look at the Departures Schedule. There is a show time of 1700 for a C-135 going to Milwaukee, Wisconsin. Twenty-three seats will be available. It is still early in the day; we have plenty of time to think about that. Right now, Ray wants to go for a long walk. Fine. Since I am really into a certain paperback, I opt to stay in the terminal. We'll discuss the situation when he gets back. He hasn't been gone ten minutes when a call comes over the loud speaker. The C-135 going to Milwaukee will be leaving early. Anyone interested should come to the passenger counter immediately! Not even a category call. I run to the window, Ray is nowhere in sight. Milwaukee is across the ocean. It is east of the Mississippi River. I run to the passenger counter and turn in our paperwork.

Finally, I see Ray walking toward the terminal and run out to meet him. "We're going to Milwaukee! We're leaving in an hour. I've ordered our meals. Hurry, we have to get our baggage checked!" Now it is 2015. It's still Thursday, but it seems like next week. We're in Milwaukee, Wisconsin, USA! Only three states north of Tennessee.

The rental car is nice, and it is smooth riding as we drive south. We arrive home early Friday evening. Home! Perhaps we'll drive our other car to Delaware. . . . Perhaps Ray will get a commercial flight. . . . Or, perhaps . . . Ray calls McGhee Tyson Air Base here in Knoxville. Yes, a C-135 is leaving tomorrow afternoon for Dover, Delaware.

It is a rainy afternoon. We have a late lunch at our favorite neighborhood restaurant before we drive across town to the McGhee Tyson Passenger Terminal. It is now 1700, Saturday, August 9, and I wave to the only passenger as he boards the plane. Our car is waiting for him in Dover.

Dover to Germany and Back
by Ellen Hart

We did it! What a challenging and exciting experience our first Space-A jaunt to Germany was. Grab a cup of coffee and I'll tell you all about it - the good and the best of it. None of it was bad. Hey. Space-A is a deal. No complaints here.

When our car broke down on the way from North Carolina to Dover, it was then we realized that the good Lord was indeed our guardian and we needn't worry about anything but to remember to trust, be patient, be flexible and use our God-given reasoning and intellect to further our journey. Thank God we were already off I-95 and on US 301 in Upper Marlboro, MD. The car died in the fast lane; my husband maneuvered to the right lane and then to the side of the road where the car expired completely at the foot of a long driveway—the home of a mechanic. Lest you think we habitually travel in an unreliable car, may I assure you we don't. We had the car in for repairs and maintenance check before we left. Alas, that's now neither here nor there.

The mechanic and his wife, literally Good Samaritans, helped move the car onto their property, invited us in and assisted in contacting our nephew in Baltimore who picked us up and drove us the 80 miles to Dover. Our nephew-another blessing on our journey.

Two C-5s to Ramstein had been posted on Dover's web page schedule for Sept. 11; however, when we arrived at the passenger terminal, we discovered one of the missions had been scratched. Uh-oh. But that's the nature of the beast. So after a hot sandwich and cup of coffee in the snack bar, we waited. At show time all categories were called, and surprisingly, many Cat VIs got on—but not us. We missed it only by a few numbers.

OK, this is a chance to be creative. What next? A flight to Rota, Spain, was going in the morning. Show time at 0400 hours. Since we had no transportation and show time was so early, we hung out in the terminal (like many others, I might add). It's important to remember to bring a book, cards, or an extra jacket to roll up under your head when you lay your head on the snack bar table.

Have patience. Be flexible. Employ a sense of humor. You will meet strangers who quickly become friends. As the clock ticks slowly forward during the wee hours, you may have already traveled to India, Africa or Australia while chatting with a seasoned Space-A traveler sitting next to you in the terminal. And, oh, by the way, you can spot those seasoned vets—they're the ones with the lightest luggage.

Waiting for the 4 a.m. showtime for the flight to Rota, Spain, Category VI spouse Ellen Hart hunkers down to catch some sleep in the Dover Air Force Base passenger terminal snack bar.

0400: A handful of us got manifested for the Rota flight. We figured let's get across the ocean and we'll worry about the next leg later. Everything we had read on this website encouraged us to take ANYTHING going in your direction. You can't progress sitting in the terminal and passing up opportunities. Swimming was not an option. Aboard the C-5, earplugs in place, pillow behind the head (no use trying to look out the windows as there are none), we settled in for the long flight - about 7 hours if I remember correctly. Twenty minutes into the flight we had to turn around because of a maintenance problem. Oh, no, I thought. This was my first inkling of doubt, of frustration. But I realized I was TIRED, having had my comfortable bed and pillow replaced with a hard snack bar table and bench earlier. Back into the terminal, weary passengers all. Breakfast sounded like a good idea. Who could remember anymore what time it was? Two hours later we boarded again and seven hours later we landed at Rota, in the wee hours of Sunday morning, Sept. 13. Hello jet lag.

At customs the rep told us when we asked about a train station, bus station, any station, that everything's closed. It's Sunday. So we hooked up with three other couples to make a plan to find a place to shower and rest until the next day's flights out. Thank God the Navy Lodge on base had vacancies! We ordered two taxis (the size of roller skates) to carry four couples and their luggage across base. Took two trips. Lighter luggage was looking better all the time.

Although not the Hyatt Regency or the Marriott, the Navy Lodge was clean, comfortable, had a hot, wonderful shower, two beds, clean sheets, and even CNN. At 3 a.m. our heads hit the pillows. Boy, did we sleep the sleep of angels. Six hours later we were showered (again), dressed and back in the terminal looking for a flight into Germany. A C-130 was scheduled to land that afternoon but seat releases were TBD, and, to our delight and hope, a C-21 into Stuttgart, Germany, with six available seats. That's the one we wanted as our final destination was Heilbronn where our German friends lived - 45 minutes away.

How's this for Space-A travel? Ellen Hart waits to board the C-21 to Stuttgart, Germany, from Rota Naval Station.

We watched in anticipation as others turned down the C-21 and gambled on the C-130 which hadn't yet landed. But we never found out if those folks got on the C-130. We were already aboard the C-21 - a two-hour champagne flight without the champagne - it sure felt good. What impressed me most though about the C-21 flight was its two Air Force pilots - Captains Matt Beebe and Will Snyder flying out of the U.S. Army Airfield, Stuttgart. It was Sunday evening and, I'm sure they were eager to return to their families. But first they helped unload and carry our bags to the airfield headquarters, called a taxi for the other passengers who flew with us, helped send an e-mail to my daughter in the states to let her know we had arrived safely in Germany, loaded our bags into their car and drove us to the front gate so that we could be picked up by our German friends who were on their way. Truly above and beyond the call of duty. It's people like Captains Beebe and Snyder who make me proud to be connected to our military services.

After three weeks of good German wine, Swiss alps and chocolate, brotchen and beer, good friends and fun, we drove to Ramstein where only a KC-10 was on the schedule that day. But you never know, we were learning quickly, what can happen from day to day. We were blessed (again) to get on a C-5 that had been on maintenance delay from the day before - with seats available. Went through customs at Dover at midnight, grabbed an airport taxi to BWI where we rented a car, drove to Annapolis where our nephew had towed our car for repair, spent a few hours at Denny's over coffee and breakfast (it's only 4 a.m. folks), waited for the dealership to open, picked up our car, returned the rental, and headed back to North Carolina.

Thanks to this website and the efforts of those of you who continue to share your experiences and knowledge, we ventured into the unknown, all the while saying, "It will be an adventure." Maybe we'll see you on our next trip. We'll be the ones with the lighter luggage.

Space-A to the Royal Tattoo - RAF Fairford, UK
by Bob Wolfson, Pittsburgh, PA

Dear Ann, Roy, RJ:
Vilma and I returned last night from the Royal International Air Tattoo '98 celebrating 80 years of the Royal Air Force (1918-1998) which was held at RAF Fairford, UK during July 25/26. Over 550 planes covering this 80-year period either were static displays or flew sky and airfield level missions with 38 countries participating.

We departed Pittsburgh, PA IAP/ARS Space-A on a KC-135 on July 21st. Although we were 50th on the list with only 40 spaces allocated, 12 did not show, so it does pay to wait on standby. We arrived the morning of the 22nd, picked up our rental car at the terminal KEMWEL - 1-800-678-0678 at a weekly rate of $161, VAT included. (Caution: When the car is reserved use a gold or platinum credit card and refuse the insurance. When you pick it up, you will be required to use the same credit card to cover a $50 deposit if the car is not returned with a full tank of gas. Refuse any insurance on the rental certificate you sign when you pick up the car.)

As you can imagine, over 100,000 visitors were on hand for the ceremonies and neither base quarters nor local hotels/B&B's were available. We phoned RAF Croughton and drove about 65 miles to get the last rooms available at the Shepherd's Inn there. We lucked out and got the DV suite for $32/night. Similar quarters would run $200-350 at the local hotels. The base has a communications mission and is relatively small, but it does have a class six/ shoppette/ commissary/ bowling alley/ consolidated club. We had dinner at the club the first night and the four course meal was the equivalent of a local four star restaurant at a fourth of the price. The 200 ml bottles of quality wine were priced at $2.00.

We showed up at RAF Fairford two hours before departure time and after lunch of fish & chips, which was served on the flight line by RAF caterers, we boarded our return flight. We refueled a C-130 in flight and arrived back in Pittsburgh after a 9-hour flight.

Traveling the Romantic Road
with Tom & Regina Dinges

We have always considered ourselves "Space-A" junkies, as we love exchanges, commissaries and overnight stops on new bases, so a trip to Europe using the Space-A system was the next logical move for us. When traveling in the U.S. we carry the Military Living books and route ourselves close to a base for an overnight stop. We have even gone out of our way to spend a night or two at such spots as Short Stay (SC), The Mugu Lagoon Beach Motel (CA) and the Pacific Beach Resort (WA). The time had come for us to spread our wings and take the long anticipated trip to Germany and travel the Romantic Road. Yes, we are true romantics but this was the old Roman Road with many beautiful and historical sights.

We believe in the division of labor, so Tom did the research on sights to see by reading the commercial travel books and Regina scoured the Internet. Planning our itinerary and obtaining information about our destinations were our first priority. We relied heavily on the internet and the Space-A books

Tom & Regina Dinges, at an overlook en route to Innsbruck.

to make our plans. Our first thoughts were to try BWI or Dover; in fact, we did send an e-mail both places and got on their lists.

Tom remembered that he had heard there were flights out of Westover, MA. We live about 100 miles from there, so that seemed like a good option. Late in October we started looking in earnest at Westover's web site and found just what we needed—a flight to Ramstein scheduled for November 17, 1998. Tom called and had us manifested on the list for Ramstein.

We had never been to Westover, so we took a day trip out there to get the lay of the land and find out what else we needed to know for our adventure. It was a very productive day. The retirees manning the desk were very helpful with information about long-term parking on base, lodging if we needed it, and meals on the plane.

In the meantime, we contacted AFRC (Vacation Planning Center) Europe in Garmisch and Chiemsee to make reservations, and ordered their video describing their Resort Schedule of Trips. The video came just before we left and it heightened our anticipation as we prepared to go. Fortunately we were able to get reservations at both places and would be in Chiemsee over the Thanksgiving holiday so we wouldn't be eating sauerkraut alone in some biergarten. The AFRC address of the site on the net is trol.redstone.army.mil/mwr/afrcs/index.html. It is a great place. They are very efficient in answering e-mail requests, and provide good brochures and information. They encourage retirees to come, and they welcome children with all sorts of packages for them.

Once we had our flight date we still had other things to think about such as a return flight, how to rent a car and the need for international driving licenses. We went on line and used the Remote Sign-Up System via e-mail to notify both Ramstein and Rhein-Main that we would be flying back from either one of those bases. Tom also went into a military chat room to get info from anyone who had recently rented a car in Europe. He received very helpful information and we then rented a car on base at Ramstein. Luggage was the next thing we had to consider—we promised ourselves we would travel light. We bought light, flexible backpacks without heavy support to carry the things we would have put into a carry-on and each packed a smaller roller bag. Since it was late November it could be cold. Luckily we prepared for it with layered clothing. We both had Polartec jackets with a Gore-Tex® outside shell, wool pants and silk underwear, which was great, as it is light and can be washed and dried quickly.

The day of our flight we left home around 8:00 am and arrived about 10:00 am for a noon show time. Our luggage was weighed and checked in. We went to the exchange and then had a buffet lunch at the club. Back at the terminal, while waiting to board, it was interesting to learn where others were going and how they planned their trips. When the time to board arrived there were about 15 including us retirees, mothers and their children, and active duty military. We were glad we had the backpacks so our hands were free to hold on as we climbed the inner steps on the C-5A—it's a long way up.

Soon we were all settled in and on our way to Dover where we deplaned after the short flight. We were driven to the terminal where we waited about three hours before the flight continued on to Germany. During that time we were re-checked in and paid $3 for a hot meal to be served in flight over the Atlantic. The stopover was another good chance to get more acquainted with our traveling companions and chat with those who had experience in flying Space-A. We met a couple who were returning to Germany after spending some sick leave time with an ill relative. They told us about contract flights out of Rhein-Main to BWI and this information came in handy later in our trip.

The plane held 73 people and was filled to capacity with active duty military, dependents with children, and retirees. It was a smooth flight with good service including the delicious hot meal. We arrived in Ramstein in the middle of the day and soon found out that due to much troop traffic, there were no available rooms on base. The clerks at Ramstein South were very helpful and provided us with a list of hotels/motels in town where we could stay at the military rate. They made a reservation for us at the Gruner-Woog. We realized our small suitcases weren't small enough at this point, because there is no place to leave luggage—security measures. You carry or drag your suitcase wherever you go or you get your companion to guard it. Since the trip, Santa has taken care of us by bringing even smaller roller bags for our next trip.

We had planned to relax for the rest of the day and pick up our rental car the next day at the base. Before we left the base we checked on our Space-A sign-up which we had submitted early in November via e-mail. We used the DSN phone in the terminal and called Rhein-Main to check on our sign-up there. We were on both lists and had a Julian date. Then we called a cab and headed for the motel which was only about five minutes from the base. After we checked in, we decided to go for a walk, as the weather was clear and crisp. Regina had seen a small shopping area and wanted to check on the stores.

That evening we had a delicious meal at our hotel and a wonderful breakfast the next morning. Snow had fallen overnight and the roads were a mess as it was the first snow of the season in that area. Ramstein was in a traffic jam! When the roads finally cleared, we returned to the base, picked up our car and headed for Heidelberg and the Romantic Road. Tom had discovered that our American Express travelers checks in Deutsch Marks were not accepted every place. The best bets are credit cards and ATMs. We had brought about $300 in DM so we had something with which to start our adventure.

A friend of ours had stopped off at our home in Weymouth before we left and given us a road atlas of Germany, which proved to be invaluable. It had all the main and back roads, so Tom drove the Ka (a car much too small) and Regina navigated us through the Bavarian hills. We were only lost once at the end of our trip as we were going back to Ramstein. We headed north instead of south but it was soon corrected.

Heidelberg was our first stop-off at the Patrick Henry Village. We were feeling the effects of jet lag by now so we got off the road early and relaxed at the base. We had a great meal that night at a place called Lexington's, in which there was a food court where you could order your meal and have it delivered to your table. It was nothing formal but there was a wide variety of foods offered. We found the help very courteous and friendly at the Patrick Henry Guest House.

The next day we headed for Wurzburg. It was a very cold and damp day. We visited the Residenz and Cathedral. It was amazing to see what had withstood the bombs of World War II. The Christkindle shops were beginning to open, as it was close to Advent. It was so cold Regina's boots cracked and she had to buy a new pair in Wurzburg. She and the clerk got along quite well in spite of the fact that neither could speak the other's language.

We tore ourselves away from Wurzburg and went on to Rothenburg. Rothenburg was much farther than we realized and when we arrived it was dark and cold. At the tourist phone and bulletin board just out of town, we stopped and found a hotel. It proved to be the least desirable place to stay, as the room was cold and the innkeeper not very hospitable. The next day we did enjoy the walled city but were disappointed we could not see the altars of the Jakobskirche carved by Tilman Riemenschneider because the church was closed for the season. Rothenburg is such a delightful city—we plan to go back and see it in better weather.

We reluctantly left Rothenburg and continued to drive south to Augsburg. By now the weather had gotten much colder and it was snowing off and on. In Augsburg we used the Tourist Information Service in the bahnhof and made a reservation at an Ibis Hotel. It was close to the bahnhof and much nicer than the one the night before in Rothenburg. The next morning we were on our way early to Garmisch and it was snowing much harder. We planned to stop off in Oberammergau, but just short of it our brakes gave out. We limped on into Garmisch using the hand brake and stick shifting into low gear.

Garmisch is all you expect of a Bavarian ski town in the Alps. We stayed at the Von Steuben, AFRC hotel, which was very nice. The clerks were very accommodating by helping us call the car rental agency, and we were able to leave the keys and rental agreement with them while we took a tour to Innsbruck. There were many other tours out of Garmisch but we were not there long enough to take another one.

It was about a 60-mile drive further northeast to Chiemsee which is on the edge of Lake Chiemsee near the Bavarian Forest. While in Chiemsee we took a tour to Salzburg. It is a very sophisticated city in which the people dress beautifully and has wonderful coffee shops and restaurants. The highlight of the tour for us was a visit and tour of Mozart's birthplace. It is a city you would want to see again in the spring. We met an active duty family on the island while visiting King Ludwig's Schloss Herrenchiemsee. It is modeled on Versailles and quite elaborate. We later enjoyed a Thanksgiving buffet dinner with them in the dining room at Chiemsee.

It was time for us to pack up and head for Ramstein and get a flight back home. As we left Chiemsee Monday morning, it started to snow but before long we were out of the mountains and the roads were clear. We had made a reservation at Ramstein South Inn so we felt pretty comfortable heading back. To be on the safe side we took the suite for two nights after we got there, even though there seemed to be plenty of flights. There were about three flights that were scheduled to leave late in the day on Tuesday for Dover. Tom thought we might want to relax before we flew out so we went to the O Club for dinner. When we returned from dinner we went to the terminal and found that one of the flights for the next day had been canceled. There were many retirees milling about looking at the schedule and talking.

Tuesday morning there were quite a few people in the terminal waiting for news of a flight. At the show time of three o'clock they announced that the flight had overflown Ramstein and there were no more flights until Wednesday. We were happy we had not given up our room as many of the others had and were now scrambling for places to stay. While in the terminal, we talked with a retired army widower who had made many trips through Ramstein. He suggested we all go to Rhein-Main and try to get on the contract flight to BWI. The next morning we were out at the military bus stop with our luggage at 5:30 am and were on our way to Rhein-Main long before the sun was up.

The bus stopped at other military sites and picked up people who worked at Rhein-Main and some who wanted to fly out. Most of the trip was in darkness through the countryside but when we got close to the city the traffic really built up. It didn't look good at Rhein-Main because there were so many dependents but we did make it onto the plane because we had sent our sign-up in advance and had a good Julian date. We traveled with a couple who had been trying to get out for a few days from Ramstein but had never signed up in Rhein-Main; they didn't get on the plane. We came back on a DC-10, which was quite large. The fee was $23.40 each and we had a wonderful flight and a great meal.

The plane was filled to capacity with families, active duty and a few retirees. We weren't able to get seats together but a soldier offered to swap so we could be together. The plane arrived in BWI around 2:00 PM EST. We knew from the *R&R Travel News*® (Sept/Oct 98) that the airport and AMTRAK station were close together and there was a shuttle bus. Since our car was in Westover, MA, AMTRAK seemed the best way for us to get home. We arrived at the AMTRAK ticket window with 10 minutes to spare. We sank into seats and enjoyed the ride to Boston. En route Tom learned that we would be stopping for 20 minutes in New Haven and he would be able to make a phone call on the platform. When we reached New Haven he hopped off and called our local taxi company in Weymouth and arranged for them to meet us at South Station in Boston when the train arrived there. Around 11:30 PM, we came out of the AMTRAK station to our waiting taxi and we were home by midnight. Thanks to Military Living, no travel agent could have planned it any better.

What Did We Do Right? 1. Good planning, 2. Obtained and used information.

What Would We Do Differently? 1. Get a bigger car. 2. Have a smaller roller bag. 3. Leave the car home—be car free and be able to land anywhere along the East Coast and get back via Amtrak, car rental or fly.

Tom and Regina Dinges
Weymouth, MA

Space-A Flights at NFARS, NY
by John Caruso LtCol USAF (Ret.)

The Niagara Falls Air Reserve Station, NY is an active base for reservists and the Air National Guard. There are two flying wings on base: the 914th Airlift Wing with C-130H transports and the 107th Air Refueling Wing with KC-135R tankers.

The Retiree Activities Office (RAO) maintains information on Space-A travel for both units and serves as a contact for direct service with Base Operations. We have the flight schedules for both units and will be able to answer questions regarding flights.

Flights operating from both units are not on a regularly scheduled basis as to date and destination. Flight schedules are given to the RAO usually a month in advance as to destination, departure date, show time, number of seats, and arrival date back to NFARS. They cannot guarantee movement in the time frame you may wish and changes in scheduling are made. Some flights are one-way and won't be carrying passengers on return to Niagara.

The 914th AW flights have gone to Alaska, Hawaii, Germany, and to many bases in the U.S. The 107th ARW flights have gone to Germany, Hawaii, Alaska, England, Puerto Rico and bases in the U.S.

The RAO services all Space-A calls for the two units on base. You can call C-716-236-2389 or stop in at the office in the Headquarters Bldg 800, 2720 Kirkbridge Dr; Rm 101. Office hours are M-F 1000-1400.

John and Gayle Caruso Visit the Azores!

After Gayle and I decided to go back to the Azores, I proceeded to make the necessary preparations. One difference this time, Fred and Rosemary Depew of Montour Falls, NY would be traveling with us. We met them at a Fort Drum Retiree Activities Day four years ago.

We were going to depart from the Baltimore/Washington International Airport (BWI) on Tuesday 10 Nov 98. They have flights that depart on Tuesday and Saturday and departures from Lajes Field, Azores to BWI on Thursday and Sunday.

Fred and I made reservations for billeting at Abrams Hall Guest House (C-301-677-5660) at Fort George G. Meade, MD for Monday 9 Nov. Reservations can be made 60 days in advance. Monday morning before leaving home, I called the Mid-Atlantic Lodge at Lajes Field and was able to reserve rooms for Fred and me and our wives for three days.

We left for Fort Meade Monday and were to meet Fred and Rosemary at Abrams Hall. The rate for Space-A travelers was $34.75 double occupancy, $30.75 single. The base has a big PX, commissary, and service station.

Upon arrival at BWI Tuesday morning, we parked both cars in the "Satellite Lot" for long-term parking. The rate is $7.00 a day with the seventh day free. There is a shuttle bus every ten minutes that will take you to the AMC terminal. It is at the far end of the BWI Terminal. Show time is two hours before departure. Our flight was a contract carrier, American Trans Air, L1011 type aircraft. There were 70 open seats; no problem being boarded. We departed with empty seats. There is a $12 custom/tax fee for each person flying on contract carriers. It is well worth it. Free meal (excellent), and movies.

We stopped at Norfolk NAS, VA and picked up more passengers but still had 86 empty seats. Our arrival at Lajes Field on Terceira Island was at 0100 Wednesday. We checked in at billeting (C-001-351-2-95-540100 Ext. 25178). Rates were VOQ & VAQ-$12, DV-$17, and TLF $35. We had DV rooms that had stocked refrigerators and extra snacks available.

Whatever you do at Lajes Field, plan on having breakfast at "The Tradewinds." Breakfast consists of anything you wish the chef to put together. The hours are 6:30 to 8:30 am. Also, if you are a golfer, take along your clubs. I was told the Terceira Island Golf Club course is really worthwhile to visit. Tours of the island can be scheduled in the Community Center.

There are four car rental services available across the field at the Lajes International Airport, or in Juncan, outside the gate. Fred and I were picked up at billeting and transacted the rental at the airport. We had two days rental at $50 and unlimited mileage and filled the tank at drop off. You can purchase gas on base; big savings. You can also shop in the BX and Commissary. They are more than adequate.

Terceira is twelve miles wide and eighteen miles long. It is the third largest of nine islands that make up the Azores. Ninety percent of the Portuguese speak English. Money exchange at this time was 1.68 Escudos to $1 American.

We drove along the northern coast and then headed south into the island interior. The natural beauty of mountains, sea, and flowers as you travel along well-worn narrow roads is breath-

Lajes AFB, Terceira Island, Azores

taking. You cannot escape the rock walls dividing the land-scape, farmers riding their donkeys, and making way for cows on the roads. One thing that was unique, we noticed donkeys were being used to herd the cows.

We visited Serreta on the west coast and then headed northeast on the main highway along the coast to Biscoitos, where we stopped to see the Casa Agricola Brum Winery & Museum. The owner gave us a personal tour of the property and saved the wine tasting for last. The winery goes back one hundred years. You won't regret making this a primary visit.

Praia Da Vitoria (Beach of Victory) is the second largest city on the island. It is five miles from Lajes Field. One of the streets bars all traffic because the roadway is made of mosaic tiles. This street has many shops and restaurants. Nearby is the "O Pescador," a restaurant with excellent seafood and meat specialities.

A street with mosaic tile in the city of Praia Da Vitoria, which means "beach of victory."

Thursday morning, Angra Do Herosimo (Bay of Heroism), the largest city on the island was our destination. There are two forts protecting the city and from their sites you can see the beauty of the city and the shoreline. This city also has streets laid out in mosaic tile with shops and restaurants. Elio's Restaurant (family-owned) was recommended to us for our lunch or dinner. The food was excellent, serving fresh fish or meat and very reasonably priced. More sightseeing was in order on our way back to the base.

Fishing along the rocks is a popular activity.

Checking in at the terminal, I was told the Sunday flight to BWI was already filled with cargo and passengers. No seats for Category VI. Two flights were scheduled for McGuire AFB the next day, Friday; a KC-10 tanker with 58 seats and a C-141 (cargo) with no other information available. There wouldn't be another flight to the states until the following Thursday.

Fred and I returned the rental car and they drove us back to billeting. All of us shopped at the store in the billeting office. Our last night together was spent at the new "Top of the Rock Club"- Officers & Enlisted. Don't miss visiting it.

The KC-10 tanker left Lajes for McGuire AFB with 39 empty seats. Box lunches were $3. It's a very comfortable airplane with airline seats. The crew was very attentive and helpful to make our trip enjoyable. Flight time was six hours.

From the time we left the states to our return, there were four flights that departed with many empty seats. November could be a month to keep in mind for traveling to warmer climates.

After arriving at McGuire AFB, NJ, we rented a car to drive to BWI where our cars were parked. One-way drop offs are hard to come by and when you find one, it tends to be expensive, We found one at Hertz Rental. The parking lot fee at BWI was $28 for four days. We went to Ft. Meade to spend the night at Abrams Hall. Reservations were made from Lajes.

Saturday morning after breakfast, we said our goodbyes to Fred and Rosemary. We enjoyed our trip with them very much. This being their first Space-A venture made it all the more enjoyable for us. The opportunities for Space-A travel are better than ever and have vastly improved since our first experience in 1987. As I have said many times before, try it - you'll like it!

TSgt Michael P. Bocchicchia Visits Pearl Harbor

On Friday 6 Nov 1998, I arrived at the 107th Operations. There were 40 seats available at briefing; only 31 PAX showed up with 9 no-shows. We departed Niagara Falls at 1000 on board a KC-135 and arrived at Hickam AFB at 1500 hrs Honolulu time after a 10-hour flight. Upon arrival at Hickam AFB, I checked in at the flight counter and signed up for the return trip.

I proceeded to the Enterprise car rental, which was right in the terminal, to pick up my vehicle. After learning there were none, five of us were transported to Honolulu where I received a small Dodge compact at the cost of $100 for three days.

Back at Hickam, I went directly to the TML office and checked in; $36 for three days at the Royal Alaska. The rooms were great, equipped with a refrigerator, which was well stocked, and snacks.

Early Saturday morning, I went to breakfast at the dining hall before making an acquaintance tour of the base, which is quite large. The AMC Terminal is only five minutes from the lodging office. I found the NCO Club, called "The Tradewinds" and dined there at the dining hall while at Hickam. Both the NCO Club and the Officers' Club are large and beautiful. The food was delicious at both facilities. At the dining hall I paid $2.65 for my meals. They have a very large commissary on base and the BX is fantastic, like nothing I have ever seen. It is in two sections; a BX and a BXtra, a large two-story building. They have everything imaginable. I made a two-hour tour of the BX.

I departed for Pearl Harbor, only 15 minutes from the base. I proceeded to the Visitors Center to pick up my ticket for the trip to the USS Arizona Memorial by U.S. Navy launch. Prior to departing on the launch, we were shown a 30-minute film depicting the actual attack on Pearl Harbor from an American film and a captured Japanese film. There were approximately 100 of us on board the launch to the USS Arizona. We were on the memorial approximately 30 minutes, during which time I was able to see the full length of the battleship with a section of the forward gun turret above water. You could see oil seepage at the far end of the memorial. There was a large backing in gold, lettering the names of the 1,177 entombed in her hull. There are monuments of other battleships that were sunk at their moorings; the Oklahoma, which went down with 400 men entombed in her hull, the West Virginia, the California, the Utah, Pennsylvania, Maryland, Tennessee, and the Nevada. This was called "Battleship Row." What an ominous feeling to know that there are those personnel entombed below you, never to be forgotten (the day that will live in infamy).

Not far from the USS Arizona Memorial, you could see the USS Missouri docked at Ford Island. They are preparing this battleship as a memorial to be opened to the public sometime in January 1999. I plan to be there. For $40 I purchased a flag that was flown over the USS Arizona on October 29, 1998. They have quite a large souvenir center.

I visited the USS Bowfin submarine nearby. You were given a tape and player to listen to as you walked through the submarine. There was a $6 charge for this. There is also a gift/souvenir shop at the completion of the tour. I returned to Hickam AFB NCO Club for dinner. I devoured a 12 oz. Hawaiian steak, baked potato, veg, and soup for $13.95. I returned to my room for the evening to watch TV. On channel 5, you are able to view all incoming and outgoing aircraft at Hickam AFB.

Sunday morning I went to the club for breakfast, then decided to go to the terminal to check on our departure and show time. I was informed that the aircraft had broken down and they had no idea when it was going to be repaired or if we would need to take a C-141 to Charleston AFB or a C-5 to Dover AFB. Monday at 0300, I reported to the AMC terminal and was informed that our A/C was still down, so I proceeded to get on the manifest that was rescheduled for a C-5 to Dover AFB, DE. 9 Nov.

While awaiting my flight, I ran into a couple who were on the Dover flight. Their vehicle was parked in the long-term lot at Dover, AFB. When I told them I was from Niagara Falls and was planning to take a train, they invited me to ride with them. I said fine and offered to help with the gas and tolls. They wouldn't take it. Instead I bought them breakfast where we spent the night at Clark Summit, PA. Their names were Bruce and Sylvia Wotherspoon from Colden, NY. Bruce is a TSgt USAF RET. The flight back on the C-5 to Dover took 9 hours. The Wotherspoons drove me right to the Niagara Falls Air Reserve Base.

It was a short trip but so much was accomplished. I am looking forward to returning to Hawaii in the very near future.
Michael P. Bocchicchia TSgt USAF RET.

Fred and Rosemary Depew's Space-A Experience

We had attended Space-A meetings at RAD days given by LtCol Caruso. He and his wife, Gayle, were very gracious and helpful in giving us the guidance to prepare for our trip to the Azores.

Our tour of the Azores was enhanced by the knowledge gained by the Carusos on a previous visit. We rented a car and toured the island. We visited many scenic areas, picturesque towns and villages. The scenery was very beautiful and the people very friendly. We were impressed with the Space-A planes, the smooth flights, and the friendly, accommodating crews. We want to thank the Carusos for all their help and advice in making this trip a great success.

Interested persons should try this experience and we are looking forward to our next Space-A trip.
TSgt Fred Depew USA (Ret.)

Bob Graham Takes Us on His January 1999 Trip to Singapore

Space-A to Singapore and return is a snap this time of year (January). At least it was for me. On every flight I was either the sole passenger or the plane was only two thirds full. And billeting was never a problem at any military base or civilian hotel.

At Travis I took a KC-10 non-stop, 13 hours to Kadena A.B., Okinawa, Japan. The reserve crew from McGuire AFB, New Jersey was extremely friendly, accommodating, and highly professional. They took me on a tour of the flight deck and the refueling boom-control compartment.

The next morning got an empty C-9, USAF MEDEVAC to Yokota A.B., Japan, near Tokyo. Showed up "bright eyed and bushy tailed" for the 0410, morning, Space-A call. Rode another McGuire AFB KC-10 seven hours to Singapore.

Now if you go to Singapore pay close attention to the following: Get from the AMC staff complete directions on getting back to that military airfield at Paya Lebar as taxi drivers will want to take you to Changi Int'l Airport. The only English some of the drivers know is "Sure I know it, get in." Then they hand you a directory of Singapore and ask you to point it out. Fortunately I saw a familiar landmark and pointed the way. The City-State island of Singapore is fun. Had a cola in the famous Raffles Hotel Long Bar where Rudyard Kipling used to hang out. Fascinating clientele there.

Visited Kuala Lumpur, Malaysia, then back to the AMC folks at Singapore for a DC-8 flight to Yokota then an L-1011 the next day for a 24-hour trip with long stopovers at Iwakuni &

Misawa, Japan, Anchorage and Seattle before arriving at Los Angeles (LAX) then commercial back home.

After 47 years going Space-A, I am still learning the ropes, and having fun.
Bob Graham
St. Louis, Missouri

Editor's note: Bob had a problem with a van company going from Oakland to Travis. He recommends you get a firm price BEFORE getting into the vehicle.

The DeLoziers' Trip to Hawaii

Dear Ann:
My wife, Shirley, and I took a hop with the TN Air National Guard (KC-135) to Hawaii on January 4th for 10 days. We stopped at Edwards AFB, CA for the night. The runway we set down on was 7-1/2 miles long and the base contains 301,000 acres.

The base OPS bus took us to the lodging office (High Desert Inn-Bldg # 5602) which was about 5 miles from the PAX terminal. The base is really spread out in the desert.

Some passengers were placed in the Desert Inn and the rest of us (a total of 23) were taken to the TML Bldgs # 7022 & 7031. They were very nice one-bedroom suites, double bed and sleeper couch in living room, TV in living room and bedroom. A/C, kitchen, microwave, washer & dryer. The rate: $24.00.

From the TML building, the exchange is 1/4 mile across the field or you can walk the road. In the Exchange Bldg # 7210, you can eat at five different places or walk across the parking lot to Burger King Bldg # 6005. Base OPS sent a bus the next morning to take us to the plane.

We left at 0830 with a group of Fighters (F-4s) for Hawaii. About every 1,000 miles the F-4s needed refueling and the ladies on the plane got a kick watching them being refueled. On arrival at Hickam AFB, I called Alamo car rental and they picked us up at the AMC terminal. They had the best prices by the week. I always stay at one of the Outrigger Hotels at a good price since my friend is the vice president of the 31 Outriggers. They also give a good military rate at most of them. I stopped at the Hale Koa parking garage and purchased a parking permit for the week ($5.00 per day). The hotels charge $5-$10 per day. You can walk to all the hotels downtown from the parking lot. The Hale Koa Hotel stays full most of the time and you can't get a room unless you want a sea view for $120.00 per night. They want you to check back every day to see if there is a cheaper room. So, the best way is to make reservations if you know ahead of time on your vacation. Our ten days in Hawaii were well-spent visiting friends, etc. We took a boat ride to see the whales jump and toured Pearl Harbor. They have the U.S.S. Missouri tied up at Ford Island and anyone can tour it for $10.00.

We drove around the Island and stopped at Bellows Air Force Station, which is very nice beach with white sand. Rental cottages are still real nice and retirees can make reservations up to 75 days in advance. Reservations Office is now located in the Bellows Beach Club and open 24 hours. On our way around the island we stopped at the Crouching Lion Restaurant for a snack. The food is still excellent and at good prices. The surf on the north shore was about 25 feet high or more. Still, there were fools on surfboards getting wiped out. We flew to Lihue, Kauai for one day, rented our car from Dollar. Drove to the end of the road to the wet caves and the beach where "South Pacific" was filmed. We stopped at Princeville on our way back and ate at Chuck's Steak House. The food was outstanding in price and plentiful. Our next day flight took us to the big island of Hawaii. Picked up our Alamo rental at Nib and stopped at the macadamia nut factory (good price) and on to Kilauea Military Camp. Now every car has to pay $10.00 to enter the Volcanoes National Park if you are going to KMC to stay. If you are not staying in the park or KMC, just tell the gate ranger you are only going to KMC to get something to eat or get gas. They have let me pass free the past two times. KMC used to have their own back gate, but no more. Veterans are getting less every year around the globe. KMC camp still has good food in the mess hall and lots of souvenirs and wine, etc., in the country store. My first time there was back in 1966 and the place hasn't changed much except the personnel. Mostly civilians run the place.

Only one day on the big island and back to Waikiki. We took the same plane back to Knoxville, TN since I signed up 55 days before. Everyone got on the plane coming back. We came back with a KC-10 and a squadron of F-15s. Refueled on the way back. When we got close to Oklahoma City, the pilot called Knoxville and they were having freezing rain. We sat down in Tinker AFB, OK and refueled in case we could not land at Knoxville. Only took one hour and we were on our way to Tennessee. Upon arrival the ice had turned to rain and we landed. It was a nice trip and enjoyed by all. It was about my 65th time to Hawaii since May 1954. Plan to go back in 2000. Military Living's *Temporary Military Lodging Around the World* was "RIGHT ON" and everyone who travels should buy a TML book and the *R&R Travel News®* to be on top of all the changes taking place at all the bases around the world. Keep up the good work. It is very much appreciated.

Sincerely,
Robert K. DeLozier AK1 (AC) USN (Ret.)
Sevierville, TN

The Conroys Share Their Space-A Trip to Germany

Dear Ann & Roy:

We recently completed another Space-A trip (our sixth in two and a quarter years) and had just a few brief comments. We flew from BWI to Rhein-Main on a Friday. With some advance phone calls we found over 100 Space-A seats anticipated. There were about that many folks in the terminal the night we arrived. I figured that about 25 of those were Category 6. Everybody got on the flight with open seats left. We deplaned at Rhein-Main and were able to secure quarters at the base hotel due to an advance phone call from CONUS before we left. My purpose in writing this letter is to reaffirm your recommendation about the Waldrestaurant Unterschweinstiege at the Steinberger Hotel. It was thoroughly delightful and was maybe the finest meal we had while in Germany. Prices were fairly reasonable. It's just out the back gate from the hotel on base.

We took a leisurely trip through the Alsace region of France, Luzerne Switzerland, and Germany. I found a unique place to stay in Strasbourg, France due to a conversation with the USO at Ramstein. They provided me with the name and address of a French Officers' Mess that allowed U.S. military, active and retired, to use their facilities at a very reasonable price. It was the Cercle des Officiers Mess. (Editor's Note: Cercle des Officiers de Garnison 17, Place Broglie, 67071, Strasbourg CEDEX, Tel: C-011-31-88-36-49-04. Closed Sunday nights, holidays and first weekend (Saturday, Sunday and Monday) of each month). The food there was also unbelievably good.

On our return we couldn't get space at Rhein-Main but arranged quarters at Darmstadt, about 15 minutes away. We planned our return on a Sunday. While only 37 Space-A seats were showing they ended up taking over 60 people with open seats left. All categories made the flight although it took two Space-A calls.

One change made at the Frankfurt terminal was in providing six trays in which to place your status form once you check in. This allows the crew to presort individuals by sign-up date. This was new to me and had not been explained when I signed in. Because I did not submit my sign-up sheet in the correct bin I found I was not included in the first round of Category VI individuals called even though I had a very senior sign-up date. I think time of sign-up still controls the order of selection but a number of folks were called before I checked on my status. It was a wake up call and it was a new procedure.

Our success with flights might have been due to time of year (early Oct). The trips on the contract flights were great and very comfortable. I also can't say enough about the crew and facilities at BWI and the smooth operation they run there. Keep up the great work.

Sincerely, CAPT. John P. Conroy, USNR (Ret.)
Pittsburgh, PA

Tom & Cherry Carnell Visit RAF Mildenhall

Dear Ann,

My husband, Tom (CDR, USN, Ret), and I recently returned from our first-ever overseas Space-A trip, from BWI to RAF Mildenhall and back on March 2/3 and 11/12. Although we'd read up in your books and from others, it was still a learning experience. For one thing, next time we'll go after April 1 or Easter, because many "great houses" and castles are not open for the season till then. However, we got to see a great deal and enjoyed ourselves very much despite the almost constant (gentle) rain and the cold weather. It was hard to believe that daffodils and some flowering trees were in full bloom as we donned our winter coats, long underwear, hats and lined gloves!

Here are some notes on Mildenhall and vicinity that might be helpful to your readers:

*RAF Mildenhall base is on Threatcon Bravo.

*Be prepared to show your ID card in every building you enter and at several newly established gates. Because of all the new fences and gates it's usually quicker to walk somewhere than to drive, because vehicles have to go the long way around but pedestrians can cut across.

*No luggage can be left anywhere on the base so if you arrive early and are waiting for a billet you will have to sit with your bag(s) or haul them everywhere with you.

*Many buildings have had their identifying signs removed so for example the Dining Hall is not labeled as such, but is still marked as Building 436.

*RAF Lakenheath, 10 minutes away by free shuttle bus, is NOT on such heightened security—go figure.

*At Mildenhall all distances are surprisingly (to us) walkable—a very compact base, especially for the Air Force!

*Billeting/Lodging Office has a much better map of the base than the one available at the passenger terminal—worth stopping by to pick one up.

*TLF price went up as of March 1, 1999 to $19.50 per room per night plus $5 for each additional occupant. (The slightly apologetic printed notice in the room stated that this was in part to make fees consistent among bases and apologized for "any inconvenience" caused.)

*If traveling with a companion with whom you are not used to sleeping in a standard (54-inch wide) double bed be sure to ask the lodging office for a room with a larger bed or else two beds (both seem to be very rare) OR ask for one that is large enough so that a rollaway can be brought in. Our best room for this purpose was in a Senior Enlisted transient billet (Building 238) -- really much nicer (because of the extra space and the free washers/dryers across the hall) than the elegantly decorated but small room we first were assigned in the Officers' Club (Building 464).

*The Travel & Tours Office personnel (Building 404, "Bob Hope Rec Center," at east end of building, with access from outside when Rec Center is still closed but travel office opens at 8 a.m.) are very nice and extremely helpful. They publish a little booklet of very useful and accurate bus schedules to nearby towns and cities. There's a 25% discount on Cambridge Coach line buses for over-60s, and other lines sometimes offer other kinds of "concessions" (that's what the Brits call "discounts") such as a "Family Rover" pass or "day-return" tickets. As you get on, ask the driver if you qualify for any of them. Riding the local buses through villages and past farms was time consuming but much more interesting to us than getting into a car and speeding off on the limited access highways -- not to mention less stressful, because we didn't have to struggle with maps or driving on the left on narrow and unfamiliar roads.

*The Dining Hall (Building 436, facing Washington Square) is open to retirees at all mealtimes; prices are extremely reasonable even with the 33% surcharge for cash customers.

*Retirees cannot use the on-base bank (north side of Building 436) BUT just outside it there is a 24-hour ATM with no such restrictions, linked to many major credit cards and banking networks, where anyone can withdraw daily up to $500 worth of either U.S. or British money.

*Retirees cannot use the commissary or BX—EXCEPT we can be admitted to the "Mini Mall" if planning to shop at the fast food stands (Baskin Robbins, Robin Hood sandwiches, Burger King, Pizza, Taco Bell) and/or the concessions (Turkish gold, English china, very nice selection of miscellaneous souvenirs in several shops).

*While waiting around for a flight or a room, the base library (Building 425) was a wonderful haven with nice people, comfortable seating, plenty of reading material (!) including a good variety of newspapers, AND a chance to sign up for their computer to check e-mail or do internet-based research, all free of charge. They take advance reservations for the computer for one hour at a time but if the person with the reservation does not show up within five minutes of the appointed hour, or leaves early, they will let the next person on the waiting list use it instead. Remove your name from the waiting list if you go out (such as for a meal) and then put it back on if you return.

On this trip we concentrated on eastern England, doing a little exploring around the bases and Mildenhall village and also taking day trips by bus to Ely (wonderful cathedral and town—be sure to take one of the free guided tours of the cathedral), Bury St. Edmund (charming town, nice shopping, fascinating ruins), Newmarket (horse country) and Kings Lynn (old port city with fascinating streets). Market Days are especially good days to visit the towns—the Tours office can tell you which days they are for each location.

Then we transferred to Cambridge by bus and stayed there four nights in the Gonville Hotel, very nice "3-crown" rated and well-located establishment that we found through the city's tourist information bureau (it's at the back side of the "Guildhall" town hall, within walking distance of the bus station) where they negotiated a half-price room deal for us, about $88 per night for a lovely room with king-sized bed, tea/coffee/cocoa-making equipment, private bath and full English breakfast in the charming dining room! Cambridge is about as expensive as London so we thought this was a good deal for a place within such easy walking distance of the colleges, museums, rail and bus stations. We could have spent less but at our ages we like to treat ourselves to a private shower and toilet, so we compensated by eating in tea shops or pubs or getting take-out snacks in grocery stores or on the street (Tom loved those hand-held pork pies!) rather than splurging in expensive restaurants. Whenever we travel we like to get close to the local culture so this kind of "dining" suits us just fine.
Cherry Carnell, Fairfax, VA

MSG Charlie Brough Tells About Space-A Air Stateside

Dear Ann and Roy,
Golf, anyone? Since turning 60 years of age, I have done some extensive traveling by Space-A travel to see the world and especially to play golf. I give credit for most of my success to Ann and Roy Crawford of Military Living. Their books *Military Space-A Air Opportunities Around the World* and *Temporary Military Lodging Around the World* are just as important to my travel as the right tools are to an expert mechanic. (Thanks!)

On 19 March I called a friend in Conroe, Texas and asked if he would be home on Tuesday, the 23rd of March. He said he would be so I told him I would probably be in Conroe by the evening of the 22nd and would give him a call when I got there. I had researched my Space-A Air book and found that Kelly AFB was the closest I could fly to Conroe, which is near Houston.

At show time 0415, 22 March, when I checked in at McChord AFB, there were 15 or so passengers with 40 seats available. I boarded Flight F025 at 0600 and was on my way to Kelly AFB, San Antonio TX. Cost on my boarding pass $0.00. At the base I checked to see if my faxed return was in their book. It was, so I knew I had a way home.

I then called Enterprise Rent-A-Car, (they come pick you up) and was soon on my way to Conroe. I arrived there at 2000, rented a room, called John, my golfing friend, to let him know I was in town. At 0800 on 23 March, I met John at the Panorama Country Club where he lives and is a member there. We had a fine breakfast at the club, caught up on old times when we were golfing in Scotland and went out to play golf. We didn't qualify for the U.S. Open or anything but had a great time anyhow and later enjoyed a fine lunch together.

I then headed back to Kelly AFB where I had, with the help of my Temporary Military Lodging book, reserved a room for the night of the 23rd. I was in my room at 1800. The hospitality was just super as was my very clean room. I learned that the bowling alley nearby had food and went there for dinner. A nice night's sleep and I got up at 0600 and went to the La Hacienda Dining Facility for a very fine breakfast, which consisted of eggs, hashbrowns, bacon, sausage, yogurt, toast, milk and coffee for $1.80.

Show time was at 0830 for the C-9 MEDEVAC to Travis AFB and boarding time was 1200 hrs. Flight 1654 cost $0.00. The weather was very nasty at Travis AFB. Getting a room was touch and go but finally got settled in. Morning of 25 March we had a show time of 0305 but that got revised a few times. Seems our C-5 Galaxy flight #0305 had a slight problem. They did get it fixed though and I was on my way home. There were only 7 of us so we got what I call First Class in the forward compartment with the crew. My boarding pass once again read $0.00. By early afternoon I was back at McChord AFB, Washington and only minutes from home. I had a wonderful reunion with an old friend, thanks to the combined efforts of the Air Mobility Command (AMC) and Military Living. The only (sensible) way to fly.
Charlie E. Brough MSG (Ret.)
Olympia, WA
Editors Note: If you are a golfer, you will find a section with military golf courses listed in our newest edition of *Military RV Camping & Outdoor Recreation Around the World*.

Yokota Terminal Closed During Night
by Senior Airman Cindy York, Air Force Print News

YOKOTA AIR BASE, Japan - Travelers passing through Yokota's passenger terminal will have to find another place to go between the hours of 10 p.m. - 4 a.m.

Air Mobility Command decided to close the terminal during the night to coincide with the nightly runway closure. By closing, security costs of watching the terminal when planes are not flying are eliminated.

The closure will not affect travel, according to Master Sgt. Gregory A. Scruggs, passenger service operations manager. He said even though the terminal would basically close in conjunction with the current airfield closure hours of 10 p.m. - 6 a.m., it will re-open at 4 a.m. to process passengers for daily flights.

"If a plane comes in after 10 p.m. or leaves before 6 a.m., which happens occasionally, we will keep the terminal open late or open it earlier than 4 a.m. to accommodate duty and space-available passengers on that aircraft," Scruggs said.

Currently, the terminal is open 24 hours a day and patrons are able to eat in the Army and Air Force Exchange Service cafeteria, and can shop in a small shoppette inside the terminal, at any hour. This service will change March 31 as well because AAFES isn't doing enough business to constitute paying their employees during the night.

Opening early does not mean the cafeteria will open, however. The cafeteria will maintain the hours of 6 a.m. - 10 p.m. daily.

For those wanting something to eat during the night, the Samurai Café Dining Facility is open 11 p.m. - 1 a.m. for midnight meal service. Anyone on subsistence-in-kind rations is able to eat in the dining hall whether on official orders or on leave. Also, E-4s and below and their families are allowed to visit the Samurai Café, according to Staff Sgt. LaRessa Keller Griffin, food service accountant.

Travelers are reminded to bring extra money for off-base hotels in case they need overnight lodging accommodations.

"Right now our lodging space is very limited," said Paul Freund, manager of the Kanto Lodge. "Due to the upcoming construction of our new lodging facility, there will be a massive shortage. In fact, lodging for people flying Space-A will virtually be nonexistent from April to June. After June, some space will open, but not much. Our situation will not get much better until the new facility is open a few years from now.

"Our job is to help people find a place to stay whether they are on official orders or on leave," Freund said. "Sleeping in the Kanto Lodge lobby is not an option for anyone, so we will be more than happy to call around to find somewhere for travelers to stay."

Freund said people should plan to spend $80-120 a night for a hotel room and they should also bring enough money for a taxi ride to and from the hotel.

For those who don't mind some discomfort, on base there is a lounge in the Jugo Annex, where Space-A travelers can wait overnight for $5.00 during the time that Yokota passenger terminal is closed. To get to the Jugo Annex, walk out of the terminal toward the front gate. Cross to the other side of the street, where you will see the BX and commissary. Close to the BX is a gift shop, Tommy China. The Jugo Annex is behind Tommy China.

Stewart Wolfe Space-A to Germany

Dear Ann and Roy,
I wanted to drop you a quick note and let you know how much your Space-A guide helped me in my travels back and forth to Europe.

With my trusty credit card in hand (just in case I got stuck, though I never used it), I decided to try the Space-A system, to see my wife, who had recently moved over to Germany. Unlike most travelers, I did not heed your warnings to use Space-A when I had time to wait for a flight. I'm a high school teacher and I didn't have any time to waste, but I figured "nothing ventured, nothing gained." I did the trip three times in three months.

The first time I went alone (had to see if this really worked), the second time, I took my 17-year-old son (Fasching), and the third time, I took both my 17-year-old son and my 16- year-old daughter. Each time, the itinerary was the same, Friday evening flight from Baltimore Washington International (BWI) to Rhein-Main with a return on Monday morning to BWI. I did the trip in January (Martin Luther King's birthday), February (St. Valentine's Day, also Fasching) and March (just a regular weekend) and met with success each time.

AMC runs a number of charter flights out of BWI each week (currently run by World Airways). Fridays they go to Rhein-Main, Aviano, and Incirlik. The flights are great! For a $12.00 airport tax fee you get on a civilian airliner with two meals, two movies and everything else you would spend $300.00+ for traveling on a commercial flight. They get you to Rhein-Main around 11:00 AM Saturday morning, so you can spend the weekend with your loved ones (like I did), or traveling around Germany. These flights are the best kept secret in the military (at least during the winter months). I should note that it cost more to park the car than it did to fly to Europe.

Coming back was no problem either. AMC has a flight that originates in Atlanta and does an immediate turnaround on Monday mornings to BWI and Charleston, SC. Again, you have to pay airport and customs fees ($23.40), but in return you get two meals, two movies and even a complimentary beer or wine with lunch. During the winter months there was no problem getting on. I expect that summer will prove to be a different story, but since my teaching contract is up in June, and my wife has announced that she really wants me to get over to Germany on a permanent (at least for three years) basis, I'm not worried about that.

My students think that I'm independently wealthy, traveling back and forth to Europe for the weekend. The favorite question is "Where are you going this weekend, Mr. Wolfe?" I almost hate to admit to them that there is very little cost involved in traveling the "military way." Thank you for publishing the books that give me the information, and "guts" to attempt these trips. This is probably the best use I've made of my retired ID card since I got it. I guarantee that I will try to "hop" around Europe, starting this fall.

Sincerely,
Stewart C. Wolfe YNC, USN (Ret.)

The Wyands' 25th Wedding Anniversary Trip

Dear Ann and Roy,
At long last - time for our 25th wedding anniversary trip to Germany, Switzerland, and Austria, courtesy of the USAF. What fun! Our pocket notebook had the following: to convert kilometers to miles, multiply by .6, to convert Deutsche marks to dollars, multiply by .6, to convert Swiss Francs to dollars multiply by 2/3.

The Wyands

Fifty days ahead of time, we faxed Dover and McGuire and e-mailed Rhein-Main and Ramstein for our Space-A sign-up to

Europe. As of that time, Dover still had its flight schedules on the internet (www.Dover.AF.Mil/Space-A) and we accessed the site right up until the time we boarded our USAF flight to Germany in early May. Travel hint: The Dover BX has an electric adapter kit for all European outlets.

After an overnight flight to Rhein-Main (pronounced Rhein-MINE) our first act was to call Ramstein (pronounced RAM-stine) Billeting. Positively NO Cat-Six retiree rooms available. Our next shock was that the free and frequent shuttle bus from FRF to RMS now cost $20 per person and only ran three times a day (often not on time).

Remembering the old Space-A rule of never taking "NO" as final, we checked Ramstein Billeting in person, and -YES- found a room for two "up-all-night" travelers. Thus, recheck base and billeting, in person, between 1100 and 1200 hrs - check-out time. Meals were available at the Community Center, only minutes away.

The AAFES Sixt Car-Rental Agency was only six minutes away from Billeting. We had a four-door German OPAL Vectra for two weeks for only $342 (unlimited mileage). We declined the expensive auto insurance because we had USAA Visa Gold credit card coverage. Further we saved the expensive VAT Tax because we rented on base from AAFES. Since the usual tour guide maps are inadequate, be sure and purchase a good road map. Editor's Note: Or *Military Living's European U.S. Military Road Atlas, Plus Near East Areas,* ISBN-0-914862-73-1.

Now, for the record -yes- the Germans drive fast on the autobahns - but - no - we didn't feel uncomfortable, because the drivers are rule abiding and predictable. The slow drivers stay in the right lane and when they change lanes they signal. No road rage, no horn honking, no weaving in and out. So - yes - we drove at 90/100 mph, but we weren't nervous wrecks. Indeed, we felt safer than driving in England or the USA!

We headed south to Switzerland via Calw and the Black Forest. We were stopped at the Swiss border and had to pay a mandatory $28 fee to drive on the autobahn. Nowhere were we stopped at any European borders for passports or customs - indeed, the only time we showed our passport was while exiting and entering the USA. German Deutsche marks were accepted almost everywhere and most prices were doubled listed in Euros - the coming European currency in 2002.

Colonel Martin J. Wyand USAF (Ret.)
State College, PA

Eppie and King Tell Us About Using an RV & Space-A Air

Dear Ann and Roy,
With the motto Still Alive at 65, my wife Eppie and I planned an ambitious travel adventure for the spring and summer of 1999. We have retired in the Denver metropolitan area so when Eppie's family decided to have a big reunion in New Brunswick, Canada in August, we decided that since we would be going east for that event we would just tack on a trip to England before the reunion and a hike on the northern 100 miles of the Appalachian Trail in Maine after the reunion.

Let me explain that for the last four years we have traveled in a pickup truck with an eight and one-half foot pop-up camper on the back. This setup has proven to be very comfortable for us. In fact we often spend as much as four to five months living in our camper. Behind the truck we tow a small Geo Metro sedan which we use for local transportation when we camp for a prolonged time at one place. Being retired, having no pets, and living in a townhome, we can up and leave on short notice which makes such travel possible.

For the last two years we have worked during March and April as volunteer rangers at the Grand Gulch Primitive Area in southeastern Utah. So when we set off in late February this year, we packed for an extended time away with warm clothing for our ranger job, travel clothes and suitcase packs for England and backpacking equipment for our hike in Maine. While in southern Utah we used e-mail to sign up at several East Coast terminals for Space-A flights to Europe. From our reading of your *R&R Travel News®* it seemed that Dover with its frequent C-5s to Europe would be our best bet, so we made advance reservations at the Dover AFB FAMCAMP.

On the 20th of April we left Blanding, Utah and headed for Kirtland AFB in Albuquerque, New Mexico. After setting up at the FAMCAMP we went to the commissary and stocked up on groceries for the cross-country drive. Worth mentioning are the Corps of Engineers (CE) Campgrounds we stayed at in Arkansas and Tennessee. CE campgrounds are beautifully maintained, usually have showers and electrical hookups, and to holders of the Golden Age Pass they give a 50% discount to an already low cost of between $12-$15 per night.

After a brief stay in Asheville, NC visiting family and friends we headed toward Dover via Fort Pickett Travel Camp southwest of Richmond, VA off I-85. We located Fort Pickett in your *Military RV, Camping & Outdoor Recreation Areas Around the World* and were pleased to get full hookups in a quiet, shaded corner of this post for only $10 per night.

We arrived at Dover, set up in the FAMCAMP and excitedly checked out the flight schedule monitor in the lovely new terminal. My journal notes indicate that the next day there were four planes to Europe with possible seats. However, we watched the first three of those planes get canceled and on the fourth plane, a KC-135 to Germany, our number came up for the last seat. Since there were two of us we had to wait another day. We spent a noisy night in our camper as C-5s did touch-and-go right next to the campground.

After our noisy night we moved our camper to the long-term parking right next to the terminal into one of the several spaces reserved for RVs that are 19 feet or longer. Although there are no hookups it is an ideal setup for waiting for a couple of days. The terminal, less than 100 yards away, is open 24 hours, has a snack bar, restrooms and showers.

By 1630 we were taxiing down the runway on a C-5 headed for Ramstein. Since there were 32 passengers and 73 seats, after dinner many of us were able to convert 3 seats into a bed and sleep all the way across the Atlantic.

At Ramstein those of us headed for England were manifested on a C-141 and were in Mildenhall by late afternoon. Eppie and I got a room at the Farleigh Guest House (25 pounds sterling), a short walk from the terminal, and crashed for some jet lag slumber. It was nice to be able to eat at the base dining hall.

For five weeks we romped around England using National Express buses for travel between areas of England where we wanted to hike. For hiking we converted our suitcases to back-packs and ambled along the southwest coast of Cornwall, the Lake District, and along the Penine Way and Hadrian's Wall in Northumberland staying in B&Bs and youth hostels.

In most of the youth hostels we were able to book a double room with two bunk beds and a shared bath. On rare occasions we had to accept a bed in a dormitory, but we lived through those nights thanks to ear plugs provided on the flight over. Most British youth hostels include breakfast in the cost of the room and also have a kitchen where the guests can cook other meals. We found that by cooking our evening meal we saved a considerable amount of money.

After spending time in Glasgow, Edinburgh and London seeing the sights and experiencing the big cities, we were ready to return home. We determined when the base schools in England would be out for the summer and timed our return to occur a few days before that date. We spent a day waiting at Mildenhall for a flight, only to see all flights to Dover canceled. But next day, after most of the terminal cleared out on a flight to McChord, we and 18 others boarded a C-5 to Dover. Again we ate, made our beds and slept over the Atlantic.

Arriving at Dover about 9:00 p.m., we went through customs, walked out to our camper in the long-term parking lot, opened it up and went to bed for the night. This had been another enjoyable Space-A trip.

Our stateside travels in New England included stops at New Boston Air Station FAMCAMP outside Manchester, NH, Hanscom AFB FAMCAMP outside of Boston, and the Naval Security Group near Winter Harbor, ME where we gave up a campsite and got a beautiful cabin that had become available when rain set in for several days. The hike in northern Maine, strenuous but enjoyable, and a last minute trip to Isle Royale National Park rounded out our Still Alive at 65 adventure. On the way home we stayed at the newly expanded FAMCAMP at Offutt AFB, NE and visited the impressive SAC Museum nearby.

King and Eppie Hastings
USAF Retired

1SG Norman Baggett, USA, RET. Lives a Fantastic Life!

Dear Ann and Roy,
I imagine you have wondered what happened to me. Well, we have been on the road for the past two years. We spent 16 months up in Alaska and just got home last September. The trip to Alaska was really great. We drove our old motor home back up there and took a side trip up into the Yukon and Northwest Territories of Canada on the way up the Alaskan Highway. The first summer we traveled around over Alaska. We traveled just about everywhere we could drive, except up to the oil fields.

When we arrived at Fort Wainwright in June we were both sick with chest and head colds. We went to the Fort Wainwright post hospital and they really gave us good service. My wife went right into the emergency room as she was really feeling bad. I waited until the next day and went to the post medical center.

We spent quite a bit of time at Fort Wainwright. The RV facilities there were about like they were when we were there in 1995. They did build a new restroom and raised the daily rate from $3.00 per day to $5.00 per day. Glass Park is a pretty nice, quiet place to park and we really enjoyed it. There is water available there, but no electricity or dump station. The dump station was over at the post service station.

In November of 1997 we drove from Anchorage up to Fairbanks. When we left Anchorage the temperature was about 20 degrees above zero and light snow. When we got to Wasilla we hit black ice for about 20 miles and for the next 300 miles we drove on packed snow and ice. We were driving our Jeep Wrangler so we got along just fine. It was 5 below zero when we arrived in Fairbanks at about 1600 hours. We stayed in the guest quarters at Fort Wainwright. They were very nice—a bedroom, sitting room and private bath for $20.00 a night. At that time of year there are plenty of rooms available.

I had my amateur radio equipment on board the motor home and talked back to New Boston almost every day. When we were on the road that was the only way our family could contact us in an emergency. We met one of our amateur radio friends in Anchorage. His folks own the Orca Inn Bed and Breakfast. They wanted to go outside for the winter so we moved in and managed the bed and breakfast for them. It was a beautiful big house that sat up on the foot of the mountain at the corner of Lake Oatis Parkway and O'Malley Road. While we were there that winter I talked to several of the amateurs out at Elmendorf Air Force Base. They were really a great bunch of guys. I used the medical facilities out at Elmendorf, but it was really hard to get in to see a doctor since I am on Medicare, but they did fill my prescriptions. We used the ski facilities out at Elmendorf. My wife fell on her ski pole and bruised her rib, so she did not ski the last time we went. We had not been skiing in about 10 years. It was amazing how much we had forgotten, how hard it was to do, what we remembered. Being in our 60s we do not fall as gracefully as we used to.

We stayed at the Military Recreation Camp down at Seward a few nights during the winter. The motel units are very nice and clean and very well-equipped. The whole camp has been rebuilt since we were there in 1995. They have a lot of facilities. They seem a little expensive, especially for our younger service members. They have charter fishing boats that are pretty reasonable when compared with the private charters.

In April we left the motor home parked in Anchorage and drove down to Seward. We caught the ferry out of Seward and had a very nice trip out to Kodiak. We spent three months doing volunteer work at the Kodiak Baptist Mission. I did maintenance work and my wife worked in the thrift shop and taught food classes for the day camp children. We shopped at the Coast Guard commissary. It is not a very big facility, but the prices were much better than in the outside stores. My wife thought they had a very good selection of foods and produce. We went to the commissary and identified ourselves as retired military and they really gave us good service. While we were at Kodiak we took the ferry out to Dutch Harbor. It was a three-day trip. The last 18 hours were rough. The Captain said we had 30-foot seas. My wife did not take her seasick pills and got pretty sick. I managed to hold out until about two hours before we got into Dutch Harbor before I got a little seasick. I had been through seas like that when I went to Korea in 1951. It was a great trip, and we really enjoyed the people we met.

ON THE ROAD AGAIN IN THEIR RV

We went to Arizona this winter and stayed at Davis-Monthan Air Force Base for a few nights. The first night we stayed in the overflow "cow pasture." This was no problem for us as we had plenty of water on board and ran the generator for power. The next morning they had spaces available so we moved over in the family park. The facilities were very nice. Full hookup for our motor home was $12.00 a night. It took us a while to get our vehicles registered at the front gate, but other than that it was a very pleasant stay.

AND ON TO CANADA

A couple of years ago we took a trip through eastern Canada. We stopped at one of the Canadian Forces bases and shopped at their post exchange. They allowed us to shop with no problems.

BACK IN THE USA

Later we were in Boston, Massachusetts and stayed at Hanscom Air Force Family Camp. The facilites were very nice. This was the latter part of October and they had plenty of space. We found the directions you gave in your RV/camping book were excellent in guiding us into all of the family camps we visited.

Schultz's Recent Trip to Incirlik AB

Dear Ann & Roy,

We arrived in Incirlik, via C-9 from Ramstein, on the 22nd of September. We were traveling with a retired Navy Capt and his wife (Tim & Jo Falkenstein), who we met in the Azores several years ago. As to the gate pass, we had been alerted that they were difficult to obtain and that we may not be able to get one. One of the problems is that you can only get them for a 24-hr period and they must be obtained from 1700 hrs till 0600 hrs only. We started by going to the main gate, asking a Turkish gate guard, who sent us to the MP guard shack in the middle of the gate entrance. There a female U.S. Air Patrol person checked our IDs/Passports and filled out the paperwork for us. She then had a motorized patrol carry the paper to the Turkish pass/ID building. For simplicity we put the four of us on one pass. The roving patrol brought the pass back and we were squared away until 2300 the following evening.

The next day I thought we would save the U.S. personnel some time so we went direct to the Turkish pass/ID point to request another 24 hours. However, this was too easy and the Turks sent us back to the main gate to get the paperwork filled out again (the gate and the pass/ID office are about a block apart). Once the same, very friendly female AP had filled out the paperwork then we walked it back over to the pass/ID office. The clerk pondered the request and then went in to see the officer in charge. After some discussion I was told to go in and see the Turkish officer, who we think was a COL. He asked me how

I had got on the base, where I had flown in from and when I was leaving. He explained to me that the SOFA agreement made no recognition of retirees being allowed on the base and therefore I was complicating his day. But he finally stated, "You are not supposed to be here, but here you are so I guess we will issue a gate pass." I thanked him and departed.

I told the clerk we would like to have the pass extended through the 26th and he put what we thought looked like the 26th. The next day we toured Adana, to include the beautiful mosque which has been under construction since 1989. Upon returning by taxi from Adana we drove through a better looking part of Incirlik than we had seen the evening before so we decided to check it out the next day. Before leaving the gate the next day we asked the Turkish guard if the gate pass we had was good to get us back in the base. That confused him and he sent us to the MP shack again. They looked at the pass and said the date could be read as either 24 or 26!?!? Our wives weren't privy to this comment so we decided to risk it. However, we decided to return by taxi so that a Turkish driver could be involved in getting us back in the gate. It worked, however the Turkish outpost guard questioned the date. We told him it said the 26th and the Turkish driver supported our statement. We were home free!!

The town of Incirlik has a 2300 curfew and many weapons are visible. I understand there is much concern with security in the area. It appears Izmir would be a better choice for retiree travel in Turkey.

Returned on 26th from great trip which originated at BWI. BWI to Mildenhall, three days later departed to Ramstein on C-9. Toured, played golf and four days later departed for Turkey on C-9. Spent four days in Turkey but did face challenge getting gate pass. Ran into a retiree living in the area who said we were the first retirees he had seen off base in more than two years!! Will go to Izmir in Feb and spend more time. Now that we have rediscovered Cat B flights (contract), will attempt to fly nothing else.

Security concerns are building in the Incirlik area, but travel to Turkey is still available and I recommend it to all retirees. Thanks for all your good efforts with the newsletters and other pubs.

Ed & Myrtle Schultz
COL, USA, (Ret.)

DeLoziers Enjoy Visiting Germany

Dear Ann,
I wanted to tell you about our fabulous trip to Germany. Shirley and I flew to Munich on 2 Sep and came back to Tennessee on 18 Sep. Another couple went with us as our guests. We had

reservations at AFRC Van Steuben Hotel in Garmisch for ten days, then moved to the Lake Hotel at Chiemsee. We took your advice and stayed at the Von Steuben instead of the General Patton—it was a very good choice since we were near the shopping center and train station.

Shirley and Robert DeLozier at Garmisch
Train Station (with friend).

After arriving at Munich airport we took the train to the main train station in Munich, bought our tickets to Garmisch and were there in 1.5 hours. We took a taxi from the Garmisch train station to the hotels—only a $7 taxi fare for all four of us (with luggage). The rooms in Von Steuben were excellent, as was the food in the restaurant. The hotel is in the process of refurbishing (carpet, upholstery, etc.). Hotel and restaurant personnel were outstanding; so were the AFRC tour guides. We took most of all the tours that were listed in your *R&R Travel News®* of May/June 1999. We took the train to the Zugspitz and rode the cable car back down. The weather all 17 days was bright and clear, with above average temperatures.

Building in Oberammergau.

Zugspitze Mountain Restaurant.

After our ten days in Garmisch, we took the train back to Munich and transferred to the train for Chiemsee Lake Hotel. The train to Lake Chiemsee stops at Bernau train station. We took a taxi from Bernau to the Lake Hotel - $8. We had a good variety of food, and prices in the hotel dining room and cafeteria were very reasonable. Our tours to Hitler's Eagle's Nest, Berchtesgaden, and Salzburg were outstanding—again great guides. King Ludwig II's Herrenchiemsee castle is only a short boat ride in the middle of Chiemsee Lake. The castle is a copy of Versailles. This tour continued to Frauen Island, another little island in the lake—no cars are allowed on the island of only 400 inhabitants.

All AFRC hotels have security guards at the front door. ID cards must be shown and packages checked. Our last night we moved to a hotel in Munich across from the main train station since we had an early flight the next morning. The hotel was Hotel Europaischer Hof, a very nice 3-star hotel, reasonable rates. We received a discount by making the reservation by e-mail. Our flight back to Atlanta on Lufthansa airlines was very nice, with good food and drinks. Military Living tips and information made this trip one of the best—a fantastic and relaxing trip!

Robert DeLozier, USN (Ret.)

Space-A Travel
by John Caruso, LTC USAF (Ret.)

Sometimes good things happen on the spur of the moment. After hearing about flights from Niagara scheduled for Geilenkirchen Base, (GB), Germany, I had our names put on the list. It is a NATO base close to the Netherlands (Holland) border. A great opportunity to visit Holland, Belgium, or France (Paris).

After much discussion with Gayle, we decided to take the second flight (of two) for six days (instead of twelve) and concentrate on visiting just Holland.

Our flight was on a 107th Air Refueling Wing KC-135 tanker from Niagara on Sunday 12 September. There were four active duty and personnel dependents going back to GB and three retirees, (Frank Burisino COL USA, Gayle, and myself). We departed at 8:00 PM and arrived Monday, 10:20 AM, (having to circle due to visibility); time difference is +6 hours. Flight time was seven hours. Geilenkirchen Base has no base exchange, commissary, or billeting for Space-A travelers unless you have a sponsor who lives on base.

Gayle and I have always said that you meet some wonderful people traveling Space-A. The active duty people were informative and very helpful. Nancy Geiger (active duty dependent) was a godsend for us. She was a reservoir of information and offered to drive us to the railroad station at Sittard, Holland. It would do away with two train changes between GB and Sittard. Nancy said it wasn't too far out of her way because she lived near the Sittard railroad station. Believe me, this woman did go out of her way. She was a "helper" and had a great outlook on life. Her parents live in Kenmore, NY and I'm sure they are proud of her.

At Sittard, I purchased train tickets to Amsterdam, Holland. The trains are fast and punctual. Language is not a barrier here; 95% of the people speak English. It is taught as the second language in the schools.

Amsterdam was a city beyond all my expectations. Population is about 750,000 but it is known as the tourist capital of the world. The old heart of the city consists of canals, with narrow streets radiating out like the spokes of a wheel. The hub of this wheel and the most convenient point to begin sightseeing is Centraal Station. Amsterdam's key points of interest can be covered within two to three days. The city center is broken up into districts that are easily covered on foot. You supposedly are able to see everything within 20 minutes' walking distance.

This is the end of the tourist season, but you wouldn't know it. It was really difficult to get a room in the city. We did luck out after two attempts. This was accomplished at the train station along with purchasing tour tickets for the Canal Cruise, Circle Tram 20 and the Dutch Village Windmill tours. I found prices at the station were very favorable compared to other agencies. The money exchange was very favorable; a little over 2 guilders to $1.00. Expenses as to room, food, transportation and entertainment were very reasonable. We spent the rest of the day and night walking along the Dam Strasse enjoying the sights and restaurants.

Tuesday morning, our first stop was a cafe to have pafferties (bite-size pancakes). These, along with the Dutch Pancake (pizza size) which is served between noon and dinner time, are traditional in Holland. Also, french fries, with a creamy mayonnaise topping was as popular as pizza is in the U.S. Many small food stands along the street sell this "specialty" and people eating as they promenade seems to be the way to go. We then walked to our Canal tour launch across from the Centraal Station. It proceeds through the old center of the city where you see merchants' mansions, canal houses, churches, and warehouses, dating back to the 16th century. A worthwhile tour.

After lunch, we started our Circle Tram 20 tour. It goes both ways around a loop that passes close to most of the main attractions and offers a hop-on, hop-off ticket for one to three days. This "tour" was a disappointment in that the brochure does not show exactly where the sights are. After getting off the tram, you are on your own to find the attraction or sight. This tour is being considered for termination at the end of 1999.

We ate dinner at one of the many restaurants on the Dam (Main St). Prices were reasonable and about the same value as ours here in the States.

The next morning we boarded our tour bus for a 30-minute ride to the Zaanse Schans. Its traditional houses, windmills, and warehouses give an impression of what a Dutch village looked like in the 17th and 18th centuries. The picturesque village offers a variety of windmills and green-timbered houses. Midway, we stopped at a typical Dutch farmhouse where Edam cheese is still made in the traditional way.

After entering the village, we visited a clog maker's shop. The worker places a 4" x 12" piece of poplar wood in a lathe to form the shoe; then in another to hollow out the inside. Within 5 minutes, he completed the entire wooden shoe (klompen). Ordinarily, it would take three hours by hand. The village is made up of six windmills, shops, homes, and warehouses. I did get to visit one of the working windmills which was very interesting.

Then on to Volendam, a fishing village on the Zuiderzee where we boarded a boat to the picturesque peninsula of Marken. In both villages, traditional costumes are still worn, evident in one of the fisherman's houses we were able to visit. The bus was our mode of transportation back to Amsterdam.

We did find the Anne Frank House where Anne wrote her diary and hid with her family during the German Occupation of World War II. There were exhibitions on wartime persecution of the Jews and contemporary fascism, racism and anti-semitism. She died in 1945. Restoration and expansion of the Anne Frank House is nearly completed.

Thursday morning it was back to the Centraal Station to leave for Geilenkirchen. This time we did have to change trains twice. Upon arrival, our objective was to find a hotel. With the help of a local German woman, we were led to the City Hotel on the square. The rate was $74 and well worth every penny. It was a suite, including a split king-sized bed, dinette, kitchen, and two mini refrigerators (one stocked with juice, beer, wine, soda, and liquor). It was ironic that we were to meet COL Frank Brusino, LTC Torgeir Fadum and his wife, Mary (Mac), and MAJ Robert McGuire staying at the same hotel. All are fellow Space-A travelers from Niagara. I highly recommend your stay at this hotel if you are in the vicinity. The town and its surrounding area are beautiful.

We departed Friday morning, 17 September for home. A refueling mission was scheduled with an EC-3 AWAC aircraft. All who wanted were able to be with the boom operator and watch the procedure involved. The flight to Niagara was 9 hours.

Space-A to Germany

Dear Ann and Roy,

My wife, Kathy, and I recently (April-May, 97) enjoyed a five-week Space-A trip to Germany and Austria. We signed up 45 days in advance. Should sign up for Space-A return flight at the same time (60 days in advance is permitted). Took a leisurely drive to Dover AFB, arriving on April 15th, and were immediately whisked off to Ramstein AB, Germany, four hours later. About 20 empty seats. Regular long-term parking at Dover is difficult, and I noticed they were repaving the overflow lot, so it may have been expanded. There was no charge for parking or anywhere to leave the $5 mentioned in *Military Space-A Air Opportunities Around the World* book.

Overnight accommodations at both Ramstein North (officer) and Ramstein South (enlisted) were excellent. Several other military places were Sembach AB, Vogelweh AS and Landstuhl Army Hospital, all within 30-minute shuttle from Ramstein. Ramstein South is directly across from the AMC terminal and a little noisy, but most convenient for Space-A travelers. New AMC terminal planned for construction near the flight line. Can take free base shuttle-bus to North (about 1 1/2 miles away and close to Officers' Club, food courts, commissary/BX. On base shuttle does not run on Sundays and holidays. Taxi fare is $5 from AMC terminal to BOQ. By the way, in accordance with Status of Forces Agreement, transient retirees cannot use commissary/BX or Mini Marts. Many other eating places at Ramstein: Officers' and Enlisted Club, bowling alley, Popeyes, pizza, Italian, Greek, German (for lunch only), ice cream. Allowed to shop at German vendor stores on base. There were also two movie theaters on base.

Prearranged Hertz rental car awaiting at Ramstein North BOQ. Make prepayment from CONUS . . . considerably cheaper, especially with AAA discount. Gas expensive (about $4-$5 a gallon) and gas coupons not available for transient retirees.

Went to Stuttgart to meet German friends and stayed at Patch Barracks, an Army base. Robinson Barracks guest facilities were being renovated. Patch Swabian Inn was excellent with video rentals, fresh brewed coffee (free) and professional reception staff. O Club facilities were excellent. Cost for double was $39.

Traveled throughout Southern Germany and Bavaria. Visit to Garmisch was lovely, but both General Patton and Von Steuben hotels (room rate $63 for 0-5) were filled with military conferences and active duty tour groups. Stayed in a German pension, a bed and breakfast called Marlene Karg, very comfortable and quiet. Much cheaper than the Army facilities at Garmisch. Room and breakfast at B&B about $50. Ate dinner at Von Steuben hotel and meal was excellent.

Spent two weeks at time-share hotels near Salzburg, Austria, and loved the "Sound of Music" country. Every village and vista is a postcard shot. Drove to Berchtesgaden to see "Eagles' Nest," Hitler's mountaintop fortress bunker, but couldn't get up there due to heavy snow barring access. Continued to Lake Chiemsee Army Recreation Area to check it out. It is a beautiful spot . . . a bit pricey for spoiled travelers spending between $17-$43. Room rates varied by pay grade . . . 0-5 was about $63 for a double room with beautiful lake view.

Not bad for what you got, but we were hurrying to rendezvous with more German friends. Someday, we'll return. Rooms were available, but many book months in advance. Tour office there is very active with forays into Bavaria, Austria and Italy.

Also stayed at Augsburg (Army) Kaserne Guest House. Base appears to be drawing down on facilities. O Club is closed. Room was big and clean . . . cost $43. (Editor's Note: Base is now closed.) Then on to Ansbach (Army) Kaserne, home of the Big Red One. Base was busy with activity . . . eating facilities were good and familiar . . . ate at Burger King. Bamberg VOQ seemed very nice but our reservations got messed up, and we were "sans" room for the night. We found a room at a small base named Kitzingen. Cost was $35. Room was on second floor of Rod & Gun Club/Restaurant. Toilet and shower facilities down the hall (about 30 feet). Eating tip—look for German Cantina. Caters to German on-base employees; breakfast and lunch only. Food is considerably cheaper and excellent German cuisine. Ate there at Ramstein and Ansbach.

Then back to Ramstein, and there we bogged down. Waited four days to get out. Tried to arrange our return to beat the exodus of dependent wives and school children; however, many spouses took kids out of school early. Of course, they are higher priority than retirees, and that's the way it should be. The key to Space-A travel is patience and flexibility. We had an uneventful return to Dover; my awaiting chariot was dusty but unbowed and turned over with a roar. Dover overflow lot was closed to incoming vehicles, but had been relocated on base.

Tony DeMarco
CDR, USN (Ret.)
Homestead, FL

First Space-A Trip with Tips

Dear Ann and Roy,
My wife and I completed our first ever Space-A trip on 28 April. I am now finally getting around to passing on to you a few of the lessons we learned, as well as some comments which may be helpful to others considering venturing forth as we did.

First off, we requested travel by fax for both going to and returning from Europe/Germany making sure we had plenty of leeway with the time we could be gone. I think this is a must—not costly and worth every penny.

We got a C-5 out of Kelly AFB on 15 April. After a short three-hour stop at Dover AFB to refuel, we went on to Rhein-Main AB. For anyone who hasn't been there recently, be warned: It is not the bustling air base it used to be. On landing, we found that if you don't have some local currency, hope that you can find a friendly cab driver as we did. The base doesn't offer a lot of services to transient retirees and it is a 15-20 minute walk from the air terminal to the bank. No mean distance if you have baggage to be concerned about. There was a military shuttle-bus stop outside the front door of the terminal for the main commercial terminal for those going to Ramstein. We were heading for the main commercial terminal to pick up a car. The cabbie that we found was kind and trusting enough to take us to the bank where I was able to get DMs from an ATM machine. (Having an ATM card is a virtual necessity and the exchange rate is the best.) Our cab ride cost about $30 and was worth it. As we were headed north to Holland, and we had been up for a long time, we thought it would be best for up to get a little rest before going on. We headed for the American Arms Hotel in Weisbaden. Had I known—or remembered—I would have gotten a reservation before leaving the states. It's possible through 1-800-GO-ARMY-1. Fortunately they had room for us. ($69.95 per night per room with a full breakfast.) We were able to rest up, pick up some needed maps at the military shopping area, tour a little downtown and plan our route for the following days. I must add, Ann had her hair done at the concession in the hotel and was extremely pleased with the results. As our trip was geared towards tracing my family tree in Holland and later visiting Ann's relatives in Alsace (Colmar, France, south of Strasbourg), we did not plan on using military bases for billeting. We found no problem getting rooms for the night with the help of the appropriate local government tourist offices. We chose places that also provided breakfast. One thing we also found is that when selecting a place, be sure you also consider parking for your car. It is worth a little extra for a safe place.

There is no question we picked the right time to visit. Although it was cool, we had eleven straight days of sunshine, traveling through the Netherlands, a corner of Luxembourg, down the "Rue du Vin" to Colmar, France, and back to Ramstein via the Black Forest route.

The only problem we encountered was with our rental car. It broke down in northern Holland (Freisland). It took a couple of extra days for Avis to get us a replacement. When we got home, I called Auto Europe (we booked the car through them) and explained and complained about the situation. They were very sympathetic and helpful. Yesterday, I got a letter of apology, a refund for three days' car rental and was advised that the Avis people in Germany had given us a credit refund for the extra night we had in the hotel in Workum, Holland, waiting for the replacement car. All's well that ends well.

Now for things learned: I never really realized how steep and narrow that ladder was from cargo deck to passenger deck in the C-5. Next time my carry on baggage will be a whole lot smaller and lighter.

A. Try to have at least some local coins in case you need to use the phone no matter what country you're in.

B. Make sure that you have the emergency road service phone number for your rental car. It would have saved us much time if we had had it in the car that we picked up at the Frankfurt terminal.

C. There is a hotline for Avis and Hertz in the Ramstein AB terminal where all you have to do is call them, tell them you are there, lock the car and put the keys in a metal box on the wall. They will do the rest. We showed up eight minutes before a show time for a flight to Dover AB and made the flight.

D. If you will need commercial air when you arrive in the states and don't have your ticket yet, there is a SATO right in the terminal. If I had had time, I could have saved about $350 buying my ticket there.

E. We arrived at Dover AFB after 1 a.m. I can assure you there is not much happening there at that time of the night. We were under the mistaken impression that there was a scheduled shuttle to the Philadelphia Airport. Not so. Need to call a limo. The folks in the terminal will help you put a group together to cut down the cost (about $25-$30 per person). To go it alone is about $60.

All in all it was a very good trip, and we are planning for more Space-A adventures and wondering why we didn't start traveling this way a long time ago.

Thanks to Military Living, traveling is not nearly as worrisome as it could be. Keep up the good work.

Merle Vernone
Major, USAF (Ret)
San Antonio, TX

If At First You Don't Succeed ...

Dear Ann and Roy,
For many years, I have wanted to make a trip to Australia. In 1990, my wife and I drove to Norton AFB in hopes of getting a Space-A flight to Australia. I had made a special trip about a

month earlier to sign up for the trip. On the day we hoped to get a flight, we were informed that only seven seats would be designated for Australia and the remaining seats would be designated for Hawaii. The seven seats for Australia were quickly filled with active duty personnel and it was obvious that no retirees would be making the trip. Being flexible, we went to March AFB and caught a flight to Alaska.

In 1995, I made another attempt to make the trip down under. I caught a flight to Hawaii but had no luck in getting a flight to Australia. I returned to Travis AFB and took a trip to England instead.

I decided to try again in April 1997. My wife was not in good health, so she suggested that I make the trip alone.

I bought a rail pass for Australia for 8 flexible days prior to leaving home which cost about $350. I had decided that I would go even if I had to purchase a ticket for a commercial flight. I bought the latest copy of your book *Military Space-A Air Opportunities Around the World* and noticed that flights to Australia originate from McChord AFB in Tacoma, WA and Travis AFB near Sacramento, CA.

I decided to drive to Tacoma to visit some friends and relatives along the way. When I got to McChord AFB, I was informed that they did not have flights that originate from there for Australia and had not for a long time. Also, they would not manifest passengers to Hawaii from there.

I signed up for a flight to Travis AFB. While I was waiting for the flight, I met an Air Force pilot on leave and told him of my desire to go to Australia. He informed me that a number of flights were going to Australia from Guam due to a military exercise that was almost over. He stated that the planes were going there to pick up troops and were not carrying much cargo so this would be my best opportunity.

I took the flight to Travis. The next day, there were four flights scheduled to go to Hawaii. Two of these were cancelled and the other two were quickly filled with active duty personnel. There were many other active duty personnel waiting to go to Hawaii who were turned down. I realized that I was going to have trouble getting to Guam.

I noticed that a C-5 was scheduled to go to Alaska with a 24-hour layover; then it would go to Korea and then Okinawa. Then it would go to Guam, to Hawaii and back to Travis AFB. I decided to take my chances on this flight as I could not get manifested further than Okinawa.

There was a 24-hour layover planned at Okinawa, but due to mechanical problems, it turned out to be two days. I asked to be manifested back to Travis in the event I did not find any flights scheduled to go to Australia from Guam.

When I arrived at Guam, I found that there were two flights scheduled the following morning for Australia. One to Darwin and Perth and the other to Amberly RAAF base near Ipswich located close to the NE coast. I knew that Darwin and Perth were very far from the East Coast (about three days one way on the train), so I decided to go to Amberly. There was no problem getting on the flight and I enjoyed nine days of traveling and sightseeing in Australia. Getting back was not difficult. I caught a flight to Hawaii and then to McChord AFB, where I had left my vehicle.

Howard Cooper
WO, USA (Ret.)
Ruidoso, NM

First Space-A Trip

Dear Ann and Roy,
As first time Space-A travelers, we have been reading your **R&R Travel News®** for two years. Finally, we decided to go to Germany in April. We faxed requests to Dover about 50 days before we intended to leave and also faxed to Ramstein our request for a return flight 20 days later. For your information, when we were in Ramstein, signs stated that they no longer accept sign-ups for Rhein-Main.

We drove from Syracuse, NY to Dover, DE on April 26, 1997, hoping to get on a flight scheduled for that evening. Only 30 of us showed up for that flight, so we all got on. We arranged for a rental car to be waiting for us on Monday the 28th, a day later than our expected arrival in case we were tired or delayed en route. By arranging for the car before we arrived, we avoided paying some extra fees in Germany.

Since we didn't have transportation, we thought we would eat at the NCO Club, as it was right around the corner from the Ramstein lodging. The NCO Club was a surprise, requiring us to pay $3 per person to get in for that day. When we returned to Ramstein in May, the price had increased to $4 per person so we didn't go back.

We started across Germany heading for the Romantic Road across Bavaria. Thank goodness we had read in your paper about the military hotels in Garmisch and Chiemsee. You gave us confidence to try to get rooms without reservations, and because it was between seasons we were able to stay in the Patton one night, the Von Steuben the second night and in the Chiemsee the third night. The scenery was beautiful and we were able to arrange day tours to castles at each place. The lake and hotels at Chiemsee were very nice, but eat in town, not at the hotel.

We definitely will travel Space-A again. I learned to always take the fax we sent, as on arrival at Ramstein they had no record of the fax requesting Space-A to the United States. We signed up that day and were able to get out on the day we tried to leave. Leaving Ramstein was interesting. We checked out of the Inn for a 0900 show time. It was postponed to 1130 then to 1345 then to 1730. We hadn't turned in the rental car yet, so we debated about leaving and doing some sightseeing around Ramstein and Landstuhl. Decided we had better stay at the airport when showtime was moved up to 1645. We were almost the last ones called for the plane. Some people who left returned after the plane was full and missed the flight.

After our baggage was all checked in, they announced a change in the schedule—we were going to Iceland instead of England, and if the unloading and refueling took more than two hours, we would have to spend the night. We were only on the ground for one and a half hours, so we continued on to Dover without further problems.

Thanks for all the letters you print. Little details in them gave us confidence to try traveling without definite plans as to where, when or what to do when we got there.

James & Rachel Kindon
MSG, USA (Ret.)
Kirkville, NY

A Tale From the South Pacific

New Zealand was our goal. We first attempted to get a Space-A trip there in 1995 but managed to get no further than Australia. So in February we decided to try again.

From Columbia, Missouri, the 190th Air Refueling Group (ANG) Forbes Field, Topeka, Kansas, was our closest base to get a flight to Hawaii, which is generally considered the place that is the best bet for getting to New Zealand or Australia. The C-135 tanker was piloted by Captain Joel Darbro. He recognized us because he was also the pilot on our flight to Iceland in April 1997 on which we had been the only Space-A passengers. This time there were others.

"When we go to Alaska or Hawaii," one crew member confided, "retirees come out of the woodwork."

When we landed at Hickam Air Force Base, luck was with us. SrA Steven Sigley, a bright young lad at the AMC counter, informed us that a C-5A was leaving for RAAF Richmond, Australia in two hours. There were more seats available than there were people desiring to go. Unusual. The plane, commanded by Captain Benjamin "Big Ben" Miller, was going via Andersen AFB, Guam. On the way it developed fuel cell problems which could not be repaired at Andersen. The closest available specialist skilled in repairing that particular problem was at Yokota AB, Japan. The plan was to RON at Andersen and proceed to Yokota the next day. There was no room in the Inn and we were advised that taxis and motels were expensive, so all Space-A travelers elected to spend the night in the terminal.

When we arrived in Yokota the billeting office had room for us all. The following day, one of the couples on the flight, Lt. Col. Gene and Sue Fleming, just happened to walk out of the VOQ where and MWR bus was waiting. It seems the bus was on its way to downtown Tokyo for a brunch. Gene asked if retirees could go. "Sure, climb aboard," the driver told him. The rest of us were not lucky enough to be at the right place at the right time.

When we were being logged in for the flight to Australia the passenger service agent, a redheaded staff sergeant named Carreon asked who was getting off at RAAF Richmond and who was flying on to Perth. A Mr. Know-It-All among the Space-A passengers pipes up and with all the authoritative voice of a General Patton says, "The Air Force doesn't go to Perth anymore."

"Well, maybe there's a special mission to Perth," I offer.

"The Air Force doesn't go to Perth anymore," he repeats.

This guy sounds like he knows what he is talking about and Carreon doesn't pursue it. After arriving at RAAF Richmond the passenger service agent there, SSgt Vince Britton, says, "Now who's staying here and who's going on to Perth?"

This dork who had first surfaced at Yokota again lectures the AMC rep, "Air Force planes don't go to Perth anymore."

"Well, the pilot said they were going to Perth," Britton replies.

Mary and I reasoned that if there was a chance of going to Perth we would postpone New Zealand until another day. It was not every day that a Space-A traveler got a chance to go to Western Australia. At this point I announce in my best General Patton voice: "Look, if that plane even points its nose in the direction of Perth, my wife and I want to be on it." The dork leaves and we never see him again. The C-5A leaves for Perth and we were on it. The moral of that story is this: If it doesn't sound quite right, double and triple check what other Space-A travelers tell you, even if they sound like they know what they are talking about. There are indeed special missions to just about any place in the world and we had Saddam Hussein to thank for this one. The C-5A had picked up six Australian Army and Air Force officers at Richmond and was picking up the main contingent of Aussie troops at Perth to transport to Kuwait. This was Australia's offering to help keep the world safe from Saddam. We knew things were serious when we found out one of the officers was a chaplain and another was a lawyer!

We ran into one other dork on the trip. He was the kind of guy that my Space-A-ing buddy Major Ray Sanders and I abhor—the retiree who likes to play the "rank card."

This guy was telling the AMC personnel that he was a full colonel—he throws in O-6 for good measure—and he needed to get to such and such a place to do something by a certain date. They listened politely until he ran out of gas then told him to get on the airplane. He would have been manifested on that C-5A if he had been a retired corporal, E-4, because there were plenty of seats. It was embarrassing just to stand there and listen to him. This was an example of not being tuned in to what's going on around you.

Most Americans, when they go to Australia, go to Sydney and the eastern coast. We were presented with the rare opportunity to go where few Americans have gone before. In fact, we never saw another American the four days we were in the Western Australia city. There are a lot of Australians who have never been there.

Having gotten to Perth so easily gave us the opportunity to do something we had talked about for a long time, and that was traversing the continent on the Trans-Australian Railway, the second longest in the world. The Trans-Siberian is the longest. In case anyone is interested in doing this, the cost at the time was $790 (U.S.) per person. This was first class, which included three meals a day and your own compartment. The trip takes three days and nights. However, we elected to stop over in Adelaide for three days. The city is named for Queen Adelaide. While there we met two of the best policemen you'll ever want to know—Andy Dunn and Jane Reed. Dunn was also a captain in the Australian Army Reserve.

An unusual thing took place between Adelaide and Sydney. The brakes went out on the locomotive. Since they couldn't fix them on the spot and we couldn't take the locomotive to Yokota, we were stuck in one spot for nine hours while another locomotive was sent to rescue us.

The thing they wouldn't let us do was get off the train and walk around. We figured the conductor was thinking that if he let the "seasoned citizens," as Rush Limbaugh calls us, off the train and one of them broke a leg he would have more to worry about than a broken locomotive. The conductor did let us phone RAAF Richmond on the train phone to let them know we wanted on the manifest for New Zealand if a plane was going that way in the next 12 hours. There wasn't.

While waiting for a flight to New Zealand we ran into a couple from Oregon who had been on the plane with us from Hickam. He had developed kidney problems and was admitted to an Australian hospital for a few days. Yes, the doctor did inquire about his ability to pay before treating him. The total doctor and hospital bill was $900, which was cheaper than it would have been in the U.S.

A week would pass before we caught a C-141 to Christchurch, New Zealand. That week was spent seeing the sights of Sydney and making another train trip, this time to the capital city, Canberra. One of the most beautiful capitals in the world, Canberra is a planned city. In 1912, the international design contest for it was won by the American architect, Walter Burley Griffin. The Australian War Memorial, opposite the parliament building is, in our opinion, the most extensive in the world and admittance is free.

There were eight Space-A travelers on the flight to Christchurch. This city is one of the main gateways to Antarctica. Since 1955 the U.S. Navy has handled the flight operations to Antarctica in what became known as Operation Deep Freeze. In February of this year that mission was turned over to an Air National Guard detachment operating out of Schenectady, New York. I asked one of the ANG people at their Christchurch headquarters why the mission had been turned over to the Air Guard. His response was that he didn't have the slightest idea. So much for keeping the troops informed.

We were in New Zealand a week. While there we did what we consider one of the ten most exciting things we have ever done—and that was land on a glcier in a ski-equipped airplane. It was the Tasman Glacier near Mount Cook and the airplane, a six place Cessna 185. Flying through the valleys and between the peaks, the pilot landed on the snow-covered glacier and shut down the engine. We got out of the plane, walked around, took pictures, threw snowballs and marveled about where in the world we were. There were two other passengers on board. We stayed on the glacier about 20 minutes before taking off for the airport in the valley below. Everyone experienced a happy, exhilarating feeling. The cost, $135 (U.S.) per person, at that time.

Now our mission was to get back to Missouri. When we returned to the Christchurch airport we tried to find the AMC flight information desk to double check if our name was on their sign-up list. When we first arrived at the Christchurch airport the AMC rep had given us an information sheet but it was an old one and the flight info desk was not where the sheet indicated. It had been moved and nobody seemed to know where it was. If my Julian date had expired or if they had never received my sign-up fax then I wanted to get on the list as soon as possible. It was almost like they were playing "find me if you can." The ANG guy I had talked to earlier told us he thought the AMC desk had been moved to a tin building he pointed at just beyond a chain-link fence. When we were within 50 yards of the fence gate a man in civilian clothes walked out of the building, strode through the gate, locked it, crawled into his car and drove off into the sunset. Had he seen us coming and knew that we wanted information?

We deduced that the information desk and a live person with information was there beyond the chain-link fence, somewhere in space and time, somewhere in . . . the Twilight Zone!

At 8 o'clock the next morning we were there at the chain-link fence to get to the bottom of it. We walked through the now unlocked gate and opened the unlocked door of the tin building. There in the middle of this long tin building stood three men in civilian clothes. We moved toward them. They could see it in our eyes. They could sense that we wanted information and were not about to give up until we got it. At last one of them broke and asked the magic question, "Are you looking for the information desk?" There in the middle of this warehouse-of-a-looking building was the elusive information desk. What an intelligent place to put it!

There was good news and bad news. The bad news was that they didn't have our names on the AMC sign-up sheet. The good news was that they were going to put them on it.

"There'll be no problem," the guy in civilian clothes said. "There are plenty of seats on the plane to the Royal Australian Air Force Base at Richmond."

At Richmond it took us a week to get a plane to the U.S. We had hoped for a base near the middle of the States but our "bird in the hand" was Travis AFB, CA, so we took it. At Travis we rented a car and drove to Topeka, KS, where we dropped it off, then picked up our car at Forbes Field and proceeded on to Missouri. We were gone a total of six weeks.

William & Mary Hobbs
Major, USAF (Ret.)
Columbia, MO

Germany Space-A

Dear Ann and Roy,
Carol and I have returned from our first Space-A flight which we both enjoyed very much. After reading your *R&R Travel News®* we decided to take advantage of this benefit of service and fly to Germany for possible genealogy research.

We drove from Columbus, OH, to Dover, DE April 14, arriving around 1800. Brought luggage in, attached ID tickets, and signed in at the counter. Luggage is x-rayed; suggest you hand pass cameras and film.

Checked the monitors for flight information and left for dinner as no flights scheduled to Ramstein. Checked in at one of many motels along US 113 to wait and try tomorrow (Wednesday). Checked flight monitors Wed. a.m. and nothing expected til evening. We toured several museums in Dover before checking again at terminal. Nothing going our way so decided to try Space-A housing. Main gate is closed while building overpass to family housing, and south gate closes at 17 or 1800. Gave a couple a lift to housing office and back to Space-A housing, which is close to the bowling alley and dining hall. (All ranks club did not serve food weekdays.)

Thursday spent visiting commissary and BX and touring air museum on base. Spen time at museum listening to ex-bomber pilot talk about flying B-17 during WWII (not everybody gets a living history lesson!) Finally a C-5 takes us. Off at 2110 for 9 hour flight. We arrive at 1130 (0530 Dover time) and take contract bus to Frankfurt. I forgot a piece of luggage so we ride to the end and back again. We decide to stay overnight and get quarters at Vogelweh. After breakfast at bowling alley (approximately one minute from room) we start out to Frankfurt again.

To go from the Flughafen (air terminal) to the Hauptbahnhof (main rail station) we asked about the connecting train at the USO, which is down one level at the Flughafen. One more level and we bought tickets. How? First check the yellow timetable posted on the wall. Then take the reference number to the ticket machine, press the English button, the reference number, and number of tickets. The machine prints the ticket and makes change.

I had used the internet to locate hotels in Frankfurt, and after checking with the information office that made the reservation for 5 DM in the Hauptbahnhof, we walked to the hotel. Please note that 50 pfennigs is requested to use restrooms in most public places, including McDonald's!

We used our German Rail Pass (purchased via internet) to ride an ICE train to Munich. It was a smooth three-hour trip, and we had the railroad information office make our reservation at a hotel in the suburbs. We took U-5 U-bahn and U-6 to the hotel. Tuesday, April 21. Found EuroAide office on left side of rail station (looking at train entrance) and purchased tickets to tour Linderhof and Newschwanstein.

Included on tour was a stop in Oberammergau. Carol walked up and through Newschwanstein while I took a horse carriage about three fourths of the way up. April 22 we used our rail pass to take the Romantic Road tour back to Frankfurt. At lunch in Dinklesbuhl, the guide offers to make reservations for rooms in Rothenburg O.T. (on the Tauber River). We accept and stay in new private house for 35 DM each! This included breakfast and luggage delivered to tour stop next day. Wonderful time walking Old Town and shopping.

Concluding tour in Frankfurt, we ride Sbahn to Darmstadt and check in at Hotel Hornung (one block from Bahnhof). April 24 we return to Frankfurt and take train to Mainz for Rhine River cruise. We are too late for regular trip, so we pay supplement and ride hydrofoil jet boat! We get off at St. Goarshausen for train trip back to Frankfurt and on to Darmstadt. Saturday, April 25 we meet with relatives and spend the day driving through the state of Hesse.

April 27 on to Walldorf by train and visit with other relatives. Monday, businesses are closed in Germany, so we are driven to see Heidelberg and also visit Frankenstein's Castle.

April 28 we drive to Schwetzinger Castle and tour English garden on foot then drive to Speyer to see Cathedral and Evangelish Church. Cathedral 60% destroyed in WWII, but now completely rebuilt. Walked to Rhine riverbank and watched barges pass.

April 29 we say goodbyes and are driven back to Ramstein 1830, too late for Space-A room at Ramstein South, so we stay at Hotel Gruene Laterne in Landstuhl.

April 30. We are offered a ride back to Ramstein and check flight monitors. We have one seat and a possible second. We are bumped, so we try Landstuhl and find room for two nights. Lunch is in the snack bar in hospital with late snack at bowling alley.

May 1 and laundry day for us (it's free!) in next building. The bus that loops (one hour) from Ramstein, Landstuhl and Vogelweh deposits us at terminal. No flights, so back to Landstuhl. We then walked down the hill into town and saw a street fair before stopping at Pizza Hut for supper.

Saturday, May 2. Breakfast in dining hall: pancakes, eggs, bacon for two cost $1.47! To terminal where no Cat-6 seats available today. We get room in Ramstein South (across street from terminal).

May 3. Find a flight at 0630 was cancelled. Flight with show time of 1700 and we are ticketed and board the bus to the plane when the flight is cancelled. We rush and get a room in Visiting Airmen's Quarters.

May 4, Monday. After several delays we finally take off for Dover, DE at 1500. Arrive at 0100 Ramstein time (1900 Dover). Check in at motel.

May 5. Up early and drive to Columbus and arrive at 1800.

It was an exciting trip. While not planned quite the way it happened, we did practically everything we wnted thanks to many helping hands and friendly people.

Fred & Carol Scior
PO1, USN (Ret.)
Columbus, OH

Space-A Trip to Germany & England

Dear Ann & Roy,
Along with your books *Military Space-A Opportunities Around the World* and *Temporary Military Lodging Around the World,* we arrived at Dover AFB on September 21. Spent night on base, as I needed a new ID card. After getting new ID, which is a breeze with automation, went to terminal and saw that a C-5 was posted with 70 seats. All Space-A passengers got a seat. We had faxed our request 50 days earlier, so we had a good number. We had also faxed Mildenhall and Ramstein for our return flights. Arrived at Ramstein at 11 a.m. No rooms at any base around Ramstein as some kind of troop movement was in progress. Rented a car—Hertz picked us up at terminal and we turned car in at terminal. Drove to Spangdahlem AB close to Bitburg on our way to Brussels. A nice room at Eiffel Arms for $17, refrig/micro/clean. Toured Luxembourg and then on to Mons where we had reservations at Hotel Maisieres across from SHAPE Hq. Nice room with refrig/micro. Toured several days in Belgium and across N. France back into Germany. B&Bs were all clean for $45/55. Toll roads in France on Saturday and traffic was quite congested due to festivals. Found Patch Barracks and a nice room, $39. Delicious Italian food at Le Rose Rest at O Club next to hotel.

We spent eight days in Germany in 1996 (Space-A) and did the Romantic Road which we still talk about. I might add that in 1996 we spent each night in Germany using TML. Several bases have since closed but if you plan using your book, most nights can be at military bases.

This time we did the Black Forest area. Germany is a beautiful country with very good road signs. Most all B&B owners speak enough English to communicate. The German B&Bs are spotlessly clean, some with private baths at a cost of $45/55. Ate some delicious German food. Did a quick driving tour of Switzerland, Basel, and Zurich. Cities crowded but country beautiful. Back into Germnay and the lake area and on to Augsburg and the base* for two nights to catch our breath and do laundry. Walked into Augsburg and visited some churches and historical sites and did some shopping. This is another base that will close in 1998. Drove back to Ramstein and lucked into room on base; they are hard to get. *(Editor's Note: Now closed.)

Turned in car and got on MEDEVAC flight to Mildenhall. Mildenhall has excellent accommodations for $17. Air Force has best prices and good facilities. Rented car and drove 1500 miles through northeastern England, up to Scotland; Bill had to do St. Andrews Golf Course, quite a site. Over to Glasgow and down northwestern England and across midland. There is so much history and things to see it's difficult to decide what to do. Hadrian's Wall, Stratford-Upon-Avon, Oxford, all the castles, abbeys, cathedrals, small villages with their market days.

All the B&Bs were nice with friendly hosts who had many tales to tell about local history. Most of them invite guests to join them for tea or drinks. Again from $40/55. Spent two nights at RAF Fairford. Nice facility with club next door for dining. Did some day tours, Avon and Oxford from Fairford.

On to RAF Alconbury, small nice room with shared bath. Back to Mildenhall with plans to take three-day Paris tour through travel agency on base. Trip filled so will have to wait until next trip. Checked terminal, KC-10 with 59 seats to Dover in two hours. Only 19 people waiting so we all had two seats each and it was quite omfortable. Spent night at Dover AFB and drove to South Carolina next day.

We did London last year and stayed at the Victory Services Club. Rooms were adequate and the convenience to downtown London, the train and buses was well worth the shared bath.

We highly recommend Space-A. Don't try it if you are in a hurry. Take a book and consider any delays a chance to meet many interesting retirees with lots of helpful information.

Joyce & Bill Pierce
MSgt, USAF (Ret.)
Greenville, SC

Space-A Air and TML Stateside

Dear Ann & Roy,
I just returned from a Space-A trip from Norfolk, VA to Phoenix, AZ and back. I am reporting in to you in case any of my experience is useful to you. As usual, your Space-A book was indispensible.

Itinerary: Tuesday 28 April—Langley to Andrews, C-21. Andrews to Randolph, C-21. Wednesday, 29 April–Auto ride across San Antonio from Randolph to Kelly. Thursday, 30 April—Kelly to Davis-Monthan, C-141 MEDEVAC. Did not make scheduled stop at Luke, my destination. So took taxi to van terminal, then commercial van to Phoenix Sky Harbor commercial field for $22. Monday, 4 May—Luke to Kelly, C-9 MEDEVAC. (Probably should have continued on to Scott to catch

Wednesday MEDEVAC to Norfolk, but MEDEVAC schedules are not dependable.) Tuesday, 5 May—Kelly to Charleston, C-5. Charleston to Dover, C-17. Wednesday, 6 May—Dover to Andrews, C-5. Thursday, 7 May—Andrews Navy terminal to Norfolk NAS, P-3. (An alternative was Davison to Langley—four flights per day, which I would have taken if I had not gotten a room at Andrews.) This would require getting to Metro bus stop in MD, across DC by Metro, and then bus #9 to Belvoir housing.

Comments: Kelly facilities are excellent—TML and dining facilities are within walking distance of air terminal and inexpensive room and meals. Officers may eat at enlisted dining facility. Also frequent commercial bus (route 62) for 75 cents from housing area to downtown San Antonio well worth staying over an extra day to visit the river walk in heart of the city; also the Alamo.

C-21 scheduled from Andrews to Kelly went to Randolph instead. I was told this is a common occurrence because Randolph is the home base for the C-21. So be prepared to have to cross to Kelly by bus or by bumming a ride. Bus from Randolph to San Antonio is NOT frequent; two early morning and two late afternoon. So get up early to catch the morning bus.

Dover housing is terribly inconvenient. Bachelor quarters are within walking distance from the terminal, but you have to go several miles off base to the housing office to check in (and again if you have to extend your stay). Highway construction adds to this distance and prevents walking, so take a taxi unless some kind person offers a ride. Housing staff is frustrated because of this condition and because tenants extend without informing office, and they cannot inform by telephone for sure whether rooms are available. (Two Air Force college ROTC girls had to make the trip twice because they were assgined to an occupied room.)

Andrews TML was tight and will be for several weeks because of an air show coming up. Only by much persistence and patience did we manage to get Air Force rooms, after being told several times there was nothing available. Navy enlisted housing there will not take officers even when there are enlisted vacancies. Andrews Officers' Club supper buffet for $10 is highly recommended—especially if you have not eaten all day!

The C-17 seating was very uncomfortable—rough benches (plastic formed seats) along the sides. We had sore backs when we finished. All of the other aircraft were better than commercial flights for comfort and space.

John Tinkham
LCDR, USN
Virginia Beach, VA

Space-A Trip to Iceland

We love to read reports of travel by other CAT-6s. Since we have never read one about an extended trip to Keflavik NAS, I decided that I must write about ours.

We first heard of the trip when we were in Meridian, MS early in June and checked by the ANG there to see what was scheduled for the summer. We were told then about the July 25 flight to Keflavik.

As we had spent a night there several years ago while getting back to the U.S. from England, our interest was immediate. My husband said, "Sign us up." We were first on the list.

When we got back to Starkville, MS, where we live, Irvin immediately sent a fax to Keflavik NAS signing us up for the return trip. He also at that time found the billeting number in our Military Living book and called to see about availability in July. He was told that there would be none since a multi-country military exercise would be going on at that time. Next he called the 1-800-NAVY LODGE number and was told that he would have to call direct himself. He called the number given for Keflavik Navy Lodge and made reservations for July 26-August 10. He was not required to give a credit card number. Had he not made the reservation that far in advance, we could not have stayed there either. If you cannot stay on base it would be quite expensive. In about two weeks he called the terminal at Keflavik and was told that our name was in the return sign-up book. He also called the Lodge and found our reservations still okay.

While waiting for the time to pass, I began my investigation of things to do and see in Iceland. I found that Keflavik MWR had a web page and an e-mail address. Since I had lots of questions about the base, weather, trips offered from the base, car rental, etc., I just e-mailed that address and was thrilled to get a reply that answered most of my questions. I had a new best friend in Iceland! We corresponded throughout the month and were able to sign up for a trip that left on the Sunday morning after we arrived on Saturday by just giving our credit card number. Otherwise we could not have gone since the MWR office is closed on weekends. Their e-mail address is webmaster@mwr.is. They also told me that reservations for the Navy Lodge can be made through them at a reduced rate. Had we known that earlier, we could have saved ourselves the expense of phone calls. there was also much good information about the country, people and things to see and do on their web page. It can be reached at www. mwr.is/index.htm.

We flew out of Meridian ANG July 25 at 10:00 p.m. on a KC-135. There is a five-hour time difference. We flew non-stop and arrived there about 10:30 a.m. July 26. On arrival we went at once to check the sign-up book. Our name was not on it, but by having a copy of our sign-up fax the problem was resolved pretty quickly.

The Navy Lodge is next door to the terminal. It was so easy to walk there across the parking lot even with luggage. We checked right in and for $46 a night got a great room with two double beds, TV, VCR, microwave, refrigerator, coffeemaker and coffee. It also had a table and chairs for dining. The windows overlooked the terminal so we could keep up with what was coming and going.

After we got settled in our room, we took our map of the base and began orienting ourselves. It was a blue sky day with a temperature in the low sixties. We walked and found Wendy's and the Mini-Mart, both of which are in the same building with the barber shop, beauty shop, post office, video rental, and bowling alley. The MWR office is right across the street as is the gym. The church is just down the street, and the commissary is in the same area. After finding that we could not shop in the commissary, we got staples at the Mini-Mart and found that we could get apples and bananas from the vending machine at the terminal. Later in the day we found the USO. It had a good collection of souvenir things that we could buy there. They did not take credit cards, however. At the NEX we could only buy in the mall area. These were mainly gift items, but they did have a good selection of Icelandic knitwear.

The base had shuttle buses that ran regularly and sheltered stops. Each bus circled the entire base on each trip, so sometimes you could walk and get there faster. There were base taxis that would take you anywhere on the base for $5.00 and into Keflavik town, about three or four miles off base, for $11.00. There was no public transportation from the base into town. We walked into Keflavik one day and found it possible to do, but just barely.

Places to eat on base were numerous. There were Wendy's, the USO with burgers and fries, etc., the Three Flags Club, former O Club, with a bar and a good buffet, a pizza and Chinese food place, the bowling alley with fast food. The NEX had a small cafeteria and Coconut Alley, former NCO Club, had a bar and fast food. Our favorite place was the Enlisted Galley. It was centrally located and had good, good food. It had meat, veggies, salad and fruit bar, dessert and drinks for $2.75 at lunch. It also served breakfast and dinner. There was also an Icelandic bakery and a place to get Icelandic hot dogs and ice cream across the street from the Lodge. I feel sure that this rather extensive variety of eating places is due to the fact that everyone stationed at Keflavik lives on base and does the majority of shopping and eating on base.

There was an ATM machine in the terminal that gave either dollars or Icelandic currency (Kronur), but we found that you could use plastic most anywhere on or off base. You could buy a hot dog and use it. Iceland is big into the use of credit cards.

We were so lucky to have taken that Sunday bus trip from MWR. It was to Thorsmork, a must-see area between two glaciers. The bus used a glacier riverbed for a road much of the way. It was the one place that you had to be in a large-wheeled vehicle in order to get where you wanted to go. The other favored sites—Thingvillar, the site of the first Icelandic parliament, the geysers, waterfalls, geothermal areas, lava fields and fjords were easily accessible by rental car. We rented a car two different days, one from the Lodge and one from MWR. The cost was $80.00 a day each place and included the insurance. We found MWR to have a little better selection. There, an automatic was the same price as a straight shift. With the long hours of daylight we were able to see everything that we had planned to see in those two days. The roads were very varied. The highways with one number were great, with two numbers fair and with three numbers you just closed your eyes and hoped for the best. The road sign that we saw most was a red sign with a big ! on it. You knew that it meant BE READY FOR ANYTHING.

The Blue Lagoon thermal power plant in Iceland.

Through MWR we also found out that the Family Services Office sponsored a free bus trip into Reykjavik, the capital of Iceland, every Thursday. It was primarily for new duty arrivals, but if there was room anyone could go. It was a great all-day trip on a very comfortable bus with a well-informed guide. We had a good introduction to the city, spending time in downtown shops, the largest church around, a very sophisticated mall, the home of the president of Iceland and many other places of interest. We were able to take the trip both Thursdays that we were there and enjoyed it very much each time.

The weather was great compared to Mississippi in late July. Except for the first two days when the temperature was in the sixties, most days were in the low fifties. Coats and caps felt good. The wind blew pretty briskly a lot of the time and an umbrella was totally useless. We learned to walk in the rain and love it. The climate is a good example of saying, "If you don't like the weather, wait ten minutes." Each day had some of it all—sunny, cloudy, windy, rainy—you name it. The sun rose at about 4:15 a.m. and set about 10:45 p.m. at that time of year. You just drew the drapes about 10:00 p.m. and told yourself it was bedtime. Of course in the winter that changes to only four hours or so of daylight.

The plane that we flew over on stayed at the base for the entire two weeks and participated in the exercise. We had high hopes of flying back with them also. Therefore we were not too interested in what other flights flew in or out during that time. There were several contract flights and several C-5s going to the U.S., but there were lot of families going too. We were the only Space-A'ers around for most of the stay.
Of course we had to worry a little at the end of our stay when what had been 40 seats changed to 10. The plane had to take on extra fuel to help two F-15s get back to the U.S. Our luck held, however, and only six people got on before us.

It was an experience of a lifetime. We came home with knowledge of a part of the world that we never expected to see.

Irvin E. and Betty Griffin
Maj, USAF (Ret.)
Starkville, MS

Report on Melbourne, Australia's Naval and Military Club

Dear Ann, Roy and R.J.,
My wife and I recently returned from a very pleasant trip to Melbourne, Australia, where we stayed one week in the Naval and Military Club* in downtown Melbourne. We would unhesitatingly recommend this service club to any reader requiring accommodations while in Melbourne. We traveled space available from Grand Forks Air Force Base, ND to Hickam, HI and then to Melbourne. We were lucky enough to catch the same plane back to Grand Forks. *(Editor's Note: This is a membership club where reciprocal membership in a dues-paying club, such as Marines' Memorial Club, San Francisco, CA, or Army Navy Club, Washington, D.C., is required.)

We did make advance reservations with the club from the U.S. before arriving in Melbourne. It was a good thing because hotel space was at a premium in mid-January due to the Australian Open Tennis Tournament. The rate was very reasonable- $AU 95.00 per night or slightly less than $U.S. 70.00 for a double with private shower and toilet. A full breakfast was included in the price as well. Our air crew stayed several blocks down the street where the normal nightly rate started at $AU 270.00

Our rooms were comfortable and clean. The interior of the club is filled with interesting Australian military memorabilia. One enticing document was the original surrender agreement between Australia and Japanese forces in New Guinea at the end of WWII. The walls are arrayed with with many wonderful Sir Arthur Streeton paintings. We found the staff to be exceedingly helpful and friendly assisting us with such things as fax, laundry and local tours. The club is located in the hub of the city just one block from Parliament House. Melbourne has one of the most advanced tram systems in the world. We caught the City Circle tram and rode free around the main business district. My wife and I decided to visit the Victoria Market, where I was lucky enough to find an Australian showerhead. We loved some of the Australian showers because the water comes straight down rather than hitting one full in the face or chest. This market is a wonderful place for bargains of all kinds.

Because of congestion, poor road signs and numerous construction projects, most travel books advise against renting a car in Melbourne. With this in mind, we opted to explore the city on foot and take a number of bus tours of the surrounding countryside. Via comfortable motor coach, we toured the Great Ocean Road with its Twelve Apostles. The following day we visited the Blue Dandenongs before pushing ahead to Phillip Island to witness fairy penguins come ashore and troop nightly up a darkened beach to the safety of their burrows. By subway and bus, we visited a wildlife animal sanctuary outside of Melbourne. Later we took a sunny afternoon cruise on the Yarra River. From our perspective, we had the advantage of exploring both downtown Melbourne as well as some of the rural areas of Victoria. However, another couple traveling with us from Grand Forks stayed at a motel near the airport and rented a car. They, too, had a nice time, concentrating mostly on the rural areas of Victoria. They reported that driving was not a major problem outside of Melbourne.

One important tip may be in order for any space-available passenger going to Australia. While a visa is still required for Australia, the Australian government has moved to a paperless visa system. Simply call an Australian consulate or embassy with your passport number and receive full clearance without any further processing. Your passport will be scanned upon arrival in Australia. Space-A travelers, however, must produce written documentation of the existence of an Australian visa. Without written proof, Space-A passengers are denied passage by the U.S. military. Usually, such written proof may be obtained from the local SATO travel office before departure.

Thanks to a wonderful KC-135 aircrew, we made the long flight to Hickam, HI and Grand Forks, ND, in one piece, going space available all the way. We have our new Australian showerhead installed and my only regret about our trip was that I could not bring back several cases of Victoria Bitters—a wonderful, delightful Australian beer. The club may be contacted at Navy and Military Club, 27 Little Collins Street, Melbourne, Victoria Australia, phone: C-011-61-3-9650-4741, fax: C-011-61-3-9650-6529, email: nmclub.wa2000.com.au

Sincerely,

Davis and Pat Cummings
MSG, USA (Ret.)

Dover AFB to London, England, Via Ramstein AB, Germany, 20 October-4 November

By Edgar Delong

Rate of exchange varied during this period and the dollar was dropping, but generally \$1.62 US=£1.00 or \$1.00 US=£0.617. Purpose of this trip was primarily to attend shows in London's West End and to try staying at the Victory Services Club in London. A separate facility report was written on the club. Shows seen during this trip were: Smoky Joe's Café, Maddie, Oliver, Martin Guerre, Phantom of the Opera, Stepping Out, Chicago and Beauty and the Beast.

Preparation: Signed up by e-mail at Dover for flight over, about 50 days in advance, and two weeks later at Mildenhall, Ramstein, Aviano, Sigonella and Rhein-Main for return flights. Ordered tickets via the internet from Lashmers Agency in London for Phantom, since they are difficult to get. Purchased a seven out of fifteen British rail pass from a travel agent that we knew would be useful. Exchanged some U.S. dollars for pounds sterling to add to what we already had from a previous trip. Also dug out German marks from earlier trip. Checked passports to make sure they were still in force. Spent several hours on the internet every evening checking out shows in London and other events during the period we expected to be there. Sent membership application and reservation request to Victory Services Club via e-mail and faxed credit card information for security purposes. Attained listings of Lions Clubs in London area and other areas where I wanted to do research, such as the Theater Museums archives, which is an extension of the Victoria and Albert Museum. Reviewed maps of area we were to visit and made sure we had passport-sized photos for transit/tube passes.

Trip Over: Drove from Virginia Beach, VA to Dover AFB, DE in about three hours. The new AMC terminal at Dover AFB is very nice looking and has dining facilities but appeared to have less overall space than the older terminal. Another new concept in use now is that you are checked by security each time you enter the terminal and there is no requirement for further x-ray checks prior to boarding the aircraft. There is more short-term parking available in front of the terminal, but the close-by long-term area is still very crowded. We happened to hit it lucky and got very convenient long-term parking. There are several other long-term lots but they area a long way off.

There were many flights scheduled for Ramstein, DE (RMS), which we decided to forego in favor of catching a direct flight to Mildenhall, UK (MHZ) at 1810 hours. We could have been on any of the Ramstein flights, had we wanted to. It was good that we did not take the first one, since after two hours airborne, the C-5 returned to Dover due to mechanical problems. The MHZ flight was fully booked and we didn't make that one so we decided to try for the next RMS flight that was scheduled for 2200 hours.

As a matter of interest, those passengers who were returned on the earlier RMS flight were not allowed to bump passengers on the later flights, but were guaranteed seats on the same flight the next day or they could start all over and re-qualify for later flights. Several passengers did try to bump others, but were not allowed to do so.

We made the flight to RMS, which was airborne by 2245 hours on 20 October. This was a KC-135 tanker which was dead-heading back to Europe and had no in-flight refueling scheduled. There were canvas bucket seats on the sides and loads of cargo. We 12 passengers were given a detailed safety briefing by a very competent crewman and told that after we got to our flight altitude we could climb up on the cargo to sleep. There is hardly any control of climate on this type aircraft. If you stay in the bucket seats you freeze and if you are on top of the cargo you boil. My wife did the seats, and I did the cargo, so we speak from experience. There were coffee, water and box lunches available. The toilet facilities on these aircraft are similar to camping facilities with only a curtain separating the user from the rest of the aircraft. We arrived at RMS at 1235 hours local time after about eight and a half hours.

The terminal at RMS was packed and many people had been trying to get out for days. Fortunately, our early sign-up date from the U.S. was still valid, as we had listed England as our final destination. Although there was a C-9 MEDEVAC sched-uled for 1640 hours to MHZ, we felt there was little chance of getting it, since the counter thought they would have only about 12 seats. We started investigating possible alternatives.

One was to catch a bus the next morning from Rhein-Main to London, via a ferry that took about 12 hours and cost only $65.00. A second was to take a train from Kaiserslautern to Paris, then change trains to the Eurostar and go to London via the Chunnel We opted to make reservations on this one at the SATO office just in case we didn't make the C-9 flight. It cost about $300 for two with a 10% penalty for cancellation.

Fortunately, we did make the C-9, which took off with a total of 47 seats occupied. We took off at 1905 hours and arrived at Mildenhall after about and hour and a half flight. This is a great aircraft with real commercial-style seating and lots of attendants. We called the SATO office and were told to turn in our tickets at Mildenhall the following morning.

As we arrived at Mildenhall, many passengers were loading on a C-5 for RMS and informed us that they had just checked out of the Gateway Inn (Air Force operated) and that rooms were available there. It's a long walk pulling suitcases, even though we had a cart from the terminal. At $17.00 a night for a great room with all kinds of amenities it is well worth it.

There are two shuttle buses from the AMC terminal to Heathrow Airport in London at 0530 and 0830 each day, but we were so tired that we decided to skip them and try another method. We slept late and found that there was no other way except to take a taxi to Cambridge and a train to London. Taxis to Cambridge from Mildenhall AMC are easy to get but cost £25, which at current rates amounted to about $40 U.S. If there are several people, its worth it. We had no other way, so we took the taxi. The driver was friendly and told us all about the area and pointed out interesting buildings along the way. At Cambridge, we exchanged our British Rail Pass for tickets and took a train into Kings Cross Station (they run every half-hour and take about an hour and a half from Cambridge.)

Kings Cross Station has all sorts of facilities for tubes, buses and trains. We purchased weekly transport passes for zones 1 and 2 only (£15.70), (you need a passport size picture- and travel agents will try to sell you zones 1 through 6 at much higher prices), which get you nearly anywhere in greater London you'd like to go. There is a number 10 bus which goes from Kings Cross to Marble Arch and beyond, but we were not aware of it, so we took the Victoria Line tube (subway) to Oxford Circus, where you transfer to the Central Line and get off at Marble Arch. There are many steps, and some escalators were out of order. It was a very trying and difficult trip. We found later that a direct taxi from Kings Cross to Victory Services Club would only have cost about £7. Maybe our misfortune will be someone else's good luck. As a matter of interest—the word "subway" in England means underground passageways from one side of the street to the other. The "tube" is the transportation we think of, so be careful what you ask for.

Checked in at VSC and paid using VISA card. Just a note—we had been very big users of Diners Club but found that on this trip, not many places took that card any more.

London - Mildenhall - Dover

We did learn from our trip in, and took a taxi from Victory Services Club to Kings Cross station for £7.00. Much easier and quicker without the hassle of climbing up and down tube stairs and escalators. Trains run to Cambridge every half hour and the ride takes about an hour and a half. We tried again to locate bus service from Cambridge to Mildenhall, but there are only a few trips a day, and we ended up taking a taxi. The driver asked for £35 but came down to £26 after a bit of haggling. We arrived at Mildenhall's terminal at about 1200 and found that there were all kinds of flights scheduled for Dover. Two were KC-135s and a later one at 1600 was a C-5. We thought about waiting for the C-5 but decided that a bird in the hand is better, as the old saying goes. This aircraft too was deadheading and did not refuel in flight, but was carrying mostly empty pallets back to Dover. Still very uncomfortable and the climate situation was no better than the flight over. The crew was exceptionally friendly and helped all they could. We were airborne at 1530 local time and arrived Dover at 1930 local after an 8-hour flight. Customs checked a few bags this time but not many. Found our car in good shape and returned to Virginia Beach, pleased at having successfully used the Space-A system once again.

Our First Space-A Adventure

Dear Ann & Roy,
Our first attempt at Space-A was not successful in 1997, when the flight from Tinker AFB, OK to England was cancelled at the last minute, so we were somewhat apprehensive about catching the April, 1998 flight from TAFB to Rhein-Main, Germany. However, this time everything went smoothly. Show time on April 18th was delayed an hour, but this gave us additional time to grab a snack and park our car in long term parking at Tinker.

We caught a ride with the 507th Air Refueling Wing, a reserve unit at TAFB, flying KC-135 tanker. We took off at 1645 and headed directly to Rhein-Main (no stopover at Dover). There were ten Space-A seats available but only four were taken- two by wife and me and two by GIs returning to their bases in Germany. Also on board was an Air Force Reserve unit going to Rhein-Main for two weeks training, hence the direct flight.

We landed in Rhein-Main at 0900 on Sunday the 19th after a smooth flight. We were taken to the terminal by a shuttle. We used the DSN line to reserve a suite at the Rhein-Main hotel at the Gateway Gardens area. We were fortunate to be able to get a room, as we later discovered, since they had to refer many to alternate quarters elsewhere. (Cost for the small DV suite was $43.25.) We caught a shuttle bus to the hotel after signing up for a return trip at the terminal.

We subscribe to the Military Living's *R&R Travel News®* and this helped us in a number of ways: First, the heating system on the KC-135 is not comparable to a commercial flight, so we were well prepared with several layers of clothes to shed or put on as the flight progressed. Second, we had a flashlight which came in handy for my wife to read a book en route. We forgot to order a box lunch; however the reserve unit's First Sergeant was resourceful and had an extra which he gave us. We usually pack some dried fruit, peanut butter and crackers, so we wouldn't have starved, but the box lunch was most welcome. Also, Space-A reports alerted us to sign up for a return flight upon arrival, in order to get on the list.

We had heard stories about the personnel at Rhein-Main Hotel, but we found them to be most helpful. We saw signs posted that indicated that the previous contractor system had been replaced by Air Force civilian personnel, who were friendly and helpful.

We had also heard of the Unterschweinstiege Restaurant near the hotel, so we decided to walk to it. It is just outside the back gate but is hidden behind the Steigenberger Airport Hotel. But we found it and had a delightful meal (about $46 for the two of us). One suprise: My wife asked for some water and the waitress brought out a large bottle of mineral water- the charge was DM12.50 (a little over $7). Next time we will ask for a smaller bottle.

Prior to departing the U.S., I called Armed Forces Recreation Center at Chiemsee and made reservations for three nights. It is very popular, so we were fortunate to get reservations on relatively short notice, but we were still in the off-season in late April. I had thought about renting a car and driving down, but my wife wanted to take the train. When I saw the price of gas (about $1 per liter) I concurred completely. To get to the train station was a little tricky—taxi to the adjacent commercial airport (DM22), train to the Haupbahnhof downtown (DM 5.80 each), then a train to Prien-a-Chiemsee, via Munich. One side note here—in 1954, I was stationed in Schweinfurt and met my new bride at this same station in Frankfurt. I had left for Germany 4 days after our marriage, so you can imagine our feelings of nostalgia 44 years later.

Our rail fare was $137.50 each round trip from Frankfurt to Prien-a-Chiemsee, going through Mannheim, Stuttgart, Ulm, and Augsburg to Munich. We changed trains in Munich and went to Rosenheim to Prien-a-Chiemsee. One thing to notice about German trains: They are absolutely on time. If it is scheduled to arrive at 11:01 and depart at 12:03, it will and you can almost set your watch by it. We learned to get a baggage cart at the station when we changed trains in order to be able to make it to the connecting rail line in time. There are no conductors to yell "all aboard." Snacks and beverages are sold in the trains and they also have a dining car available, with reservations preferred.

Total time for the train trip was about five hours one way. Prien-a-Chiemsee is a ways from the AFRC "Lake Hotel," located on the lake near a delightful village "Bernau." We hailed a taxi (DM32) and settled in. We had a small but nice room with television (much to my wife's horror). Cost was $58 per night. The hotel has a very nice dining room (Lakeside) plus a fast food service (Reggies Express). Dinner cost about $12 each at Lakeside and about $7 each at Reggies.

We checked at the travel service at the hotel and discovered that it had a day trip to Salzburg, Austria the next day. We hadn't been to Salzburg in more than 40 years, so we decided to go. Cost was $35 each and included bus and guide service walking tours. Lunch was on our own so we went to the St. Peter Stiftskeller, the oldest continuously operating restaurant in Europe, having started in AD 803. My wife and I had eaten there with friends many years ago and it was as good and expensive as ever. We also took the elevator up the cliff to Cafe Winkler, which has a spectacular view of Salzburg. This also brought back memories from the 50s.

Two surprises in Austria—1. The border between Austria and Germany is open. 2. They will take Austrian shillings or German marks for payment; I did not ask about U.S. dollars.

The next day, we walked around Chiemsee and then in to Bernau—about 3 km from the hotel. We had a nice luncheon in a cafeteria-like establishment. Instead of going to a tourist-like restaurant, we wanted to see where the workmen were having lunch, and liked our choice. Thursday, the 23rd, we returned to Frankfurt by rail and succeeded in getting accommodations at the Rhein-Main Hotel again. This time there were no DV suites, so we settled for a room with shared bath ($23.25). There are facilities at the hotel for doing laundry and we were also able to get some TV dinners to prepare in our room so we didn't have to go out. We checked on flight schedules to the U.S. and found that a World Airways contract flight was going to Atlanta on Friday morning, so we signed up for it. As it turned out, the DC-10 was only about two-thirds full, so there was plenty of room and nobody was left behind. Each of us was charged $23.40—I'm not sure what it was for, but it certainly beat commercial rates. En route, we were served two meals and the service was comparable to any tourist class commercial flight.

We arrived in Atlanta about 1430 on Friday after an 8-hour flight. We were checked through immigration and customs at Atlanta; something we had not had to do on the entire trip except for passport and ID checks at Tinker prior to our USA departure. Now the problem was that our car was at Tinker at Oklahoma City and no military related flights were available from Atlanta to OKC on Friday afternoon. Plane tickets exceeded $500 each, so we ended up renting a car and driving the 750 miles in two days. This was our first Space-A adventure in our retirement and almost everything worked out smoothly. We credit the *R&R Travel News®* for cluing us in on items we would not have thought of. We also made the decision (a wise one, I think) not to try to see all of Europe in one trip, but rather to concentrate on one area at a time. It lessens complications on what to pack and gives a bit more leisure time. Total cost of the trip for the two of us was about $160 per day for an 8-day German vacation—not bad, in my way of thinking.

Some lessons learned:
1. Dress appropriately for the aircraft.
2. Get some money exchanged in the U.S. before getting to Germany. The exchange rate may be okay but the service charges are significant (even with travelers checks).
3. Charge to your MasterCard or whatever—you will end up with the best available rates of exchange with no commissions.
4. Consider getting a Eurorail pass in the U.S. for flexibility in traveling.
5. Stay at military facilities insofar as possible. It is simply less expensive for food and lodging and you are generally with friends.
6. Be flexible and carry some extra money for contingencies.
Do we plan to go again? YOU BET.

Lee and Charlotte Holder
Col. AUS-RET
Oklahoma City, OK

Space-A to England

Dear Roy and Ann:
We have just returned from a 23-day Space-A trip to England and would like to share some of our experiences along the way. Enclosed is a copy of our trip log.

Your *Military Space-A Opportunities Around the World* publication is outstanding, particularly your addition of a base facilities map.

ThreatCon A in CONUS and ThreatCon B in England are presenting some additional requirements for the Space-A traveler. Bases are requiring a 100% ID check at main gates. McGuire AFB restricted us to a separate room in the terminal; you could not go to the exterior of the building to smoke and no vending machines around.

RAF Mildenhall ThreatCon requires 100% ID Check at the entrance of all major base buildings. There are no luggage storage lockers. You cannot leave any personal item unaccompanied anywhere, thus you are married to your luggage while on base, unless you have base quarters or stay in the Bird In Hand Motel (incorporates a pub with good food for lunch and dinner for $7-$10 USD).

The bus stop for Lakenheath shuttle is now located behind the Marauder Club and local bus stops are across from Mickey's and between the VOQ and The Bird In Hand Motel. Taxis are adjacent to the Billeting Office. Be prepared to do considerable walking, while assuming the role of a Red Cap. Also, beware of British advice that it is ONLY A 5-MINUTE WALK. Five-minute walks are usually 10-15 minutes and quite often 20 or more!

The ATMs on base at RAF Mildenhall and Lakenheath will deliver dollars or pounds on specified ATM cards, without a special service charge, not so with ATMs in the city! Both currencies may be exchanged at the O Club.

The existing RAF Mildenhall terminal building is under extensive renovation and expansion, to be completed +/- February 1999. An adjacent temporary terminal is about a 100-yard walk from the existing terminal parking lot. This terminal has a Retiree Activities Office (free hot coffee), DSN: 238-2039 and Fax:238-2250; C-01638-542039. Helpful people. Terminal amenities are limited: Toilets, a coffee and snack vending machine and bottled water! Retirees are not allowed to shop at the BX or commisary, thus you are out of luck for rolls, fruit, etc.

Dover AFB has a new terminal and incorporates a cafeteria, accessible from the secure waiting room, and has storage lockers. Apparently they are still working the kinks out of the new building and systems, as processing is extremely slow, with considerable delay in departure time! If billeting cannot be obtained on base, it appears advisable to make reservations directly with motels at a military rate, rather than go across the highway to the Billeting Office for contract civilian quarters and then on to the same motel. Saves time.

Arriving in the evening at Travis AFB poses some problems, particularly ground transportation. Cabs or an airporter have to be called from Fairfield or Vacaville, which necessitates a 20-30 minute wait and the potential a cab may pick up a fare other than you. The airporter is another story suffice to say; I witnessed an airman and his wife being returned from halfway to Sacramento airport for a flight reservation, to pick up another fare at the terminal for first delivery to San Francisco!

As our car was at McChord AFB, the wife had to return to Portland commercial anyway. Space-A to McChord was a five stop milk run two days later, so I opted for commercial to SEATAC. Even with the above glitches, it was a great trip to and through England and the price is still right!

Robert S. Furrer
Major USAF (Ret.)
Lake Oswego, OR

Major Furrer's Space-A Log
England-09/10/98 to 10/03/98

08/17/98 Faxed AMC Form 140 to McChord and Fairchild AFBs.
09/09/98 McChord Flt. recording: MIS #1152 (C-141) 09/10/98, RAF Fairford, GB, Show 1000 PDT LV 1300. MIS #06XS (C-

141), 1130 PDT show, McGuire>Azores>Ramstein. 24 HR Space-A VOQ reservations ($15.30).

09/10/98 #1152 40 seats, #06XS 35 seats. Show for #1152 $3.20 box lunch, 1st plane abort, 2nd plane LV: 1355 PDT. Mission parameters change AR: McGuire 2145 EDT, deplane for fuel, due to ThreatCon A restricted to one sterile room of terminal, no amenities!

09/11/98 LV: McGuire 0016 EDT, AR: RAF Mildenhall 1108 local time @ temporary terminal (Existing terminal being remodeled and expanded, finish +/- February 1999) under ThreatCon B, 100% ID checks and married to baggage, NO LOCKERS! Signed up for return trip (Pointed out by a more seasoned Space-A traveler that I could have also faxed Mildenhall from the States to establish an earlier return sign-up date.) NO POUNDS-NEVER COME TO ENGLAND W/O POUNDS. Walked to O Club for money exchange. Called base cab £8.3 ($13 USD), to Mildenhall Village, joined fellow travelers @ bus stop, taxi £20 ($33 USD) for four people to Cambridge. Tourist Info office, Gonville Hotel £55 ($90 USD) including breakfast.

09/12/98 Free bus to Duxford & American Air Museum in England at Holiday Inn (LV 1000). An outstanding building and addition to the Duxford Museum complex. Returned by bus £1.95 ($3.20 USD)

09/13/98 One hour morning Cambridge bus tour. Local bus to Ely £2.95 ($5 USD). Lamb Hotel £84 ($140 USD) including breakfast, one block from Ely Cathedral, a most impressive piece of architecture.

09/14/98 Morning walking tour of Ely, AM train to Coventry £27.4 ($46 USD), taxi recommended Britannia hotel £55 ($95 USD- USD dropping in value) including breakfast, adjacent to cathedral. The remains of the old bombed-out cathedral tastefully combined with the new cathedral.

09/15/98 Walk central Coventry, British Motor Museum. Pub lunch. Healthy pub lunch £3.75 ($6.50 USD).

09/16/98 Train to Maccelsfield 19.5 P($33 USD), picked up by British friend/host at RR Station pub. Pub dinner.

09/17/98 +/- 200 mile drive through country side to Blackpool seaside resort, picnic lunch and return for dinner at Ploughman Pub.

09/18/98 Shopping at downtown Maccelsfield, city museum and silk factory museum. First bit of rain. Home-cooked curry dinner.

09/19/98 Direct train to Carlisle £29 ($49 USD), picked up at RR Station by British friend/host. Tour castle and church and pub lunch. Buy your liquor at local supermarket, not liquor store, save up to 50%!

09/20/98 Car tour to Lanercost Prior (1100 AD Norman), on to Hadrian's Wall (300 AD), Birdswald and Housesteads Roman Forts.

09/21/98 Visited Carlisle Cathedral and museum, with a few pub stops. Host took wife to library to research IGI for purported Graham ancestors and Netherby family estate. Side trip to check out Netherby Estate, now for sale.

09/22/98 Quiet day in central market, antique shops and pub lunch.

09/23/98 Off with host by car to Edinburgh. Stop at Gretna Green marriage museum, Dryfsdale and Lockerbie PanAm Memorial Cemetery. Pub lunch. Hotel reservations Kew Guest House £75 ($128 USD) with breakfast. Bus to downtown and Dome Restaurant, all booked. Wandered around Rose Lane and finally picked a bad seafood restaurant.

09/24/98 Host dropped us off downtown and returned to Carlisle. Took bus tour of city and wife shopped for Scottish woolens.

09/25/98 AM train to Berwick-on-Tweed £10.8 ($19 USD) and as usual, taxi driver directed us to a good hotel, Queens Head at £36 ($57 USD) with breakfast. Walked city and old city wall, Berwick Barracks Museum and pub lunch.

09/26/98 Taxi to Bamburg castle £20 ($34 USD) and bus return, £2.8 ($5USD). Walked most of town and Saturday Market on Main St.

09/27/98 AM train to York £28.4 ($49 USD). Hotel poor choice, £45 ($77 USD) with breakfast. Advertised as 5-minute walk to old city center. A 5-minute British walk is always 15-20 minutes and many times, 25! Bus tour of city, walked medieval shopping street, tour York Cathedral and dinner @ Russell's Carvery, just adequate!

09/28/98 York and British Railway Museums. Mildenhall flight check, mission to Fairchild AFB C-135 @ 1355 on the 29th. Rushed to train station to reschedule to a 0735 departure to Cambridge.

09/29/98 AM train to Cambridge, AR 1000, taxi 33P ($56 USD) to RAF Mildenhall. 1355 flight dropped through cracks! We are unaware there is heavy stateside AF troop rotation from Saudi to Fairchild AFB. No Space-A @ Mildenhall, score @ Lakenheath VOQ ($20). ThreatCon B alert has caused various base service relocations, i.e., base shuttle bus stop to Lakenheath relocated from PAX terminal parking lot to bus stop behind Marauder Club @ center of support base. Long walk with bags! Shuttle at 5 minutes past the hour to Lakenheath hospital drop. Four block walk to billeting office and about the same from billeting to VOQ, but good quarters. Excellent steak dinner @ adjacent O Club!

09/30/98 AM taxi to Mildenhall £6 ($10 USD), flight finally shows @ 1210 with 10 seats, 9 go CAT 3 and one single CAT 6! Tomorrow three C-135s to Fairchild AFB with show @ 0640, 0710 and 0740. Mildenhall VOQ for $20.

10/01/98 Troops gobble up two C-135s and CAT 3 eat the other! Night at The Bird In Hand Motel adjacent too VOQ 39.99 P ($69 USD), adjacent pub. Bus to Mildenhall Village for R&R.

10/02/98 C-135 with 6 seat release, all taken by CAT 3 and 5. Still heavy troop rotation. Three C-135 to Fairchild tomorrow, each with 10 seats, show @ 0640, 0710 and 0740, also C-5 showing @ 1220 for Dover/Travis. Back to Bird In Hand Motel.

10/03/98 All C-135 taken by troop rotation. C-5 with 51 seat show @ 1220. Bingo, LV 1356 (all but three seats are taken), AR Dover 1654 EDT. Base housing zero, can contract through billeting @ $48 for motel. Reserve directly with Howard Johnson, Days Inn, etc., at military rate and save stop @ billeting and standing in line! Stayed @ Howard Johnson Inn, along with our flight crew, $55. Show tomorrow @ 1320. Restaurant about 4 block walk.

10/04/98 Show time deteriorates to 1430, LV Dover at 1705 EDT, 19 aboard. Flight diverted south over Texas to miss violent weather. First in-flight hot meal and goood! AR Travis 2024 PDT. Outstanding flight #03R2 in Travis 0002 aircraft, handled by a sharp and helpful crew.

Travis found transportation, spastic, long waits for Fairfield or Vacaville cabs. A very sad event occurred with the Fairfield Airporter and an airman and his wife who were due back in McChord the following day. They had reserved the airporter from Dover which was waiting when they arrived and were immediately off to catch the last flight out of Sacramento Airport @ 2230. Halfway to the airport, the dispatchcer told the airporter to go back to Travis and pick up and deliver a San Francisco fare first! Needless to say this left the couple stranded at Travis!

Made Alaska Air reservations for 1005 the next day, wife to Portland ($141) and myself to SEATAC ($121). Yellow Cab/Vacaville $20 to Vacaville Best Western, $55 military rate, continental breakfast. 10/05/98 $75 cab fare (35-40 minute running time) to SAC, AR SEATAC 1300 PDT. Pick up McChord/Ft. Lewis shuttle for $10 @ Gate #26 (North end of baggage claim area) and retrieve my car form long term parking around 1460 PDT.

Space-A to Germany and Italy

Dear Ann & Roy,
Our 50-day advance sign-up had ZERO influence on being selected for any of the flights on this trip. Either no Cat 6 or all Cat 6 made each flight we "showed" for.

We all got on the ATL-FRF (6 of us) flight as hoped on March 1st, a DC-10. Seats were comfortable, service good, and the movie also.

We planned to travel from Germany to Aviano, Italy ASAP, and thought we knew that the first chance would be on Tuesday from Ramstein, so we planned to take the free shuttle from FRF (Rhein-Main) to Ramstein at 1110 (we had arrived and cleared customs by 0740 and were then snoozing in the comfortable DV lounge at FRF). At 1000 I telephoned Ramstein AMC and learned that a C-5 was leaving for Aviano with many available seats one hour later. We should have checked earlier, rented a car for the 75-minute drive there and would have been en route, but were too late by then. The Tuesday KC-135 was full before Cat 6. We were selected on Thursday for the C-5 to depart around 1300, then it was postponed for an 0330 Friday showtime; fortunately due to our snoozing, we learned before retiring Thursday that show time was rescheduled for 0445.

We had been able to get Space-A rooms at Ramstein for all four nights there and did some driving trips—Heidelberg is plus or minus 65 miles, and we also visited Saarbrucken. The former is a great visit. Saarbrucken never again—skip it—Trier would be better. Other super side trips from FRF/Ramstein are Rothenberg and Limburger.

Upon arrival at Aviano, we rented a large (9 passenger) Fiat van (diesel-powered) and toured Italy for 11 days. Military lodging was available at Vicenza—beautiful hotel—and Camp Darby, costing $59 to $90 (the Camp Darby DV suite for four persons). Darby is six miles from Pisa; we made day trips from there to St. Gimignano and to Portofino, both excellent destinations. We went on from St. G to Siena but ran short of time before finding anything of interest there. Returned to Vicenza for four nights total—DV can be reserved through Protocol if available, but other Space-A rooms are first come, first served. you must sign up any time after 0600, but can't be assured a room until 1800 roll call. Venice was a fantastic day trip from Vicenza—can be done by public transportation or by shuttle to the Venice airport, then the water bus into the city. We also spent two nights at a Florence hotel, (reserved by SATO at Aviano). That's also a fabulous city for visitors. We returned to Aviano on Monday, March 16, stupidly missed a C-21 (Lear jet) to Ramstein by failing to inquire about the "pop-up" flight, then stayed at a Pordenone hotel, the Villa Ottoboni—about $100 per couple including breakfast. Returned to Aviano for an 0800 show time for a DC-8 with 10 seats to Ramstein—FULL! There were two other Ramstein flights later—a C-9 with 10 seats and a C-21 with 5 seats, but we elected to take the scenic train (beautiful trip) through the Alps to Salzburg, then Frankfurt, about $215 per person, arriving at 0400 on Wednesday. Called Rhein-Main lodging and to our surprise DV suites were available.

The next available public transportation to FRF airport was the 0138 train (5 DM each); arrived there at 0149, then tried to reach the Rhein-Main taxi service but they only had recordings saying "call back later—we are open." Don't believe it. Took a regular taxi which is not allowed onto Rhein-Main AB, but we were able to get it to the gate of the housing area and a 500-yard walk to lodging.

Finally into our room after 0345, we arose to shuttle to the AMC terminal on the 0820 bus for the DC-10 to BWI and ATL, which reportedly would have 100 Space-A seats Wednesday, 18 March. They ran out during Cat 4, so we checked back into lodging (one DV and two rooms with shared baths) for two more nights, hoping to get the DC-10 to ATL on 20 March (Friday)—it actually had 170 Space-A seats and we got it. It was four hours late arriving, but it was a great flight.

In the future, I'd not bother competing for the Wednesday flight—this makes twice that we missed it, but easily made it on Friday. Just relax and enjoy Germany for two more days. Also learned we probably would have made the C-9 Aviano-Ramstein later on Tuesday, but the train trip was great anyway. For planning purposes, an L-1011 from Saudi - Aviano - FRF - BWI goes every Sunday. We're told it has many more Space-A seats on the third or fourth Sundays generally than on the first or second. All in all, it was a great trip.

R.E. and Mrs. Hamilton
COL, USA (Ret.)
Marietta, GA

Flying to Europe?

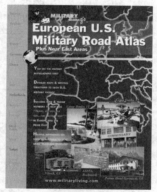

Take Military Living's New Atlas with You and $ave!

You may order by credit card from your online military exchange and save! Call 1-800-527-2345 (USA) and order catalog item number T 023X.

If not available, you may order online through our secure web order system at www.militaryliving.com or call 703-237-0203 to place a credit card order by phone. You may also order by fax at 703-237-2233. Be sure to give the name on the credit card, card number, expiration date and credit card billing address, as well as ship-to address and daytime phone number.

Visit us online at

www.MilitaryLiving.com
and learn more about our $$$-saving publications!

R&R Travel News™

By subscription. Published six times yearly. Subscription rate, shipped by business standard mail*:

1 year	$18.00	2 years	$28.00
3 years	$38.00	5 years	$57.00

*For first class delivery, mailed in an envelope, add $1 per issue ($6 per year extra)

To subscribe
using Visa, Mastercard, American Express or Discover
call 703-237-0203
or visit our secure web order online at
www.MilitaryLiving.com.

To keep costs down, billing is not available–pre-payment is required.

Military Living's **R&R Travel News** covers all facets of military leisure travel, including Space-A air travel, Temporary Military Lodging and RV Camping and outdoor recreation worldwide. We also include reader trip reports so that you can get the info "first-hand." **If you would like to receive 2 previous issues for $5, call 703-237-0203 and request 2 R&R samples for $5 (charged to your credit card) as mentioned in Military Living's *Space-A Air Basic Training and Reader Trip Reports*.**

This special offer expires 1 December 2001. Please note: We are not able to provide specific back issues covering specific locations/topics.

R&R Travel News™
keeps you up-to-date on all facets of
military leisure travel, including
Space-A air travel, Temporary
Military Lodging and RV Camping
and outdoor recreation worldwide.

APPENDIX A: Space-A Passenger Regulations

DOD 4515.13-R Air Transportation Eligibility

CHAPTER 6: SPACE-AVAILABLE TRAVEL

A.   GENERAL POLICY

1. Definition and Scope. Space-available travel is the specific program of travel authorized by this Chapter allowing authorized passengers to occupy DoD aircraft seats which are surplus after all space-required passengers have been accommodated. Space-available travel is allowed on a non-mission interference basis only. DoD aircraft shall not be scheduled to accommodate space-available passengers. No (or negligible) additional funds shall be expended and no additional flying hours shall be scheduled to support this program. In order to maintain the equity and integrity of the space-available system, seats may not be reserved or "blocked" for use at en route stops along mission routes.

2. Purpose of the Space-Available Program. Space-available travel is a privilege (not an entitlement) which accrues to Uniformed Services members as an avenue of respite from the rigors of Uniformed Services duty. Retired Uniformed Services members are given the privilege in recognition of a career of such rigorous duty and because they are eligible for recall to active duty. The underlying criteria for extending the privilege to other categories of passengers is their support to the mission being performed by Uniformed Services members and to the enhancement of active duty Service members' quality of life.

3. Leave Status for Travel. Uniformed Services members on active duty must be in a leave or pass status to register for space-available travel, remain in a leave or pass status while awaiting travel, and be in a leave or pass status the entire period of travel. DoD civilian employees, when afforded space-available privileges listed in table 6-1, below, must be in a leave or non-duty (i.e., weekend or holiday) status to register for space-available travel. If in a non-duty status, leave must have been approved for the first normal working day following the non-duty period. A leave status must then be maintained while awaiting travel and for the entire period of travel. Those members in appellate leave status are not authorized space-available travel privileges.

4. In Conjunction with Space-Required Travel or to Restricted Tour Areas. Space-available travel may not be used instead of space-required travel, such as TDY, TAD and PCS travel, except emergency leave type travel (see Chapter 2, subsection A.4., above). Space-available travel may be used in conjunction with space-required travel as long as space-available travel does not substitute for any single leg for which the traveler has

a space-required entitlement (except emergency leave type travel). For example, a Uniformed Services member may take leave with a TDY or TAD, as allowed by Service regulations, and may travel space-available while on leave. Travel from the PDS to the TDY or TAD location shall be space-required with the traveler in a duty status; any space-available travel from the TDY or TAD duty location shall return to the TDY or TAD location, with the traveler in a leave status; and the final leg shall be space-required from the TDY or TAD location to the PDS with the traveler in a duty status. Dependents may not use space-available travel options in this Regulation to accompany their sponsor on space-required travel or to travel to or from a sponsor's restricted or all others (unaccompanied) tour location.

5. Registers and Sign-Up Procedures

a. Each base, installation or post from which space-available travel is accomplished shall maintain a single space-available register and all space-available passengers accepted for airlift from that location must have been selected from the register's roll. The maintenance of such a roster shall be the responsibility of the AMC passenger activity, where established. Where no AMC passenger activity is established, it shall be the responsibility of the base, installation, or post commander to designate the Agency responsible for maintaining the space-available roster.

b. To compete for space-available travel, eligible personnel must sign up on the space-available roster in person and present all required documentation (see subsection A.6., below). The DoD Components and the USTRANSCOM may also accept sign-up information in writing from eligible space-available travelers (through mail, fax transmission, or courier). When adopted, the DoD Components and the USTRANSCOM shall provide detailed guidance outlining procedures for using "remote sign-up" services. Passengers shall declare their final destination when they sign up for space-available travel. The original date and time of sign-up shall be documented and stay with the traveler until his or her destination is reached. On reaching the destination, the traveler may again sign up for space-available travel to return to home station. Those registered are not required to accept any seat offered, and failure to accept an offered seat shall not jeopardize a passenger's position on the space-available register. All but Category VI passengers (see table 6-1, below) are automatically removed from the space-available register on expiration of leave, pass or after 60 days, whichever is sooner. Category VI passengers are removed from the list after 60 days. All space-available passengers dropped from the register may sign up again in their respective categories (see table 6-1, below) with a new date and time of sign-up.

c. Eligible travelers who arrive at an air terminal seeking space-available transportation shall sign a document certifying compliance with the rules for eligibility and conditions of space-available travel, and be provided access to documentation showing the date and time their request for movement was entered onto the installation space-available roster.

d. Reservations shall not be made for any space-available passenger. Travel opportunity shall be afforded on an equitable basis to officers, enlisted personnel, civilian employees, and their accompanying dependents without regard to rank or grade, military or civilian, or branch of Uniformed Service.

6. Required Documentation. Unique documentation required for specific types of individuals (e.g., Medal of Honor recipients) is cited in table 6-1, below, on a case-by-case basis. Additionally, the following types of travelers shall present the documentation listed below to air terminal personnel, and shall have all the documentation in their possession during travel:

a. Active Duty Uniformed Services Members (includes National Guard and Reserve members on active duty in excess of 30 days)

(1) DD Form 2 (Green) U.S. Armed Forces Identification Card (Active), or Form 2 NOAA (Green) Uniformed Services Identification and Privilege Card (Active), or PHS Form 1866-3 (Green) United States Public Health Service Identification Card (Active).

(2) A valid leave authorization or evidence of pass status as required by the Service concerned.

b. Retired Uniformed Services Members. DD Form 2 (Blue) U.S. Armed Forces Identification Card (Retired), or DD Form 2 (Blue) NOAA Uniformed Services Identification Card (Retired), or PHS Form 1866-3 (Blue) United States Public Health Service Identification Card (Retired).

c. National Guard and Reserve Members

(1) Authorized Reserve Component Members (National Guard and Reserve) of the Ready Reserve. and members of the Standby Reserve who are on the Active Status List; On presentation of the following valid:

(a) DD Form 2 (Red), "Armed Forces of the United States Identification Card (Reserve).

(b) DD Form 1853, "Verification of Reserve Status for Travel Eligibility."

(2) Retired Reservists Entitled to Retired Pay at Age 60; On presentation of the following valid:

(a) DD Form 2 (Red).

(b) A notice of retirement eligibility as described in DoD Directive 1200.15, (reference (kk)). If the automated DD Form 2 (Red) has been issued, the member is registered in his or her Service personnel system as a Reserve retiree entitled to retired pay at age 60, and a notice of retirement eligibility is not required.

(3) Retired Reservists Qualified for Retired Pay; Documentation, as prescribed in subsection A.6.b., above. For space-available travel eligibility, no distinction is made between members retired from the Reserves and members retired from active duty.

(4) On Active Duty for 30 Days or Less; On presentation of the following valid:

(a) DD Form 2 (Red).

(b) Orders placing the Reservist on active duty.

(c) A valid leave authorization or evidence of pass status as required by the Service concerned.

(5) ROTC. Nuclear Power Officer Candidate (NUPOC). and Civil Engineer Corps (CEC) Members; When enrolled in an advanced ROTC, NUPOC, or CEC course or enrolled under the financial assistance program, on presentation of the following valid:

(a) DD Form 2 (Red).

(b) DD Form 1853.

d. Dependents of Uniformed Services Members. DD Form 1173, "United States Uniformed Services Identification and Privilege Card."

e. EML Travelers. Besides any documentation required by paragraphs A.6.a. through A.6.d., above, EML orders issued in accordance with Unified Command procedures (see paragraph B.4.a., below).

7. Categories of Travel and Priorities of Movement

a. Categories. There are six categories of space-available travel. Space-available travelers are placed in one of the six categories based on their status (e.g., active duty Uniformed Services member, and DoDDS teacher, etc.) and their situation (e.g., emergency leave, and ordinary leave, etc.). Once accepted for movement, a space-available passenger may not be "bumped" by another space-available passenger, regardless of category. See table 6-1, below, for a list of specific travelers and the category in which they fall.

b. <u>Priority of Movement</u>. The numerical order of space-available categories indicates the precedence of movement between categories; e.g., travelers in Category III move before travelers in Category IV. The order in which travelers are listed in a particular category in table 6-l, below, does not indicate priority of movement in that category. In each category, transportation is furnished on a first-in, first-out basis.

c. <u>Changes to Movement Priorities</u>. Wherever the issue may arise, the local installation commander may change the priority of movement of any space-available traveler for emergency or extreme humanitarian reasons when the facts provided fully support such an exception. The installation commander may delegate the authority to
make such changes to no lower than the Chief of the Passenger Service Center or its equivalent when a movement priority is changed, the passenger shall be moved no higher than the bottom of the Category I space-available list. Where AMC units are tenants, the senior local AMC authority shall advise the installation commander of this authority and offer technical assistance, as needed.

8. <u>Destinations and international Restrictions</u>

a. If authorized by this Chapter for a particular traveler's status and situation (see table 6-1, below), transportation may be between overseas stations, between CONUS stations, and between overseas and CONUS stations where adequate border clearance facilities exist or can be made readily available. Theater or international restrictions shall be observed and all requirements pertaining to passports, visas, foreign customs, and immunizations shall be met.

b. Individuals traveling to or from the CONUS, and who are not otherwise eligible to travel space-available in the CONUS, may travel on any CONUS leg segment (i.e., on a flight with en route stops) when no change of aircraft or mission is involved.

9. <u>Conditions of Travel</u>. There is no guaranteed space for any traveler. The Department of Defense is not obligated to continue an individual's travel or return him or her to point of origin, or any other point. Travelers shall have sufficient personal funds to pay for commercial transportation to return to their residence or duty station if space-available transportation is not available. Space-available travel shall not be used for personal gain, for a business enterprise or outside employment, when theater or international restrictions prohibit such travel, or to establish a home overseas or in the CONUS (except for permissive TDY house hunting trips as authorized in table 6-1, below).

10. Dependent Travel. Except where specifically noted in this chapter, dependents may travel space-available only when accompanied by their sponsor.

B. EML TRAVEL

Except as noted, unfunded EML travel is subject to the space-available travel program rules and guidance outlined in this section A., above, and table 6-l, below. Funded EML travel is discussed in Chapter 2, sections B.l.e. B.3.a.(14).

1. Definition. EML is leave granted with an EML program, as prescribed in DoD Directive 1327.5 (reference (d)), established at an overseas installation where adverse environmental conditions require special arrangements for leave in more desirable places at periodic intervals.

2. Program Description For a complete description of the EML program, see reference (d).

   a. EML Locations and Destinations. Specified locations where adverse environmental conditions exist and at which EML is authorized, are called "EML locations" The Under Secretary of Defense (Personnel and Readiness) designates Funded EML (FEML) locations and relief destinations. Unified commanders designate locations under the unfunded EML program. Under the EML program, not more than two relief destinations shall be designated unless additional destinations are needed to provide a reasonable prospect of relief. The CONUS shall not be designated an "EML destination" except when such designation is necessary to provide a realistic opportunity for relief.

   b. Priority, Timing, and Frequency. Passengers traveling space-available under the EML program are given a higher priority than those traveling on ordinary leave (see table 6-1, below). The timing and the frequency of EML is limited by DoD Directive 1327.5 (reference (d)). Transportation officials are not responsible for monitoring this timing and frequency, but rather are responsive to EML documentation issued by the commanders concerned.

3. Responsibilities. Unified commanders shall ensure that administrative controls are in place to ensure that all eligible travelers are able to participate in the EML space-available travel program on a fair and equitable basis. The unified commanders concerned shall forward two copies of each implementing directive, and of any modifications to such directive, to The Department of the Army (DAPE-MBB-C), the Commandant of the U.S. Marine Corps (LFT), the Chief of Naval Operations (N4l), HQ USAF/LGTT, NOAA Corps (NC), and the USTRANSCOM (TCJ3/J4).

4. Policy and Procedures

a. Unified command procedures shall include the issuance of a separate set of EML orders each time an individual is approved for EML.

b. Unfunded EML travelers may travel in Category II status (See table 6-1, below) to only one EML destination for each set of EML orders. This does not preclude several approved EML destinations being included in a single set of EML orders as long as procedures are in effect to ensure that the individual is provided Category II status only for travel to and from the first authorized EML destination actually reached. Subsequent space-available travel; e.g., from the EML destination to a third location and return, or from the third location to another EML location, may only be provided in Category III status (table 6-1, below).

c. When traveling under EML orders, dependents who are 18-years of age or older may travel unaccompanied by their sponsor. Dependents who are under 18-years of age traveling under EML orders must be accompanied by an EML eligible parent or legal guardian who is traveling in an EML status.

C. ELIGIBILITY
The travelers listed in table 6-1, below, are eligible to travel space-available in the categories and over the geographical segments cited, subject to any limitations cited in table 6-1, below, under "Traveler's Status and Situation," or elsewhere in this Regulation.

ELIGIBLE SPACE-AVAILABLE TRAVELERS, PRIORITIES, AND APPROVED GEOGRAPHICAL TRAVEL SEGMENTS

This table lists travelers who are eligible to travel on DoD aircraft according to the space-available program outlined in paragraphs A. and B., above. "Item" is a sequential numbering and is for reference purposes only. "Cat" is the category of travel as explained in section A.7.a., above. These are used to determine priority of movement as explained in section A.7.b., above. "Traveler's Status and Situation" lists specific travelers and conditions under which space-available travel may be authorized. The approved geographical travel segments, i.e., origin and destination combinations, are C-C (CONUS to CONUS), O-O (overseas to overseas), C-O (CONUS to overseas) and O-C (overseas to CONUS) (reference section A.8.). A "yes" in the column headed by one of these abbreviations indicates that travel is authorized in that particular geographical travel segment for the particular type traveler cited in that item number, and subject to any limitations cited. Lack of a "yes" indicates travel is not authorized in that particular geographical travel segment.

Item	Category	Traveler's Status & Situation	C-C	O-O	C-O and O-C
1		**Category I - Emergency Leave Unfunded Travel** Transportation by the most expeditious routing only for bona fide immediate family emergencies, as determined by DoD Directive 1327.5 (reference(d)) and Service regulations, for the following travelers:			
2				yes	
3	I	Uniformed Services members with emergency status indicated in leave orders (for space-required option see Chapter 2, sections B.1.L and B.1.b., above).	yes		
4	I	Civilians, U.S. citizens, stationed overseas, employees of: (1) Uniformed Services; or (2) NAF activities and whose travel from the CONUS, Alaska or Hawaii was incident to a PCS assignment at NAF expense (for space-required option see Chapter 2, sections B.2.a. and B.4.a., above		yes	yes
5	I	Dependents of members of the Uniformed Services, command sponsored, accompanied or unaccompanied (for space-required option see Chapter 2, sections B.3.a(1), B.3.a(2), and B.3.a.(4), above).		yes	yes

6	I	Dependents of members of the Uniformed Services, noncommand sponsored, residing overseas with the sponsor, one-way only to emergency destination (for space-required option see Chapter 2 sections.3.b.(1) and B.3.b.(2), above.	yes	C-O no O-C yes
7	I	Dependents, command sponsored, of: (1) U.S. citizen civilian employees of the Uniformed Services stationed overseas;(2) U.S. citizen civilian employees of the DoD stationed overseas and paid from NAF; or (3) American Red Cross full-time, paid personnel, serving with a DoD Component overseas (for space-required option see Chapter 2, section B.3.a. 2 above).	yes	yes
8	I	Professional Scout leaders, and American Red Cross full-time, paid personnel, serving with a DoD Component overseas (for space-required option see Chapter 2 section B.6., above).	yes	yes
9		**Category II - EML**		
10	II	Sponsors in an EML status and their dependents traveling with them, also in an EML status. "Sponsors" includes: (1) Uniformed Services members. (2) U.S. citizen civilian employees of the Armed Forces who are eligible for Government-funded transportation to the United States at tour completion (including NAF employees).(3) American Red Cross full-time, paid personnel on duty with a DoD Component overseas. (4) USO professional staff personnel on duty with the Uniformed Services. (5) DoDDS teachers during the school year and for Employer-approved training during recess periods.	yes	yes

Item	Category	Traveler's Status & Situation	C-C	O-O	C-O and O-C
11		**Category III - Ordinary Leave, Close Blood or Affinitive Relatives, House Hunting Permissive TDY, Medal of Honor Holders and Others**			
12	III	Uniformed Services members in a leave or pass status other than leave (use Category I) or excess appellate leave, for which space-available travel is not authorized. This includes members of the Reserve components on active duty, in a leave or pass status.	yes	yes	yes
13	III	Dependents of a member of the Uniformed Services accompanied by their sponsor in a leave status other than emergency leave (use Category I) or excess appellate leave, for which space-available travel is not authorized.		yes	yes
14	III	Close blood or affinitive relatives who are permanent members of the household and dependent upon a Military Service member, a DoD civilian employee, or American Red Cross employee serving with a DoD Component overseas, when the sponsor is authorized transportation of dependents at Government expense. Travel must be with the sponsor's, or his or her dependent's, PCS move.			yes

15	III	Dependent spouses of military personnel officially reported in a missing status under 37 U.S.C.551 (reference (11)), and accompanying dependent children and parents, when traveling for humanitarian reasons and on approval on a case-by-case basis by the Head of the Service concerned (Chief of Staff of the Army, the Chief of Naval Operations, the Chief of Staff of the Air Force, and the Commandant of the Marine Corps) or their designated representative. Travelers shall present an approval document from the Service concerned.	yes	yes	yes
16	III	Uniformed Services members traveling under permissive TDY orders for house hunting incident to a pending PCS.	yes	yes	yes
17	III	Uniformed Services members traveling under permissive TDY orders for house hunting incident to a pending PCS and one accompanying dependent.	yes	yes	yes
18	III	Medal of Honor recipients. Except for active duty, traveler shall present a copy of the Medal of Honor award certificate.	yes	yes	yes
19	III	Dependents of Medal of Honor recipients when accompanied by their sponsor.		yes	yes

Item	Category	Traveler's Status & Situation	C-C	O-O	C-O and O-C
20	III	Command sponsored dependents of Uniformed Services members accompanying their sponsor on approved circuitous travel. Commanders authorized to publish circuitous travel orders for members under current policy of their Uniformed Service, where extenuating circumstances prevail, may approve requests for space-available travel of their dependents within and between overseas areas and the CONUS, incident to approved circuitous travel of the member. (For space-required option see Chapter 2, section B.3.a.(7), above.)		yes	yes
21	III	Cadets and midshipmen of the U.S. Service academies, and foreign cadets and midshipmen attending U.S. Service academies, in a leave status. Foreign cadets' and midshipmen's native countries must be identified in the leave authorization.			yes
22	III	Civilian U.S. Armed Forces patients who have recovered after treatment in medical facilities and their accompanying nonmedical attendants. Travel is permitted by the most expeditious routing to return the recovered patient and nonmedical attendant to the overseas post of assignment. (During the death or extended hospitalization of the patient, the nonmedical attendant retains the space-available travel authority to return to the patient's overseas post of assignment.)		yes	C-O yes O-C no
23	III	Foreign exchange service members on permanent duty with the Department of Defense, when in a leave status.	yes	yes	yes

24	III	Dependents of foreign exchange service members on permanent duty with the Department of Defense, when accompanying their sponsor.	yes	yes	
25		**Category IV - Unaccompanied Dependents on EML and DoDDS Teachers on EML During Summer**			
26	IV	Dependents traveling under the EML Program, unaccompanied by their sponsor, traveling under subsection B.4.c., above ("Sponsor" as defined in item 10, above).	yes	yes	
27	IV	DoDDS teachers or dependents (accompanied or unaccompanied) traveling under the EML Program during the summer break.	yes	yes	
28		**Category V - Permissive TDY (Non-householding), Foreign Military, Students, Dependents & Others**			
29	V	Military personnel traveling on permissive TDY orders other than for house hunting.	yes	yes	yes

Item	Category	Traveler's Status & Situation	C-C	O-O	C-O and O-C
30	V	Dependents (children) who are college students attending in residence an overseas branch of an American (U.S.) university located in the same overseas area in which they reside, command sponsored, stationed overseas with their sponsor who is: (1) A member of the Uniformed Services; (2) A U.S. citizen civilian employee of the Department of Defense (paid from either appropriated funds or NAF); or (3) An American Red Cross full-time, paid employee serving with the Department of Defense. Unaccompanied travel is permitted from the overseas military passenger terminal nearest their sponsor's permanent duty station to the overseas military passenger terminal nearest the university, and to return during school breaks.		yes	
31	V	Students must present written authorization from an approving authority and only one round trip each year is authorized. Unused trips may not be accumulated from school year to school year. Dependents, command sponsored, stationed overseas with their sponsor who is: (1) A member of the Uniformed Services; (2) A U.S. citizen civilian employee of the Department of Defense (paid from either appropriated funds or NAF); or (3) An American Red Cross full-time, paid employee serving with the Department of Defense. Unaccompanied travel is permitted to and from the nearest overseas military academy testing site to take scheduled entrance examinations for entry into any of the U.S. service academies.		yes	
		Dependents of active duty U.S. military personnel stationed overseas who, at the time of PCS, were not entitled to transportation at Government expense. Travel is to accompany or join their sponsor at his or her duty station. Travel			

No.	Cat.	Description			
32	V	may be unaccompanied and is limited to travel from the APOE in the CONUS, Alaska, or Hawaii to the overseas APOD serving the sponsor's duty station. Before travel, approval of the overseas major commander is required. (For space-required option see Chapter 2, section B.3.(8), above.)			C-O yes O-C no
33	V	Noncommand sponsored dependents, acquired in an overseas area during a military member's current tour of assigned duty, not otherwise entitled to transportation at Government expense. Travel must be with the member's PCS, may be unaccompanied, and is limited to travel from the overseas APOE to the APOD in the CONUS, Alaska, or Hawaii. Member's PCS orders are required for travel. Command regulations pertaining to the acquisition of dependents must have been followed. (For space-required option see Chapter 2, section B.3.b. (2) above.)			C-O no O-C yes
34	V	Unaccompanied spouses of Uniformed Services members stationed in overseas areas in response to written requests from school officials for personal consultation on matters about the needs of family members attending school at an overseas location away from the Uniformed Service member's PDS.		yes	
35	VI	**Category VI - Retired, Dependents, Reserve, ROTC, NUPOC, and CEC**			
36	VI	Retired Uniformed Services members.	yes	yes	yes
37	VI	Dependents of retired Uniformed Services members, when accompanying their sponsor.	yes	yes	yes

Item	Category	Traveler's Status & Situation	C-C	O-O	C-O and O-C
38	VI	Dependents, command sponsored, stationed overseas with their sponsor who is: (1) A member of the Uniformed Services; (2) A U.S. citizen civilian employee of the Department of Defense (paid from either appropriated funds or NAF); or (3) An American Red Cross full-time, paid employee serving with the Department of Defense. Unaccompanied travel is permitted to the U.S. for enlisting in one of the Armed Forces when local enlistment in the overseas area is not authorized. If an applicant for Military Service is rejected, return travel to the overseas area may be provided under this eligibility.		yes	yes
39	VI	Authorized Reserve component members and authorized Reserve component members entitled to retired pay at age 60, traveling in the CONUS and directly between the CONUS and Alaska, Hawaii, Puerto Rico, the U.S. Virgin Islands, Guam, and American Samoa (Guam and American Samoa travelers may transit Hawaii or Alaska); or traveling within Alaska, Hawaii, Puerto Rico or the U.S. Virgin Islands.	yes		
40	VI	NUPOC, CEC, and ROTC students of the Army, Navy, or Air Force, receiving financial assistance or enrolled in advanced training, in uniform, during authorized absences from the school. Travel is authorized within and between the CONUS, Alaska, Hawaii, and the U.S. territories.	yes		

Rhein-Main Lodging - This air base is scheduled for closure when the base is turned back to the German government. If going to Germany, check to see if it is still open as it is a great facility.

Garmisch Loisach Inn -If you find no room at AFRC, the Loisach Inn has rooms near the housing area.

Lake Hotel- Go now before Chiemsee closes and enjoy this beautiful military recreation area run by AFRC.

Ederle Inn - Perhaps the only military lodging in Europe which has a swimming pool. It is conveniently located to visit Venice.

How can you find great military lodging to use when traveling?

Military Living's Temporary Military Lodging Around the World lists military lodging of all services, worldwide!

All new edition available Summer 2000

ADDITIONAL SPACE-A INFORMATION FROM CHAPTER 1

C. USE OF MILITARY AIRCRAFT, INELIGIBLE TRAFFIC, AND RESTRICTIONS

1. Commanders' Responsibility. The commanders at all levels shall exercise prudent judgment to ensure that only authorized traffic is transported and that they do not misuse the authority delegated to them by this Regulation. The commanders and other officials responding to requests for transportation not specifically authorized by this Regulation shall make no commitments concerning prospective travelers or cargo until they receive all required approvals.

2. Ineligible Traffic Procedures

    a. When an order or authorization for movement of traffic (passenger or cargo) which is neither authorized by this Regulation nor approved according to the procedures in this Regulation is presented, transportation shall be denied. The station making the determination shall document the case and forward it through channels to USTRANSCOM TCJ3/J4-LP, 508 SCOTT DRIVE, SCOTT AFB IL 62225-5357 for necessary action.

    b. Any traffic transported by DoD aircraft which is ineligible, even though documentation may have been issued, is liable for reimbursement at the non-U.S. Government rate tariff according to APR 76-28 (reference (f)) for all transportation furnished. If any passenger or cargo is challenged for eligibility or authority, every effort shall be made to provide assistance short of delaying a scheduled aircraft.

3. Restrictions on Use of Unit or Operational Support Aircraft. Unless requested and authorized under DoD Directive 4500.43 (reference (t)), unit aircraft shall not be utilized to transport DoD passengers and cargo. Similarly, the use of unit or operational support airlift aircraft to provide PCS transportation for DoD members or their dependents is not authorized.

4. Pregnant and Post-Partum Mothers and Newborn Infants

    a. Pregnant women up to the 34th week of gestation may be accepted for air transportation unless medically inadvisable.

    b. Women who are 6 weeks, or more, postpartum and infants at least 6 weeks old may be accepted for air transportation unless medically inadvisable. Infants under 6 weeks old and women who are less than 6 weeks post partum may be accepted if considered medically sound and so certified in writing by a responsible medical officer or civilian physician.

5. Unaccompanied Minors. Restrictions on travel by unaccompanied minors vary with types of travel (see Chapters 2, 5, 6, and 7).

6. Passengers on "Non-Transport-Type" Aircraft. Aircraft not designed or normally configured for passenger (nonaircrew personnel) carrying capability, such as, but not limited to, fighter aircraft, are not to be used for passenger travel. This does not restrict use of these type aircraft for orientation flights, as prescribed in Chapter 4 below.

7. Disabled Passenger. Every effort shall be made to transport passengers with disabilities who are otherwise eligible to travel. Passenger service personnel and crew members shall provide assistance in loading, seating, and unloading the disabled passenger. Travel may be disapproved by the chief of the passenger travel section or the aircraft commander if there is an unacceptable risk to the safety of the disabled passenger, other passengers or the crew, or if operational necessity or equipment or manpower limitations preclude accepting disabled passengers. Such disapprovals shall be rare. In such cases, air terminal personnel must ensure that the passenger understands why air transport is not possible on the mission in question. When a disabled passenger is denied transportation for the above reasons, and when his or her sponsor or dependent, who is otherwise eligible to travel, accompanies the disabled passenger to assist in his or her needs, travel shall be approved if such assistance will eliminate the reasons for denying travel.

D. BAGGAGE

1. Timeliness. Baggage must arrive at the APOE either with the traveler or sufficiently in advance to permit the owner to document and offer it for movement as "accompanied baggage."

2. Allowances

a. Normal Free Checkable Baggage Allowance. Duty and space-available passengers are authorized two pieces of checked baggage and one carry-on piece. Checked baggage may not exceed 62 linear inches (length plus width plus height) or 70 pounds for each piece. Carry-on baggage must fit under the seat and may not exceed 45 linear inches (length plus width plus height). For duty passengers only, a duffel bag, sea bag, B-4 bag, flyer's kit bag, or diver's traveling bag, any of which exceeds 62 linear inches, may be substituted for one of the 62 linear inch items.

b. Excess Baggage Allowance. When authorized by service regulations or directives, an excess baggage allowance may be included in an individual's orders. Excess baggage shall be stated in terms of number of pieces, not by weight. Use the formula of 70 pounds for each piece and round to the next highest whole piece to determine the number of pieces necessary. For example, if 100-pounds excess is needed, then two pieces of excess baggage are authorized. Excess baggage is not authorized for space-available passengers.

c. <u>Unauthorized Excess Baggage</u>. Baggage which exceeds the normal baggage allowance without proper authorization may be accepted for shipment at the discretion of air terminal representatives. Passengers owning such baggage will be charged the appropriate excess baggage fee. Air terminal representatives are authorized to refuse to accept baggage in excess of that authorized. Disposition of unauthorized baggage not accepted for shipment shall be the personal responsibility of the owner. Shipment may be made at personal expense through postal facilities or commercial transportation companies. If shipment is otherwise authorized to be made at Government expense, arrangements for forwarding may be made with the APOE transportation office.

d. <u>Patients</u>. Patients are limited to two pieces of baggage not to exceed 70-pounds each.

e. <u>Baggage Allowance Restriction</u>. To maximize seat availability, terminal personnel may further restrict passenger baggage allowances when air transportation services are provided by an activity not financed through the DBOF-T.

f. <u>Other Modes</u>. This Regulation limits only the baggage that may be carried by passengers traveling on DoD aircraft. It does not restrict or increase the baggage allowance that may be prescribed by other directives for shipment by other modes.

3. <u>Firearms and Ammunition</u>. Unloaded personal firearms and small arms ammunition may be carried as checked baggage within the authorized weight allowance as long as they are in compliance with the laws and regulations of the United States, foreign governments, the Department of Defense, and the Military Departments. The Military Departments shall establish procedures which require the passenger to identify the items to passenger service personnel or their equivalent at the time of processing for flight and which ensure that the items are in checked baggage, or otherwise adequately secured, so as to be inaccessible to passengers while they are aboard the aircraft.

E. DRESS, CONDUCT, AND STANDARD OF SERVICE

1. <u>Dress</u>. The wearing of the uniform on DoD aircraft by members of the Uniformed Services on active duty, members of the Reserve components not on active duty, and authorized foreign military personnel shall be governed by the directives of the Service concerned and by DoD 4500.54-6, "Foreign Clearance Guide" (reference (u)). When civilian clothing is

worn, it shall be in good taste and not in conflict with accepted attire in the overseas country of departure, transit, or destination.

2. Conduct. Under no circumstances shall a passenger be accepted for transportation or be permitted to board an aircraft if he or she is unruly, under the influence of alcohol or narcotic, may create a hazard to the safety of the aircraft or passengers, or is a disruptive influence.

3. Standard of Service. The DoD Components shall establish and maintain standards of appearance, conduct, and service for flight and ground personnel who come in contact with customers of the airlift system which shall ensure professional, courteous, and responsive service.

F. ANIMALS

1. Seeing Eye Dogs

a. Transportation of a dog properly trained to lead the blind, and officially identified by a bona fide organization which trains or registers such dogs, is authorized without charge when accompanying its blind owner who is otherwise authorized transportation under this Regulation.

b. The dog must be properly harnessed to lead a blind person, muzzled to safeguard other passengers and crew members, remain at the blind person's feet, and not create a safety hazard to others by being in the aisle. The dog shall be permitted to accompany the owner in the cabin, but may not occupy a seat or be in the galley area. Sanitation must be maintained at all times.

c. Transportation of seeing eye dogs shall be subject to country quarantine procedures. When it is necessary to detain the animal pending determination of its admissibility, the owner shall provide detention facilities satisfactory to the cognizant quarantine officer. The owner shall bear the expense of such detention, including necessary examinations and vaccinations, and other expenses incurred due to the dog's accompanying the owner.

2. Pets. Passengers traveling under PCS orders may be allowed to ship their pets at their own personal expense. For this privilege, pets are defined as "dogs and cats only," and are limited to two for each family. Requests to deviate from this policy, i.e. number, type, or weight of pets, will be submitted through Service Headquarters to AMC for consideration.

a. Owner Responsibilities. The owner of the pet(s) is responsible for the preparation and care of the animal and for all documentation, immunization, and border clearance requirements including quarantine. The owner shall provide a pet shipment container approved by the International Air

Transport Association of sufficient size to allow the animal to stand up, turn around, and lie down with normal posture and body movements.

b. <u>Aircraft Operator Responsibility</u>. The DoD Component operating the aircraft shall ascertain that the means and facilities exist at origin and destination to permit the owner to accomplish his or her responsibilities before accepting the animal for shipment. The operator of the aircraft shall establish procedures to ensure that the pets accepted for movement are stowed in areas heated and pressurized adequately to sustain health and comfort according to accepted commercial industry practice.

3. <u>Other Animals</u>. There is no restriction on shipping other animals aboard DoD aircraft for official purposes if they meet all criteria for shipment of official cargo established by this Regulation. Animals shall be housed, caged, and shipped in a humane fashion consistent with law and industry standards.

G. <u>FORMS</u>

1. <u>DD Form 1381. "Air Transportation Agreement."</u> Before travel aboard aircraft operated by an activity not financed through DBOF-T, the DD Form 1381 shall be executed by the non-DoD personnel specified in Chapters 2, 3, 4,5, 8, and 10, below, when their flight originates in a foreign country. NATO member national personnel traveling in the performance of official duties are exempt from this requirement. The completed DD Form 1381 shall be attached to the passenger manifest and filed at the point of origin. Sponsors will execute DD Form 1381 for minor dependents or individuals incapable of signing for themselves.

2. <u>DD Form 1839. "Baggage Identification."</u> All checked and carry-on baggage shall be identified with required data clearly annotated on the DD Form 1839. When the DD Form is unavailable, substitute tags, such as those used in the commercial aviation industry, may be used.

3. <u>DD Form 1853. "Verification of Reserve Status for Travel Eligibility."</u> Members of the Reserve components traveling under the provisions of Chapter 6, below, shall have a completed DD Form 1853 in their possession at all times.

4. <u>Boy Scouts of America. "Parent/Guardian Consent Form for Aviation Flights."</u> Explorer Scouts participating in an orientation flight under the provisions of Chapter 4, below, shall present a completed Parent/Guardian Consent Form for Aviation Flights before the flight.

5. <u>Supply of Forms</u>. DD Forms 1381, 1839, and 1853 shall be made available to users by forms management officers of the DoD Components. To ensure availability to users, forms

management officers are encouraged to permit local reproduction of these forms. The Parent/Guardian Consent Form for Aviation Flights shall be obtained from the individual's Scout Troop.

AUTHOR'S NOTE: This Appendix (chapter 6, SPACE AVAILABLE TRAVEL, of DoD 4515.13-R and related) contains references to other related documents which are independent of DoD 4515.13-R and other chapters in DoD 4515.13-R all of which are not published here because of space limitations. In most cases, this documentation amplifies, provides background information and further explains chapter 6 of DoD 4515.13-R. Although not completely essential to the understanding of the Space Available Travel directive, persons wishing to view the entire DoD 4515.13-R and related documents may do so upon request and presentation of appropriate entitlement identification at military Space-A departure locations and Uniformed Services Personnel Offices. The following chapter 6, SPACE AVAILABLE TRAVEL and part of chapter 1, DoD 4515.13-R was released to Military Living Publications by the Office of The Under Secretary of Defense, Jan 1995.

Space-A Expands for Active Duty Family Members

The following unclassified message, p 210939Z OCT 95, from HQ AMC SCOTT AFB IL//DOJ// to AIG 8521, dated 20 October 1995, regarding: change 1 to DoD 4515.13-R, Air Transportation Eligibility.

"1. The following changes to DoD 4515.13-R are effective immediately: changes appear on pages 6-7, 6-9, and 6-11. New page changes will be sent to all locations on requirement for this regulation through normal distribution channels. In the interim, use this message as authorization to execute movement for all eligible passengers under this change. A. Page 6-7 add: Item 5A CAT I. Dependents of members of the uniformed services when accompanied by their sponsor. (CONUS to CONUS) Yes.

B. Page 6-9 add: Item 17 CAT III. Uniformed services members traveling under permissive TDY orders for house hunting incident to a pending PCS and one accompanying dependent. (CONUS to CONUS) Yes; (OVERSEAS to OVERSEAS) Yes; (CONUS to OVERSEAS) and (OVERSEAS to CONUS) Yes.

C. Page 6-11 add: Item 34A CAT V. Command-sponsored dependents of uniformed services members who are stationed overseas. Travel restrictions may apply to certain overseas destinations as determined by the appropriate unified commander. Documentation signed by the sponsor's commander verifying command sponsorship shall be presented to air terminal personnel and shall be in the dependent's possession during travel. This documentation is valid for one round-trip from sponsor's PCS duty location. Dependents under 18 years af age must be accompanied by an eligible parent or legal guardian. (OVERSEAS to OVERSEAS) Yes; (CONUS to OVERSEAS) and (OVERSEAS to CONUS) Yes.

2. These changes are effective immediately."

Travel on AMC Flights by Non U.S. Citizens

Non U.S. citizens are not authorized to travel on AMC flights unless they are in possession of a valid visa of the country being visited (if required). For those traveling to the U.S., passengers must have an immigration visa, green card or a tourist visa. This prohibition for travel to the U.S. has taken place within the past year.

Infants and Infant/Car Seats Aboard Aircraft

1. When traveling on an AMC (CAT B) flight, children under the age of 2, below the weight of 40 pounds, and under the height of 40 inches are accepted as passengers, **the parent or guardian must provide their own FAA-approved infant/car seat (ICS).** This requirement does not preclude a passenger from temporarily holding an infant during the cruise portion of a flight when safety considerations are not violated.

2. The approved infant/car seat must bear one or more labels as follows:

a. Seats manufactured to U.S. standards between 1 Jan 81 and 25 Feb 85 must bear the label: "this child restraint system conforms to all applicable federal motor vehicle safety standards."

b. Seats manufactured to U.S. standards on or after 26 Feb 85 must bear two labels:

(1) "this child restraint system conforms to all applicable federal motor vehicle safety standards."

(2) "this restraint is certified for use in motor vehicles and aircraft" (printed in red lettering).

3. Infant/car seats that do not qualify under paragraph 2 above must bear either a label showing approval of a foreign government or a label showing the seat was manufactured under the standards of the United Nations. Booster-type child restraint systems (as defined in federal motor vehicle standard no. 213 (49 CFR 571.213)), vest- and harness-type child restraint systems, and lap-held child restraints are not approved for use in aircraft.

Air Mobility Command (AMC) Passenger Reservation Procedures

1. Public law (14CFR Part 243) requires emergency next of kin information for all international airline passengers. As such, AMC is modifying their procedures for making passenger

reservations on AMC aircraft to comply with this law. AMC has announced that effective immediately, AMC passenger reservations will require the names and social security numbers (SSAN) of all passengers including dependents. While dependent SSANs are not required by public law, inclusion of this information at the time reservations are made will help expedite passenger processing for travelers at AMC aerial ports and commercial gateways. The dependent SSAN will be used as a link to Defense Eligibility Enrollment Report System (DEERS) to positively identify the travelers and obtain next of kin notification information in the event of an emergency.

2. To assist AMC with their efforts, we are requesting that the MPF be the collection point for this vital information. Please provide the full name and SSAN in the remarks portion of section VI on the AF Form 1546 for all dependents requesting international travel prior to submitting the request to the traffic management office (TMO).

3. Failure to comply with this requirement could result in departure delays while TMO attempts to obtain the required information. All personal information collected is subject to the Privacy Act of 1974 and will be protected as required under the act.

Excerpts From the Coast Guard Military Space Available Travel Program Regulations Relevant to 100% DAV Passengers

This regulation excerpt is applicable only to 100% DAVs paid by Dept of Veteran Affairs.

5. USCG Military Space Available Travel Program. Title 10 USC §4744 authorizes a Military Space Available Travel Program . . .

b. Military Space Available Travel Program Categories.

(1) Category A: Transportation of Military Space Available Passengers Between the CONUS and Overseas Areas by Coast Guard Aircraft.

(d) Priority 4.

1/ Retired military members and veterans rated totally disabled by the Department of Veteran Affairs.

(2) Category B: Transportation of Military Space Available Passengers Within CONUS by Coast Guard Aircraft.

(d) Priority 4.

1/ Unaccompanied retired military members and veterans rated totally disabled by the Department of Veteran Affairs.

(3) Category C: Transportation of Military Space Available Passengers Within and Between Overseas Areas by Coast

Guard Aircraft.

(d) Priority 4.

1/ Unaccompanied retired military members and veterans rated as totally disabled by the Department of Veteran Affairs (VA).

Last modified: Sat Mar 9 22:35:41 1996

Exception to Policy for Space-Available Travel Upgrade for Unaccompanied Family Members of Deployed USEUCOM Service Members

Effective 19 Nov 1998 some unaccompanied family members may be eligible for Space Available Upgrade from Category V to Category III. Requirements of DoD 4515.13R, *Air Transportation Availability,* for unaccompanied travel are still valid but with additional documentation the unaccompanied family member may travel at a higher priority. The following are requirements for the travel:

1. Military Sponsor must be on a USEUCOM Command Sponsored tour.

2. This entitlement is good for one round trip during the sponsors 120 day or longer TDY.

3. Unaccompanied dependents must present a letter signed by the sponsor's commander verifying command sponsorship and sponsor's TDY status. The letter must include:

      a. Sponsor's name, social security number, date assigned unit, statement to the effect that the military member has been deployed and that 120 days has lapsed since the last use of the Cat III entitlement by the family member

      b. Statement of understanding from family member

      c. List all command sponsored traveling dependents by name

      d. Commander's signature

4. Other documentation required for travel by each dependent include a military ID (for all dependents 10 years and older) and passport with appropriate Visa(s) if required.

5. Dependents must have documentation signed by sponsor's commander in their possession during the entire travel period.

6. Dependents are allowed upgraded travel within USEUCOM or to and from CONUS to the USEUCOM area of responsibility.

7. Family members are eligible for this entitlement effective the first day of the deployment as indicated on the member's deployment orders and will remain on the Space Available List for 30 days only.

USEUCOM Dependent Upgrade Sample Letter

Department of the (your Service)
Unit or Command

Memorandum for AMC Terminal

From (Unit ID) Example HHC 3/25th Armor

Subject: Authorization for Command Sponsored Dependents and USEUCOM Upgrade

1. The following individuals are command-sponsored dependents of Doe, John A, USA (branch of service), Sgt 123-45-6789:

a. Jane Doe	SSN: 012-34-5678		German Passport
b. John Doe Jr	SSN: 098-76-5432	DOB 2/12/96	US Passport
c. Jeff Doe	SSN: 345-67-8910	DOB 3/16/97	US Passport

2. Sgt Doe has been assigned to this unit since 3 Nov 96. On 6 Dec 98, he deployed to __(Location)__ to support __(name of deployment)__.

3. Sgt Doe will be deployed 120 days (or more) and his/her command sponsored family member(s) understand that this is a one time entitlement per 120 day or more deployment.

Signature _____ Date_____.

4. This upgrade entitlement has not been used in the last 120 days.

5. Please direct any questions to Maj. Help at DSN: XXX-XXXX

I.L. Help, Maj, USA

Commander*

Or Acting Commander

Or By Direction (US Navy)

Notes:
* Commanders whose name is typed on the form must sign the form. Having someone sign in lieu of the commander is NOT authorized.
-Please include all above information on all requests for dependent travel.
-Please make sure you include the SSN of each dependent and Date of Birth for children.
-Include the nationality of dependents. Those without U.S. passports may encounter difficulties when traveling to certain countries without their sponsor.
-Traveling dependents must keep original copy of the letter on their person at all times during travel.

APPENDIX B: Procedures for Remote Space-A Travel Sign-up and One-Time Sign-up
(Use AMC Form 140, Feb 95 APPENDIX D)

The Assistant Secretary of Defense (OSDUSD-TP), gave approval to USCINCTRANS on 30 March 1994 to implement remote sign-up for Space-available (Space-A) travel and sought service headquarters planned implementation instructions/guidelines. The following (summarized) procedures for this initiative became effective 1 July 1994.

1. ACTIVE DUTY MEMBERS OF THE SEVEN UNIFORMED SERVICES:

A. Fax a copy of the applicable service leave (or pass) **(OF Form 988, DA Form 31, NAVCOMP 3065 and NAVMC 3) and other service leave (or pass) forms from USCG, USPH and NOAA or use AMC Form 140, Feb 95 (Appendix D).**

B. A statement that required border clearance documents are current, i.e., I.D. cards for sponsor and eligible dependents (family members); passports for sponsor (if required) and dependents (family members); visas for sponsor and dependents (family members) and immunizations (PHS-731, I. International Certificates of Vaccination and II. Personal Health History), as required for all travelers.

C. A list of five desired country destinations (5th may be "ALL" to take advantage of opportune airlift).

D. The fax should be sent on the effective date of leave (or pass): **Therefore, the fax header will establish the basis for date/time of sign-up.**

E. Members will remain on the Space-A travel register for a period of 60 days or upon expiration of leave (or pass), whichever is sooner. As an option the Services (USA, USN, USMC, USCG, USAF, USPH, NOAA) may designate a central point of contact to assist members by answering basic questions and ensuring information is correct to minimize delayed sign-up. (NOTE: none have been so designated.)

F. Mail (United States Postal Service) and Courier (Base/Installation official distribution) entries will be permitted. The Air Mobility Command (AMC) has indicated that commercial courier/delivery services such as United Parcel Service (UPS), Federal Express (FEDEX), and e-mail on the worldwide web (where available) are acceptable media for filing your application for Space-A air travel. Upon receipt, the service leave (or pass) form can then be stamped with the current date/time (please keep in mind that mail on military installations goes through distribution channels and may take longer than normal mail). NOTE: Active duty members on pass may utilize this enhancement. Fax a request indicating desired destination, name, rank and inclusive dates of pass.

2. ACTIVE STATUS MEMBERS OF THE RESERVE COMPONENTS:

A. Fax a current copy of their DD Form 1853, **"Authentication of Reserve Status For Travel Eligibility"** and use AMC Form 140, Feb 95.

B. A statement that border clearance documents are current, if applicable for United States possessions.

C. A list of five desired destinations (no foreign country destinations; 5th destination may be "ALL" to take advantage of opportune airlift).

D. Active Status members will remain on the Space-A register for a period of 60 days. NOTE: Active Status members of the Reserve components may only register for travel to/from the CONUS and Alaska, Hawaii, Puerto Rico, the U.S. Virgin Islands, American Samoa and Guam. **Dependents (family members) of an Active Status Reservist do not have a Space-Available travel eligibility.**

E. Mail and Courier entries will be permitted. Upon receipt the DD Form 1853 can then be stamped with the current date/time (please keep in mind, mail on military installations goes through distribution channels and may take longer than normal mail).

3. ELIGIBLE RETIRED MEMBERS OF THE SEVEN UNIFORMED SERVICES:

A. Fax a request to the desired aerial port(s) (station) of departure giving five desired destinations (5th destination may be "ALL" to take advantage of opportune airlift). **The fax data/time header will be the basis for the date/time of Space-A travel sign-up, or use AMC Form 140, Feb 95.**

B. Retirees may remain on the Space-A travel register for a period of 60 days.

C. Mail, e-mail and courier entries will be permitted. Upon receipt the request can be stamped with the current date/time (please keep in mind that mail on military bases goes through distribution channels and may take longer than normal mail).

4. MEMBERS OF THE RESERVE COMPONENTS (GRAY AREA RETIREES) WHO HAVE RECEIVED NOTIFICATION OF RETIREMENT ELIGIBILITY BUT HAVE NOT YET REACHED AGE 60:

A. These members are limited to the same travel destinations as Active Status Reserve Members. Dependents (family members) of these Reservists do not have a Space-Available travel eligibility. Use AMC Form 140, Feb 95.

5. Appendix C has a list of AMC Terminals (Stations) having the best capability of providing Space-A travel. Units listed in USAF, AMCP 76-4 will also provide remote Space-A travel sign-up. The Services (other than USAF/AMC, USA, USN, USMC, USCG and other USAF) are requested to augment this listing with their Base/Installation manifesting agencies capable of providing this service. **NOTE: Remote Space-A travel sign-up is the sole responsibility of each member unless a (Uniformed) Service designates a single Point of Contact (POC) for a specific installation. Uniformed Services have not designated single POCs.**

6. Please note that **worldwide Space-A sign-up in person and at self-service counters remains available at Services terminals and stations which operate Space-A registers.** Times available for registration in person are based on local operating hours.

ONE-TIME SIGN-UP FOR SPACE-AVAILABLE PASSENGERS

Passengers traveling Space-A on military and contract charter aircraft **now can retain their initial date/time (Julian date) of sign-up when traveling through more than one destination/station (traveling in the same general direction, i.e., east to west, north to south) to reach their final destination.** The new procedure is the result of a recommendation made by the U.S. Air Force's Air Mobility Command (AMC) and approved by the Assistant Under Secretary of Defense.

In the past, travelers received a new sign-up date at each stop on their way to their final destination, which caused some to say that those stationed or living at or in the vicinity of the en route location had an unfair advantage. **Under the new rules, passengers still are required to sign up at all en route stops, but they keep their date and time of sign-up from their originating location.** For example a passenger who originates his/her travel at Incirlik AB (ADA), TR to Rhein-Main AB (FRF), DE, and plans to continue straight through to CONUS, will get priority over people starting their flights at Rhein-Main AB, DE.

The process is not automatic. Passengers must still sign up at all stops to continue their Space-A flights and retain their original sign-up date. However, passengers receive an "in transit" stamp on their travel order or boarding pass indicating date, time and location where they entered the system. This stamp identifies en route travelers to terminal personnel and gives the travelers priority on subsequent flights.

*Ed's Note: Message from HQ AMC Scott AFB, FL / / DOJP / /, R 51515Z Aug 96--paragraph 1-D "One-time Space-Available sign-up. We continue to receive inquiries on this subject. Apparently, some passenger terminals have procedures to honor other terminals' date / time of sign-up for passengers who do not arrive in-transit on DoD aircraft. This is a misapplication of the one-time sign-up rules. Unless arriving your station via DoD aircraft, passengers desiring Space-Available transportation must sign up with a new date / time of sign-up in person or use established remote means, i.e,. fax or e-mail. **We are exploring future implementation of a one-time/round-trip Space-A sign-up. We will be soliciting your input in the near future. Until then, all passenger terminals must consistently follow current guidance."***

There are restrictions. **Passengers traveling (hopping) by Space-A air through terminals/bases for extended visits will lose their transient status.** For example, if the above passenger gets to Rhein-Main, AB, DE and takes six days of leave/pass/vacation there, he/she will get a new date and time for his next Space-A flight.

Fly Space-A Air to Europe and then tour the Italian countryside by car. This is Camp Darby near Livorno, Italy.

APPENDIX C: Space-A Air Travel Remote Sign-up

The following is a list of Air Mobility Command Terminals/ Stations providing Space-A Travel and their fax numbers and e-mail addresses (where available) for Remote Space-A Travel sign-up. Telephone numbers are also provided for voice contact. Complete mail addresses for these stations are contained in *Military Space-A Air Opportunities Around the World*. **NOTE:** Fax numbers are constructed for dialing from the North American touch tone dial code system. Please pause where there are dashes located in number groups.

Terminal/Stations
LI/ICAO
Phone Number
Fax Number
E-mail

Al Dhafra Airfield, AE
DHF/OMAM
Tel: C-011-971-2-436-691
Fax: C-011-971-2-434-771

Al Fujayrah IAP, AE
FJR/OMFJ
Tel: C-011-971-9-165
Fax: C-011-971-9-229-045

Alexander Hamilton APT, VI
STX/TISX
Tel: C-340-778-2165
Fax: C-340-778-9261

Alice Springs APT, AU
ASP/YBAS
Tel: C-011-61-245-78-3309
Fax: C-011-61-245-88-5366

Andersen AFB, GU
UAM/PGUA
Tel: C-671-366-5165/5135
Fax: C-671-366-3984
E-mail:
spacea@andersen.af.mil

Andrews AFB, MD
ADW/KADW
Tel: C-301-981-1854/3526
Fax: C-301-981-4241
E-mail:
passenger@andrews.af.mil

Ascension Auxiliary Airfield, GB
ASI/FHAW
Tel: C-407-494-5631

Ataturk IAP(Istanbul), TR
IST/LTBA
Tel: C-011-90-212-663-0925/0917
Fax: C-011-90-212-663-0925

Atsugi NAF, JP
NJA/RJTA
Tel: C-011-81-3117-64-3118/3803
Fax: C-011-81-3117-64-3149

Augusto C. Sandino IAP (Managua), NI
MGA/MNMG
Tel: C-011-505-2-666-039
Fax: C-011-505-2-668-022

Aviano AB, IT
AVB/LIPA
Tel: C-011-39-0434-66-7680
Fax: C-011-39-0434-66-7782
E-mail: spacea@aviano.af.mil
or
spacea@nsanaples.navy.mil

Bahrain IAP, BH
BAH/OBBI
Tel: C-011-973-727-347/368
Fax: C-011-973-727-360
E-mail:
nielsenk@bahrain.navy.mil

Baltimore/Washington IAP, MD
BWI/KBWI
Tel: C-410-918-6900
Fax: C-410-918-6932
E-mail:
bwipax@mcguire.af.mil

Bangor IAP/ANGB, ME
BGR/KBGR
Tel: C-207-990-7018

Barking Sands Pacific Missile Range Facility, HI
BKH/PHBK
Tel: C-808-335-4310

Barksdale AFB, LA
BAD/KBAD
Tel: C-318-456-3226/5630/4978
Fax: C-318-456-2918

Ben Gurion IAP(Tel Aviv), IL
TLV/LLBG
Tel: C-011-972-3-971-2267
Fax: C-011-972-3-972-1989

Biggs AAF (Fort Bliss), TX
BIF/KBIF
Tel: C-915-568-8097

Birmingham IAP/ANG, AL
BHM/KBHM
Tel: C-205-714-2208
Fax: C-205-714-2610

Brasilia IAP, BR
BSB/SBBR
Tel: C-011-55-61-226-0172
Fax: C-011-55-61-322-4795

Brunswick NAS, ME
NHZ/KNHZ
Tel: C-207-921-2692/2682
Fax: C-207-921-2152

Bucholz AAF/KMR (Kwajalein Atoll), KA
KWA/PKWA
Tel: C-808-449-1515
Fax: C-808-448-1503

Bush Field APT (Fort Gordon), GA
AGS/KAGS
Tel: C-706-791-5811

Cairo IAP/Cairo East AB, EG
CAI/HECA
Tel:C-011-20-2-357-3212/2596
Fax: C-011-20-2-357-2273

Campbell AAF (Fort Campbell), KY
HOP/KHOP
Tel: C-270-798-7146
Fax: C-270-798-9288

Cannon AFB, NM
CVS/KCVS
Tel: C-505-784-2935/2801/2
Fax: C-505-784-4658

Capodichino APT (Naples), IT
NAP/LIRN
Tel: C-011-39-081-568-5283/5247
Fax: C-011-39-081-568-5259/5499
E-Mail:
spacea@naples.navy.mil

Carrasco IAP (Montevideo), UY
MVD/SUMU
Tel: C-011-598-2-408-77-77
Fax: C-011-598-2-408-8581

Charleston AFB, SC
CHS/KCHS
Tel: C-843-963-3083
Fax: C-843-963-3060
E-Mail:
spacea@charleston.af.mil

Charleston IAP, SC
CHS/KCHS
Tel: C-843-963-5794/5795
Fax: C-843-963-3845
E-Mail:
spacea@charleston.af.mil

Cherry Point MCAS, NC
NKT/KNKT
Tel: C-252-466-3232/2379
Fax: C-252-466-4518/6526

Cheyenne Municipal APT, WY
CYS/KCYS
Tel: C-307-772-6347, ext 71
Fax: C-307-772-6000
E-Mail:
chooper@wycys.ang.af.mil

Chievres AB, BE
CHE/EBCU
Tel: C-011-32-68-27-5411
Fax: C-011-32-68-27-5573

Christchurch IAP, NZ
CHC/NZCH
Tel: C-011-64-3-358-1455/7
Fax: C-011-64-3-358-1458

Corpus Christi NAS, TX
NGP/KNGP
Tel: C-361-961-2505
Fax: C-361-9613774

Cumaovasi Apt (Izmir), TR
ADB/LTBJ
Tel: C-011-90-232-484-5360 ext 3442
Fax: C-011-90-232-441-7044

Dakar Leopold S. Senghor APT, SN
DKR/GOOY
Tel: C-011-221-823-65-27/20 ext 2300/2301
Fax: C: 011-221-822-29-91

Davis-Monthan AFB, AZ
DMA/KDMA
Tel: C-520-228-3641
Fax: C-520-228-7229
E-Mail: spacea@dm.af.mil

Davison AAF (Fort Belvoir), VA
DAA/KDAA
Tel: C-703-806-7224/7682
Fax: C-703-806-7538

Don Muang APT, TH
BKK/VTBD
Tel: C-011-66-2-287-1036 ext 166 or ext 333
Fax: C-011-66-2-287-1036 ext 167

Dover AFB, DE
DOV/KDOV
Tel: C-302-677-4088
Fax: C-302-677-2953
E-Mail: spacea@dover.af.mil

Dyess AFB, TX
DYS/KDYS
Tel: C-915-696-4505
Fax: C-915-696-2943

Eareckson AS, AK
SYA/PASY
Tel: C-907-392-3401/3471/3064

Eastern West Virginia Regional APT, WV
MRB/KMRB
Tel: C-304-262 5110
Fax: C-304-262-5250

Eglin AFB, FL
VPS/KVPS
Tel: C-850-882-4757/2636
Fax: C-850-882-1461
E-Mail: gatesb@eglin.af.mil

Eielson AFB, AK
EIL/PAEI
Tel: C-907-377-1854/1250
Fax: C-907-377-2287

El Dorado IAP(Bogota), CO
BOG/SKBO
Tel: C-011-57-1-315-2125
Fax: C-011-57-1-315-2179

Elizabeth City CGAS, NC
ECG/KECG
Tel: C-252-335-6333

Ellsworth AFB, SD
RCA/KRCA
Tel: C-605-385-1181
Fax: C-605-385-1181

Elmendorf AFB, AK
EDF/PAED
Tel:C-907-552-3781/4616/8588
Fax: C-907-552-3996
E-Mail: spacea@elmendorf.af.mil

Esenboga APT, (Ankara), TR
ESB/LTAC
Tel:C-011-90-312-468-6110/6111/6112/6113 ext 2300
Fax:C-011-90-312-467-0148/1366

Ezeiza APT (Buenos Aires), AR
BUE/SAEZ
Tel: C-011-54-1-777-1207
Fax: C-011-54-1-777-0673

Fairchild AFB, WA
SKA/KSKA
Tel: C-509-247-5435
Fax: C-509-247-4909

Fallon NAS, NV
NFL/KNFL
Tel: C-775-426-3415
Fax: C-775-426-3482

Fort Worth NAS/JRB, TX
NFW/KNFW
Tel:C-817-782-6288

Fukuoka IAP/Itazuke AB, JP
FUK/RJFF
Tel: C-011-81-92-451-2558
Fax: C-011-81-611752-2421

General Mitchell IAP/ARS, WI
MKE/KMKE
Tel: C-414-944-8732

Grand Forks AFB, ND
RDR/KRDR
Tel: C-701-747-4409/10
Fax: C-701-747-3169

Grantley Adams IAP, BB
BGI/TBPB
Tel: C-011-246-436-4950
Fax: C-011-246-429-5246

Great Falls IAP/ANGB, MT
GTF/KGTF
Tel: C-406-453-7613
E-Mail:
quentin.larson@malmstrom.af.mil

Guantanamo Bay NAS, CU
NBW/MUGM
Tel: C-011-53-99-6204/6408
Fax: C-011-53-99-6170/6398

Halim Perdanakusuma AB, ID
HLP/WIIH
Tel: C-011-62-21-344-2211 ext 2621
Fax: C-011-62-21-386-2259

Hanscom AFB, MA
BED/KBED
Tel: C-781-377-1143/3333
Fax: C-781-377-2383

Hato APT, Curacao, AN
CUR/TNCC
Tel: C-011-599-9-461-3066
Fax: C-011-599-9-461-6489

Hickam AFB, HI
HIK/PHIK
Tel: C-808-449-1515
Fax: C-808-448-1503

Hill AFB, UT
HIF/KHIF
Tel: C-801-777-2887/3088
Fax: C-801-775-2677

Ilopango AB, SV
SAL/MSSS
Tel: C-011-503-295-0240
Fax: C-011-503-295-0240

Incirlik AB (Adana), TR
ADA/LTAG
Tel: C-011-90-322-316-6424/6425
Fax: C-011-90-322-316-3420
E-Mail:
spacea@incirlik.af.mil

Iwakuni MCAS, JP
IWA/RJOI
Tel: C-011-81-827-21-4171 ext 5509/3947
Fax: C-011-81-827-21-4171 ext 3301

Izmir AS, TR
IGL/LTBL
Tel: C-011-90-232-484-5360 ext 3442
Fax: C-011-90-232-441-7044
E-Mail:
425abs.lgta.@izmir.af.mil

J.F. Kennedy IAP (La Paz), BO
LPB/SLLP
Tel: C-011-591-2-432-253
Fax: C-011-591-2-433-900

Jackson IAP/Allen C. Thompson Field, MS
JAN/KJAN
Tel: C-601-936-8761
Fax: 601-936-8509

Jacksonville NAS, FL
NIP/KNIP
Tel: C-904-542-3956/3825
Fax: C-904-542-3257

Johan A. Pengel IAP (Paramibo), SR
PBM/SMJP
Tel: C-011-597-477-937
Fax: C-011-597-410-565

Johnston Atoll, JO
JON/PJON
Tel: C-808-621-3044 ext 2252
Fax: C-808-621-3044/2343

Jomo Kenyatta IAP (Nairobi), KE
NBO/HKNA
Tel: C-011-254-2-338218
Fax: C-011-254-2-230201

Jorge Chavez IAP (Lima), PE
LIM/SPIM
Tel: C-011-511-434-0199

Juan Santamaria IAP (Alajuela), CR
OCO/MROC
Tel: C-011-507-442-1121
Fax: C-011-507-255-1791
E-Mail:
ciscoamc@sol.racsa.co.cr

Kadena AB(Okinawa), JP
DNA/RODN
Tel: C-011-81-611-734-2159/4673
Fax: C-011-81-611-734-4221
E-Mail:
spacea@kadena.af.mil

Kaneohe Bay MCB, HI
NGF/PHNG
Tel: C-808-257-0777
E-Mail:
smbmcbhmcaf@exemh1.mcb
h.usmc.mil

Keesler AFB, MS
BIX/KBIX
Tel: C-228-377-4538/2120
Fax: C-228-377-2459

Keflavik APT, IS
KEF/BIKF
Tel: C-011-354-425-6139
Fax: C-011-354-425-4649
E-Mail: air.terminal@
naskef.navy.mil

Kelly AFB, TX
SKF/KSKF
Tel: C-210-925-8714/5
Fax: C-210-925-2732
E-Mail: spacea@kelly.af.mil

Key West NAS, FL
NGX/KNGX
Tel: C-305-293-2769
Fax: C-305-293-2126

Kimhae AB, KR
KHE/RKPK
Tel: C-011-82-51-801-3584

**King Abdullah AB
(Amman), JO**
AMM/OJAF
Tel: C-011-962-6-489-0972
Fax: C-011-962-6-489-0972
E-Mail: ajayme@san.osd.mil
or wrahhal@san.osd.mil

King Salmon APT, AK
AKN/PAKN
Tel: C-907-552-8744
Fax: C-907-552-3474

Kinshasa N'Djili APT, ZR
FIH/FZAA
Tel: C-011-243-12-
46929/21532/21628
Fax: C-011-243-12-43467

Kirtland AFB, NM
IKR/KIKR
Tel: C-505-
846-7000/7001/6184
Fax: C-505-846-6185

Kodiak CGAS, AK
ADQ/PADQ
Tel: C-907-487-5149
Fax: C-907-487-5273

**Kulis ANGB/Anchorage
IAP, AK**
ANC/PANC
Tel: C-907-249-1225
Fax: C-907-249-1477

Kunsan AB, KR
KUZ/RKJK
Tel: C-011-82-654-470-
4666/5403
Fax: C-011-82-654-470-7550
E-Mail:
spacea@kunsan.af.mil

Kuwait IAP, KW
KWI/OKBK
Tel: C-011-965-487-8822 ext
2447
Fax: C-011-965-434-0496

**La Aurora APT
(Guatemala City), GT**
GUA/MGGT
Tel: C-011-502-331-
7804/5747
Fax: C-011-502-339-
4301/332-2844

Lajes Field AB (Azores), PT
LGS/LPLA
Tel: C-011-351-2-95-540-
100 ext 23227/23582
Fax: C-011-351-2-95-540-100
ext 5110
E-Mail: spacea@lajes.af.mil

**Lawton/Fort Sill Regional
APT, OK**
LAW/KLAW
Tel: C-580-442-2815/2215

**Lincoln Municipal
APT/Nebraska ANGB, NE**
LNK/KLNK
Tel: C-402-458-1291
Fax: C-402-458-1272

Little Rock AFB, AR
LRF/KLRF
Tel: C-501-987-3342/3393
Fax: C-501-987-6726

Los Angeles IAP, CA
LAX/KLAX
Tel: C-310-
363-0714/0715/0716
Fax: C-310-363-2790
E-Mail:
spacealax@travis.af.mil

**Louisville IAP/Kentucky
ANGB, KY**
SDF/KSDF
Tel:C-502-364-4459
Fax: C-503-364-9605

Luke AFB, AZ
LUF/KLUF
Tel: C-623-856-7035/7131

March ARB, CA
RIV/KRIV
Tel: C-909-655-2397
Fax: C-909-655-3887
E-Mail:
452amw.apsf@riv.afrc.af.mil

**Mariscal Sucre APT
(Quito), EC**
UIO/SEQU
Tel: C-011-593-2503-822
Fax: C-011-593-2-561-344

**Marshall AAF/Manhattan
Municipal Apt, KS**
FRI/KFRI
Tel: C-785-239-7740
Fax: C-785-239-7405

Maxwell AFB, AL
MXF/KMXF
Tel: C-334-953-7372/6454
Fax: C-334-953-6114

McChord AFB, WA
TCM/KTCM
Tel: C-253-512-4260/4259
Fax: C-253-512-3815
E-Mail:
eagle@mcchord.af.mil

McConnell AFB, KS
IAB/KIAB
Tel: C-316-759-3701/3840
Fax: C-316-759-4957

MacDill AFB,FL
MCF/KMCF
Tel: C-813-828-2485
Fax: C-813-828-7844
E-Mail:
spacea@macdill.af.mil

McGhee Tyson ANGB, TN
TYS/KTYS
Tel: C-865-985-4404/4419
Fax: C-865-985-4397

McGuire AFB, NJ
WRI/KWRI
Tel: C-609-724-3070
Fax: C-609-724-4621
E-Mail:
wripax@mcguire.af.mil

Memphis IAP/ANGB, TN
MEM/KMEM
Tel: C-901-541-7221
Fax: C-901-541-7230

**Minneapolis St.Paul
IAP/ARS, MN**
MSP/KMSP
Tel: C-612-713-1701

Minot AFB, ND
MIB/KMIB
Tel: C-701-
723-1854/2347/2348
Fax: C-701-723-3637

Miramar MCAS, CA
NKX/KNKX
Tel: C-858-577-4277/9/4285
Fax: C-858-577-4261/1721

Misawa AB, JP
MSJ/RJSM
Tel: C-011-81-3117-66-
2370/71 Fax: C-011-81-3117-
66-4455

Moron AB, ES
OZP/LEMO
Tel: C-011-34-955-84-8111
Fax: C-011-34-955-84-8008

Mountain Home AFB, ID
MUO/KMOU
Tel: C-208-828-4747
Fax: C-208-828-4128

N'Djamena IAP, TD
NDJ/FTTJ
Tel: C-011-235-51-7009/6211
Fax: C-011-235-51-56-64

**New Orleans NAS/JRB,
LA**
NBG/KNBG
Tel: C-504-678-3213
Fax: C-504-678-3156

Niagara Falls IAP/ARS, NY
IAG/KIAG
Tel: C-716-236-2475
Fax: C-716-236-2380
E-Mail:
kurt.novak@iag.afres.af.mil

Niamey IAP, NE
NIM/DRRN
Tel: C-011-227-72-26-
61/62/63/64, ext 262 or 245
Fax: C-011-227-73-31-67

Norfolk NAS, VA
NGU/KNGU
Tel: C-757-
444-4118/4148/3947
Fax: C-757-445-7501

Norman Manley IAP (Kingston), JM
KIN/MKJP
Tel: C-011-809-929-4850
Fax: C-011-809-926-6743

OAFB Thumrait, OM
TTH/OOTH
Tel: C-011-968-698-989
Fax: C-011-968-699-779

Oceana NAS, VA
NTU/KNTU
Tel: C-757-433-2903
Fax:C-757-433-2711

Offutt AFB, NE
OFF/KOFF
Tel: C-402-294-7111/8510
Fax:C-402-294-4070

Olbia/Costa Smeralda APT (Sardinia), IT
OLB/LIEO
Tel: C-011-39-0789-69516
Fax: C-011-39-0789-68874

Osan AB, KR
OSN/RKSO
Tel: C-011-82-333-661-1854
Fax: C-011-82-333-661-4897
E-Mail: spacea@osan.af.mil

Pago Pago IAP, AS
PPG/NTSU
Tel: C-011-684-699-1515
Fax: C-011-684-699-1515

Patrick AFB, FL
COF/KCOF
Tel: C-407-494-5631
Fax: C-407-494-7991

Peterson AFB, CO
COS/KCOS
Tel: C-719-556-4521/4707
Fax: C-719-556-4979

Phillip S.W. Goldson IAP (Belize City), BZ
BZE/MZBZ
Tel: C-011-501-25-2454
Fax: C-011-501-25-2453
E-Mail: usmlo@btl.net

Piarco IAP (Port Of Spain), TT
POS/TTPP
Tel: C-809-622-6372/6, 6176
Fax: C-809-628-5462

Pittsburgh IAP/ARS, PA
PIT/KPIT
Tel: C-412-474-8163
Fax: C-412-474-8156

Prince Sultan AB (Al Kharj), SA
EKJ/OEKJ
Tel: C-011-966-1-488-3800 ext 1275
Fax: C-011-966-1-488-7809

Point Mugu NAS, CA
NTD/KNTD
Tel: C-805-989-7731/7305
Fax: C-805-989-4085

Polk AAF, LA
POE/KPOE
Tel: C-318-531-4831/7328
Fax: C-318-531-4633

Pope AFB, NC
POB/KPOB
Tel: C-910-394-6527/8
Fax: C-910-394-6526
E-Mail:
3aps.spacea@pope.af.mil

Port-Au-Prince IAP, HT
PAP/MTPP
Tel: C-011-509-23-9697
Fax: C-011-509-23-1641

Pudahel APT/Arturo Merino Benitez IAP (Santiago), CL
SCL/SCEL
Tel: C-011-56-2-522-5000
Fax: C-011-56-2-522-5000

Quonset Point State Apt, RI
OQU/KOQU
Tel: C-401-886-1420
Fax: C-401-886-1412

RAAFB Richmond, AU
RCM/YSRI
Tel: C-011-61-245-87-1651/2
Fax: C-011-61-245-87-1663
E-Mail:
space@teamrichmond.org

RAF Mildenhall, GB
MHZ/EGUN
Tel: C-011-44-1-638-54-2248/2526
Fax: C-011-44-1-638-54-2250
E-Mail: sa@mildenhall.af.mil
or
spacea@mildenhall.af.mil

RAFB Akrotiri, CY
AKT/LCRA
Tel: C-011-357-2-476100 ext 2536/2537
Fax: C-011-357-2-477833

Ramstein AB, DE
RMS/ETAR
Tel: C-011-49-6371-47-2433/5364/2120
Fax: C-011-49-6371-47-2364
E-Mail:
spacea@amc.ramstein.af.mil

Rhein-Main AB, DE
FRF/EDAF
Tel: C-011-49-69-699-6567/8
Fax: C-011-49-69-699-6309
E-Mail:
spacea@rheinmain.af.mil

Rickenbacker IAP/ANGB, OH
LCK/KLCK
Tel: C-614-492-4595
Fax: C-614-492-3580

Rio De Janeiro IAP, BR
RIO/SBGL
Tel: C-011-55-21-220-8880
Fax: C-011-55-21-262-7844

Robert Gray AAF, TX
GRK/KGRK
Tel: C-254-288-1432
Fax: C-254-288-1930

Roosevelt Roads NS, PR
NRR/TJNR
Tel: C-787-865-4374/3296
Fax: C-787-865-3257/4208

Rota NS, ES
RTA/LERT
Tel: C-011-34-956-82-2411
Fax: C-011-34-956-82-1734/2968
E-Mail:
spacea@exchange.rota.af.mil
or
spacea@navsta.rota.navy.mil

RSAF Paya Lebar, SG
QPG/WSAP
Tel: C-011-65-381-3653
Fax: C-011-65-382-3614

Sacramento CGAS, CA
MCC/KMCC
Tel: C-916-643-2081

Salt Lake City IAP, UT
SLC/KSLC
Tel: C-801-595-2274
Fax: C-801-595-2271

Sangster IAP, Montego Bay, JM
KJS/MKJS
Tel: C-011-809-935-6021
Fax: C-011-809-935-6020

San Isidro AB, DO
SDQ/MDSI
Tel: C-809-682-4835/1953
Fax: C-809-682-3991

Scott AFB, IL
BLV/KBLV
Tel: C-618-256-2014/3017/4042
Fax: C-618-256-1946
E-Mail:
paxterminal@scott.af.mil

Seattle/Tacoma IAP, WA
SEA/KSEA
Tel: C-1-877-863-1463
Fax: C-253-512-5557
E-Mail:
eagle@mcchord.af.mil

Selfridge ANGB, MI
MTC/KMTC
Tel: C-810-307-5322

Seymour Johnson AFB, NC
GSB/KGSB
Tel: C-919-722-4170
Fax: C-919-722-4162

Shaw AFB, SC
SSC/KSSC
Tel: C-803-895-1741/1738
Fax: C-803-668-4156

Sherman AAF (Fort Leavenworth), KS
FLV/KFLV
Tel: C-913-684-2396
Fax: C-913-684-5241

Sigonella NAS/APT, (Sicily), IT
SIZ/LICZ
Tel: C-011-39-095-86-6725/6726/5576
Fax: C-011-39-095-86-5211/6729

Silvio Pettirossi IAP (Asuncion), PY
ASU/SGAS
Tel: C-011-595-21-645-457
Fax: C-011-595-21-645-815
E-Mail:
andresc@highway.com.py

Simon Bolivar IAP (Caracas), VE
MIQ/SVMI
Tel: C-011-58-2-977-0103
Fax:C-011-58-2-977-2908

Sitka CGAS, AK
SIT/PADQ
Tel: C-907-966-5580
Fax: C-907-966-5428

Sky Harbor IAP/Phoenix ANGB, AZ
PHX/KPHX
Tel: C-602-302-9162
Fax: C-602-302-9288

Soto Cano AB, HN
PLA/MHSC
Tel: C-011-504-237-88-33 ext 4148
Fax: C-011-504-237-88-33 ext 4887

Souda Bay NSA (Crete), GR
CHQ/LGSA
Tel: C-011-30-821-66200 ext 1275/1383
Fax: C-011-30-821-66200 ext 1525

Stewart IAP/ANGB, NY
SWF/KSWF
Tel: C-914-563-2965
Fax:C-914-563-2228

Theodore Francis Green State APT (Newport), RI
PVD/KPVD
Tel: C-401-841-3409

Thule AB (Greenland), DK
THU/BGTL
Tel:C-011-299-50-636 ext 2711
Fax: C-011-299-50-636 ext 2314

Tinker AFB, OK
TIK/KTIK
Tel: C-405-739-4339
Fax: C-405-739-3826
E-Mail:
rebecca.davidson@tinker.af.mil

Toncontin IAP (Tegucigalpa), HN
TGU/MHTG
Tel: C-011-504-33-4618

Travis AFB, CA
SUU/KSUU
Tel: C-707-424-5703/3161
Fax: C-707-424-4021
E-Mail:
60aps.sa@travis.af.mil

V.C. Bird IAP(St. John's), AG
SJH/TAPA
Tel: C-268-462-0368/3223
Fax: C-268-461-4884

Viru Viru IAP (Santa Cruz), BO
VVI/SLVR
Tel: C-011-591-2-430251
Fax: C-011-591-2-433900

Wake Island AAF, WK
AWK/PWAK
Tel: C-808-424-2210
Fax: C-808-424-2190

Washington NAF (Andrews AFB), MD
NSF/KNSF
Tel: C-240-857-2740/2744

Waterkloof AB, ZA
LMB/FAWK
Tel: C-011-27-12-342-1048
Fax: C-011-27-12-342-2244

Waynesville Regional APT at Forney AAF, MO
TBN/KTBN
Tel: C-573-596-0165
Fax: C-573-596-0166

Westover ARB, MA
CEF/KCEF
Tel: C-413-557-2622
Fax: C-413-557-3147
E-Mail:
derek.quimette@cef.afres.af.mil

Wheeler-Sack AAF (Fort Drum), NY
GTB/KGTB
Tel: C-315-772-5681

Whidbey Island NAS, WA
NUW/KNUW
Tel: C-360-257-2604
Fax: C-360-257-1942
E-Mail: web-airterm@naswi.navy.mil

Whiteman AFB, MO
SZL/KSZL
Tel: C-660-687-3101
Fax: C-660-687-6106

William B. Hartsfield
Atlanta IAP, GA
ATL/KATL
Tel: C-843-963-5794/5795
Fax: C-843-963-3845
E-Mail:
spacea@charleston.af.mil

Willow Grove NAS/JRB, PA
NXX/KNXX
Tel: C-215-443-6215/6/7
Fax: C-215-443-6188

Wright-Patterson AFB, OH
FFO/KFFO
Tel: C-937-257-7741
Fax: C-937-656-1580
E-Mail: spacea@wpafb.af.mil

Yaounde/Nsimalen IAP, CM
NSI/FKYS
Tel: C-011-237-23-45-52
Fax: C-011-237-23-07-53

Yokota AB, JP
OKO/RJTY
Tel: C-011-81-3117-55-9540/5661
Fax: C-011-81-3117-55-9768
E-Mail:
space.available@yokota.af.mil

APPENDIX D: Space Available Travel Request
(AMC Form 140)

SPACE AVAILABLE TRAVEL REQUEST *(This form is affected by the Privacy Act of 1974-See below)*	*INSERT HERE*

This information is required for space available travel registration. Upon completion, place the upper right corner of this form, and the back of your leave form into the Date/Time validator. Be sure to deposit one copy of this request into the box; retain carbon copy for the Space Available roll call. Space A sign-up is good for a 60-day period, or when your leave expires, whichever comes first. For facsimile (fax) requests, telefax header will establish date/time of sign-up.

PLEASE PRINT CLEARLY

1. NAME *(Last, First, MI)*

2. RANK/GRADE	3. SSN	4. SEATS REQUIRED

5. TRAVEL STATUS *(Type of Leave)*	FOR OVERSEAS TRAVEL:
CATEGORY I -- Civ or Mil Dependent on Emergency Leave	Border Clearance Documents Current?
CATEGORY II -- Environmental Morale Leave (EML)	
CATEGORY III -- Active Duty on Ordinary Leave / House Hunting	YES ☐ ☐ NO
CATEGORY IV -- (EML) Unaccompanied Dependents	
CATEGORY V -- Permissive TDY or TAD / Student Travel	*(See Appendix O)*
CATEGORY VI -- Retired Military / Reserves	

6. SERVICE:	ARMY	NAVY	AF	MARINES	OTHER

7. DATE LEAVE BEGINS *(Active Duty Only)*	8. DATE LEAVE ENDS *(if extended, you must notify us before this date)*

9. COUNTRY CHOICES *(List up to 5; one choice may be all)*

10. LIST NAMES OF DEPENDENTS TRAVELING AND TYPE OF PASSPORT *(US or Foreign)*

11. I CERTIFY THAT I AM ON LEAVE OR PASS STATUS AT THE TIME I REGISTER FOR SPACE AVAILABLE TRAVEL AND WILL REMAIN IN SUCH STATUS WHEN AWAITING AND/OR HAVE BEEN ACCEPTED FOR SPACE AVAILABLE TRAVEL. IF ACCOMPANIED BY DEPENDENTS, I FURTHER CERTIFY THAT MY TRAVEL IS NOT IN CONJUNCTION WITH TDY/TAD AND THAT I AM NOT USING SPACE AVAILABLE TRAVEL TO TRANSPORT MY DEPENDENTS TO OR FROM MY RESTRICTED DUTY STATION OF ALL OTHERS (UNACCOMPANIED) TOUR LOCATION STATION. I CERTIFY THAT MY REQUEST FOR, AND ACCEPTANCE OF, TRANSPORTATION VIA DOD-OWNED OR CONTROLLED AIRCRAFT IS NOT FOR PERSONAL GAIN, NOR FOR, OR IN CONNECTION WITH BUSINESS OF ANY NATURE AND THAT THIS TRIP WILL NOT RESULT IN ANY FORM OF RENUMERATION TO MYSELF OR TO MY FAMILY. I UNDERSTAND VIOLATION OF ANY OF THE ABOVE COULD RESULT IN BILLING AND/OR PUNITIVE ACTION.

12. DATE	13. SIGNATURE

PRIVACY ACT STATEMENT
AUTHORITY: 10 U.S.C. 8013; EO 9397, 22 November 1943.
PRINCIPAL PURPOSE: To apply for air travel. SSN is needed for positive ID.
ROUTINE USE(S): Records from this system of records may be disclosed for any of the blanket routine uses published by the Air Force.
DISCLOSURE IS VOLUNTARY: Failure to proved the information may result in member not being accepted for travel on military aircraft. Disclosure of SSN is voluntary.

AMC FORM 140, FEB 95 *(EF) (PerFORM PRO)*   AMC COPY

**Note: This image is approximately 60% actual size.
Enlarge and copy at 140%.**

APPENDIX E: International Civil Aviation Organization (ICAO) Location Identifiers and Federal Aviation Administration (FAA) Location Identifiers (LI) Conversion Tables

The location identifiers (LI) used in this book are the Federal Aviation Administration coordinated three letter LIs for the United States, its possessions and Canada. Foreign country LIs have been coordinated by the Department of Defense. An LI represents the name/location of an airport/air base. They are considered permanent (changes are made for air safety only) and cannot be transferred. The original LI remains in effect even if it becomes necessary to change the name of a given facility.

The International Civil Aviation Organization (ICAO) has established an international location indicator which is a four letter code used in international telecommunications. If the ICAO is shown on the departure board or other displays, look under the **encode** for the ICAO listed alphabetically to find the three letter Location Identifier (LI), the local standard time (LST) and the clear text name and location of the airport. If the LI is shown on the departure board or other display, look under the **decode** for the LI listed alphabetically to find the four letter ICAO, LST and the clear text name and location of the airport.

The ICAO/LIs listed below are primarily used to identify military stations/locations around the world. Some of the stations listed may not be active at all times, and all worldwide stations may not be listed. Local standard time (LST) gives the difference in LST from Greenwich Mean Time (GMT).

ENCODE (ICAO vs LI)

ICAO	LI	LST	STATION
BGTL	THU	-04:00	Thule AB (Greenland), DK
BIKF	KEF	+00:00	Keflavik Apt, IS
CYQX	YQX	-03:30	Gander IAP (Newfoundland), CA
CYYR	YYR	-04:00	Goose Bay AB (Newfoundland), CA
CYYT	YYT	-03:30	St. John's Apt, (Newfoundland), CA
DRRN	NIM	+01:00	Niamey IAP, NE
EBCU	CHE	+01:00	Chievres AB, BE
EDAF	FRF	+01:00	Rhein-Main AB, DE
EDAS	SEX	+01:00	Sembach Annex (Ramstein AB), DE
EDDS	STR	+01:00	Stuttgart AAF, DE
EGUL	LKZ	+00:00	RAF Lakenheath, GB
EGUN	MH	+00:00	RAF Mildenhall, GB
EINN	SNN	+00:00	Shannon Apt, IE
ETAD	SPM	+01:00	Spangdahlem AB, DE
ETAR	RMS	+01:00	Ramstein AB, DE

FAWK	LMB	+01:00	Waterkloof AB, ZA
FHAW	ASI	+00:00	Ascension Auxiliary Airfield, GB
FJDG	NKW	+06:00	Diego Garcia Atoll (Chagos Archipelago), GB
FKYS	NSI	+00:00	Yaounde/Nsimalen IAP, CM
FTTJ	NDJ	+01:00	N'Djamena IAP, TD
FZAA	FIH	+01:00	Kinshasa N'Djili Apt, ZR
GOOY	DKR	+01:00	Dakar Leopold S. Senghor Apt, SN
HECA	CAI	+02:00	Cairo IAP, Cairo East AB, EG
HECW	CIR	+02:00	Cairo West IAP, EG
HKNA	NBO	+03:00	Jomo Kenyatta IAP, KE
KADW	ADW	-05:00	Andrews AFB, MD
KAEX	AEX	-06:00	Alexandria IAP, LA
KAGS	AGS	-05:00	Bush Field Apt, GA
KAPN	APN	-05:00	Alpena Combat Readiness Training Center/Alpena County Regional Apt, MI
KATL	ATL	-05:00	William B. Hartsfield Atlanta IAP, GA
KBAB	BAB	-08:00	Beale AFB, CA
KBAD	BAD	-06:00	Barksdale AFB, LA
KBED	BED	-05:00	Hanscom AFB, MA
KBGR	BGR	-05:00	Bangor IAP/ANGB, ME
KBHM	BHM	-05:00	Birmingham IAP/ANG, AL
KBIF	BIF	-06:00	Biggs AAF, TX
KBIX	BIX	-06:00	Keesler AFB, MS
KBKF	BKF	-07:00	Buckley ANGB, CO
KBKT	BKT	-05:00	Blackstone AAF, VA
KBLV	BLV	-06:00	Scott AFB, IL
KBNA	BNA	-06:00	Nashville IAP/Tennessee ANGB, TN
KBOI	BOI	-07:00	Boise Air Terminal/Gowen Field Apt, ID
KBWI	BWI	-05:00	Baltimore/Washington IAP, MD
KBYS	BYS	-08:00	Bicycle Lake AAF, CA
KCBM	CBM	-06:00	Columbus AFB, MS
KCEF	CEF	-05:00	Westover ARB, MA
KCHS	CHS	-05:00	Charleston AFB/IAP, SC
KCLT	CLT	-05:00	Charlotte/Douglas IAP, NC
KCMY	CMY	-06:00	Fort McCoy Aviation Support Facility, WI
KCOF	COF	-05:00	Patrick AFB, FL
KCOS	COS	-07:00	Peterson AFB, CO
KCRW	CRW	-05:00	Yeager Apt, WV
KCUB	CUB	-05:00	Columbia Owens Downtown Apt, SC
KCVS	CVS	-07:00	Cannon AFB, NM
KCYS	CYS	-07:00	Cheyenne Municipal Apt, WY
KDAA	DAA	-05:00	Davison AAF, VA
KDLF	DLF	-06:00	Laughlin AFB, TX
KDMA	DMA	-07:00	Davis-Monthan AFB, AZ
KDOV	DOV	-05:00	Dover AFB, DE
KDPG	DPG	-07:00	Michael AAF, UT
KDYS	DYS	-06:00	Dyess AFB, TX

KECG	ECG	-05:00	Elizabeth City CGAS, NC
KEFD	EFD	-06:00	Texas ANG/Ellington Field, TX
KEND	END	-06:00	Vance AFB, OK
KFAF	FAF	-05:00	Felker AAF, VA
KFBG	FBG	-05:00	Simmons AAF, NC
KFCS	FCS	-07:00	Butts AAF, CO
KFEW	FEW	-07:00	F.E. Warren AFB, WY
KFFO	FFO	-05:00	Wright-Patterson AFB, OH
KFHU	FHU	-07:00	Libby AAF, AZ
KFLV	FLV	-06:00	Sherman AAF, KS
KFMH	FMH	-05:00	Otis ANGB, MA
KFOE	FOE	-06:00	Forbes Field IAP/ANGB, KS
KFOK	FOK	-05:00	Francis S. Gabreski IAP/ANG, NY
KFRI	FRI	-06:00	Marshall AAF, KS
KFSI	FSI	-06:00	Henry Post AAF, OK
KFTK	FTK	-06:00	Godman AAF, KY
KFTY	FTY	-05:00	Atlanta Regional Flight Center/Fulton County Apt , GA
KGRF	GRF	-08:00	Gray AAF, WA
KGRK	GRK	-06:00	Robert Gray AAF, TX
KGSB	GSB	-05:00	Seymour Johnson AFB, NC
KGTB	GTB	-05:00	Wheeler-Sack Army Airfield (Fort Drum), NY
KGTF	GTF	-06:00	Great Falls IAP/Montana ANGB, MT
KGUS	GUS	-05:00	Grissom ARB, IN
KHGT	HGT	-08:00	Fort Hunter Liggett, CA
KHIF	HIF	-07:00	Hill AFB, UT
KHMN	HMN	-07:00	Holloman AFB, NM
KHOP	HOP	-06:00	Campbell AAF, KY
KHRT	HRT	-05:00	Hurlburt Field, FL
KHST	HST	-05:00	Homestead ARS, FL
KHUA	HUA	-06:00	Redstone Arsenal AAF, AL
KIAB	IAB	-06:00	McConnell AFB, KS
KIAG	IAG	-05:00	Niagara Falls IAP, NY
KIKR	IKR	-07:00	Kirtland AFB, NM
KILG	ILG	-05:00	New Castle County Apt, DE
KJAN	JAN	-06:00	Jackson IAP/Allen C. Thompson Field, MS
KLAW	LAW	-06:00	Lawton/Fort Sill Regional Apt, OK
KLAX	LAX	-08:00	Los Angeles IAP, CA
KLCK	LCK	-05:00	Rickenbacker ANGB, OH
KLFI	LFI	-05:00	Langley AFB, VA
KLHW	LHW	-05:00	Wright AAF, GA
KLMT	LMT	-08:00	Kingsley Field, OR
KLNK	LNK	-06:00	Lincoln Municipal Apt/Nebraska ANGB, NE
KLRF	LRF	-06:00	Little Rock AFB, AR
KLSF	LSF	-05:00	Lawson Army Airfield (Fort Benning), GA
KLSV	LSV	-08:00	Nellis AFB, NV
KLTS	LTS	-06:00	Altus AFB, OK
KLUF	LUF	-07:00	Luke AFB, AZ
KMCC	MCC	-08:00	Sacramento Coast Guard Air Station, CA
KMCF	MCF	-05:00	MacDill AFB, FL

KMCI	MCI	-06:00	Kansas City IAP, KS
KMEI	MEI	-06:00	Key Field Apt, MS
KMEM	MEM	-06:00	Memphis IAP/ANGB, TN
KMFD	MFD	-05:00	Mansfield Lahm Apt, OH
KMGE	MGE	-05:00	Dobbins ARB, GA
KMHK	MHK	-06:00	Marshall AAF/Manhattan Municipal Apt, KS
KMIB	MIB	-07:00	Minot AFB, ND
KMKE	GMF	-06:00	General Mitchell IAP/ARS, WI
KMMT	MMT	-05:00	McEntire ANG Station, SC
KMOB	MOB	-06:00	Mobile CG Aviation Training Center, AL
KMRB	MRB	-05:00	Eastern West Virginia Regional Apt, WV
KMSP	MSP	-06:00	Minneapolis-St. Paul IAP/ARS, MN
KMTC	MTC	-05:00	Selfridge ANGB, MI
KMTN	MTN	-05:00	Martin State Apt, MD
KMUI	MUI	-05:00	Muir AAF, PA
KMUO	MUO	-07:00	Mountain Home AFB, ID
KMXF	MXF	-06:00	Maxwell AFB, AL
KNBC	NBC	-05:00	Beaufort MCAS, SC
KNBG	NBG	-06:00	New Orleans NAS/JRB, LA
KNCA	NCA	-05:00	New River MCAS, NC
KNCQ	NCQ	-05:00	Atlanta NAS, GA
KNEL	NEL	-05:00	Lakehurst NAWC, NJ
KNFL	NFL	-08:00	Fallon NAS, NV
KNFW	NFW	-06:00	Fort Worth NAS/JRB, TX
KNGP	NGP	-06:00	Corpus Christi NAS, TX
KNGU	NGU	-05:00	Norfolk NAS, VA
KNHK	NHK	-05:00	Patuxent River NAWC, MD
KNHZ	NHZ	-05:00	Brunswick NAS, ME
KNID	NID	-08:00	China Lake NWC, CA
KNIP	NIP	-05:00	Jacksonville NAS, FL
KNJK	NJK	-08:00	El Centro NAF, CA
KNKT	NKT	-05:00	Cherry Point MCAS, NC
KNKX	NKX	-08:00	Miramar MCAS, CA
KNLC	NLC	-08:00	Lemoore NAS, CA
KNMM	NMM	-06:00	Meridian NAS, MS
KNOM	NOM	-05:00	Miami CGAS, Opa Locka Apt, FL
KNPA	NPA	-05:00	Pensacola NAS, FL
KNQA	NQA	-06:00	Millington Municipal Apt/Mid-South NSA, TN
KNQI	NQI	-06:00	Kingsville NAS, TX
KNQX	NQX	-05:00	Key West NAS, FL
KNRB	NRB	-05:00	Mayport NS, FL
KNSF	NSF	-05:00	Washington NAF, DC
KNTD	NTD	-08:00	Point Mugu NAS, CA
KNTU	NTU	-05:00	Oceana NAS, VA
KNUW	NUW	-08:00	Whidbey Island NAS, WA
KNXX	NXX	-05:00	Willow Grove NAS/JRB, PA
KNYG	NYG	-05:00	Quantico MCB, VA
KNYZ	YUM	-07:00	Yuma MCAS, AZ
KNZY	NZY	-08:00	North Island NAS, CA
KOFF	OFF	-06:00	Offutt AFB, NE
KOKC	OKC	-06:00	Will Rogers World Apt/ANGB, OK

KOQU	OQU	-05:00	Quonset State Apt, RI
KOZR	OZR	-06:00	Cairns AAF, AL
KPAM	PAM	-05:00	Tyndall AFB, FL
KPDX	PDX	-08:00	Portland IAP/ANGB, OR
KPHX	PHX	-07:00	Sky Harbor IAP, AZ
KPIA	PIA	-06:00	Greater Peoria Regional Apt, IL
KPIE	PIE	-05:00	Clearwater CGAS, FL
KPIT	PIT	-05:00	Pittsburgh IAP/ARS, PA
KPOB	POB	-05:00	Pope AFB, NC
KPOE	POE	-06:00	Polk AAF, LA
KPSM	PSM	-05:00	Pease ANGB, NH
KPVD	PVD	-05:00	Theodore Francis Green State Apt, RI
KRCA	RCA	-07:00	Ellsworth AFB, SD
KRDR	RDR	-06:00	Grand Forks AFB, ND
KRIV	RIV	-08:00	March ARB, CA
KRND	RND	-06:00	Randolph AFB, TX
KRNO	RNO	-08:00	Reno/Tahoe IAP, NV
KSAN	SAN	-08:00	San Diego CGAS, CA
KSAV	SAV	-05:00	Savannah IAP, GA
KSCH	SCH	-05:00	Stratton ANGB, NY
KSDF	SDF	-05:00	Louisville IAP/Kentucky ANGB, KY
KSEA	SEA	-08:00	Seattle/Tacoma IAP, WA
KSKA	SKA	-08:00	Fairchild AFB, WA
KSKF	SKF	-06:00	Kelly AFB, TX
KSLC	SLC	-07:00	Salt Lake City IAP, UT
KSLI	SLI	-08:00	Los Alamitos AAF, CA
KSPS	SPS	-06:00	Sheppard AFB, TX
KSSC	SSC	-05:00	Shaw AFB, SC
KSTJ	STJ	-06:00	Rosecrans Memorial Apt, MO
KSUU	SUU	-08:00	Travis AFB, CA
KSVN	SVN	-05:00	Hunter AAF, GA
KSWF	SWF	-05:00	Stewart IAP/ANGB, NY
KSYR	SYR	-05:00	Syracuse-Hancock Field IAP, NY
KSZL	SZL	-06:00	Whiteman AFB, MO
KTBN	TBN	-06:00	Forney AAF, MO
KTCM	TCM	-08:00	McChord AFB, WA
KTIK	TIK	-06:00	Tinker AFB, OK
KTYS	TYS	-05:00	McGhee Tyson ANGB, TN.
KUBG	VBG	-08:00	Vandenberg AFB, CA
KVAD	VAD	-05:00	Moody AFB, GA
KVKS	VKS	-06:00	Vicksburg Municipal Apt, MS
KVOK	VOK	-06:00	Volk Field ANGB, WI
KVPS	VPS	-05:00	Eglin AFB, FL
KWRB	WRB	-05:00	Robins AFB, GA
KWRI	WRI	-05:00	McGuire AFB, NJ
KWSD	WSD	-07:00	Condron AAF, NM
KYNG	YNG	-05:00	Youngstown/Warren Regional Apt/ARS, OH
LCRA	AKT	+02:00	RAFB Akrotiri, CY
LEMO	OZP	+00:00	Moron AB, ES
LERT	RTA	+00:00	Rota NS, ES
LGRX	GPA	+02:00	GAFB Araxos, GR
LGSA	CHQ	+02:00	Souda Bay NSA (Crete), GR

LICZ	SIZ	+01:00	Sigonella NAS/Apt (Sicily), IT
LIEO	OLB	+01:00	Olbia/Costa Smeralda Apt, IT
LIPA	AVB	+01:00	Aviano AB, IT
LIRN	NAP	+01:00	Capodichino Apt (Naples), IT
LLBG	TLV	+02:00	Ben Gurion IAP (Tel Aviv), IL
LPLA	LGS	+00:00	Lajes Field AB (Azores), PT
LPPT	LIS	-01:00	Lisbon IAP, PT
LTAC	ESB	+02:00	Esenboga Apt (Ankara), TR
LTAG	ADA	+02:00	Incirlik AB (Adana), TR
LTBA	IST	+02:00	Ataturk IAP (Istanbul), TR
LTBJ	ADB	+02:00	Cumaovasi APT (Izmir), TR
LTBL	IGL	+02:00	Izmir AS, TR
LWSK	SKP	+01:00	Skopje Apt, MK
MDSI	SDQ	-04:00	San Isidro AB, DO
MGGT	GUA	-06:00	La Aurora Apt, GT
MHSC	PLA	-06:00	Soto Cano AB, HN
MHTG	TGU	-06:00	Toncontin IAP, HN
MKJP	KIN	-05:00	Norman Manley IAP, JM
MKJS	KJS	-05:00	Sangster IAP, Montego Bay, JM
MNMG	MGA	-06:00	Augusto C. Sandino IAP, NI
MPTO	PTY	-05:00	Tocumen IAP, PA
MROC	OCO	-06:00	Juan Santamaria IAP, CR
MSSS	SAL	-06:00	Ilopango AB, SV
MTPP	PAP	-05:00	Port Au Prince IAP, HT
MWCR	WCR	-05:00	Owen Roberts IAP, Cayman Islands (GB)
MUGM	NBW	-05:00	Guantanamo Bay NAS, CU
MZBZ	BZE	-06:00	Phillip S.W. Goldson IAP, BZ
NFFN	NAN	+12:00	Nandi IAP, FJ
NTSU	PPG	-11:00	Pago Pago IAP, AS
KNYG	KNYG	-05:00	Quantico MCB, VA
NZCH	CHC	+12:00	Christchurch IAP, NZ
OBBI	BAH	+03:00	Bahrain IAP, BH
OEKH	EKJ	+03:00	Prince Sultan AB (Al Kharj), SA
OJAF	AMM	+02:00	King Abdullah AB, JO
OKBK	KWI	+03:00	Kuwait IAP, KW
OMAM	DHF	+00:00	Ad Dafrah Airfield, AE
OMFJ	FJR	+04:00	Al Fujayrah IAP, AE
OOTH	TTH	+04:00	OAFB Thumrait, OM
PABI	BIG	-09:00	Allen AAF, AK
PACL	CLF	-09:00	Clear AS, AK
PADQ	SIT	-09:00	Sitka CGAS, AK
PADQ	ADQ	-10:00	Kodiak CGAS, AK
PAED	EDF	-09:00	Elmendorf AFB, AK
PAEI	EIL	-09:00	Eielson AFB, AK
PAFB	FBK	-09:00	Wainwright AAF/Fort Wainwright, AK
PAKN	AKN	-09:00	King Salmon Apt, AK
PANC	ANC	-09:00	Kulis ANGB/Anchorage IAP, AK
PASY	SYA	-10:00	Eareckson AS, AK
PGSN	SPN	+10:00	Saipan IAP, MP

PGUA	UAM	+10:00	Andersen AFB, GU
PHBK	BKH	-10:00	Barking Sands Pacific Missile Range Facility, HI
PHHI	HHI	-10:00	Wheeler AAF, HI
PHIK	HIK	-10:00	Hickam AFB, HI
PHNG	NGF	-10:00	Kaneohe Bay MCB, HI
PJON	JON	-10:00	Johnston Atoll, JO
PKWA	KWA	-12:00	Bucholz AAF/KMR (Kwajalein Atoll), KA
PTKK	TKK	+10:00	Truk IAP, MC
PTPN	PNI	+11:00	Pohnpei IAP, FM
PTRO	ROR	+09:00	Babelthuap IAP, PW
PTSA	KSA	+12:00	Kosrae IAP, FM
PWAK	AWK	+12:00	Wake Island AAF, WK
RJCB	OBO	+09:00	Obihiro Apt, JP
RJCJ	CTS	+09:00	Chitose Apt, JP
RJFF	FUK	+09:00	Fukuoka IAP/Itazuke AB, JP
RJOI	IWA	+09:00	Iwakuni MCAS, JP
RJSM	MSJ	+09:00	Misawa AB, JP
RJTA	NJA	+09:00	Atsugi NAF, JP
RJTY	OKO	+09:00	Yokota AB, JP
RKJJ	KWJ	+09:00	Kwang Ju Republic of Korea AFB, KR
RKJK	KUZ	+09:00	Kunsan AB, KR
RKPC	CJU	+09:00	Cheju IAP, KR
RKPK	KHE	+09:00	Kimhae AB, KR
RKSO	OSN	+09:00	Osan AB, KR
RODN	DNA	+09:00	Kadena AB (Okinawa), JP
ROTM	NFO	+09:00	Futenma MCAS, JP
RPLC	CRK	+08:00	Clark IAP, PH
RPMM	MNL	+08:00	Ninoy Aquino IAP (Manila), PH
SAEZ	BUE	-03:00	Ezeiza Airport, Buenos Aires, AR
SBBR	BSB	-03:00	Brasilia IAP, BR
SBGL	RIO	-03:00	Rio de Janeiro IAP, BR
SCEL	SCL	-04:00	Pudahel Apt/Arturo Merino Benitez IAP, Santiago, CL
SEQU	UIO	-05:00	Mariscal Sucre Apt, EC
SGAS	ASU	-04:00	Silvio Pettirossi IAP, PY
SKBO	BOG	-05:00	El Dorado IAP, CO
SLLP	LPB	-04:00	J.F. Kennedy IAP, La Paz, BO
SLVR	VVI	-04:00	Viru Viru IAP, BO
SMJP	PBM	-03:00	Johan A. Pengel IAP, SR
SPIM	LIM	-05:00	Jorge Chavez IAP, PE
SUMU	MVD	-03:00	Carrasco IAP, Montevideo, UY
SVMI	MIQ	-04:00	Simon Bolivar IAP, VE
TAPA	SJH	-04:00	V.C. Bird IAP (St. John's), AG
TBPB	BGI	-04:00	Grantley Adams IAP, BB
TIST	STT	-04:00	Cyril E. King Apt, VI
TISX	STX	-04:00	Alexander Hamilton Apt, VI
TJBQ	BQN	-04:00	Borinquen CGAS, PR
TJNR	NRR	-04:00	Roosevelt Roads NS, PR
TJSJ	SJU	-04:00	Luis Munoz Marin IAP, PR

TNCC	CUR	-04:00	Hato Airport, Curacao, AN
TTPP	POS	-04:00	Piarco Apt (Port-of-Spain), TT
VTBD	BKK	+07:00	Don Muang Apt, TH
VTBU	VBU	+07:00	RTN U-Tapao, TH
WIIH	HLP	+07:00	Halim Perdanakusuma AB, ID
WSAP	QPG	+08:00	RSAF Paya Lebar, SG
WSSS	SIN	+08:00	Singapore Changi IAP, SG
YBAS	ASP	+09:00	Alice Springs Apt, AU
YSRI	RCM	+10:00	RAAFB Richmond, AU

DECODE (LI vs ICAO)

ICAO	LI	LST	STATION
ADA	LTAG	+02:00	Incirlik AB (Adana), TR
ADB	LTBJ	+02:00	Cumaovasi APT (Izmir), TR
ADQ	PADQ	-10:00	Kodiak CGAS, AK
ADW	KADW	-05:00	Andrews AFB, MD
AEX	KAEX	-06:00	Alexandria IAP, LA
AGS	KAGS	-05:00	Bush Field Apt, GA
AKN	PAKN	-09:00	King Salmon Apt, AK
AKT	LCRA	+02:00	RAFB Akrotiri, CY
AMM	OJAF	+02:00	King Abdullah AB, JO
ANC	PANC	-09:00	Kulis ANGB/Anchorage IAP, AK
APN	KAPN	-05:00	Alpena Combat Readiness Training Center/Alpena County Regional Apt, MI
ASI	FHAW	+00:00	Ascension Auxiliary Airfield, GB
ASP	YBAS	+09:00	Alice Springs Apt, AU
ASU	SGAS	-04:00	Silvio Pettirossi IAP, PY
ATL	KATL	-05:00	William B. Hartsfield Atlanta IAP, GA
AVB	LIPA	+01:00	Aviano AB, IT
AWK	PWAK	+12:00	Wake Island AAF, WK
BAB	KBAB	-08:00	Beale AFB, CA
BAD	KBAD	-06:00	Barksdale AFB, LA
BAH	OBBI	+03:00	Bahrain IAP, BH
BED	KBED	-05:00	Hanscom AFB, MA
BGI	TBPB	-04:00	Grantley Adams IAP, BB
BGR	KBGR	-05:00	Bangor IAP/ANGB, ME
BHM	KBHM	-05:00	Birmingham IAP/ANG, AL
BIF	KBIF	-06:00	Biggs AAF, TX
BIG	PABI	-09:00	Allen AAF, AK
BIX	KBIX	-06:00	Keesler AFB, MS
BKF	KBKF	-07:00	Buckley ANGB, CO
BKH	PHBK	-10:00	Barking Sands Pacific Missile Range Facility, HI
BKK	VTBD	+07:00	Don Muang Apt, TH
BKT	KBKT	-05:00	Blackstone AAF, VA
BLV	KBLV	-06:00	Scott AFB, IL
BNA	KBNA	-06:00	Nashville IAP/Tennessee ANGB, TN
BOG	SKBO	-05:00	El Dorado IAP, CO
BOI	KBOI	-07:00	Boise Air Terminal/Gowen Field Apt, ID

BQN	TJBQ	-04:00	Borinquen CGAS, PR
BSB	SBBR	-03:00	Brasilia IAP, BR
BUE	SAEZ	-03:00	Ezeiza Airport, Buenos Aires, AR
BWI	KBWI	-05:00	Baltimore/Washington IAP, MD
BYS	KBYS	-08:00	Bicycle Lake AAF, CA
BZE	MZBZ	-06:00	Phillip S.W. Goldson IAP, BZ
CAI	HECA	+02:00	Cairo IAP, Cairo East AB, EG
CBM	KCBM	-06:00	Columbus AFB, MS
CEF	KCEF	-05:00	Westover ARB, MA
CHC	NZCH	+12:00	Christchurch IAP, NZ
CHE	EBCU	+01:00	Chievres AB, BE
CHQ	LGSA	+02:00	Souda Bay NSA (Crete), GR
CHS	KCHS	-05:00	Charleston AFB/IAP, SC
CIR	HECW	+02:00	Cairo West IAP, EG
CJU	RKPC	+09:00	Cheju IAP, KR
CLF	PACL	-09:00	Clear AS, AK
CLT	KCLT	-05:00	Charlotte/Douglas IAP, NC
CMY	KCMY	-06:00	Fort McCoy Aviation Support Facility, WI
COF	KCOF	-05:00	Patrick AFB, FL
COS	KCOS	-07:00	Peterson AFB, CO
CRK	RPLC	+08:00	Clark IAP, PH
CRW	KCRW	-05:00	Yeager Apt, WV
CTS	RJCJ	+09:00	Chitose Apt, JP
CUB	KCUB	-05:00	Columbia Owens Downtown Apt, SC
CUR	TNCC	-04:00	Hato Airport, Curacao, AN
CVS	KCVS	-07:00	Cannon AFB, NM
CYS	KCYS	-07:00	Cheyenne Municipal Apt, WY
DAA	KDAA	-05:00	Davison AAF, VA
DHF	OMAM	+00:00	Al Dhafra Airfield, AE
DKR	GOOY	+01:00	Dakar Leopold S. Senghor Apt, SN
DLF	KDLF	-06:00	Laughlin AFB, TX
DMA	KDMA	-07:00	Davis-Monthan AFB, AZ
DNA	RODN	+09:00	Kadena AB (Okinawa), JP
DOV	KDOV	-05:00	Dover AFB, DE
DPG	KDPG	-07:00	Michael AAF, UT
DYS	KDYS	-06:00	Dyess AFB, TX
ECG	KECG	-05:00	Elizabeth City CGAS, NC
EDF	PAED	-09:00	Elmendorf AFB, AK
EFD	KEFD	-06:00	Texas ANG/Ellington Field, TX
EIL	PAEI	-09:00	Eielson AFB, AK
EKJ	OEKH	+03:00	Prince Sultan AB (Al Kharj), SA
END	KEND	-06:00	Vance AFB, OK
ESB	LTAC	+02:00	Esenboga Apt (Ankara), TR
FAF	KFAF	-05:00	Felker AAF, VA
FBG	KFBG	-05:00	Simmons AAF, NC
FBK	PAFB	-09:00	Wainwright AAF/Fort Wainwright, AK
FCS	KFCS	-07:00	Butts AAF, CO
FEW	KFEW	-07:00	F.E. Warren AFB, WY
FFO	KFFO	-05:00	Wright-Patterson AFB, OH

FHU	KFHU	-07:00	Libby AAF, AZ
FIH	FZAA	+01:00	Kinshasa N'Djili Apt, ZR
FJR	OMFJ	+04:00	Al Fujayrah IAP, AE
FLV	KFLV	-06:00	Sherman AAF, KS
FMH	KFMH	-05:00	Otis ANGB, MA
FOE	KFOE	-06:00	Forbes Field IAP/ANGB, KS
FOK	KFOK	-05:00	Francis S. Gabreski IAP/ANG, NY
FRF	EDAF	+01:00	Rhein-Main AB, DE
FRI	KFRI	-06:00	Marshall AAF, KS
FSI	KFSI	-06:00	Henry Post AAF, OK
FTK	KFTK	-06:00	Godman AAF, KY
FTY	KFTY	-05:00	Atlanta Regional Flight Center/Fulton County Apt , GA
FUK	RJFF	+09:00	Fukuoka IAP/Itazuke AB, JP
GMF	KMKE	-06:00	General Mitchell IAP/ARS, WI
GPA	LGRX	+02:00	GAFB Araxos, GR
GRF	KGRF	-08:00	Gray AAF, WA
GRK	KGRK	-06:00	Robert Gray AAF, TX
GSB	KGSB	-05:00	Seymour Johnson AFB, NC
GTB	KGTB	-05:00	Wheeler-Sack Army Airfield (Fort Drum), NY
GTF	KGTF	-06:00	Great Falls IAP/Montana ANGB, MT
GUA	MGGT	-06:00	La Aurora Apt, GT
GUS	KGUS	-05:00	Grissom ARB, IN
HGT	KHGT	-08:00	Fort Hunter Liggett, CA
HHI	PHHI	-10:00	Wheeler AAF, HI
HIF	KHIF	-07:00	Hill AFB, UT
HIK	PHIK	-10:00	Hickam AFB, HI
HLP	WIIH	+07:00	Halim Perdanakusuma AB, ID
HMN	KHMN	-07:00	Holloman AFB, NM
HOP	KHOP	-06:00	Campbell AAF, KY
HRT	KHRT	-05:00	Hurlburt Field, FL
HST	KHST	-05:00	Homestead ARS, FL
HUA	KHUA	-06:00	Redstone Arsenal AAF, AL
IAB	KIAB	-06:00	McConnell AFB, KS
IAG	KIAG	-05:00	Niagara Falls IAP, NY
IGL	LTBL	+02:00	Izmir AS, TR
IKR	KIKR	-07:00	Kirtland AFB, NM
ILG	KILG	-05:00	New Castle County Apt, DE
IST	LTBA	+02:00	Ataturk IAP (Istanbul), TR
IWA	RJOI	+09:00	Iwakuni MCAS, JP
JAN	KJAN	-06:00	Jackson IAP/Allen C. Thompson Field, MS
JON	PJON	-10:00	Johnston Atoll, JO
KEF	BIKF	+00:00	Keflavik Apt, IS
KHE	RKPK	+09:00	Kimhae AB, KR
KIN	MKJP	-05:00	Norman Manley IAP, JM
KJS	MKJS	-05:00	Sangster IAP, Montego Bay, JM
KSA	PTSA	+12:00	Kosrae IAP, FM
KUZ	RKJK	+09:00	Kunsan AB, KR

KWA	PKWA	-12:00	Bucholz AAF/KMR (Kwajalein Atoll), KA
KWI	OKBK	+03:00	Kuwait IAP, KW
KWJ	RKJJ	+09:00	Kwang Ju Republic of Korea AFB, KR
LAW	KLAW	-06:00	Lawton/Fort Sill Regional Apt, OK
LAX	KLAX	-08:00	Los Angeles IAP, CA
LCK	KLCK	-05:00	Rickenbacker ANGB, OH
LFI	KLFI	-05:00	Langley AFB, VA
LGS	LPLA	+00:00	Lajes Field AB (Azores), PT
LHW	KLHW	-05:00	Wright AAF, GA
LIM	SPIM	-05:00	Jorge Chavez IAP, PE
LIS	LPPT	-01:00	Lisbon IAP, PT
LKZ	EGUL	+00:00	RAF Lakenheath, GB
LMB	FAWK	+01:00	Waterkloof AB, ZA
LMT	KLMT	-08:00	Kingsley Field, OR
LNK	KLNK	-06:00	Lincoln Municipal Apt/Nebraska ANGB, NE
LPB	SLLP	-04:00	J.F. Kennedy IAP, La Paz, BO
LRF	KLRF	-06:00	Little Rock AFB, AR
LSF	KLSF	-05:00	Lawson Army Airfield (Fort Benning), GA
LSV	KLSV	-08:00	Nellis AFB, NV
LTS	KLTS	-06:00	Altus AFB, OK
LUF	KLUF	-07:00	Luke AFB, AZ
MCC	KMCC	-08:00	Sacramento Coast Guard Air Station, CA
MCF	KMCF	-05:00	MacDill AFB, FL
MCI	KMCI	-06:00	Kansas City IAP, KS
MEI	KMEI	-06:00	Key Field Apt, MS
MEM	KMEM	-06:00	Memphis IAP/ANGB, TN
MFD	KMFD	-05:00	Mansfield Lahm Apt, OH
MGA	MNMG	-06:00	Augusto C. Sandino IAP, NI
MGE	KMGE	-05:00	Dobbins ARB, GA
MHK	KMHK	-06:00	Marshall AAF/Manhattan Municipal Apt, KS
MHZ	EGUN	+00:00	RAF Mildenhall, GB
MIB	KMIB	-07:00	Minot AFB, ND
MIQ	SVMI	-04:00	Simon Bolivar IAP, VE
MMT	KMMT	-05:00	McEntire ANG Station, SC
MNL	RPMM	+08:00	Ninoy Aquino IAP (Manila), PH
MOB	KMOB	-06:00	Mobile CG Aviation Training Center, AL
MRB	KMRB	-05:00	Eastern West Virginia Regional Apt, WV
MSJ	RJSM	+09:00	Misawa AB, JP
MSP	KMSP	-06:00	Minneapolis-St. Paul IAP/ARS, MN
MTC	KMTC	-05:00	Selfridge ANGB, MI
MTN	KMTN	-05:00	Martin State Apt, MD
MUI	KMUI	-05:00	Muir AAF, PA
MUO	KMUO	-07:00	Mountain Home AFB, ID
MVD	SUMU	-03:00	Carrasco IAP, Montevideo, UY
MXF	KMXF	-06:00	Maxwell AFB, AL

NAN	NFFN	+12:00	Nandi IAP, FJ
NAP	LIRN	+01:00	Capodichino Apt (Naples), IT
NBC	KNBC	-05:00	Beaufort MCAS, SC
NBG	KNBG	-06:00	New Orleans NAS/JRB, LA
NBO	HKNA	+03:00	Jomo Kenyatta IAP, KE
NBW	MUGM	-05:00	Guantanamo Bay NAS, CU
NCA	KNCA	-05:00	New River MCAS, NC
NCQ	KNCQ	-05:00	Atlanta NAS, GA
NDJ	FTTJ	+01:00	N'Djamena IAP, TD
NEL	KNEL	-05:00	Lakehurst NAWC, NJ
NFL	KNFL	-08:00	Fallon NAS, NV
NFO	ROTM	+09:00	Futenma MCAS, JP
NFW	KNFW	-06:00	Fort Worth NAS/JRB, TX
NGF	PHNG	-10:00	Kaneohe Bay MCB, HI
NGP	KNGP	-06:00	Corpus Christi NAS, TX
NGU	KNGU	-05:00	Norfolk NAS, VA
NHK	KNHK	-05:00	Patuxent River NAWC, MD
NHZ	KNHZ	-05:00	Brunswick NAS, ME
NID	KNID	-08:00	China Lake NWC, CA
NIM	DRRN	+01:00	Niamey IAP, NE
NIP	KNIP	-05:00	Jacksonville NAS, FL
NJA	RJTA	+09:00	Atsugi NAF, JP
NJK	KNJK	-08:00	El Centro NAF, CA
NKT	KNKT	-05:00	Cherry Point MCAS, NC
NKW	FJDG	+06:00	Diego Garcia Atoll (Chagos Archipelago), GB
NKX	KNKX	-08:00	Miramar MCAS, CA
NLC	KNLC	-08:00	Lemoore NAS, CA
NMM	KNMM	-06:00	Meridian NAS, MS
NOM	KNOM	-05:00	Miami CGAS, Opa Locka Apt, FL
NPA	KNPA	-05:00	Pensacola NAS, FL
NQA	KNQA	-06:00	Mid-South NSA, TN
NQI	KNQI	-06:00	Kingsville NAS, TX
NQX	KNQX	-05:00	Key West NAS, FL
NRB	KNRB	-05:00	Mayport NS, FL
NRR	TJNR	-04:00	Roosevelt Roads NS, PR
NSF	KNSF	-05:00	Washington NAF, DC
NSI	FKYS	+00:00	Yaounde/Nsimalen IAP, CM
NTD	KNTD	-08:00	Point Mugu NAS, CA
NTU	KNTU	-05:00	Oceana NAS, VA
NUW	KNUW	-08:00	Whidbey Island NAS, WA
NXX	KNXX	-05:00	Willow Grove NAS/JRB, PA
NYG	KNYG	-05:00	Quantico MCB, VA
NZY	KNZY	-08:00	North Island NAS, CA
OBO	RJCB	+09:00	Obihiro Apt, JP
OCO	MROC	-06:00	Juan Santamaria IAP, CR
OFF	KOFF	-06:00	Offutt AFB, NE
OKC	KOKC	-06:00	Will Rogers World Apt/ANGB, OK
OKO	RJTY	+09:00	Yokota AB, JP
OLB	LIEO	+01:00	Olbia/Costa Smeralda Apt, IT
OQU	KOQU	-05:00	Quonset State Apt, RI
OSN	RKSO	+09:00	Osan AB, KR
OZP	LEMO	+00:00	Moron AB, ES
OZR	KOZR	-06:00	Cairns AAF, AL

PAM	KPAM	-05:00	Tyndall AFB, FL
PAP	MTPP	-05:00	Port Au Prince IAP, HT
PBM	SMJP	-03:00	Johan A. Pengel IAP, SR
PDX	KPDX	-08:00	Portland IAP/ANGB, OR
PHX	KPHX	-07:00	Sky Harbor IAP, AZ
PIA	KPIA	-06:00	Greater Peoria Regional Apt, IL
PIE	KPIE	-05:00	Clearwater CGAS, FL
PIT	KPIT	-05:00	Pittsburgh IAP/ARS, PA
PLA	MHSC	-06:00	Soto Cano AB, HN
PNI	PTPN	+11:00	Pohnpei IAP, FM
POB	KPOB	-05:00	Pope AFB, NC
POE	KPOE	-06:00	Polk AAF, LA
POS	TTPP	-04:00	Piarco Apt (Port-of-Spain), TT
PPG	NTSU	-11:00	Pago Pago IAP, AS
PSM	KPSM	-05:00	Pease ANGB, NH
PTY	MPTO	-05:00	Tocumen IAP, PA
PVD	KPVD	-05:00	Theodore Francis Green State Apt, RI
QPG	WSAP	+08:00	RSAF Paya Lebar, SG
RCA	KRCA	-07:00	Ellsworth AFB, SD
RCM	YSRI	+10:00	RAAFB Richmond, AU
RDR	KRDR	-06:00	Grand Forks AFB, ND
RIO	SBGL	-03:00	Rio de Janeiro IAP, BR
RIV	KRIV	-08:00	March ARB, CA
RMS	ETAR	+01:00	Ramstein AB, DE
RND	KRND	-06:00	Randolph AFB, TX
RNO	KRNO	-08:00	Reno/Tahoe IAP, NV
ROR	PTRO	+09:00	Babelthuap IAP, PW
RTA	LERT	+00:00	Rota NS, ES
SAL	MSSS	-06:00	Ilopango AB, SV
SAN	KSAN	-08:00	San Diego CGAS, CA
SAV	KSAV	-05:00	Savannah IAP, GA
SCH	KSCH	-05:00	Stratton ANGB, NY
SCL	SCEL	-04:00	Pudahel Apt/Arturo Merino Benitez IAP, Santiago, CL
SDF	KSDF	-05:00	Louisville IAP/Kentucky ANGB, KY
SDQ	MDSI	-04:00	San Isidro AB, DO
SEA	KSEA	-08:00	Seattle/Tacoma IAP, WA
SEX	EDAS	+01:00	Sembach Annex (Ramstein AB), DE
SIN	WSSS	+08:00	Singapore Changi IAP, SG
SIT	PADQ	-09:00	Sitka CGAS, AK
SIZ	LICZ	+01:00	Sigonella NAS/Apt (Sicily), IT
SJH	TAPA	-04:00	V.C. Bird IAP (St. John's), AG
SJU	TJSJ	-04:00	Luis Munoz Marin IAP, PR
SKA	KSKA	-08:00	Fairchild AFB, WA
SKF	KSKF	-06:00	Kelly AFB, TX
SKP	LWSK	+01:00	Skopje Apt, MK
SLC	KSLC	-07:00	Salt Lake City IAP, UT
SLI	KSLI	-08:00	Los Alamitos AAF, CA
SNN	EINN	+00:00	Shannon Apt, IE
SPM	ETAD	+01:00	Spangdahlem AB, DE

SPN	PGSN	+10:00	Saipan IAP, MP
SPS	KSPS	-06:00	Sheppard AFB, TX
SSC	KSSC	-05:00	Shaw AFB, SC
STJ	KSTJ	-06:00	Rosecrans Memorial Apt, MO
STR	EDDS	+01:00	Stuttgart AAF, DE
STT	TIST	-04:00	Cyril E. King Apt, VI
STX	TISX	-04:00	Alexander Hamilton Apt, VI
SUU	KSUU	-08:00	Travis AFB, CA
SVN	KSVN	-05:00	Hunter AAF, GA
SWF	KSWF	-05:00	Stewart IAP/ANGB, NY
SYA	PASY	-10:00	Eareckson AS, AK
SYR	KSYR	-05:00	Syracuse-Hancock Field IAP, NY
SZL	KSZL	-06:00	Whiteman AFB, MO
TBN	KTBN	-06:00	Forney AAF, MO
TCM	KTCM	-08:00	McChord AFB, WA
TGU	MHTG	-06:00	Toncontin IAP, HN
THU	BGTL	-04:00	Thule AB (Greenland), DK
TIK	KTIK	-06:00	Tinker AFB, OK
TKK	PTKK	+10:00	Truk IAP, MC
TLV	LLBG	+02:00	Ben Gurion IAP (Tel Aviv), IL
TTH	OOTH	+04:00	OAFB Thumrait, OM
TYS	KTYS	-05:00	McGhee Tyson ANGB, TN
UAM	PGUA	+10:00	Andersen AFB, GU
UIO	SEQU	-05:00	Mariscal Sucre Apt, EC
VAD	KVAD	-05:00	Moody AFB, GA
VBG	KVBG	-08:00	Vandenberg AFB, CA
VBU	VTBU	+07:00	RTN U-Tapao, TH
VKS	KVKS	-06:00	Vicksburg Municipal Apt, MS
VOK	KVOK	-06:00	Volk Field ANGB, WI
VPS	KVPS	-05:00	Eglin AFB, FL
VVI	SLVR	-04:00	Viru Viru IAP, BO
WCR	MWCR	-05:00	Owen Roberts IAP, Cayman Islands (GB)
WRB	KWRB	-05:00	Robins AFB, GA
WRI	KWRI	-05:00	McGuire AFB, NJ
WSD	KWSD	-07:00	Condron AAF, NM
YNG	KYNG	-05:00	Youngstown/Warren Regional Apt/ARS, OH
YQX	CYQX	-03:30	Gander IAP (Newfoundland), CA
YUM	KNYZ	-07:00	Yuma MCAS, AZ
YYR	CYYR	-04:00	Goose Bay AB (Newfoundland), CA
YYT	CYYT	-03:30	St. John's Apt, (Newfoundland), CA

APPENDIX F: Julian Date Calendars
and Military (24 Hour) Clock

Julian Date Calendar: The following tables will be used to convert the Gregorian (official United States Commerce Calendar) calendar dates to a three numerical digit Julian Date. The first Julian Date Calendar table is a perpetual calendar for all years except leap years. The second Julian Date Calendar table is a perpetual calendar for leap years only, such as 2000, 2004, 2008, etc.

How to use Julian Date Calendars: The calendars are constructed in a matrix with the days of the month in the left hand column from 1 through 31. The months are displayed in rows

JULIAN DATE CALENDAR ENCODE/DECODE TABLE

DAY	JAN	FEB	MAR	APR	MAY	JUN	JUL	AUG	SEP	OCT	NOV	DEC
1	001	032	060	091	121	152	182	213	244	274	305	335
2	002	033	061	092	122	153	183	214	245	275	306	336
3	003	034	062	093	123	154	184	215	246	276	307	337
4	004	035	063	094	124	155	185	216	247	277	308	338
5	005	036	064	095	125	156	186	217	248	278	309	339
6	006	037	065	096	126	157	187	218	249	279	310	340
7	007	038	066	097	127	158	188	219	250	280	311	341
8	008	039	067	098	128	159	189	220	251	281	312	342
9	009	040	068	099	129	160	190	221	252	282	313	343
10	010	041	069	100	130	161	191	222	253	283	314	344
11	011	042	070	101	131	162	192	223	254	284	315	345
12	012	043	071	102	132	163	193	224	255	285	316	346
13	013	044	072	103	133	164	194	225	256	286	317	347
14	014	045	073	104	134	165	195	226	257	287	318	348
15	015	046	074	105	135	166	196	227	258	288	319	349
16	016	047	075	106	136	167	197	228	259	289	320	350
17	017	048	076	107	137	168	198	229	260	290	321	351
18	018	049	077	108	138	169	199	230	261	291	322	352
19	019	050	078	109	139	170	200	231	262	292	323	353
20	020	051	079	110	140	171	201	232	263	293	324	354
21	021	052	080	111	141	172	202	233	264	294	325	355
22	022	053	081	112	142	173	203	234	265	295	326	356
23	023	054	082	113	143	174	204	235	266	296	327	357
24	024	055	083	114	144	175	205	236	267	297	328	358
25	025	056	084	115	145	176	206	237	268	298	329	359
26	026	057	085	116	146	177	207	238	269	299	330	360
27	027	058	086	117	147	178	208	239	270	300	331	361
28	028	059	087	118	148	179	209	240	271	301	332	362
29	029		088	119	149	180	210	241	272	302	333	363
30	030		089	120	150	181	211	242	273	303	334	364
31	031		090		151		212	243		304		365

from left to right starting with January and continuing through each month to December on the extreme right.

Example: If you made an application for space available travel on 15 April 2000 (a leap year), go to the lower table for leap years and read down the date column to 15 and across to the right to April where you find the number 106, or the 106th day in the Julian Date Calendar. If this were not a leap year, i.e. 15 April 2001, check the number in the non-leap year calendar—it would be the 105th day. Please try to convert some sample dates (birthdays, holidays, etc.) until you are comfortable using this system.

The entire Julian Date is constructed using the last two digits of the calendar year, i.e., 2000 is 00, 105 for 15 April. The last four digits of the Julian date are taken from the twenty-four

JULIAN DATE LEAP YEAR CALENDAR ENCODE/DECODE TABLE

DAY	JAN	FEB	MAR	APR	MAY	JUN	JUL	AUG	SEP	OCT	NOV	DEC
1	001	032	061	092	122	153	183	214	245	275	306	336
2	002	033	062	093	123	154	184	215	246	276	307	337
3	003	034	063	094	124	155	185	216	247	277	308	338
4	004	035	064	095	125	156	186	217	248	278	309	339
5	005	036	065	096	126	157	187	218	249	279	310	340
6	006	037	066	097	127	158	188	219	250	280	311	341
7	007	038	067	098	128	159	189	220	251	281	312	342
8	008	039	068	099	129	160	190	221	252	282	313	343
9	009	040	069	100	130	161	191	222	253	283	314	344
10	010	041	070	101	131	162	192	223	254	284	315	345
11	011	042	071	102	132	163	193	224	255	285	316	346
12	012	043	072	103	133	164	194	225	256	286	317	347
13	013	044	073	104	134	165	195	226	257	287	318	348
14	014	045	074	105	135	166	196	227	258	288	319	349
15	015	046	075	106	136	167	197	228	259	289	320	350
16	016	047	076	107	137	168	198	229	260	290	321	351
17	017	048	077	108	138	169	199	230	261	291	322	352
18	018	049	078	109	139	170	200	231	262	292	323	353
19	019	050	079	110	140	171	201	232	263	293	324	354
20	020	051	080	111	141	172	202	233	264	294	325	355
21	021	052	081	112	142	173	203	234	265	295	326	356
22	022	053	082	113	143	174	204	235	266	296	327	357
23	023	054	083	114	144	175	205	236	267	297	328	358
24	024	055	084	115	145	176	206	237	268	298	329	359
25	025	056	085	116	146	177	207	238	269	299	330	360
26	026	057	086	117	147	178	208	239	270	300	331	361
27	027	058	087	118	148	179	209	240	271	301	332	362
28	028	059	088	119	149	180	210	241	272	302	333	363
29	029	060	089	120	150	181	211	242	273	303	334	364
30	030		090	121	151	182	212	243	274	304	335	365
31	031		091		152		213	244		305		366

hour clock, frequently known as the military clock, or time when the hour is a period of time equal to one twenty-fourth of a mean solar or civil day and equivalent to sixty minutes. The Julian Day is divided into a series of twenty-four hours from midnight to midnight. See the table on the next page.

Using the tables on the prior pages, along with the table below, if you are applying for Space-A air travel at 2:45pm on April 15, 2000, your complete Julian Date and time would be 00 106 1444 or the year 2000, 106th day 14th hour and 45th minute.(Note that 2000 is a leap year.)

TWENTY-FOUR HOUR CLOCK/MILITARY TIME

Conventional Clock	Military Clock	Conventional Clock	Military Clock
midnight 12am	2400 hours	noon 12pm	1200 hours
1am	0100 hours	1pm	1300 hours
2am	0200 hours	2pm	1400 hours
3am	0300 hours	3pm	1500 hours
4am	0400 hours	4pm	1600 hours
5am	0500 hours	5pm	1700 hours
6am	0600 hours	6pm	1800 hours
7am	0700 hours	7pm	1900 hours
8am	0800 hours	8pm	2000 hours
9am	0900 hours	9pm	2100 hours
10am	1000 hours	10pm	2200 hours
11am	1100 hours	11pm	2300 hours

APPENDIX G: Standard Time Conversion Table

STANDARD TIME CONVERSION TABLE

The world is divided into 24 time zones or areas. The zero time zone is known as Greenwich Mean Time (GMT), also referred to as Zulu Time, which is physically located at Greenwich, England (UK), near London. Other areas in this time zone include Iceland, Ascension Island, England and Scotland. The following table shows major areas and their respective time zones in + or - hours from Greenwich Mean Time (GMT). Across the top row of the table, each area (zone) to the right of GMT is a plus (+), meaning an hour ahead. Each zone to the left of GMT is a minus (-), meaning an hour behind. The columns down the page are simply the next 24 hours from the baseline at the top. For example, if you are in Germany, Italy or Spain (GMT +1), the local time is 0800 hours. If you want to know the local time in San Francisco, CA, USA, you read down the GMT +1 column to 0800 hours and left to GMT -8 (Pacific Time U.S, San Francisco, CA, USA) where it is 2300 hours. Practice with this table until you are proficient.Note: This chart is for planning purposes only, as local times may vary from the above due to local conditions, such as Daylight Savings Time, etc. For exact local times, consult DoD Foreign Clearance Guide, DoT Flight Information Publication or Air Almanac.

Location	Offset				
New Zealand/Wake Island	+12	0600	0700	0800	0900
Guam/Richmond (AU)	+10	0400	0500	0600	0700
Alice Springs (AU)/Woomera (AU)	+9:30	0330	0430	0530	0630
Okinawa/Japan/Korea	+9	0300	0400	0500	0600
Philippines/Taiwan/S Vietnam/Perth (AU)	+8	0200	0300	0400	0500
Thailand/Singapore	+7	0100	0200	0300	0400
Diego Garcia	+6	2330	0030	0130	0230
Dhahran/Bahrain	+3	2100	2200	2300	2400
Greece/Egypt/Johannesburg/Turkey	+2	2000	2100	2200	2300
Germany/Italy/Spain	+1	1900	2000	2100	2200
Iceland/Ascension/England/Scotland	GMT	1800	1900	2000	2100
Azores	-1	1700	1800	1900	2000
Bermuda/Puerto Rico/Greenland	-4	1400	1500	1600	1700
Eastern Time U.S.	-5	1300	1400	1500	1600
Central Time U.S.	-6	1200	1300	1400	1500
Mountain Time U.S.	-7	1100	1200	1300	1400
Pacific Time U.S.	-8	1000	1100	1200	1300
Elmendorf	-9	0900	1000	1100	1200
Hawaii/Shemya	-10	0800	0900	1000	1100
Midway/Pago Pago/Canton	-11	0700	0800	0900	1000
Kwajalien	-12	0600	0700	0800	0900

1000	0800	0730	0700	0600	0500	0330	0100	2400	2300	2200	2100	1800	1700	1600	1500	1400	1300	1200	1100	1000
1100	0900	0830	0800	0700	0600	0430	0200	0100	2400	2300	2200	1900	1800	1700	1600	1500	1400	1300	1200	1100
1200	1000	0930	0900	0800	0700	0530	0300	0200	0100	2400	2300	2000	1900	1800	1700	1600	1500	1400	1300	1200
1300	1100	0130	1000	0900	0800	0630	0400	0300	0200	0100	2400	2100	2000	1900	1800	1700	1600	1500	1400	1300
1400	1200	1130	1100	1000	0900	0730	0500	0400	0300	0200	0100	2200	2100	2000	1900	1800	1700	1600	1500	1400
1500	1300	1230	1200	1100	1000	0830	0600	0500	0400	0300	0200	2300	2200	2100	2000	1900	1800	1700	1600	1500
1600	1400	1330	1300	1200	1100	0930	0700	0600	0500	0400	0300	2400	2300	2200	2100	2000	1900	1800	1700	1600
1700	1500	1430	1400	1300	1200	1030	0800	0700	0600	0500	0400	0100	2400	2300	2200	2100	2000	1900	1800	1700
1800	1600	1530	1500	1400	1300	1130	0900	0800	0700	0600	0500	0200	0100	2400	2300	2200	2100	2000	1900	1800
1900	1700	1630	1600	1500	1400	1230	1000	0900	0800	0700	0600	0300	0200	0100	2400	2300	2200	2100	2000	1900
2000	1800	1730	1700	1600	1500	1330	1100	1000	0900	0800	0700	0400	0300	0200	0100	2400	2300	2200	2100	2000
2100	1900	1830	1800	1700	1600	1430	1200	1100	1000	0900	0800	0500	0400	0300	0200	0100	2400	2300	2200	2100
2200	2000	1930	1900	1800	1700	1530	1300	1200	1100	1000	0900	0600	0500	0400	0300	0200	0100	2400	2300	2200
2300	2100	2030	2000	1900	1800	1630	1400	1300	1200	1100	1000	0700	0600	0500	0400	0300	0200	0100	2400	2300
2400	2200	2130	2100	2000	1900	1730	1500	1400	1300	1200	1100	0800	0700	0600	0500	0400	0300	0200	0100	2400
0100	2300	2230	2200	2100	2000	1830	1600	1500	1400	1300	1200	0900	0800	0700	0600	0500	0400	0300	0200	0100
0200	2400	2330	2300	2200	2100	1930	1700	1600	1500	1400	1300	1000	0900	0800	0700	0600	0500	0400	0300	0200
0300	0100	0030	2400	2300	2200	2030	1800	1700	1600	1500	1400	1100	1000	0900	0800	0700	0600	0500	0400	0300
0400	0200	0130	0100	2400	2300	2130	1900	1800	1700	1600	1500	1200	1100	1000	0900	0800	0700	0600	0500	0400
0500	0300	0230	0200	0100	2400	2230	2000	1900	1800	1700	1600	1300	1200	1100	1000	0900	0800	0700	0600	0500

APPENDIX H: Authentication of Reserve Status For Travel Eligibility (DD Form 1853)

Active Duty Status Reserve Component members must present the form below, DD Form 1853, completed and signed by the Reserve organization commander within the previous 180 days when applying for Space-A air travel.

AUTHENTICATION OF RESERVE STATUS FOR TRAVEL ELIGIBILITY				1. DATE PREPARED (YYMMDD)
PRIVACY ACT STATEMENT AUTHORITY: 10 USC 8102, 44 USC. 3101 and EO 9397. PRINCIPAL PURPOSE: Use of your SSN is necessary to positively identify you. ROUTINE USE: Used by Reserve personnel for space available on DoD-owned or controlled aircraft. DISCLOSURE IS VOLUNTARY: However, failure to disclose it will prevent you from traveling on a DoD-owned or controlled aircraft.				
PART A. TO BE COMPLETED BY APPLICANT				
2. NAME (Last, First, MI)	3. PAY GRADE	4. BRANCH OF SERVICE		5.SSN
6. UNIT/COMMAND NAME	7. UNIT/COMMAND ADDRESS			
I hereby certify that my space-available travel on military aircraft is not for personal gain, or in connection with business enterprise or employment, or to establish a home either overseas or in the United States.				
8. SIGNATURE				9. DATE SIGNED (YYMMDD)
PART B. TO BE COMPLETED BY RESERVE ORGANIZATION COMMANDER				
The Reservist named above is an active reserve component member and is eligible for space-available transportation on DoD-owned or controlled aircraft in accordance with DoD Regulation 4515.13-R, and is authorized to so travel from _____ to _____ (Not to exceed 30 days)		10. Date (YYMMDD)		11. Date (YYMMDD)
12. NAME (Last, First, MI)	13. PAY GRADE	14. SIGNATURE		15. DATE SIGNED (YYMMDD)
DD Form 1853, 84 Apr	Previous editions are obsolete		*US Government Printing Office: 1984-460-983/23245	

APPENDIX I: Boarding Pass/Ticket Receipt
(AMC Form 148/2)

This or similar form will be used to record boarding, baggage, meals and other charges.

AMC-	BOARDING PASS/TICKET					AMC-
NAME *(Last, First, Middle)*	FLIGHT NO	GATE	BOARDING TIME	SEAT NO	TAX/INSP FEE	FLIGHT CODE/DATE
DESTINATION	DEPARTURE DATE	MEAL *(Kind/Type/Quantity)*			MEAL COST	SEAT NO
VIA	BAG WGT/PIECES	EXCESS WEIGHT			BAGGAGE COST	AGENT NUMBER
ORIGIN	REMARKS				OTHER COSTS	CASH COLLECTED
CARRIER	REASON/DATE OF REFUND				TOTAL	FROM
AGENT / SIGNATURE	PASSENGER SIGNATURE				FINAL DEST	TO

AMC FORM 148, JUN 96   PREVIOUS EDITIONS ARE OBSOLETE

APPENDIX J: Baggage Identification
(DD Form 1839, AMC Form 20-ID, and USAF Form 94)

This baggage identification tag, and others, are used to identify checked and cabin luggage.

SUU

TRAVIS AFB, CALIFORNIA

MISSION NUMBER/DATE

FROM

0 0 0 0 0 0

Strap Check - Not a Claim Check

BAGGAGE IDENTIFICATION

NAME *(Last, First, M.I.)*

STREET ADDRESS *(Home or Unit/APO)*

CITY, STATE AND ZIP CODE

| DD | FORM 80 SEP | 1839 | USE PREVIOUS EDITION. |

FOLD HERE   AND TUCK UNDER FLAP

PRINT NAME *(Last, First, Middle Initial)*   ADDRESS *(Unit/New Station)*

CITY/BASE   STATE

ZIP CODE   TELEPHONE NUMBER (COMMERCIAL/AUTOVON)

AMC FORM 20-ID, DEC 92

APPENDIX K: Air Passenger Comments
(AMC Form 253)

As a Space-A passenger you are encouraged to use this (or similar) form to report positive and negative information to managers of the system who are in a position to correct deficiencies and/or reward outstanding performance of duty. You may also be requested to participate in AMC Passengers Surveys from time to time (AMC Form 22 APR 96). (Form size adjusted to fit on this page; actual size is larger.) *Please send a courtesy copy of your comments to: Military Living's **R&R Travel News®**, PO Box 2347, Falls Church, VA 22042-0347.*

AIR PASSENGER COMMENTS

Please provide a copy to terminal management by placing in the slot marked for Squadron/Port Operations Officer. Terminal addresses are listed on the reverse in case you desire to mail your comments to a terminal you have passed through. Your comments to Squadron/Port Operations Officers will let them take immediate action. If you feel we need to know about a particular item, send a copy of your comments to us:

> HQ Air Mobility Command/DOJP
> 402 Scott Drive Unit 3A1
> Scott AFB, IL 62225-5302

COMMENTS

To assist us, please provide the following information when applicable.

NAME *(Last, First, M.I.)* *(Optional)*	GRADE *(Optional)*	DUTY ADDRESS *(Optional)*	DUTY PHONE *(Optional)*
FLIGHT NUMBER	DEPARTING FROM	DESTINATION	DATE FORM PREPARED *(Day, Month, Year)*

AMC FORM 253, MAR 95 (EF) (PerFORM PRO)   PREVIOUS EDITION IS OBSOLETE

APPENDIX L: International Certificates of Vaccination and Personal Health History (PHS Form 731)

This document provides for the recording of international certificates of vaccination and revaccination in both the English and French languages and the personal health history of international travelers. This document, with current health entries, is required as a Personnel Entrance Requirement for many foreign countries.

I. INTERNATIONAL CERTIFICATES OF VACCINATION AS APPROVED BY THE WORLD HEALTH ORGANIZATION
(EXCEPT FOR ADDRESS OF VACCINATOR)

CERTIFICATS INTERNATIONAUX DE VACCINATION APPROUVES PAR L'ORGANISATION MONDIALE DE LA SANTE
(SAUF L'ADRESSE DU VACCINATEUR)

II. PERSONAL HEALTH HISTORY

Traveler's Name—Nom du voyageur

Address—Adresse (Number—Numéro)   (Street—Rue)

(City—Ville)

(Country—Départment)   (State—Etat)

U.S. DEPARTMENT OF HEALTH, EDUCATION, AND WELFARE PUBLIC HEALTH SERVICE

PHS—731, Rev. 9-66 READ INSTRUCTIONS CAREFULLY

INTERNATIONAL CERTIFICATES OF VACCINATION AND PERSONAL HEALTH HISTORY (PHS FORM 731)

INTERNATIONAL CERTIFICATE OF VACCINATION OR REVACCINATION AGAINST SMALLPOX
CERTIFICAT INTERNATIONAL DE VACCINATION OU DE REVACCINATION CONTRE LA VARIOLE

This is to certify that . . . . .sex
Je soussigné(e) certifie que . . . . sexe
whose signature follows . . . . date of birth
dant la signature suit . . . . né(e) le
has on the date indicated been vaccinated or revaccinated against smallpox with a freeze-dried liquid vaccine certified to fulfil the recommended requirements of the World Health Organization.
a été vacciné(e) ou revacciné(e) contre la variole à la date indiquée ci-dessous avec un vaccin iyophilisé ou liquide certifié conforme aux normes recommandée par L'Organisation mondiale de la Santé.

INTERNATIONAL CERTIFICATE OF VACCINATION OR REVACCINATION AGAINST YELLOW FEVER
CERTIFICAT INTERNATIONAL DE VACCINATION OU DE REVACCINATION CONTRE LA FIEVRE JAUNE

This is to certify that . . . . .sex
Je soussigné(e) certifie que . . . . sexe
whose signature follows . . . . date of birth
dant la signature suit . . . . né(e) le
has on the date indicated been vaccinated or revaccinated against yellow fever.
a été vacciné(e) ou revacciné(e) contre la fievre jaune à la date indiquée.

INTERNATIONAL CERTIFICATE OF VACCINATION OR REVACCINATION AGAINST CHOLERA
CERTIFICAT INTERNATIONAL DE VACCINATION OU DE REVACCINATION CONTRE LE CHOLERA

This is to certify that . . . . .sex
Je soussigné(e) certifie que . . . . sexe
whose signature follows . . . . date of birth
dant la signature suit . . . . né(e) le
has on the date indicated been vaccinated or revaccinated against cholera.
a été vacciné(e) ou revacciné(e) contre la choléra à la date indiquée.

APPENDIX M: A Brief Description of Aircraft On Which Most Space-A Travel Occurs

The following transport, tanker, and special mission aircraft are used by the military services (USPHS and NOAA do not have aircraft which are suitable for Space-A travel) for missions having Space-A air opportunities. **Only the major channel and support aircraft are listed.** We have not listed minor, some special mission, and helicopter (rotary wing) aircraft due to space limitations. **We have provided for you a brief description of each aircraft with emphasis on performance and passenger accommodations.** The total number of each aircraft changes in the inventory due to acquisitions, conversions, reconfiguration, and attrition. **Our best estimate of current specific aircraft inventories are listed below.**

C-005A/B GALAXY
The C-005A/B is a long-range, air-refuelable, heavy logistics transport which is capable of airlifting loads up to 291,000 pounds. This aircraft was developed, designed and configured to meet a wide range of military airlift missions. This is the "Free World's" largest aircraft.

PROGRAM/PROJECT CONTRACTOR: Lockheed Aeronautical Systems Company.
POWER SOURCE: Four General Electric TF39-GE-1C turbofan engines. Each engine has 43,000 lbs of thrust.
DIMENSIONS: Wing span is 222 ft, 8.5 in. Length is 247 ft, 10 in. Height is 65 ft, 1.5 in.
WEIGHTS: Empty weight is 374,000 lbs. Maximum payload is 261,000 lbs. Gross weight is 837,000 lbs.
PERFORMANCE: Maximum speed at 25,000 ft is 571 mph. Service ceiling with 615,000 lbs gross weight is 35,750 ft. Range with maximum payload is 3,434 miles and range with maximum fuel is 6,469 miles. Between 1982-1987 the 77 C-005As were upgraded to C-005B capabilities. From 1985-1989, 50 C-005Bs were acquired.
FACILITIES: Aircraft crew of six. Relief crew/rest area of 15. **Seating for 75 passengers, 2nd deck airline type seats facing to the rear of the aircraft for safety purposes.** Cargo, 1st deck, 36 standard 463L pallets or mounted weapons and vehicles or a maximum of 340 passengers in a wide-body

jet configuration. There is a program to repaint all USAF C-005A/Bs flat grey. AMC has control of all C-005A/Bs.
INVENTORY: Total USAF 126.

C-009A/E NIGHTINGALE

This aircraft was designed as a commercial airliner. The DC-9 Series 30 commercial aircraft was reconfigured, modified and equipped to perform aeromedical (air ambulance) airlift transport missions. The C-009A/C performs aeromedical missions in CONUS, and in the European and Pacific Theaters.

PROGRAM/PROJECT CONTRACTOR: Douglas Aircraft Company. Division of McDonnell Douglas Corporation.
POWER SOURCE: Two Pratt & Whitney JT8D-9 turbofan engines. Each engine produces 14,500 lbs of thrust.
DIMENSIONS: Wing span is 93 ft, 3 in. Length is 119 ft, 3 in. Height is 27 ft, 6 in.
WEIGHT: Gross weight 108,000 lbs.
PERFORMANCE: The maximum cruising speed at 25,000 ft is 565 mph. Ceiling is 35,000 ft. Range is in excess of 2,000 miles.
FACILITIES: Aircraft crew of three (includes flight mechanic and spare parts) and five medical staff. There can be a combination of 40 litter (stretcher) or 40 ambulatory patients. Most MEDEVAC patients are ambulatory, that is, they can walk but may be put in a litter for comfort. The ambulatory seats are spacious airline type seats. These are the seats used by Space-A passengers.
INVENTORY: Twenty-one in CONUS, four in Europe, three in Pacific, for a total inventory of 28 aircraft configured for aeromedical missions. Three are specifically configured C-9Cs which are assigned for Presidential and related missions. **The USN has 29 each C-9B SKYTRAIN II aircraft procured in FY 1985 to meet major Navy logistics requirements. This aircraft is configured for cargo and passenger (airline type seats, up to approximately 100). Total 57.**

C-017A GLOBEMASTER III

This is a new aircraft which is now undergoing initial operational testing. It is a heavy-lift, air-refuelable, cargo transport designed to meet inter-theater and intra-theater airlift for all types of cargo and passengers. This aircraft will be

capable of using unimproved landing facilities (runways - 90 ft wide x 3,000 ft long). The initial operational capability (IOC) date is scheduled for FY 1994. A total of 40 aircraft has been funded through FY 1995. The planned total acquisition is 120 aircraft. **The passenger configurations for this aircraft have not been established.**

PROGRAM/PROJECT CONTRACTOR: McDonnell Douglas Aerospace Transport Aircraft Division of McDonnell Douglas Aerospace.

POWER SOURCE: Four Pratt & Whitney F117-PW 100 turbofans; each 40,000 lbs of thrust on each aircraft.

DIMENSIONS: Wing span is 169 ft 10 in. Length is 174 ft. Height is 55 ft 1 in.

WEIGHT: Payload 172,000 lbs, Gross weight 585,000 lbs.

PERFORMANCE: Cruising speed (estimated) 518 mph, range with 160,000 lbs payload is 2,765 miles.

FACILITIES: Up to 102 passengers or paratroops, or 48 litters.

INVENTORY: Total USAF 45.

C-21A EXECUTIVE AIRCRAFT

There is a group of executive type aircraft in use in all of the Military Services. The C-21A is typical of these aircraft. **We will list the data for the C-21A and then list the inventory and passenger capacity of executive type aircraft in the Military Services.**

PROGRAM/PROJECT CONTRACTOR: Learjet Corporation.

POWER SOURCE: Two Garrett TFE731-2 turbojet engines. Each engine has 3,500 lbs thrust.

DIMENSIONS: Wing span is 39 ft, 6 in. Length is 48 ft, 8 in. Height is 12 ft, 3 in.

WEIGHT: Gross 18,300 lbs.

PERFORMANCE: Cruising speed is Mach 0.81. Service ceiling is 45,000 ft. Range with maximum passengers is 2,420 miles and with maximum cargo load is 1,653 miles.

FACILITIES: Aircraft crew of two. **Eight passengers in airline type seats,** or cargo of 3,153 lbs. Also convertible to aeromedical (MEDEVAC) configuration.

INVENTORY: Total 556.

C-12A-J HURON (8 Pax): USAF-33, USN-100. Total-133.

HU-25A GUARDIAN (APPROXIMATELY 12 Pax): USCG-41.

C-20A/B GULFSTREAM III/IV (14-18 Pax): USAF-13, USCG-1, USN-5. Total-19.

C-21A EXECUTIVE AIRCRAFT (8 Pax): USAF-76.

C-22B (BOEING 727 (APPROXIMATELY 100 Pax): USAF-3, CV-22, OSPREY USAF-50 (planned).

C-23A SHERPA (APPROXIMATELY 8 Pax): USAF-13.

C-26-A/B FAIRCHILD METRO III (19-20 Pax): USAF -16, USN-7. Total:23. (53 ON ORDER)
C-27A STOL (53 Pax): USAF-5

C-29A (125-800 BUSINESS JET, APPROXIMATELY 8 Pax): USAF-6.

The U.S. Army operates a fleet of C-12, RC-12 Fixed-Wing Aircraft of approximately 200 in number. Each aircraft can seat approximately 8 passengers.

C130A-H HERCULES

The C-130 Hercules is a very versatile aircraft which is used to perform a wide range of missions for all of the military services. The aircraft has been used mainly in a cargo and passenger role. It has also been used in specialized combat, electronic warfare, Arctic ice cap resupply, aerial spray, aeromedical MEDEVAC, and aerial refueling among many similar missions. This aircraft is found in the inventory of all the military (Armed) services.

PROGRAM/PROJECT CONTRACTOR: Lockheed Aeronautical Systems Company.

POWER SOURCE: Four Allison T-56-A-15 turboprop engines. Each engine has 4,508 ehp.

DIMENSIONS: Wing span is 132 ft, 7 in. Length is 97 ft, 9 in. Height is 38 ft, 3 in.

PERFORMANCE: The maximum cruising speed at 20,000 ft is 374 mph. The service ceiling for 130,000 lbs is 33,000 ft. The range with maximum payload is 2,356 miles.

FACILITIES: Aircraft crew of five, **92 passengers in commercial airline type seats,** 74 litter patients, five 463L standard pallets, and assorted mounted weapons and vehicles. Seating ranges from side "bucket" seats along the sides of the aircraft to airline type seating with aisles and facing to the rear. The noise level is extremely high in this aircraft. Ear plugs are highly recommended for all passengers and crew.

INVENTORY: Total 853. C-130A-H and HC-130H/N/P: USAF-APPROXIMATELY 711. USN-26, USMC-85 (KC-130), USCG-30 (HC-130), USA-1 (EW MISSIONS).

KC-135A-R STRATOTANKER

This stratotanker was designed to military specifications. The aircraft is similar in size and design appearance to the commercial 707 aircraft but there the similarity ends. The KC-135 has different internal structural designs and materials which stress the ability to operate at high gross weights. The fuel carried in this tanker is located in the "wet wings" and in the fuel tanks below the floor in the fuselage. Passengers traveling on this aircraft are allowed, subject to mission restraints, to observe the Air to Air Refueling Operations which usually take place over the world's oceans.

PROGRAM/PROJECT CONTRACTOR: Boeing Military Airplanes.

POWER SOURCE: Four CFM international F108-CF-100 turbofan engines. Each engine has 22,224 lbs of thrust.

DIMENSIONS: Wing span is 130 ft, 10 in. Length is 136 ft, 3 in. Height is 38 ft, 4 in.

WEIGHT: Empty weight is 119,231 lbs. Gross 322,500 lbs.

PERFORMANCE: The maximum speed at 30,000 ft is 610 mph. Service ceiling 50,000 ft. Range with 12,000 lbs of transfer fuel is 11,192 miles.

FACILITIES: Aircraft crew of 4 or 5. **Maximum of 80 passengers in airline type seats facing to the rear of the aircraft.**

INVENTORY: USAF 552.

C-135B STRATOLIFTER

This aircraft is similar to the KC-135 Stratotanker without the refueling equipment. These aircraft were initially purchased as an interim cargo/passenger aircraft placed in service before delivery of the C-141s. The appearance of this aircraft is similar to the KC-135.

PROGRAM/PROJECT CONTRACTOR: Boeing Military Airplanes.

POWER SOURCE: Four CFM international F108-CF-100 turbofan engines. Each engine has 22,224 lbs of thrust.

DIMENSIONS: Wing span is 130 ft, 10 in. Length is 134 ft, 6 in. Height is 38 ft, 4 in.

WEIGHT: Empty 102,300 lbs. Gross 275,000 lbs.

PERFORMANCE: Maximum speed 600 mph. Range with 54,000 lb payload is 4,625 miles.

INVENTORY: USAF 6.

VC-137B/C STRATOLINER

This is a special mission aircraft which has been modified from the commercial Boeing 707 transport. Two of these aircraft were the original "Air Force One" aircraft used by past United States Presidents.

PROGRAM/PROJECT CONTRACTOR: The Boeing Company.

POWER SOURCE: Four Pratt & Whitney JT3D-3 turbofan engines. Each engine has a 17,200 lb thrust.

DIMENSIONS: VC-137B: Wing span is 130 ft, 10 in. Length 144 ft, 6 in. Height 42 ft, 10 in. VC137-C: Wing span is 145 ft, 9 in. Length is 152 ft, 11 in. Height is 42 ft, 5 in.

WEIGHT: VC-137B: Gross 258,000 lbs. VC-137C: Gross 322,000 lbs.

PERFORMANCE: VC-137C: Maximum speed 627 mph. Service ceiling 42,000 ft. Range 5,150 miles.

FACILITIES: This is a special mission aircraft with a variety of configurations. There are full-service galleys, dining, sleeping berths, and airline type seating.

INVENTORY: USAF 2.

C-141A/B STARLIFTER

The C-141A/B STARLIFTER transport has undergone extensive modification to extend the airframe and modernization to all aspects of the aircraft. The result is a modern air transport which is fully capable of performing many missions from routine cargo and passengers to intertheater MEDEVAC and humanitarian missions around the world. All of the C-141A/B fleet are scheduled for repainting to a flat grey.

PROGRAM/PROJECT CONTRACTOR: Lockheed-Georgia Company.

POWER SOURCE: Four Pratt & Whitney TF33-P-7 turbofan engines. Each engine has 21,000 lbs of thrust.

DIMENSIONS: Wing span is 159 ft, 11 in. Length is 168 ft, 3.5 in. Height is 39 ft, 3 in.

WEIGHT: Operating 149,000 lbs. Maximum payload 89,000 lbs. Gross 343,000 lbs.

PERFORMANCE: Maximum cruising speed is 566 mph. Range with maximum payload is 2,293 miles without air refueling.

FACILITIES: Air crew of five. **200 passengers in commercial airline seats facing to the rear of the aircraft.** 103 litter patients plus attendants. Cargo on 13 standard 463L pallets or alternate mounted weapons, vehicles or other cargo.

INVENTORY: USAF 207.

KC-010A EXTENDER

This advanced tanker/cargo aircraft is based on the commercial DC-10 Series, 30 CF. It has been modified to include fuselage fuel cells, aerial refueling operator station and boom. Military avionics have been added. The aircraft is fit to perform a role of extending and enhancing worldwide military mobility. The latest modifications to this aircraft are wing-mounted air-refueling pods designed to supplement the basic system and increase capability.

PROGRAM/PROJECT CONTRACTOR: Douglas Aircraft Company, Division of McDonnell Douglas Corporation.

POWER SOURCE: Three General Electric CF-6-50C2 turbofan engines. Each engine has 52,500 lbs of thrust.

DIMENSIONS: Wing span is 165 ft, 4.5 in. Length is 181 ft, 7 in. Height is 58 ft, 1 in.

WEIGHT: Gross 590,000 lbs.

PERFORMANCE: Cruising speed Mach 0.825. Service ceiling 42,000 ft range with maximum cargo 4,370 miles.

FACILITIES: Aircraft crew of four. **75 passengers in commercial airline seats facing to the rear of the aircraft.** 27 standard 463L pallets. Maximum cargo payload 169,409 lbs.

INVENTORY: USAF 59.

P-3C-ORION

This is a propeller-driven aircraft which has been used by the U.S. Navy since 1958 in an Anti-Submarine Warfare (ASW) role. Many improvements have been incorporated in the basic airframe over the years. The latest improvements allow the aircraft to detect, track and attack quieter new generation submarines. **The replacement P-7A program, with Lockheed as the contractor, was terminated in July 1990. The USN is investigating alternative programs.**

PROGRAM/PROJECT CONTRACTOR: Lockheed.
POWER SOURCE: Four Allison T-56-A-14 turboprop engines. Each engine has 4,900 ehp.
DIMENSIONS: Wing span is 100 ft. Length is 117 ft. Height is 34 ft.
WEIGHT: Gross weight is 139,760 lbs.
PERFORMANCE: Maximum speed 473 mph. Cruise speed 377 mph. Ceiling 28,300 ft.
FACILITIES: Aircraft crew of 10. **18 passengers in airline seats.**
INVENTORY: USN-133. Seventy-three older aircraft are to be retired in the very near future, thus reducing the number of aircraft in regular and reserve P-3 squadrons. **Total-273.**

Photo Credits

Cover top   "Space-A call at Travis AFB, CA." (Ann Crawford)

Cover bottom   "C-005B - Boarding to the passenger compartment by the truck stairs."(Courtesy AMC)

Page 16   "This Space-A traveler is "travel-ready!" (Courtesy R&R subscriber)

Page 17   "Ready to make the Space-A roll call." (Ann Crawford)

Page 19   "Active duty members on a PCS may take pets on commercial contract Patriot Flights. Space-A passengers, however, may NOT take pets by Space-A air travel. Sorry, Fido." (Ann Crawford)

Page 20   "The Amnesty Box - where you can dispose of prohibited items before boarding." (Ann Crawford)

Page 20   "Snacks and meals are available on most Space-A flights." (Courtesy USN)

Page 22   "Passengers line up to go through security screening and then to the aircraft." (Ann Crawford)

APPENDIX N: Space-A Questions and Answers

One of the biggest fringe benefits, dollar-wise, for uniformed services personnel and their family members is Space-A air travel on U.S. military owned and operated aircraft. While there are some old pros who know all the ropes, having learned the hard way by flying Space-A, there are those who are a bit afraid to jump into the unknown. This appendix is especially for those who want to know as much as they can about Space-A air travel. Answers are based on information available to us at press time. Because policies can change or be interpreted differently, these general answers must be regarded only as guides - not rules. Specific questions, particularly those dealing with changes in policy, should be directed to military officials who are the final authority on the subject. We have divided the questions and answers into general functional categories. We hope that this appendix will aid readers in locating questions and answers in which they have a special interest.

GENERAL INFORMATION

01. Is Space-A travel a reasonable substitute for travel on a commercial airline? The answer depends on you! If your travel schedule is flexible and your finances permit for a stay (sometimes in a "high-cost" area), while awaiting movement, space-available travel is a good travel choice. While some travelers sign up and travel the same day, many factors could come together to make buying a commercial ticket your best or only option. Remember, Space-A travel success depends on flexibility, patience and good timing.

02. What facilities are available at AMC terminals (nursery, BX, snack bar)? Facilities at most military terminals are generally the same as commercial facilities. Facilities include exchanges, barber shops, snack bars, pay television (free television lounge in some military terminals), traveler assistance, baggage lockers or rooms, United Service Organization (USO) lounges, and nurseries (at major terminals). The type of facility available will vary according to the terminal size, passenger volume, location and military mission.

03. What documents are required for traveling Space-A? All travelers require a uniformed services ID card. Dependent family members and Retirees require a passport in most cases. Visas or visitor cards may be required for passport holders traveling to some destinations. In some cases immunization records are required. See Appendix B: Personnel Entrance Requirements in Military Living's *Military Space-A Air Opportunities Around the World* book for detailed requirements.

04. Will Space-A travel cost much? In general, no. Some terminals must collect a federal departure tax and/or a federal inspection fee from Space-A passengers on commercial contract

missions. Meals may be purchased at a nominal fee out of most air terminals while traveling on military aircraft. Meal service on AMC Category B "Patriot Flights" full plane load charters is complimentary.

05. What fees will Space-A passengers be required to pay? All passengers departing CONUS, Alaska or Hawaii on a commercial aircraft from a commercial airport must pay a $6 Airport Departure Tax that goes toward airport improvements. Also, all Space-A passengers departing on commercial contract mission inbound to the United States must pay a $12.40 Head Tax and an $11.00 Federal Inspection Fee. Some foreign departure terminals may also collect a departure tax, e.g., $30 AU when leaving Australia.

06. What are the trends in the availability of Space-A travel? Does it seem as if there will be more or less Space-A travel in the coming years? Although AMC has lead efforts to improve Space-A travel in the past few years, movement still remains a result of unused seats. Present DoD personnel and budget trends are effecting Space-A movement opportunity. AMC is dedicated to putting a passenger in every available seat.

07. How can I find where my name is on the Space-A register? Each terminal maintains a Space-A register (organized by priority and the date and time of registration for travel) that is updated daily. The register is conveniently located in the terminal and directly accessible to you. Travelers may call the terminal directly to find where they stand travelwise.

08. As a Reservist, where can I fly? Reserve members with DD Form 2 (Red) identification and DD Form 1853 may fly to, from, and between Alaska, Hawaii, Puerto Rico, the U.S. Virgin Islands, Guam, American Samoa, and CONUS. Additionally, when on active duty (for 30 days or more), members may fly anywhere overseas that AMC has flights operating.

09. As a Retiree, where can I fly? Retired members with DD Form 2 (Blue; the old form is gray) identification card may fly anywhere AMC has flights operating including CONUS, with the exception of occasional restricted areas such as Vietnam and Diego Garcia which have been restricted for many years. Some areas require special permission to enter, such as Kenya.

10. Can I have family members travel with another military member if given power of attorney, other releases, or authority? No, with the exception of Category IV EML Leave and Category V, command-sponsored dependents may only travel when accompanied by their sponsor.

11. Who determines eligibility to fly Space-A? The four services jointly establish Space-A eligibility which is published in DoD 4515.13-R "Air Transportation Eligibility." AMC's first responsibility is airlifting official DoD traffic. Space-A passen-

gers are accommodated only after official duty passengers and cargo.

12. How long does my name stay on the Space-A list? All travelers remain on the register for 60 days after registration, for the duration of their travel orders authorization, or until they are selected for travel, whichever occurs first. Revalidation has been eliminated.

13. What is country sign-up and how does it affect me? Under this program, you may sign up for five different countries rather than five different destinations. You are also eligible for the "ALL" sign-up which makes you eligible for all other destinations served. The applicant can sign up for four countries and "ALL" as the fifth destination. This gives you a greater selection of destinations from which to choose.

14. What is remote sign-up? Remote sign-up allows passengers to enter the backlog by telefaxing copies of proper service documentation along with desired country destinations and family members' first names to the aerial port of departure. The telefax data header will establish date/time of sign-up; therefore, Active Duty personnel must ensure the telefax is sent no earlier than the effective date of leave. Mail entries will also be permitted. The original date and time of sign-up shall be documented and stay with the passenger until his or her destination is reached. Also at any time the passenger may sign up for space-available travel to return to home station. NOTE: If applicable, a statement that all required border clearance documents are current is required.

15. What is self sign-up? Self sign-up is a program that allows passengers to sign up at a terminal without waiting in line. Most locations now provide self sign-up counters with easy to follow instructions for registration.

BAGGAGE

16. How much baggage can Space-A passengers check? Each Space-A passenger (regardless of age) can check two pieces of baggage totaling 140 pounds. Air Mobility Command (AMC) limits the size of each item to 62 linear inches. This measurement is obtained by adding together the item's length, width and height. The rules permit some exceptions to the 62 linear inches size limitation. For Active Duty personnel, all duffel bags, sea bags, Air Force issue B-4 bags and civilian-origin versions that have the same approximate dimensions can be checked. Similarly, the size restrictions do not apply to golf bags with golf clubs, snow skis, folding bicycles, fishing equipment, musical instruments and rucksacks. Any one of these oversized items listed above may be checked if it is the only piece checked and meets weight requirements of 140 pounds total.

17. We have heard that families and other groups can "pool" their baggage authorization. What's the story? Space-A passengers traveling together as a group (that is, listed on a single Military Transportation Authorization or AMC Form 140 (Space Available Travel Request)) may pool their baggage authorization so long as the total number of checked pieces does not exceed the number of travelers times 140 pounds, i.e., a five person family travel group could not exceed 700 pounds (5 x 140 pounds = 700 pounds) and 10 pieces (5x2=10).

18. How much baggage can I carry with me into the passenger cabins? All passengers boarding the aircraft can carry on one or more pieces so long as they fit under the passenger's seat, in the overhead compartment or other approved storage area, e.g., closets for hang-up garment bags. If available storage space is important to your baggage carrying needs, inquire at the terminal regarding storage areas for carry-on baggage before checking your baggage for a particular flight. As a guideline carry-on bags should not exceed 45 linear inches (length + width + height = 45 inches). Passengers traveling with infants can also carry on any Federal Aviation Administration (FAA) approved infant car seat regardless of any other baggage. Each AMC facility has a list of the FAA approved car seats. Passengers can call the FAA at tel: (202) 426-3800 to determine if new seats have been added to the list of approved seats.

19. Is the baggage limit the same for all aircraft? No. The baggage limit for smaller executive aircraft and the C-009A/E Nightingale is considerably less. On small two-engine executive and operational support aircraft, the baggage limit for Space-A passengers is 30 pounds. Also, on the C-009A/E aircraft the size limit for carry-on baggage is 18" long, 5" wide and 19" high or 42" overall.

20. As a Space-A passenger, may I pay for excess checked baggage over 140 pound or two pieces? No. Only duty status passengers may pay for excess baggage.

NOTE: See APPENDIX O: Space-A Travel Tips for more information on baggage.

ELIGIBILITY

21. May all Active Duty and Retired members of all the Uniformed Services fly Space-A? Yes. All Active Duty and Retired members (as well as their eligible family members) of all seven uniformed services (U.S. Army, U.S. Navy, U.S. Marine Corps, U.S. Coast Guard, U.S. Public Health Service Officer Corps, National Oceanic and Atmospheric Administration Officer Corps and U.S. Air Force) may fly Space-A as provided for in DoDD 4515.13-R as revised. Dependent family members may only accompany their sponsor on flights going overseas and in overseas areas. Dependents may not fly point to point in CONUS unless the same mission/flight continues overseas. As

the result of a recent change in the regulation, one adult Active Duty dependent may accompany the sponsor on CONUS point-to-point flights when the sponsor is on "emergency leave" and when the sponsor is on an approved house hunting trip prior to a PCS.

22. May National Guard and Reservists fly Space-A? National Guard members and Reservists in an Active paid status may fly anywhere in CONUS, Alaska, Hawaii, Puerto Rico, Guam, American Samoa and the U.S. Virgin Islands. Guard and Reserve members cannot fly Space-A to a foreign country. Congressman Tom Campbell of California (Tel: C-202-225-2631) has introduced a bill H. R. 3267, Fairness for the Military Reserve Act of 1999, which among other things, would extend Space-A air travel to selected Reservists, including National Guard to outside the United States and its possessions, to foreign countries--the same as retired military, and would give Reservists the same priority status as Active Duty personnel when traveling for their monthly drills. Caution: This is not law at press time. Guard and Reserve members must have the ID Card, DD Form 2 (Red), and DD Form 1853, Authentication of Reserve Status for Travel Eligibility (authenticated by the Unit Commander within the last six months). The same is true of Guard and Reserve personnel who have received official notification of retirement eligibility but have not reached retirement age (60). This "gray area" retirement eligible group must present their ID cards (Red) and retirement eligibility notices (letters) or possess a red DD Form 2 which has been generated from the DEERS database.

23. When may National Guard and Reservist eligible family members fly Space-A? When the sponsor retires and receives retired pay and full benefits at age 60, eligible family members may then fly Space-A. Family members must be accompanied by their sponsor when flying Space-A and may only fly on flights going overseas and in the overseas area, except CONUS legs of overseas flights.

24. Is there any difference in Space-A rules regarding eligibility for Active Duty versus Retired service members? Yes. First of all, Active Duty sponsors personnel have priority (Categories I Emergency Leave (retirees may be added to this category when approved under special circumstances), II EML, III Ordinary Leave, IV Unaccompanied Dependents on EML and V Permissive TDY) on Space-A flights at all times. Other differences include the fact that Active Duty personnel may take their "dependent" mothers and fathers (who have ID Cards DD Form 1173), with them on Space-A trips. Dependent in-laws are NOT included in this privilege. Retired members do not have this privilege, and Retired members and their families travel in Category VI.

25. I am a 100% disabled American veteran (DAV). I've heard that some of us can fly Space-A and some can't. Could you give

me more information on 100% DAVs and Space-A? Disabled American veterans must be RETIRED from a uniformed service to qualify for Space-A travel. Those members who were separated in lieu of being retired are not eligible. Here's an easy way to check your eligibility. If your monthly retired check is paid by a uniformed services finance center, e.g., Defense Finance and Accounting Service, Cleveland Center, and your ID card is DD Form 2 (old cards are gray in color; new cards are blue), you can fly Space-A. If you are paid by the Veterans Administration and your ID card is a DD Form 1173 (butterscotch in color) or the more recently issued DD Form 2765, you cannot fly Space-A. The color of ID cards and their form numbers are the key to being allowed to sign up for a Space-A flight. The DD Form 1173 is the same ID form used by dependents. In any case, dependents are not generally allowed to fly Space-A without their sponsors, so this butterscotch color card is a red flag alerting the officials at the Space-A desk that the carrier of the DD Form 1173 is not eligible to fly Space-A unaccompanied.

26. I am Retired military and disabled and carry a blue ID card. Can I have a brother, sister, or friend accompany me to help me? The only persons permitted to accompany you are your dependents (not in the CONUS) or other persons eligible for Space-A travel. Every effort shall be made to transport passengers with disabilities who are otherwise eligible to travel. Passenger service personnel and crew members shall provide assistance in boarding, seating, and deplaning passengers with special needs.

27. May a Retired service member, who relies on a guide dog because of vision deficiency, travel with the animal aboard military aircraft Space-A? Yes. This is allowed when the dog is properly harnessed and muzzled and the animal does not obstruct the aisle. Also, the dog may not occupy a seat in the aircraft, it must sit at the feet of the service member.

28. Who may fly on National Guard and Reserve flights of the Military Services? All uniformed services personnel and their eligible dependents may fly on most National Guard and Reserve flights depending upon the mission. The National Guard and Reserve have some of the best flights available. The catch is that many are not scheduled flights. Many different types of flight missions are given to National Guard and Reserve units; therefore, one can often find some very special flights to places not normally seen on flight schedules. Most National Guard and Reserve departure locations are listed in Military Living's *Military Space-A Air Opportunities Around The World* book.

29. Are Active Duty personnel in a leave or pass status traveling Space-A, always required to wear the service uniform? No. All Active Duty members (except USMC flying on USMC Marine aircraft) in a leave or pass status traveling Space-A on

military department owned and operated aircraft are not required to wear the class A or B uniform of their service.

30. May an Active Duty service member use Space-A to take dependents to his/her unaccompanied duty station overseas or back from overseas to CONUS after the unaccompanied duty tour is completed? No. Family members may use Space-A only when they are with the sponsor on an accompanied tour (on service orders) overseas. The Space-A privilege is intended only for a visit to an overseas or CONUS area on a round-trip basis with the sponsor. Space-A cannot be used to establish a home for dependents overseas or in CONUS.

31. May an Active Duty service member sign out on leave, sign up (register) for Space-A and if there is a wait for the flight, go back to work to avoid loss of leave time? When registering for Space-A travel, either by fax, mail/courier or in person, the member must have an approved leave or pass authorization effective on or before the date of registration for Space-A travel. You must show your approved leave with an effective date on or before your sign-up date. If a member registers for Space-A travel but voluntarily returns to work during the intervening days before the actual flight departure, leave will be charged for those days. You must be on leave throughout your entire Space-A leave travel period.

32. What does it mean to be "bumped?" The mission needs of space required passengers or cargo may require the removal of Space-A passengers at any point. If removed after being manifested (approved for this particular flight) on a flight or en route, you may re-register with the date and time adjusted to reflect the date and time of registration at the point of origin. The Space-A passengers will be placed no higher than the bottom of the category I on the Space-A register. Space-A passengers cannot be bumped by other Space-A passengers.

33. What can service families do if they become extremely ill while overseas and need to return to the United States? Air medical evacuation (MEDEVAC) through AMC is available to Active Duty, Retired and their eligible family members. Space-A travelers should get in touch with a U.S. military medical facility, preferably a hospital, or the American Embassy or Consulate to be considered for this service. In a change of military regulations, the remains of a retiree who died overseas may be returned on AMC aircraft to the U.S. for burial. Watch our *R&R Travel News*™ for more info.

34. What is "show time?" "Show time" is the time when a roll call of prospective Space-required and Space-A passengers, who are waiting for a specific flight, is made. The total available seats are allocated to travelers based on priority category and date/time of sign-up. See Section I for details. Failure to make "show time" will result in not making the flight and

"show times" can be changed without notice depending on operational requirements.

35. Why can't passengers arriving at the terminal after "show time" for a flight be processed for that flight? Passengers should realize that many tasks are performed before a flight departs. Every possible effort will be made to process passengers arriving after "show time" if it doesn't jeopardize the aircraft's departure time or mission safety.

36. Are there special eligibility requirements for pregnant women and infants? Yes. Children must be older than six weeks to fly on military aircraft. If the infant is younger than six weeks old, there must be written permission from a physician to fly for mother and child. Pregnant women may fly without approval until their 34th week of pregnancy. In a medical emergency, a pregnant woman of more than 34 weeks or a child younger than six weeks and the mother will be flown on a medical evacuation (MEDEVAC) flight as patients.

37. What is the scope of the DoD student travel program? Dependent students who attend school in the United States are authorized one round-trip travel per fiscal year from the school location to the parents' duty station overseas, including U.S. possessions. The student travel program began in 1984 as a quality of life initiative for service members stationed overseas who had children attending secondary or undergraduate school in the United States. The plan has fluctuated over the years. The rule for the travel program applies to service members permanently assigned outside CONUS authorized to have family members reside with them. The student dependent must be unmarried, under age 23, pursuing a secondary or undergraduate education and possess a valid DD Form 1173 ID card.

38. What is the Environmental and Morale Leave (EML) Program? This program is designed to provide environmental relief from a duty station which has some "drawbacks" and to offer a source of affordable recreation otherwise not available. In simple terms, it boils down to allowing Active Duty military personnel and their dependents to fly Space-A on military aircraft. There are, however, a couple of big differences in EML leave and regular Space-A leave. First, dependents are permitted to travel accompanied or UNACCOMPANIED by their sponsor. They may utilize "suitably equipped DoD logistic-type aircraft" as well as AMC channel and contract aircraft. Secondly, EML has a Category II classification (for sponsors and their dependents traveling together) which is higher than regular Active Duty, Category III and Retired Space-A classification (Category VI). Dependents traveling on EML leave alone are in category IV. Military sponsors and/or dependents on EML revert to ordinary leave status when they arrive in CONUS. They regain their EML status only when they depart CONUS for their EML program area. A good bit of EML travel is utilized in the Middle and Far East areas. This

means that fewer flights may be available from this area for lower category personnel. The EML program is a tremendous morale booster to those assigned in far-off places and is very popular in these areas.

39. My husband was killed in Vietnam and is buried in the Punch Bowl (National Memorial Cemetery of the Pacific) in Hawaii. The children and I would like to take a trip to Hawaii to visit his grave. Can we fly in a Space-A status? No. Sorry, but widow/ers are not afforded the privilege of Space-A air travel. The rules state that family members must be accompanied by their military sponsor, so naturally this is impossible. There have been proposals advanced, namely by the National Association of Uniformed Services/Society of Military Widows (NAUS/SMW) and others, to support a change to the DoD Space-A Directive which does not provide for widow/ers of uniformed personnel from using overseas (and any other) Space-A travel.

40. May I register (sign-up) by fax, e-mail, letter/courier or in person at the same departure terminal more than one time for five different foreign countries in order to improve my chances for selection to a particular country? Space-A passengers may have only one registration (sign-up) record at a passenger terminal specifying a maximum of five countries (the fifth country may be "ALL" in order to allow the widest opportunity for Space-A air travel). This record may be changed at any time to include adding or deleting countries to which a passenger wants to travel, but the Julian date and time will be adjusted to the date of the latest change. No passenger may have two or more records with separate information; however, you may sign-up at several departure terminals in order to improve your chances for selection for air travel. This may change in the near future if "round-trip sign-up or one-time sign up" is approved. For example, in the Mid-Atlantic States Area you can sign up at McGuire AFB, Baltimore/Washington IAP, Andrews AFB and Dover AFB for air travel to Central Europe and the Near East Area.

41. What happens to your sign-up records at a departure location when you fly from that station? Note carefully that once passengers are selected for a flight, their name will be removed from the station standby register for all destinations.

42. May pets be transported Space-A? Not by Space-A passengers. Active Duty personnel may move pets Space-A on military contract flights when the sponsor is traveling on a permanent change of station.

43. I am retired. When I was on active duty, my personnel officer issued me travel and leave orders which specified travel documents and other requirements for visiting foreign countries. Where can I now get that information? Appendix B: Personnel Entrance Requirements in Military Living's

Military Space-A Air Opportunities Around The World
book. You may also check the personnel entrance requirements
to foriegn countries and the latest changes to the DoD Foreign
Clearance Guides at local personnel offices, AMC Space-A
counters or most other air departure locations.

44. As a Space-A passenger, will I be subjected to security
screening prior to boarding a flight? Yes. In most cases you and
your baggage will receive electronic and/or personal security
screening prior to boarding the flight or entering a secure area
for aircraft boarding.

45. May adult family members who are dependent children
because of a handicap or a permanent disability, and who have
a valid DD Form 1173 military ID card, travel with their sponsor regardless of age? Yes. They may travel on the same basis
as any other dependent on flights going overseas and in the
overseas theater. Documentation of the dependent's permanent
disability may be required.

FOOD AND BEVERAGE SERVICES

46. Is food served to Space-A passengers on the flight? Food and
soft drinks are free on AMC contract "Patriot Flights". Space-A
passengers, like duty passengers, may purchase beer and wine
on AMC contract Patriot Flights. There is a charge if Space-A
passengers want to eat on other (military) flights. You can purchase healthy heart menus from the in-flight kitchen. The
snack menu, at $1.90, includes sandwich, salad or vegetables,
fruit and milk or soft drink. The breakfast menu, at $1.50,
includes cereal or bagel, fruit, danish and milk or juice. The
sandwich meal, at $3.00, includes sandwich, fruit, vegetable or
salad, snack or dessert, milk, juice or soft drink. These meals
are served at the appropriate time in the flight. Reservations
for meals are made at the time of seat assignment or other
times in the flight processing. You may bring your own snacks
(food) aboard (no alcohlic beverages). New meal prices are
established on 1 October each year.

47. Are specialized meals available to Space-A passengers?
Specialized meals are made available for duty passengers only
for medical or religious reasons. If you need special food, we
suggest you bring your own to maintain flexibility. Check with
the Air Passenger Terminals regarding any restrictions on carrying food aboard as this can differ from place to place. While
you can make your requirements known to passenger processing personnel at the time of flight processing, the chance of
having additional specialized meals available at the last
minute for passengers might be slim.

48. How are alcoholic beverages handled? Alcoholic beverages
are not served on military aircraft. All open (seals broken) containers of alcoholic beverages will be confiscated if on your person or in your carry-on baggage. In many cases, sealed alcoholic

containers may be checked. Check with the Air Passenger Terminal for more information. You may not consume alcoholic beverages from your own supply on a military aircraft. The AMC commercial contract Patriot Flights, which frequently carry Space-A passengers, offer beer and wine to everyone of legal age for a fee.

49. How is food service handled on USN, USMC, USCG, USAF (USAFR, USAG) and other non-AMC flights? Most departure terminals have food service for crews and passengers. If the flight duration is more than approximately four hours, you will be notified in time to obtain your own box of food and drinks. Most flights have coffee and tea and all flights have drinking water on board.

CHANCES OF FLYING SPACE-A

50. How about Space-A availability? Space-A air opportunities change daily and, in fact, even hourly. There are more than 300 very active locations at which uniformed personnel, their eligible family members, and others may fly Space-A. There are also many other less active locations which offer some Space-A air opportunities. We estimate that more than 800,000 Space-A flights (all services) are taken every year. Availability is subject to time of the year, air mission, needs of the military services, quantity of flights, frequency of flights and the number of people attempting to fly Space-A. This large number of interactive variables which impact Space-A Air Opportunities makes it very difficult to precisely predict the availability of Space-A seats to a particular destination at a precise time.

51. What is the best time of the year to travel Space-A? The best time is a function of departure locations, arrival locations, space-required needs and the number of people waiting for Space-A transportation. Generally the best times to travel Space-A are autumn, late winter, early spring and after 15 July. It is best to avoid travel between 1-5 January, 15 May-15 July, 15-30 November and 15-25 December when traffic is heaviest.

52. Who flies Space-A the most - enlisted personnel, officers, Retired members or dependents? Enlisted members travel Space-A more than all other groups (of course there are more Active Duty enlisted members than any other group).

53. Which uniformed service uses Space-A more than the others? Air Force members travel Space-A more than members from any other service followed by the U.S. Army, U.S. Navy and U.S. Marine Corps.

PRIORITY FOR SPACE-A TRAVEL

54. Who has priority on Space-A flights? The DoD has established a priority system for allocating Space-A air travel. This system is described in detail in Appendix A, which is taken

from Chapter 6, Space Available Travel, DoDD 4515.13-R. The general categories and their travel priorities are as follows:

Category I: Emergency Leave, Unfunded Travel.

Category II: Environmental and Morale Leave (EML).

Category III: Ordinary Leave, Close Blood or Affinitive Relatives, House Hunting Permissive TDY, Medal of Honor Holders, Cadets and Midshipmen of the U.S. Service Academies and Others.

Category IV: Unaccompanied Dependents on EML and DoDDS Teachers on EML During Summer.

Category V: Permissive TDY (Non-House Hunting), Foreign Military, Students, Dependents and Others.

Category VI: Retired, Dependents, Reserve, ROTC, NUPOC and CEC.

Note: More details concerning each category is available in Chapter VI, DoDD 4515.13-R in this book.

55. May any eligible passenger make reservations for Space-A travel? No. Space-A passengers may not make reservations and are not guaranteed seats. The application for Space-A travel is not a reservation. The DoD is not obligated to continue Space-A passengers travel or to return them to their point of origin.

56. Does rank/grade have anything to do with who gets a Space-A flight? No. Travel opportunities are available on a first-in first-out basis within DoD established categories. Travel is afforded on an equitable basis to officers, enlisted personnel, DoD/other civilian employees and their dependents without regard to rank or grade, military or civilian or branch of service.

57. Are there any circumstances under which a Retired service member in Category VI may be upgraded to a higher category? You bet there are. If you are traveling Space-A overseas and an emergency occurs at home, you may be upgraded to Category I, Emergency Leave, Unfunded Travel, by the installation commander or his representative under par 7-C, Chapter 6, DoDD 4515.13-R. However, you should have the emergency verified, in writing, by the Red Cross before attempting to obtain an upgrade.

TEMPORARY DUTY AND SPACE-A TRAVEL

58. May uniformed services personnel on official temporary duty orders (TDY) elect to travel Space-A to the TDY point (station)? No. Uniformed services personnel on official TDY orders must travel in a duty status from their permanent duty station

to the TDY point and return to their permanent duty station.

59. Is there any way family members can travel Space-A to their sponsor's TDY point? No. Family members are not authorized Space-A to and from a sponsor's TDY point. TDY personnel may not travel Space-A between their duty station and TDY point as a means to have their dependents travel with them.

60. Can the service member take leave and travel Space-A from the TDY point? Upon arrival at the TDY point, personnel must conduct their business in a TDY status. They may then take ordinary leave while at the TDY point and travel Space-A from the TDY point to another location, but leave must be terminated prior to return travel from the TDY point of origin to the service member's duty station or next TDY location.

61. May family members travel Space-A when the sponsor takes leave at the TDY point? Family members may join the sponsor at the TDY point (at their own expense) in order to travel Space-A with the sponsor while the sponsor is on leave.

62. May the service member and dependents travel Space-A between CONUS and overseas? When the service member's permanent duty station and TDY location are within CONUS, Space-A travel to an overseas area and return is authorized. Also, when the service member's duty station and TDY location are overseas, Space-A travel to CONUS and return is authorized. (NOTE: Dependents may not travel point to point Space-A within CONUS except on the CONUS legs of overseas flights, emergency leave and PCS house hunting.)

63. When the service member's duty station and TDY location are in different countries overseas, and the service member travels Space-A to CONUS, may they return Space-A to their duty station? No. The service member must return Space-A from CONUS to the overseas TDY point or to a location other than the permanent duty station. He must return to the TDY point (at personal expense, if necessary, if Space-A travel is not possible to the TDY point) in order to complete travel to the permanent duty station in TDY status.

64. What is a simple summary of the above complex guidelines? The bottom line is that service members must always travel between their permanent duty station and a TDY point or between two TDY points in a TDY status.

OTHER

65. May Space-A eligible passengers take Space-A air transportation around the world? No. There are insufficient Space-A flights to circumnavigate the earth north to south or south to north. There are adequate flights to travel around the earth east to west or west to east. However, there is one choke point,

Diego Garcia Atoll (NKW/KJDG), Chagos Archipelago, GB, through which you are not authorized to travel Space-A. The Secretary of Defense (SECDEF) has limited access to Diego Garcia to mission-essential personnel. Space-A travel through Diego Garcia, including circuitous travel for personnel on official orders, is not authorized. This prohibition is found in SECDEF message 250439Z JAN 1986 and the DoD Foreign Clearance Guides. Commercial facilities at this UK territory in the Indian Ocean are extremely limited to nonexistent. The Diego Garcia Naval Base does not have lodging, messing and other support facilities essential for non-mission essential travelers.

66. Should I expect to find more than one Space-A roster on a base? No. Only one Space-A roster shall be maintained on a base, installation or post. The maintenance of such a roster is the responsibility of the AMC passenger or terminal service activity. If there is no AMC transportation activity, then the base, installation or post commander designates the agency responsible for maintaining the Space-A roster. You may find an exception at locations where a second service has a separate facility such as Andrews AFB and the Washington NAF.

67. Can people travel Space-A to Alaska or South America? Yes. Travelers may obtain Space-A travel to Alaska, South America, and other interesting locations; i.e., Australia, New Zealand, etc. Travel to Alaska is relatively easy when departing from the West Coast (Travis AFB, California, and McChord AFB, Washington). Travel to South America and other remote areas is more difficult. Infrequent flights to remote areas are primarily cargo missions and have few seats available for passenger movement. Expect long waiting periods for movement.

68. I am retired and am traveling on a passport and my flight originated overseas. Where in the CONUS can I fly into? When traveling on a passport, (family members, Retired Uniform Service, Reserve, etc.,) you may return to CONUS only through authorized ports of entry where customs and immigration clearance is available. While you may depart CONUS literally from any military airfield, reentry locations for passport holders are limited. Active Duty passengers who do not require immigration clearance have more reentry options open.

69. Is it easier to go to some destinations? Space available travel occurs year round. However, travelers will find it is much more difficult to travel during the summer months (June-August) and the November-December holiday periods. It is particularly important that passengers be prepared to make alternate arrangements if they are not able to travel during these times.

APPENDIX O: Space-A Travel Tips

DOCUMENTS

Carry passports, military IDs and travelers checks with you and not in your luggage. Make photo copies of your ID cards, credit/debit cards, title page of passports, immunization records, title page of international driver's permit, list of travelers' checks, list of baggage contents and other important documents. Take one copy with you (not in your luggage) and leave one copy at home or at the office where it is accessible from overseas.

MEDICATIONS

Take all medications (prescriptions and over-the-counter) in their original (labeled) containers, and take any essential medications with you on the plane/train, not in your baggage. If you require prescription refills overseas, take an original physician's prescription for each drug.

If possible, and when necessary, it is recommended by physicians and travelers that you do not take Dramamine until the plane has been in the air for a while.

CLOTHING

If you are planning to launder clothes, pack a well wrapped (plastic bag) liquid laundry soap as opposed to a powder soap. Woolite works well for hand as well as machine washing and comes in both liquid and powder form. Note that laundromats overseas may not have a "permanent-press" cycle on the washer/dryer. They also have a much smaller capacity than U.S. laundry machines.

Know the climate at your destination. Travel light. In most cases you will be carrying your own bags. Wear wash-and-wear type clothes. Travel in casual clothes that are loose-fitting and comfortable. Plan your wardrobe such that you can take off or add clothes in layers. Always wear a jacket, lightweight or heavy depending on the weather at your destination. Include a light raincoat or all-purpose coat in lieu of the jacket. Always wear comfortable shoes with low heels or no heels. Pack/roll socks, underwear, etc., and place in plastic bags.

BAGGAGE

Folding luggage carriers do not count as weight against your checked baggage.

Because of security problems and other reasons, many U.S. bases may no longer have lockers available for storing your luggage. If lockers are available, they will most likely be located outside the terminal. So locations may have lockers located in the secure passenger area to which you may not have access unless you are awaiting departure.

Consider using soft-sided luggage to get more into each suitcase. Allow space for items you purchase overseas, or take a collapsible suitcase to bring gifts home.

There are very few porters at European and Far Eastern airports and train stations, and there are limited to no porters at Space-A terminals. Pack only what you can carry or roll comfortably. Can you carry your bags for one mile (15-20 minutes) without setting them down? If not, your bags are too heavy. Get a shoulder bag with small outer compartments. The bag must fit under your seat in the aircraft, and it should be stain resistant and waterproof. Never carry one large bag but split travel articles into two bags for ease in carrying. Bring less clothing and more money. As a general rule, pack a first time, and then cut your original amount of clothes in half and repack.

Always put your name and address in the inside of your bags as well as on the outside tag of each bag. If the outside tag is lost, your bag can still be returned to you. Put identifying marks (e.g., 1" wide masking tape) in bright colored tape on the outside of your bags for easy identification. (We have a large "C" on each side of our bags.) Lock your bags to protect against partial loss or to at least slow down the would-be thief. Officials (hotel bell stand and porters) have keys for different types of bags to be used in an emergency.

As said earlier, always lock and strap, if available, every bag (place straps from luggage inside before locking). Never pack cash, jewelry, medicine or other valuables or hard to get items in your bags. After you have packed your bags, never leave them unattended, anywhere, for any reason, at any time, until they are checked for travel.

CUSTOMS

Keep receipts for Value Added Tax refunds and for proof of purchase at U.S. Customs. Keep all of your dutiable items in one bag or area for ease in locating during customs inspections.

AMC PLANES AND FLIGHTS

In a C-005A/B/C, your seats are above the cargo area, and the seats are airline seats. In a C-141B, your seats are in lieu of cargo. There may be regular seats or red fabric/canvas fold down seats. Avoid seats 1A and 1B in a C-005A/B/C. They are against the bulkhead and do not recline, as well as being opposite the restroom(s).

Boarding may be quite different from commercial airlines. There may be ladders to climb, or passengers might be boarded from the open flight line rather than through an enclosed passenger gate. For these reasons slacks are better than skirts for women.

Climate in the plane may not be standard. In each type of plane there are hot spots and cold spots. Try to dress in layers for comfort and convenience. The flight crew will supply a small pillow, a blanket and earplugs (on some flights).

Planes are usually boarded and deplaned with DV/VIPs or families first. (May not be followed at all stations/locations.)

Bring something to eat, to read or games to play on the plane. You can also buy a meal to be served on the flight. The food is good, and it also gives you something to do during the seven to nine hour flight to Europe.

Usually there is a DV/VIP lounge in the AMC airport terminal available to O-6 and above of the Uniformed Services and to E-9s of the Armed Services.

MONEY

Exchange some U.S. currency for the currency of at least your first destination country before you go overseas. Exchange at least $25 for local transportation and tips.

Distribute travelers' checks among those traveling in your group. Consider travelers' checks in various U.S. denominations ($20, $50 or $100) as well as in foreign currency denominations (French francs, Italian lire, German marks, British pounds sterling, Japanese yen and other Asian currencies). Travelers checks are now available in the new Euro. The Euro currency will soon be available for the European Market Countries (less the United Kingdom).

If possible, bring foreign coins with you for telephones, tips, etc. Bring along U.S. change to use in the vending machines on U.S. bases/installations. Bring a personal check or two to cash at an Officers' Club/NCO Club overseas. (You will need a U.S. military club card to cash a check in overseas clubs.) When dealing with foreign coinage, watch for non-money coins, e.g., telephone tokens in Italy and UK.

Bring a pocket calculator to convert local prices into U.S. dollars.

Border towns will usually accept either country's money.

Bring along U.S. dollars for the flight home ($23.40 per person for head tax and federal inspection when departing on a contract mission (Patriot Flight); $3.00 per person for a dinner-meal). Be prepared to take a commercial flight home, and have enough money or credit/debit card for that type of flight.

Be aware that foreign banks may close early on some days; usually the exchanges at major airports and train stations are open 24 hours a day. Exchange your travelers' checks at banks or exchanges rather than in stores or restaurants. Hotels and stores tend to charge expensive exchange commissions.

MasterCard and Visa are widely accepted in Europe, as is American Express. Internationally accepted credit cards can be used for cash advances (execute/use with care for security reasons). Also, carry one or two airline credit cards in case of an emergency. Arrange to have funds sent to you via wire to a local bank. For tips and payment for services, carry some foreign currency and coins if available, or carry new U.S. one dollar bills which are readily accepted by service personnel in foreign countries (strongly recommended). You know how much the tip is worth and the dollar is readily accepted by service personnel in foreign countries.

BILLETING

Check for hotel/motel accommodations at post offices (AU, NZ and GB), the tourist offices at main train stations and airports. There are also computer matching services at these locations that will provide a list of accommodations, base or location, price range, length of stay and your needed accommodation.

Your room rate will most often include a continental breakfast. The room rate will vary according to the following:
Class of hotel (Deluxe, First Class, Second Class, etc.);
Type of accommodations (Double bed, King-size bed);
With or without toilet (W/C) in room;
With or without bath/shower in room;
Whether or not the hotel has a restaurant;
Whether or not the hotel has a parking lot;
Whether or not the hotel has an elevator (lift).

In Great Britain, area libraries and post offices usually have a list of local Bed and Breakfast ("B&B") establishments.

In France and its overseas territories, check with the French Armed Forces for lodging and meals/bar service in their Officer and NCO clubs. Also check with Canadian military forces for billeting and mess facilities.

Consider traveling before or after the tourist season in a country; when "in season" rates are no longer in effect. Watch out for trade or other seasonal fares/events, Book Fair in Frankfurt and Oktoberfest in Munich, that will tie up a large number of hotel rooms.

Address and telephone numbers (800) can be obtained from the research section of your local library.

Write the foreign country's tourist office; in the U.S., most are located in New York City and other gateway cities. Addresses and telephone numbers are available in base and public libraries. They will send various kinds of tourist information as well as hotel/motel price lists.

Look for different types of accommodations such as a "Bed and Breakfast" or a "Pension."

TRANSPORTATION

European and most Asian transportation runs on time!

Use the local public transportation system whenever and wherever possible. Note that there is usually a "smoking" and "non-smoking" section on public transportation.

Public transportation (buses/subways) usually accepts exact change only. You may have to buy a ticket before boarding, but frequently no one collects bus or tram tickets from you (i.e., the Frankfurt, DE light rail system). NOTE: Do not fail to buy and retain your ticket. The fine for not buying a ticket is extremely high.

Look for special tourist rates or tourist passes offered by your hotel or the local tourist office. Ask about special transportation rates for round-trip travel or time-limited travel, i.e., weekend, five, seven, or fifteen-day passes.

Most European train stations and airports are open 24 hours a day.

Note the difference between first class and second class on trains. Trains in Europe and Asia are heavily utilized, and second class may be jammed with students and vacationers during holiday times (Easter, Christmas, New Year's, school breaks, etc.). Pay for a reserved seat if you want to insure that you have a seat. The ticket is for transportation only, not a seat.

Note that in most cases you can reserve a seat on a train, etc., especially if you want a window seat or a seat facing in the same direction in which the train is traveling (many seats are reversible).

As in the U.S., food and drink aboard a train or boat is expensive. You may want to bring your own snack, drink or lunch on board.

Be aware of the different fare structures, e.g., a special rate for children (may not be based on age but height), military and animals.

A few points on rental cars: (1) Check the base MWR office for rentals, (2) rent away from the airport to save money and use low rental agencies, (3) return the car full of gas, (4) your insurance may cover the rental car, (5) consider drive-aways, (6) you pay a refundable deposit, (7) they put in the first tank of gas and you put in the rest, (8) rental car reservations are essential in most foreign countries, (9) you can make reservations from the U.S. for major car rental companies, (10) check any car damage very carefully before renting, and make sure that damages are documented on the rental agreement.

LOCAL CUSTOMS

Know if a visa is necessary for your entry into or exit from the country. See Military Living's *Military Space-A Air Opportunities Around the World* book or the DoD Foreign Clearance Guide(s) at AMC Space-A counters or military personnel offices which issue worldwide travel orders.

Know what language is spoken in the part of the country you are visiting, e.g., Switzerland has no official language of its own; rather, the Swiss speak a Swiss-German in the north, French near Geneva, Italian in the south and English everywhere.

Bring an English (foreign language) dictionary with you. Try to learn the basics in the appropriate foreign language, e.g., "Hello," "Goodbye," "Please," "Thank You," "Good Morning," "Good Evening," "Yes," "No," "One," "Two," "Toilet," "Train Station," "Restaurant," etc.

Study the local customs and manners in the country you plan to visit. For example, know when to shake hands, how to greet a guest and when to ask for the menu.

Restaurant menus are often available in English; ask the waiter or hostess for an English-language menu.

Know when the local and national holidays are in the country you are visiting. Know the stores that are open late. Get a local map and mark the location of your hotel on it, and memorize or write down the address where you are staying.

Look for an English-speaking tour. You'll get more out of it if the guide does not have to translate into multiple languages.

Plan to visit the countryside, not just the big cities.

Note the time differences between where you are and the East Coast of the U.S., especially in late April and October when our time changes. Typically, there are a telephone, telegraph and post office located in one central and several other locations.

Be sure to send postcards and other mail to the U.S. via air mail.

TOP TEN TIPS FOR TRAVELERS
(from Dept of State Publication 10541)

1. Make sure you have a signed, valid passport (and visas, if required). Also, before you go, fill in the emergency information page of your passport.

2. Read the Consular Information Sheets (and Public Announcements or Travel Warnings, if applicable) for the countries you plan to visit.

3. Familiarize yourself with local laws and customs of the countries to which you are traveling. Remember, the U.S. Constitution does not follow you. While in a foreign country, you are subject to its laws.

4. Make two copies of your passport identification page. This will facilitate replacement if your passport is lost or stolen. Leave one copy at home with friends or relatives. Carry the other with you in a separate place from your passport.

5. Leave a copy of your itinerary with family or friends at home so that you can be contacted in case of emergency.

6. Do not leave your luggage unattended in public areas. Do not accept packages from strangers.

7. Notify by phone or register in person with the U.S. embassy or consulate upon arrival.

8. To avoid being a target, try not to wear conspicuous clothing and expensive jewelry and do not carry excessive amounts of money or unnecessary credit cards.

9. In order to avoid violating local laws, deal only with authorized agents when you exchange money or purchase art or antiques.

10. If you get into trouble, contact the U.S. consul.

OTHER TIPS

Travel Preparation Time Schedule - Ninety (90) days before departure: Documents: Health, language training, guide books and maps, money requirements, travelers' checks. Sixty (60) days before departure: Documents: ID, passport, visas, international driver's permit, immunizations. Thirty (30) days before departure: Health insurance, money. Seven (7) days before departure: Clothes, insurance, luggage, medicines, glasses, film, audio/video tape.

The successful Space-A traveler has time, patience, funds and is flexible in all aspects of travel.

Have a map of your destination area for orientation purposes and to avoid becoming lost. It is also useful for measuring local travel distances and paying fares.

Be flexible in selecting your Space-A route. A direct line to your desired destination may not be the only route to your destination. If possible, select a place with frequently scheduled departures to your planned destination.

When leaving your car at a departure location, be aware that you may not be able to return via Space-A to your car's location.

Some bases are more fun than others; try to pick a fun and inexpensive base if you expect to wait for a few days before obtaining a flight.

Get information from libraries, book and map stores, tourist offices (state, regional and national), travel agents, uniformed services personnel and their families and friends about your destination. See Military Living's *U.S. Forces Travel Guide to Overseas U.S. Military Installations*, ISBN 0-914862-43-X, an excellent guide to U.S. installations in 28 foreign countries and much, much more. See the appendices which are indispensible to overseas travel. See coupon in the back of this book.

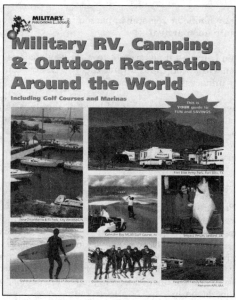

Military Living's Military RV Camping & Outdoor Recreation Around the World is an indispensible guide to worldwide U.S. military installations with RV campgrounds, tent camping, golf courses and marinas.

APPENDIX P: Before You Go - Travel Aids and Travel Publications

The Government Printing Office (GPO) prints many pamphlets which are helpful to travelers. A selection published by the United States Department of State, Bureau of Consular Affairs, Department of the Treasury, U.S. Customs Service, United States Department of Transportation, Federal Trade Commission and other government agencies and private travel organizations follows. The publishing office, International Standard Book Number (ISBN) or pamphlet number, ordering information and price are listed below. You may order most U.S. Government publications from the Superintendent of Documents, U.S. Government Printing Office, Washington, D.C. 20402-9325 or via telephone using VISA or MasterCard, Tel: 202-512-1800. Most of the pamphlets cost $1.00-$2.00; prices change frequently and are noted at press time when available.

UNITED STATES DEPARTMENT OF STATE PUBLICATIONS

---**A SAFE TRIP ABROAD**, ISBN-0-16-048791, #10399, $1.25.

---**CONSULAR INFORMATION SHEETS**, (Specify Foreign Country), Bureau of Consular Affairs, Washington, D.C. 20520, Free with a #10 self-addressed stamped envelope. For recorded travel information, Tel: 202-647-5225.

---**KEY OFFICERS OF FOREIGN SERVICE POSTS**, ISBN-0-16-049628-4, #10556, $5.50.

---**TIPS FOR AMERICANS RESIDING ABROAD**, ISBN-0-16-048784-6, #10391, $1.50.

---**TIPS FOR TRAVELERS TO THE CARIBBEAN**, ISBN 0-16-049089-8, #10439, $1.00.

---**TIPS FOR TRAVELERS TO CENTRAL AND SOUTH AMERICA**, ISBN-0-16-061911-4, #10407, $1.25.

---**TIPS FOR TRAVELERS TO MEXICO**, ISBN-0-16-049710-8, #10571, $1.50.

---**TIPS FOR TRAVELERS TO THE MIDDLE EAST AND NORTH AFRICA**, #10167, ISBN 0-16-045317, $1.50.

---**TIPS FOR TRAVELERS TO THE PEOPLE'S REPUBLIC OF CHINA**, #10271, ISBN-0-16-048376-X, $1.00.

---**TIPS FOR TRAVELERS TO SOUTH ASIA**, ISBN 0-16-048142-2, #10266, $1.00.

---**TIPS FOR TRAVELERS TO SUB-SAHARAN AFRICA**, ISBN-0-16-045390-9, #10205, $1.50.

The following publications may be ordered from the **Consumer Information Center**, Pueblo, CO 81009. They may also be accessed and read from the web page www.pueblo.gsa.gov/travel.htm.

---**FACTS ABOUT FEDERAL WILDLIFE LAWS**, DOI, #591E, Free.

---**FLY-RIGHTS**, #130G, DOT, $1.75.

---**FLY SMART**, #594G, DOT, Free.

---**FOREIGN ENTRY REQUIREMENTS**, #358G, 50 cents.

---**PASSPORTS: APPLYING FOR THEM THE EASY WAY**, #359G, 50 cents.

---**TRAVEL TIPS FOR OLDER AMERICANS**, ISBN-0-16-048762-5, #10337, $1.25.

---**USING CREDIT & CHARGE CARDS OVERSEAS**, DOC, #367E, 50 cents.

---**YOUR TRIP ABROAD**, ISBN 0-16-049506-7, #10542, $150.

DEPARTMENT OF THE TREASURY PUBLICATIONS

---**IMPORTING OR EXPORTING A CAR**, ISBN-0-16-061957-2, #520, $1.00.

---**KNOW BEFORE YOU GO, Customs Hints for Returning Residents**, #512, GPO 294-052: QL 3.

---**TRADEMARK INFORMATION for TRAVELERS**, #508.

---**UNITED STATES CUSTOMS HIGHLIGHTS for GOVERNMENT PERSONNEL, CIVILIAN & MILITARY**, #518, GPO 229-152: 90415.

OTHER GOVERNMENT AGENCIES

---**BUYER BEWARE!**, Division of Law Enforcement, U.S. Fish and Wildlife Service, PO Box 3247, Arlington, VA 22203-3247.

---**CAR RENTAL GUIDE**, Federal Trade Commission, #F025913, Free.

---**HEALTH INFORMATION FOR INTERNATIONAL TRAVEL**, HHS pub #(CDC) ISBN 0-16-061502-X, $21.00.

---**HOW TO DO IT!**, Vote Absentee, FS-13, DOD, Free.

---**NEW HORIZONS for the AIR TRAVELER with a DISABILITY**, Department of Transportation, Office of Consumer Affairs, 400 Seventh Street SW., Washington, DC 20590, Free.

---**TAX HIGHLIGHTS for U.S. CITIZENS and RESIDENTS GOING ABROAD**, #593, IRS.

---**TIPS FOR TAXPAYERS LIVING ABROAD**, #1423, Catalogue #10359A.

---**TRAVEL TIPS On Bringing Food, Plant, and Animal Products into the United States**, #1083, United States Department of Agriculture.

---**VOICE OF AMERICA (VOA) ENGLISH BROADCAST GUIDE**, Voice of America, Audience Mail Unit, 330 Independence Avenue SW, Room G-759, Washington, D.C. 20547 USA, C-202-619-2538, fax: 1-202-619-1241. Please include your postal address when writing via fax. Free. Tours of Washington Hq VOA offered Mon through Fri at 1040, 1340 and 1440 hours and can be arranged by Tel: 202-619-3919.

PRIVATE TRAVEL ORGANIZATIONS

---**AMERICAN SOCIETY OF TRAVEL AGENTS (ASTA)**, Public Relations Department, 1101 King Street, Alexandria, VA 22314, Tel: 703-739-2782, fax: 703-684-8319. To receive the following pamphlets; AVOIDING TRAVEL PROBLEMS, CAR RENTAL TIPS, DESTINATION GOOD HEALTH, HOLIDAY TRAVEL, HOTEL TIPS, OVERSEAS TRAVEL, PACKING TIPS, TRAVEL SAFETY, TIP ON TIPPING and WHY USE AN ASTA TRAVEL AGENT, send a #10 self-addressed stamped ($1.01 postage) envelope to ASTA at the above address, Free.

---**INTERNATIONAL ASSOCIATION FOR MEDICAL ASSISTANCE TO TRAVELERS (IAMAT)**, 417 Center Street, Lewiston, NY 14092-3633, Tel: 716-754-4883. This is a no-membership-fee organization that publishes a directory of English-speaking physicians at IAMAT Centers in hundreds of cities all over the world (including some very remote places). You may join this organization for a tax deductible (we believe) contribution of your choice. They will provide you with the directory, a passport-sized medical record to be completed by your physician before departure, world immunization charts, and world climate charts. The centers will have daily lists of approved physicians available on a 24-hour basis. The scheduled fees (as of January 1996) agreed to be charged are: Office call $45; house/hotel call $55; night, Sunday and local holiday call $65. These fees do not apply to consultations, hospital or laboratory fees. Free (Donation requested).

---**THE INTERNATIONAL DIRECTORY OF ACCESS GUIDES**, Rehabilitation International USA Inc., 20 West 40th Street, New York, NY 10018, Free.

---**DIRECTORY OF USOs WORLDWIDE**, United Service Organization (USO) World Headquarters, Washington Navy Yard, 1008 Eberle Place, Suite 301, Washington, D.C. 20374-5096, Tel: 202-610-5700, Free.

---**WASHINGTON POST TRAVEL INFORMATION**, by fax (24 hours a day) 1-800-945-5190 with major credit/debit cards. See the Sunday Travel Section for a list and code numbers of available articles. Variable cost $2-4.

Military Living's maps and atlases are especially designed with the military traveler in mind.

You can easily plan your trips and locate military installations from major interstates and highways using these essential trip-planning tools.

APPENDIX Q: Passports

Q. Other Than at Passport Agencies, Where Can I Apply for a Passport?

A. You can apply for a passport at many Federal and state courts, probate courts, some county/municipal offices, and some post offices. Over 2500 courts and 1100 post offices in the United States accept passport applications. Court, county/municipal offices and post offices are usually more convenient because they are near your home or your place of business. You save time and money by not having to travel to one of the 13 major U.S. cities where passport agencies are located.

Q. When Do I Have to Apply in Person?

A. You must always apply in person if you are 13 or older, and if you do not meet the requirements for applying by mail. (See "May I Apply for a Passport by Mail?") Usually, for children under 13, only a parent or legal guardian need appear to execute a passport application.

Q. What Do I Need to Do to Apply for a Passport at a Courthouse or Post Office?

A. Go to a courthouse, county/municipal office, or post office authorized to accept passport applications and complete the DSP-11 application form, but do not sign it until instructed to do so. You must present:

1. PROOF OF U.S. CITIZENSHIP—That is—a previous U.S. Passport or, if you were born in the U.S., a certified copy of your birth certificate issued by the state, city, or county of your birth (a certified copy will have a registrar's raised, embossed, impressed, or multicolored seal and the date the certificate was filed with the registrar's office).

If you have neither a U.S. passport nor a certified birth certificate issued in the U.S.—bring a notice from the registrar of the state where you were born that indicates no birth record exists; also, bring as many as possible of the following: a baptismal certificate, hospital birth record, early Census, early school record, or family Bible record. (To be considered, these documents must show your full name and date and place of birth.) Also, bring a notarized affidavit completed by an older blood relative who has personal knowledge of your birth.

If you were born abroad, bring a Certificate of Naturalization, Certificate of Citizenship, Report of Birth Abroad of a U.S. Citizen, or a Certificate of Birth (Form FS-545 or DS-1350). If you do not have these documents, check with the passport acceptance agent for documents that can be used in their place.

2. TWO PHOTOGRAPHS: Photographs must be recent (taken within the past six months), identical, 2 X 2 inches, and either color or black/white; they must show a front view, full face, on a plain, light (white or off-white) background. (Vending machine photographs are not acceptable.)

3. PROOF OF IDENTITY: That is—a previous U.S. passport, a Certificate of Naturalization or Citizenship, a valid driver's license, government or military ID.

4. FEES: $60.00 for a ten-year passport (age 16 or older); $40.00 for a five-year passport (under 16). These amounts include a $15.00 execution fee. Make your check or money order payable to **Passport Service.** Post offices (and passport agencies) accept cash, but courts are not required to do so. If you must have your passport in less than 25 business days, you will need to pay an additional $35.00 expedite fee to ensure urgent handling. (See "What If I Need a Passport in a Hurry?")

5. SOCIAL SECURITY NUMBER: Although a Social Security number is not required for issuance of a passport, Section 6039E of the Internal Revenue Code of 1986 requires that passport applicants provide this information. Passport Services gives this information to the Internal Revenue Service (IRS) routinely. Any applicant who fails to provide the information is subject to a $500.00 penalty enforced by the IRS. Questions on this matter should be referred to the nearest IRS office.

Q. Where Can I Get Passport Forms?

A. Passport forms are available from passport agencies, many post offices, and travel agencies or by calling the National Passport Information Center at 1-900-225-5674 (See **"Passport Agencies"** section for more information). They can also be downloaded via the internet at this website: travel.state.gov.

Q. May I Apply for a Passport by Mail?

A. Yes, if you already have a passport and that passport is your most recent one, and it was issued within the past 12 years, and if you were over age 16 when it was issued.

Obtain DSP-82 "Application For Passport By Mail." Fill it out, sign, and date it. **Attach to it:** Your most recent passport; two identical passport photographs (see previous section on passport photographs); and a $40.00 fee, and if applicable, a $35.00 expedite fee for urgent service. (See **"What If I Need a Passport in a Hurry?"**) Make your check or money order payable to **Passport Services.** (The $15.00 execution fee is waived for those eligible to apply by mail.)

If your name changed, enclose a certified copy of the Court Order, Adoption Decree, Marriage Certificate, or Divorce Decree, specifying another name for you to use. (Photocopies will not be accepted.) If your name has changed by any other means, you must apply in person.

Mail (if possible, in a padded envelope) the completed DSP-82 application and attachments to: National Passport Center, P.O. Box 371971, Pittsburgh, PA 15250-7971. Include the appropriate fee for overnight return of your passport. Please note that overnight service will not speed up processing time unless payment for expedited service is also included. (See **"What If I Need a Passport in a Hurry?"**)

Note: *If your passport has been **mutilated, altered or damaged,** you cannot apply by mail. You must **apply in person** using Form DSP-11, present evidence of U.S. citizenship, and acceptable identification. (If you mutilate or alter your U.S. passport, you may render it invalid and expose yourself to possible prosecution under the law [Section 1543 of Title 22 of the U.S. Code]).

Q. When Should I Apply for a Passport?

A. Apply several months in advance of your planned departure. If you will need visas from foreign embassies, allow more time.

Q. What Happens to My Passport Application After I Submit It?

A. If you apply at a passport acceptance facility, the day that you apply, your application will be sent to Passport Services for processing. Your passport will be issued within 25 business days after receipt of complete applications by Passport Services. Your passport will be sent to you by mail at the address you provided on your application.

Q. What Should I Do if My Passport Is Lost or Stolen?

A. If your passport is lost or stolen report the loss on form DSP-64, when you apply, in person, for your new passport. If you are abroad, report the loss immediately to local police authorities and the nearest U.S. embassy or consulate. Remember to write your current address in the space provided in your passport, so that, if it is found, it can be returned to you.

Q. What Else Should I know About Passports?

A. All persons, including newborn infants, are required to obtain passports in their own name. If you need to get a valid passport amended due to a name change, use form DSP-19. (See "May I Apply for a Passport by Mail" for the documentation required.)

Before traveling abroad, make a copy of the identification page so it is easier to get a new passport, should it be necessary. It is also a good idea to carry two extra passport size photos with you. If you run out of pages before your passport expires, submit Form DSP-19, along with your passport to one of the passport agencies listed below. (Please allow time for the processing of the request.) If you travel abroad frequently, you may request a 48-page passport at the time of application.

Some countries require that your passport be valid at least 6 months beyond the dates of your trip. Check with the nearest embassy or consulate of the countries you plan to visit to find out their entry requirements.

In addition to foreign entry requirements, U.S. law must be considered. With certain exceptions, it is against U.S. law to enter or leave the country without a valid passport. Generally for tourists, the exceptions refer to direct travel within U.S. territories or between North, South or Central America (except Cuba).

Q. What If I Need a Passport in a Hurry?

A. If you are leaving on an emergency trip within five working days, apply in person at the nearest passport agency and present your tickets or itinerary from an airline, as well as the other required items. Or, apply at a courthouse, county or municipal office, or post office and have the application sent to the passport agency through an overnight delivery service of your choice (include a self-addressed, prepaid envelope for the overnight return of the passport). Be sure to include dates of departure and travel plans on your application and all fees (including the $35.00 expedite fee).

For more information, contact the National Passport Information Center (NPIC). The NPIC is the only public telephone number for passport information. Callers can dial 1-900-225-5674* to receive passport applications, information on applying for a U.S. passport, or to check on the status of a passport application, or emergency passport procedures. Automated information is available 24 hours/day, 7 days/week. Operators can be reached Monday-Friday, excluding Federal holidays, 0800 to 2000 hours Eastern Standard time. Services are provided in English, Spanish, and by TDD (1-900-225-7778*).

*The cost per minute for 1-900 services is $.35 for recorded information and $1.05 for operator assisted calls. This service also includes an optional number, 1-888-362-8668 (TDD 1-888-498-3648), for those calling from telephones with blocked 1-900 service. These calls require a credit card for payment of a flat rate of $4.95 per call.

APPENDIX R: Passport Agencies

Boston Passport Agency
Thomas P. O'Neill Federal Building
Room 247
10 Causeway Street
Boston, MA 02222-1094

Chicago Passport Agency
Suite 380, Kluczynski Federal Office Building
230 South Dearborn Street
Chicago, IL 60604-1564

Honolulu Passport Agency
First Hawaii Tower
1132 Bishop Street, Suite 500
Honolulu, HI 96813-2809

Houston Passport Agency
Mickey Leland Federal Building, Suite 1100
1919 Smith Street
Houston, TX 77002-8049

Los Angeles Passport Agency
Room 1000
11000 Wilshire Boulevard
Los Angeles, CA 90024-3615

Miami Passport Agency
3rd Floor, Claude Pepper
Federal Office Building
51 Southwest First Avenue
Miami, FL 33130-1680

New Orleans Passport Agency
Postal Service Building
701 Loyola Avenue, Room T-12005
New Orleans, LA 70113-1931

New York Passport Agency
Greater Manhattan Federal Building
376 Hudson Street
New York, NY 10014-5000
Appointment line: 212-206-3500
(this line is only for individuals in
the New York City area who are
traveling in less than 14 days.)

Philadelphia Passport Agency
U, S. Customs House
200 Chestnut Street, Room 103
Philadelphia, PA 19106-2970

San Francisco Passport Agency
95 Hawthorne Street, 5th Floor
San Francisco, CA 94105-3901

Seattle Passport Agency
Room 992, Federal Office Building
915 Second Avenue
Seattle, WA 98174-1091

Stamford Passport Agency
One Landmark Square
Broad and Atlantic Streets
Stamford, CT 06901-2667

Washington Passport Agency
1111 19th Street, N. W.
Washington, D.C. 20524-5000

Do you need immediate passport assistance, passport information or the status on your pending passport application?

If so, you may call the
National Passport Information Center

Passport Services has committed itself to responding to the needs of its customers and established the National Passport Information Center (NPIC).

You may reach the center by calling 1-900-225-5674 (1-900-CALL-NPI) or TDD: 1-900-225-7778 (for the hearing impaired).

Live operators will be available 8am-8pm, Eastern Time, Monday-Friday, excluding Federal holidays. Automated Voice Response Unit (VRU) service is available 24 hours a day, seven days a week.

Live operator service is $1.05 per minute and is available from 8am to 8pm, Eastern Time, Monday through Friday, excluding Federal Holidays. If your 900 service is blocked, you may use a credit card to call 1-888-362-8668 or TDD: 1-888-498-3648 at $4.95 per call. Callers must be over 18 years old to use this service.

Information provided by the U.S. Department of State, Washington, DC.

Avoid Bringing Hazardous Items Aboard Aircraft

Hazardous materials include many common items from your home, workshop, or garage which because of the physical or chemical properties can pose a danger during air transportation. The following is a partial list common items that are strictly forbidden in carry-on or checked baggage:

Mace, tear gas, and other irritants

Aerosols containing flammable material

Loaded firearms

Gunpowder and primers

Loose ammunition

Gasoline, diesel, or kerosene

Propane, butane cylinders or lighter refills

Wet-type batteries (as used in cars)

Safety or "strike-anywhere" matches

Corrosive material

Infectious substances

Radioactive material

Any equipment containing fuel

The following hazardous articles may be transported in restricted quantities in hand-carried or checked baggage. A restricted quantity is what a passenger would use on a short trip:

Toiletry articles and medicines containing hazardous substances

Matches and lighters

Electronic wheelchairs as checked baggage

Small arms ammunition for sporting purposes when properly packaged

Catalytic hair curlers without refills

Oxygen cylinders used by individuals for medical purposes

Dry ice in small quantities

Aerosols intended for personal care (hair sprays and deodorants)

Lithium batteries located in watches, computers, etc.

Most Space-A terminals provide an "amnesty box" in which travelers may dispose of illegal/hazardous items. If you have any questions as to whether an item is allowed either as carry-on or as checked baggage, call or ask Space-A passenger services personnel. It's better to be safe than sorry!

This information courtesy of AMC

Planning on driving
while traveling in Europe?

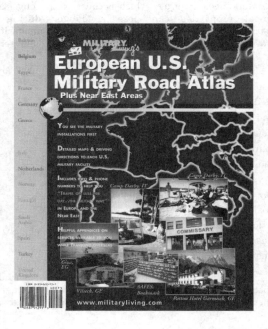

Military Living's

European U.S. Military Road Atlas
Plus Near East Areas

can show you the way!

**It's no fun getting lost- use this unique atlas to find
your way to U.S. Military Installations and major cities.**

visit Military Living online at

www.MilitaryLiving.com

to learn more abut this atlas.

APPENDIX S: Visa Information and Personnel Entrance Requirements

OBTAINING A FOREIGN VISA

A visa is a permit to enter and leave the country to be visited. It is a stamp of endorsement placed in a passport by a consular official of the country to which entry is requested. Many countries require visitors from other nations to have in their possession a valid visa obtained before departing from their home country. A visa may be obtained from foreign embassies or consulates located in the U.S. (Visas are not always obtainable at the airport of entry of the foreign location and verification of visa issuance must be made in advance of departure.) Various types of visas are issued depending upon the nature of the visit and the intended length of stay. **Passport services of the Department of State cannot help you obtain visas.**

A valid passport must be submitted when applying for a visa of any type. Because the visa is usually stamped directly onto one of the blank pages in your passport, you will need to fill out a form and give your passport to an official of each foreign embassy or consulate. The process may take several weeks for each visa, so apply well in advance. The visa requirements of each country will differ.

Some visas require a fee. You may need one or more photographs when submitting your visa applications. They should be full-faced, on white background and should not be larger than 3" x 3" nor smaller than 2.5" x 2.5."

Several countries do not require U.S. citizens to obtain passports and visas for certain types of travel, mostly tourist. Instead, they issue a simple tourist card which can be obtained from the nearest consulate of the country in question (presentation of a birth certificate or similar documentary proof of citizenship may be required.) In some countries, the transportation company is authorized to grant tourist cards. A fee is required for some tourist cards.

Some Arab or African countries will not issue visas or allow entry if your passport indicates travel to Israel or South Africa. Consult the nearest U.S. Passport Agency for guidance if this applies to you.

The official institutions (embassies or consulates) representing foreign governments in the U.S. are located in Washington, D.C. (see below) and major U.S. cities and have the most up-to-date information. They are, therefore, your best source. Double check visa requirements before you leave. **(*The Congressional Directory*, available at most public libraries, lists their addresses and phone numbers.)**

For your convenience we have listed below the names, addresses, phone numbers, website and e-mail addresses of embassies in the countries where stations are frequently used by DoD-owned or controlled aircraft. U.S. Trust territories and possessions overseas have the same requirements as the U.S. has for U.S. citzens upon return from a foreign country. If you wish to travel to a country not listed below, visa and other personnel entry requirements can be obtained from the "DoD Foreign Clearance Guides" available at most AMC (USAF) and other passenger service counters or at many military personnel offices. For complete personnel entrance requirements to foreign countries, see Appendix B in *Military Space-A Air Opportunities Around the World.*

NOTE: Embassies may close on their respective national holidays. Call before going to be sure they are open. We have listed only the Washington, D.C. based foreign embassies. There may be consulates of these embassies in other major cities which have visa-issuing authority.

The personnel entrance requirements information contained in this appendix has been extracted from the Department of Defense (DoD) FOREIGN CLEARANCE GUIDE(S): NORTH AND SOUTH AMERICA; EUROPE; AFRICA AND SOUTH-WEST ASIA; PACIFIC, SOUTH ASIA AND INDIAN OCEAN, DoD 4500.54-G. The information extracted is largely from SEC-TION II, Personnel Entrance Requirements. Some data from other sections which we believe meets the needs of Space-A travelers has also been included in this appendix. Note: Only Countries/Areas with regular space-available passenger traffic are listed in this appendix.

All Space-A passengers departing on commercial contract mission (Patriot Flights) inbound to the United States must pay a $12.40 head tax and an $11.00 federal inspection fee, for a total of $23.40. Some foreign departure terminals may also collect a departure tax, which have been noted in the respective country listings.

The data in this appendix is subject to change without notice as political situations change and new developments occur in foreign countries. When in doubt, Space-A travelers should call or write to the anticipated departure location or military personnel office (which issues official duty orders) for the latest information on personnel entrance requirements to the countries which you plan to visit.

IDENTIFICATION CREDENTIALS: NOTE: When U.S. citizens travel to a country where a valid passport is not required, they must possess documentary evidence of both their U.S. citizenship and personal identity. Proof of U.S. citizenship includes valid U.S. passport, expired U.S. passport, a certificate of Naturalization, Certificate of Citizenship, or Report of Birth Abroad of a Citizen of the United States. Proof of identity includes a valid state driver's license or government identification card provided they identify you by physical description or photograph. Travelers must prove both citizenship and identity.

AMERICAN (EASTERN) SAMOA (AS) (U. S. TERRITORY)
Identification Required: AD: ID Card, Leave orders. Ret/Civ: ID Card.

ANTIGUA & BARBUDA (AG & BD)
Identification Required: AD: ID Card, Leave orders. Ret/Civ: ID Card or Passport. Passport & visa stays over six months.
Other: All: Proof of return/onward ticket and/or proof of sufficient funds for stay up to six months. Embark/Debark Card if arriving on a civilian aircraft.
Embassy of Antigua and Barbuda, 3216 New Mexico Avenue, NW, Washington, D.C. 20016, C-202-362-5122/5166/5211.

ARGENTINA (AR)
Identification Required: All: ID Cards, Passport, No visa up to 3 months. AD: Leave orders.
Consular Section of the Argentine Embassy, 1718 Connecticut Avenue, NW, Washington, D.C. 20009, C-202-238-6460.

ASCENSION ISLAND (United Kingdom) (AI)
Identification Required: AD: ID Card, Leave orders. Ret/Civ: ID, Passport or documentary of U.S. citizenship and personal identity.

AUSTRALIA (AU)
Identification Required: AD: ID Card, Passport, visa or ETA (Electronic Travel Authority) and Leave orders. Ret/Civ: ID Card, Passport, visa or ETA. Visa or ETA must be obtained before arrival. All travelers receiving an ETA and intending to travel via Military Space-A Air must ensure that the Australian Embassy or consulate issuing the ETA provide written confirmation to the traveler that an ETA was issued or places a visa stamp in the passport. The cost of a visa stamp is $33.00 U.S. The ETA can be obtained free through the Embassy of Australia, 1601 Massachusetts Avenue, NW, Washington, D.C. 20036, C-202-797-3145/3161, WEB: www.austemb.org
Other: There is a $30 AU passenger movement charge for Space-A passengers (except age 12 or under).

AZORES (Also see Portugal) (PT)
Identification Required: AD: ID Card, Leave orders. Ret/Civ: ID Card, Passport. Visa required after 90 days.
Other: All: Passport valid for three months beyond stay.

BAHRAIN (BH)
Identification Required: All: ID Cards, Passport, visa (Three and seven day visas may be obtained upon arrival at the airport, obtaining visas before arrival is recommended).
Embassy of the State of Bahrain, 3502 International Drive, NW, Washington, D.C. 20008, C-202-342-0741.

BARBADOS (BB)
Identification Required: AD: ID cards and orders. All: Proof of U.S. citizenship and onward/return ticket required. Passport required for visits over 28 days.
Other: All: Departure tax $12.50 if staying over 24 hours.
Embassy of Barbados, 2144 Wyoming Avenue, NW, Washington, D.C. 20008, C-202-939-9200.

BELGIUM (BE)
Identification Required: AD: ID Card, Leave orders. Ret/Civ: ID Card, Passport, visa after three months (all Schengen territory countries).
Embassy of Belgium, 3330 Garfield Street, NW, Washington, D.C. 20008, C-202-333-6900, WEB: www.diplobel.org/usa, E-mail:Washington@diplobel.org

BELIZE (BZ)
Identification Required: All: Passport, ID Cards, return/onward ticket and sufficient funds required. Permit from immigration authorities required for visit over one month; visa required for stay over three months.
Other: All: Airport departure tax U.S. $11.25.
Embassy of Belize, 2535 Massachusetts Avenue, NW, Washington, D.C. 20008, C-202- 332-9636.

BOLIVIA (BO)
Identification Required: AD: ID Card, Passport, Clearance required from USMILGP, C-011-591-2-430-251-EX-2671/2672, Leave orders (except Ret/Civ), Passport stamped by immigration at airport on entry, with tourist entry permit, for 30 days. Visa not approved if passport expires within six months. Ret/Civ: ID Card, Passport. Tourist entry permit same as AD above.
Embassy of Bolivia (Consular Section), 3014 Massachusetts Avenue, NW, Washington, D.C. 20008, C-202-232-4827/28.

BRAZIL (BR)
Identification Required: All: ID Card, Passport, visa. AD: Leave orders.
Other: All: Visas required prior to arrival, not issued at airport.
Brazilian Embassy (Consular Section), 3009 Whitehaven Street, NW, Washington, D.C. 20008, C-202-238-2828, WEB: www.Brasil.emb.nw.dc.us

CAMEROON (CM)
Identification Required: ALL: ID Card, Passport, visa. AD: Leave Orders.
Carry passports at all times.
Embassy of the Republic of Cameroon, 2349 Massachusetts Avenue, NW, Washington, D.C. 20008, C-202-265-8790/8794.

CANADA (CA)
Identification Required: All: ID Card. AD: Leave orders.
Canadian Embassy, 501 Pennsylvania Avenue, NW, Washington, D.C. 20001, C-202-682-1740, WEB: www.cdnemb-washdc.org

CAYMAN ISLANDS (GB)
Identification Required: AD: ID Card and Leave orders. Ret/Civ: Passport or proof of citizenship, photo ID, onward/return ticket and proof of sufficient funds. Visa required for stays over three months.
British Embassy (Consular Section), 19 Observatory Circle, NW, Washington, D.C. 20008, C-202-588-7800.

CHAD (TD)
Identification Required: All: ID Card, Passport, visa (immunization record showing vaccination against yellow fever must be provided when applying for visa).
Other: All: Visas valid for single entry (multiple entries on request) and must be obtained prior to arrival in Chad.
Embassy of the Republic of Chad, 2002 R Street, NW, Washington, D.C. 20009, C-202-462-4009.

CHILE (CL)
Identification Required: AD: ID Card, Passport, Leave orders. Ret/Civ: ID Card, Passport, onward/return ticket. All: A tourist card obtained in the airport for $20.00 U.S., exact change only, is required, and good for 90 days.
Other: All: Visas required after 90 days. Airport departure tax $18 U.S.
Embassy of Chile, 1732 Massachusetts Avenue, NW, Washington, D.C. 20036, C-202-785-1746.

COLOMBIA (CO)
Identification Required: AD: Passport, ID card, Leave orders (visa not required for visits of less than 30 days). Ret/Civ: Passport and proof of onward/return ticket. Visa required for visits over 30 days, must be obtained in advance.
Other: AD: Departure tax $35 U.S.
Embassy of Colombia (Consulate), 1875 Connecticut Avenue, NW, Suite 218, Washington, D.C. 20009, C-202-332-7476, WEB: www.colombiaemb.org

CONGO (Democratic Republic of) (ZR) (Formerly Zaire)
Identification Required: AD: ID Card, Passport, visa, Leave orders. Ret/Civ: ID Card, Passport, visa. ALL: Immunization records.
Other: All: Visa (three month) must be obtained before arrival.
Embassy of the Democratic Republic of the Congo, 1800 New Hampshire Avenue, NW, Washington, D.C. 20009, C-202-234-7690/91.

COSTA RICA (CR)
Identification Required: All: ID card, Passport, onward/return ticket. Exit tax $6 U.S.
Other: AD: Without passport may purchase tourist card for $2 U.S. at airport but must show proof of citizenship on departure.
Embassy of Costa Rica (Consular Section), 2112 S Street, NW, Washington, D.C. 20008, C-202-328-6628.

CRETE (GR), See Greece.

CUBA (CU) (U.S. Guantanamo Bay)
Identification Required: AD: ID Card, Leave orders. Ret/Civ: ID Card.
Apply Cuban Interests Section, 2639 16th Street, NW, Washington, D.C. 20009, C-202-797-8518/797-8609.

CYPRUS (CY)
Identification Required: All: ID Card, Passport, AD: Leave orders, ALL: Visas are issued at the port of entry for a stay of up to three months (extendable).
Embassy of the Republic of Cyprus, 2211 R Street, NW, Washington, D.C. 20008, C-202-462-5772.

DENMARK (DK) (Greenland)
Identification Required: AD: ID Card, Passport, Leave orders. Passport if landing at non-U.S. base. Ret/Civ: ID Card. Passport if landing at non-U.S. base.
Other: All: Visa required for stays over three months.
Royal Danish Embassy, 3200 Whitehaven Street, NW, Washington, D.C. 20008, C-202-234-4300, WEB: www.denmarkemb.org, E-mail: ambadane@erols.com

DIEGO GARCIA (Chagos Archipelago) (IO) (United Kingdom, UK)
Identification Required: All: ID Card, Leave orders or PCS orders. Civilians: Passports.
British Embassy, 19 Observatory Circle, NW, Washington, D.C. 20008, C-202-588-7800.

DOMINICAN REPUBLIC (DO)
Identification Required: All: ID Card, Passport, visa or Purchase Tourist Card ($10 U.S.) upon arrival.
Embassy of the Dominican Republic, 1715 22nd Street, NW, Washington, D.C. 20008, C-202-332-6280, WEB: www.dom-rep.org

ECUADOR (EC)
Identification Required: All: ID card, Passports, and return/onward ticket, tourist card (valid for 90 days) issued on arrival. AD: Leave orders.
Other: Airport departure tax $25 U.S. per person. Visas required for cumulative stay more than 90 days, must be obtained in advance.
Embassy of Ecuador, 2535 15th Street, NW, Washington, D.C. 20009, C-202-234-7166, WEB: www.ecuador.org/ecuador, E-mail: mecuawaa@pop.erols.com

EGYPT (Arab Republic of) (EG)
Identification Required: AD: Leave orders. All: ID Card, Passport, visa.
Other: All: Visas (valid for six months) obtainable at airport banks for $15 U.S.

Embassy of the Arab Republic of Egypt, 3521 International Court, NW, Washington, D.C. 20008, C-202-895-5400.

EL SALVADOR (SV)
Identification Required: AD: ID cards and Leave orders. All: Passport and visa required. Tourist cards available at airport for $10 U.S. AD: Contact USDAO on arrival and departure at: C-011-503-228-2017.

Other: AD: Airport departure tax $26 U.S., if departing commercial airport.

Embassy of El Salvador, Consulate General of El Salvador, 1424 16th Street, NW, Suite 200, Washington, D.C. 20036, C-202-265-9671.

FIJI (FJ)
Identification Required: AD: ID Cards, Passport, Leave Orders, Proof of sufficient funds, and an onward/return ticket. Visa is issued upon arrival for an initial stay of up to four months. Ret/Civ: ID Cards, Passport. Visas not required; visitor permits, valid for up to one month, are issued on arrival.

Embassy of the Republic of the Fiji Islands, 2233 Wisconsin Avenue, NW, #240, Washington, D.C. 20007, C-202-337-8320, E-mail: fijiemb@earthlink.net

GERMANY (DE)
Identification Required: AD: ID Card, Leave orders. Ret/Civ: ID Card, Passport, visa after 90 days.

Other: All: Visas for stays in excess of 90 days.

Embassy of the Federal Republic of Germany, 4645 Reservoir Road, NW, Washington, D.C. 20007, C-202-298-8140, WEB: www.germany-info.org

GREECE (GR) (Includes all Greek Islands in the Aegean Sea)
Identification Required: AD: ID Card, Leave orders, or Passport. Ret/Civ: ID Card, Passport. All: Visa required after 90 days.

Other: All: Visa required for visits over 90 days and resident permit or police ID card.

Embassy of Greece (Consular Section), 2211 Massachusetts Avenue, NW, Washington, D.C. 20008, C-202-939-5818.

GUAM (GU) (U.S. TERRITORY)
Identification Required: AD: ID Card, Leave orders. Ret/Civ: ID Card.

GUATEMALA (GT)
Identification Required: AD: ID card, Passport and Leave orders. All: Passport and visa or tourist card (good for 30 days) $5 U.S. purchased in advance. Must carry identification credentials with them at all times.

Other: AD: Airport departure tax 145 quetzales (approximately $20 U.S.).

Embassy of Guatemala, 2220 R Street, NW, Washington, D.C. 20008-4081, C-202-745-4952.

HAITI (HT)

Identification Required: AD: ID Card, Passport. Ret/Civ: ID Card, Passport.

All: If departing via commercial airline, a departure tax of $25 U.S. Haitian citizens in U.S. military require Passport and Exit Permit.

Embassy of Haiti, 2311 Massachusetts Avenue, NW, Washington, D.C. 20008, C-202-332-4090, WEB: www.haiti.org/embassy, E-mail: embassy@haiti.org

HONDURAS (HN)

Identification Required: All: ID Card, Passport (valid six months), onward/return ticket.

Other: All: If departing via commercial airline, an Exit Tax of 95 lempira, (approximately $12 U.S.) is charged.

Embassy of Honduras (Consular Section), 1612 K Street, NW, Suite 310, Washington, D.C. 20006, C-202-223-0185, E-mail: embhondu@aol.com

ICELAND (IS)

Identification Required: AD: ID Card, Leave orders. Ret/Civ: ID Card, Passport

Other: All: Visas required for 90 or more days; period begins when entering the Scandinavian area (Denmark, Finland, Norway and Sweden).

Embassy of Iceland, 1156 15th Street, NW, Suite 1200, Washington, D.C. 20005, C-202-265-6653/55, WEB: www.iceland.org, E-mail: icemb.wash@utn.stjr.is

INDONESIA (ID)

Identification Required: AD: ID Card, Leave orders, Passport and onward/return tickets. Ret/Civ: ID Card, Passport and onward/return tickets.

Other: All: Visa required after 60 days.

Embassy of the Republic of Indonesia, 2020 Massachusetts Avenue, NW, Washington, D.C. 20036, C-202-775-5200.

ISRAEL (IL)

Identification Required: All: ID Card, Leave Orders, Passport, visa. (Valid 90 days, can be obtained at Ben Gurion IAP, and can be renewed)

Other: All: Onward/return ticket and proof of sufficient funds required. Visa at Ben Gurion airport for Tourist Passport (90 days). Exit reconvert up to $300 U.S.

Embassy of Israel, 3514 International Drive, NW, Washington, D.C. 20008, C-202-364-5500, WEB: www.israelemb.org

ITALY (IT)

Identification Required: AD: ID Card, Leave orders (Passport highly recommended). Ret/Civ: ID Card, Passport. Visa required for stays longer than 90 days.

Other: All: Tourist Passport highly recommended. Non-U.S. and non-European Union citizens require visa.

Embassy of Italy, 1601 Fuller Street, NW, Washington, D.C. 20009, C-202-328-5500, WEB: www.italyemb.nw.dc.us:80/Italy/

JAMAICA (JM)

Identification Required: AD: ID Card, Leave orders. Ret/Civ: ID Card, Proof of citizenship.

Other: All: Onward/return ticket and proof of sufficient funds required. Departure fee $26 U.S. each passenger at commercial airport.

Embassy of Jamaica, 1520 New Hampshire Avenue, NW, Washington, D.C. 20036, C-202-452-0660, E-mail: emjam@sys-net.net

JAPAN (JP)

Identification Required: AD: ID Card, Leave orders (Japan as destination). Ret/Civ: ID Card, Passport.(Onward/return tickets are required for passengers arriving at commercial ports; AMC passengers are exempt).

Other: All: Visa for stay over 90 days.

Embassy of Japan, 2520 Massachusetts Avenue, NW, Washington, D.C. 20008, C-202-238-6800, WEB: www.emb-japan.org, www.embjapan.org/jicc.html, E-mail: eojjicc@erols.com

JOHNSTON ATOLL (JO) (U.S.) (U.S. TERRITORY)

Identification Required: AD: ID Card, Leave orders, Entrance approval. Ret/Civ: ID Card, Entrance approval.

JORDAN (JO)

Identification Required: AD: ID Card, Leave orders, Passport, visa. Ret/Civ: ID Card, Passport, visa.

Other: All: The stated policy does not prohibit travelers whose passports contain Israeli stamps or markings. However, implementation of this change from previous policy has been inconsistent. Exit fee of ten dinar (approximately $15 U.S.) if departing from civilian airport.

Embassy of the Hashemite Kingdom of Jordan, 3504 International Drive, NW, Washington, D.C. 20008, C-202-966-2664.

KENYA (KE)

Identification Required: All: ID Card, Passport, visa.

Other: All: Transit visas are available for limited stays up to seven days. Tourist passport visas are $50 U.S. $20 U.S. departure tax paid in U.S. dollars.

Embassy of Kenya, 2249 R Street, NW, Washington, D.C. 20008, C-202-387-6101.

KOREA (Republic of) (KR)

Identification Required: AD: ID Card, Leave orders. Ret/Civ: ID Card, Passport, visa, (for 15 or more days visit).

Other: All: Airport departure tax of 6,000 won or approximately $8.40 U.S., except EML leave, funded emergency leave and overseas tour leave.

Embassy of the Republican of Korea (Consular Division), 2320 Massachusetts Avenue, NW, Washington, D.C. 20008, C-202-939-5663/60, WEB: korea.emb.washington.dc.us

KOSRAE (FM) (SEE FEDERATED STATES OF MICRONESIA)

KUWAIT (KW)
Identification Required: AD/DoD Civ: ID card, Passport, Visa, Leave orders, country clearance approval message. Ret/Civ: ID card, Passport, Visa.
Embassy of the State of Kuwait, 2940 Tilden Street, NW, Washington, D.C. 20008, C-202-966-0702.

KWAJALEIN ATOLL (KA) (U.S. ARMY KA, (USAKA)) (REPUBLIC OF THE MARSHALL ISLANDS)
Identification Required: AD: ID Card, Leave orders, Entry approval. Ret/Civ: ID Card, Entry approval.

MARSHALL ISLANDS (Republic of) (MH)
[Includes Ailinglapalap Atoll, Arno Atoll, Bikini Atoll, Ebon Atoll, Enewetak Atoll, Jaluit Atoll, Kili Island, Kwajalein Atoll (except U.S. Army Kwajalein Atoll), Majuro Atoll, Maloelap Atoll, Mili Atoll, Namorik Atoll, Ralik Chain, Ratak Chain, Rongelap Atoll, Taongi Atoll, Ujelang Atoll, Utirik Atoll, Wotje Atoll]
Identification Required: AD: ID Card, Leave orders. Ret/Civ: ID Card, Passport.
Other: All: Sufficient funds for stay of 30 days and onward/return ticket.
Embassy of Marshall Islands, 2433 Massachusetts Avenue, NW, Washington, D.C. 20008, C-202-234-5414.

MICRONESIA, (FEDERATED STATES OF) (FM)
[Includes Eauripik Atoll, Fais Island, Faraulep Atoll, Gaferut Island, Kapingamarangi Atoll, Kosrae State, Mortlock Islands, Hall Islands, Ifalik Atoll, Namonuito Atoll, Oroluk Atoll, Pingelap Atoll, Pohnpei State, Pulap Atoll, Pulusak Island, Puluwat Atoll, Chuuk State, Ulithi Atoll, West Fayu Atoll, Woleai Atoll, Yap State.]
Identification Required: AD: ID Card, Leave orders. All: ID Card, Proof of citizenship.
Other: Onward/return ticket and sufficient funds required. Departure tax of $5 U.S. for all persons.
Embassy of the Federated States of Micronesia, 1725 N Street, NW, Washington, D.C. 20036, C-202-223-4383.

NETHERLANDS ANTILLES (AN)
Identification Required: AD: ID Cards and Leave orders. Ret/Civ: ID Cards and Proof of U.S. Citizenship.
Other: All: Personnel staying over 24 hours must have orders authorizing travel outside AN, ID cards and POC, documents necessary to continue journey or return to country of origin, and means of support during stay. A visa is required for stays of more than 90 days. Tourists may be asked to show onward/return ticket or proof of sufficient funds for their stay
Embassy of the Netherlands, 4200 Linnean Avenue, NW, Washington, D.C. 20008, C-202-244-5300.

NEW ZEALAND (NZ)

Identification Required: AD: ID Card, Passport (valid for six months), Leave orders. Ret/Civ: ID Card, Passport.

Other: All: Onward/return ticket and visa for next destination; proof of sufficient funds. Visa required when stay exceeds 90 days. Military ID Card is accepted in lieu of usual outward ticket requirement for Space-A traveler.

Embassy of New Zealand, 37 Observatory Circle,NW, Washington, D.C. 20008, C-202-328-4800, WEB: www.emb.com/nzemb

NICARAGUA (NI)

Identification Required: All: Passport (valid at least six months), Tourist card in lieu of visa (paid), onward/return ticket and sufficient funds ($500 minimum).

Other: There is a $20 U.S. departure fee for all except diplomats.

Consulate of Nicaragua, 1627 New Hampshire Avenue, NW, Washington, D.C. 20009, C-202-939-6531/32.

NIGER (NE)

Identification Required: AD: Passport, visa, ID Card and Leave orders. Ret/Civ: Passport, visa and ID card.

Embassy of the Republic of Niger, 2204 R Street, NW, Washington, D.C. 20008, C-202-483-4224.

NORTHERN MARIANAS (COMMONWEALTH OF THE) (MP)

Identification Required: AD: ID cards and orders. Ret/Civ: ID Cards and Passport, DOD Civilians: Orders and personal identification card with name, status, date of birth and photo.

OMAN (OM)

Identification Required: All: ID Card, Passport, visa.

Other: All: Visa (validation for 7-90 days) not available at airport.

Embassy of the Sultanate of Oman, 2535 Belmont Road, NW, Washington, D.C. 20008, C-202-387-1980/81/82.

PALAU (REPUBLIC OF) (PW)

Identification Required: AD: ID Card, Leave orders. All: ID Card, Proof of citizenship, onward/return ticket for stay of up to 30 days. Visa for stays longer than 30 days, fee of $50 U. S.

Representative Office, 1150 18th Street, NW, Suite 750, Washington, D.C. 20036, C-202-452-6814.

PANAMA (REPUBLIC of) (PA)

Identification Required: AD: ID Card, Leave orders. Ret/Civ: ID Card, Passport (valid for six months), visa before arrival or purchase within first 3 days of visit to Panama ($10 for a 30-day stay), onward/return ticket.

Embassy of Panama, 2862 McGill Terrace, NW, Washington, D.C. 20008, C-202-483-1407.

PARAGUAY (PY)

Identification Required: AD: ID Card, Passport, visa for stay longer than 90 days, Leave orders, Immunization record. Ret/Civ: ID Card, Passport, visa for stay longer than 90 days.
Other: All: Visits less than 90 days require Tourist Card ($3 U.S.) at airport.
Embassy of Paraguay, 2400 Massachussetts Avenue, NW, Washington, D.C. 20008, C-202-483-6960.

PERU (PE)

Identification Required: AD: ID Card, Passport, Leave orders, tourist card. Ret/Civ: ID Card, Passport, onward/return ticket.
Other: All: Visa for stay longer than 90 days. Exit Tax at Lima airport $18 U.S.
Consulate General of Peru, 1625 Massachussetts Avenue, NW, 6th Floor, Washington, D.C. 20036, C-202-462-1084.

PHILIPPINES, REPUBLIC OF THE (PH)

Identification Required: All: Passport and visa if staying over 21 days, round-trip ticket and sufficient funds.
Embassy of the Philippines, 1600 Massachusetts Avenue, NW, Washington, D.C. 20036, C-202-467-9300.

POHNPEI (See FEDERATED STATES OF MICRONESIA)

PORTUGAL (PT)

Identification Required: AD: ID Card, Leave orders. Ret/Civ: ID Card, Passport.
Other: All: Visa after 90 days. Persons stationed in Azores may visit without Passport and visa up to 60 days.
Embassy of Portugal, 2310 Tracy Place, NW, Washington, D.C. 20008, C-202-322-3007.

PUERTO RICO (PR) (U.S. TERRITORY)

Identification Required: AD: ID Card, Leave orders. Ret/Civ: ID Card. Proof of citizenship if entering from other than North, South or Central America.

SAUDI ARABIA (SA) (KINGDOM OF)

Identification Required: AD: ID Card, Passport, visa, Leave orders. Ret/Civ: ID Card, Passport, visa.
Other: AD: Passport and visa are required. The Kingdom does not issue airport/plane-side visas. Saudi Arabia does not grant visas to personnel desiring leave unless they are sponsored by family members within the Kingdom or attending the Hajj.
The Royal Embassy of Saudi Arabia, 601 New Hampshire Avenue, NW, Washington, D.C. 20037, C-202-944-3126.

SENEGAL (SN)

Identification Required: AD: Passport, ID Card, Leave orders, except if arriving by Navy ships -ID card, Ret/Civ: Passport, ID Card.
Other: All: Visa required if staying over 90 days.
Embassy of the Republic Of Senegal, 2112 Wyoming Avenue, NW, Washington, D.C. 20008, C-202-234-0540.

SINGAPORE (SG)

Identification Required: AD: ID Card, Leave orders, Passport. Ret/Civ: ID Card, Passport.

Other: AD: Emergency leave do not require Passport. Personnel on EML orders may transit with EML orders and ID card, no Passport. All: Entry valid for 30 days. Visa after 30 days required.

Embassy of Singapore, 3501 International Place, NW, Washington, D.C. 20008, C-202-537-3100, WEB: www.gov.sg/mfa/washington

SOUTH AFRICA (ZA)

Identification Required: AD: ID Cards, Passport (valid for 6 months), Leave orders, and immunization record. Ret/Civ: ID Cards, Passport, Visa before arrival.

Embassy of South Africa's Consular Office, 3051 Massachusetts Avenue, NW, Washington, D.C. 20016, C-202-966-1650.

SPAIN (ES)

Identification Required: AD: ID Card, Leave orders, Passport (except if stationed in Europe). Ret/Civ: ID Card, Passport.

Other: All: Visa required after three months.

Embassy of Spain, 2375 Pennsylvania Avenue, NW, Washington, D.C. 20037, C-202-425-0100 or 202-728-2330.

SURINAME (SR)

Identification Required: AD: ID Card, Passports, visas and return airline ticket. Ret/Civ: Passport, Visa, ID card.

Other: All: Plane-side visas not available except in extreme emergency. There is an airport departure tax of $10 U.S. and a terminal fee of $5 U.S.

Embassy of the Republic of Suriname, 4301 Connecticut Avenue, NW, Suite 108, Washington, D.C. 20008, C-202-244-7488/7490, E-mail: embsur@erols.com

THAILAND (TH)

Identification Required: All: ID Card, Passport, visa, onward/return ticket.

Other: All: Stamp (good for 30 days) given at airport or border. Tourist visa (valid up to 60 days) or non-immigration visa (good for 90 days) must be obtained in advance.

Royal Thai Embassy, 1024 Wisconsin Avenue, NW, Washington, D.C. 20007, C-202-944-3608, WEB: www.thaiembdc.org/

TRINIDAD AND TOBAGO (TT)

Identification Required: AD: ID Cards, Passport, Leave orders, Ret/Civ: ID Cards, Passport.

Other: All: Departure tax of 75 TTD (approx $18 U. S.). Visa required after 3 months or pay a visa waiver fee of TTD 100 (approx $23.50 U.S.).

Embassy of Trinidad and Tabago, 1708 Massachusetts Avenue, NW, Washington, D.C. 20036, C-202-467-6490.

TURKEY (TR)
Identification Required: AD: ID Card, Passport, Leave orders, visa. Ret/Civ: ID Card, Passport, visa. Holders of tourist passports can purchase a sticker visa at the port of entry for $45 U.S. Other: All: Visa for visit of 90 days available in advance at border crossing points.
Embassy of the Republic of Turkey, 1714 Massachusetts Avenue, NW, Washington, D.C. 20036, C-202-659-0742, WEB: www.turkey.org, E-mail: embassy@ turkey@org

UNITED ARAB EMIRATES (AE)
Identification Required: All: Passport and visa (obtained in advance).
Embassy of United Arab Emirates, 3000 K Street, NW, Washington, D.C. 20007, C-202-338-6500.

UNITED KINGDOM (GB)
[England, Northern Ireland, Scotland, & Wales]
Identification Required: AD: ID Card, Leave orders. Ret/Civ: ID Card, Passport, visa (not required for six months).
British Embassy (Consular Section), 19 Observatory Circle, NW, Washington, D.C. 20008, C-202-588-7800.

URUGUAY (UY)
Identification Required: AD: ID Card, Passport, Leave orders. Ret/Civ: ID Card, Passport.
Other: All: Visa required after three months.
Embassy of Uruguay, 1918 F Street, NW, Washington, D.C. 20008, C-202-331-4219, WEB: www.embassy.org/uruguay, E-mail: uruguay@embassy.org

VENEZUELA (VE)
Identification Required: All: ID Cards, Passport and tourist card (issued by commercial airlines).
Other: Visas required if remaining over 72 hours, not available plane side. Departure tax of $15 U.S. will be charged to all DoD travelers and crew arriving via military air and remaining over 72 hours in country.
Embassy of Venezuela (Consular Section), 1099 30th Street, NW, Washington, D.C. 20007, C-202-342-2214, E-mail: despacho@embavenez-us.org

U.S. VIRGIN ISLANDS (VI) (U.S. TERRITORY)
Identification Required: AD: ID Cards, Leave orders. Ret/Civ: ID Card.

WAKE ISLAND (WK) (U.S. TERRITORY)
Identification Required: AD: ID Card, Leave orders. Ret/Civ: ID Card.

APPENDIX T: Customs and Duty

DECLARATIONS: You must declare all articles acquired during your trip and in your possession at the time you return. This includes: 1) Articles you purchased; 2) Articles given to you while abroad, such as gifts or inherited items; 3) Articles purchased in the duty-free shops or on board carrier; 4) Repairs or alterations made to any articles taken abroad and returned, whether they were performed free of charge or not; 5) Items you have been requested to bring home for another person; 6)All articles you intend to sell or use in your business (Promotional items and samples for Customs purposes are only those items valued at $1.00 or less.) Any articles acquired in the U.S. Virgin Islands, American Samoa, Guam or a country of the Caribbean Basin Economic Recovery Act and not accompanying you when you return. The price actually paid for each article must be stated on your declaration in U.S. currency or its equivalent in the country of acquisition. The stated price must include any value-added tax (VAT) unless it was refunded prior to your arrival in the U.S. If the article was given to you, obtain an estimate of its fair retail value in the country in which it was acquired. *Note: Wearing or using an article acquired abroad does not exempt it from duty. It must be declared at the price you paid for it.*

Oral Declarations: A Customs declarations form will be distributed on your plane on the return trip. Fill it out before your arrival so that you can give it to Immigration and Customs inspectors when you disembark. You may make an oral declaration of the articles you acquired abroad if they accompany you and if you have not exceeded the duty-free exemption. A Customs officer may, however, ask you to prepare a written list of the articles.

Written Declaration: A written declaration will be necessary when: 1) The total fair retail value of articles acquired abroad exceeds your personal exemption; 2) More than 1 liter (33.8 fl oz) of alcoholic beverages, 200 cigarettes (one carton), and 100 cigars are included; 3) Some of the items are not intended for your personal or household use, like commercial samples, items for sale or use in your business, or articles you brought home for another person; 4) Articles acquired in the U.S. Virgin Islands, American Samoa, Guam or a Caribbean Basin Economic Recovery Act country are being shipped to the United States; 5) A Customs duty or Internal Revenue tax is collectible on any article in your possession; 6) You have used your exemption within the last 30 days.

Family Declaration: The head of a family may make a joint declaration for all members residing in the same household as long as they return to the United States together. Family members making a joint declaration may combine their personal exemptions; for example, if Mrs. Smith bought $600.00 worth of merchandise but Mr. Smith only purchased $200.00 worth, Mr. and Mrs. Smith may combine their $400.00 exemptions and will not have to pay any duty on their purchases. **Infants and children** returning to the United States are entitled to the same exemptions as adults, except for alcoholic beverages. Children born abroad, who have never lived in the United States, are entitled to the customs exemptions granted nonresidents.

Visitors to the United States should obtain the leaflet **Visiting the U.S.: Customs Requirements for Non-Residents.**

Military and civilian personnel of the U.S. government should obtain the leaflet **Customs Highlights for Government Personnel** for information about their customs exemptions when returning from an extended duty assignment abroad.

WARNING! If you understate the value of an article you declare, or if you otherwise misrepresent an article in your declaration, you may have to pay a penalty in addition to payment of duty. That article may also be subject to seizure and forfeited if the penalty is not paid. You may find that some merchants abroad offer travelers invoices or bills of sale showing false or understated values. The Customs Service is well-aware of this practice, which can not only delay your Customs examination, but could also result in civil or even criminal penalties. If you fail to declare an article acquired abroad, not only is it subject to seizure or forfeiture, but you will also be liable for a personal penalty in an amount equal to the article's value in the United States. You may also be liable for criminal prosecution. Be very careful about advice given by individuals outside the Customs Service. It could be misleading, and could even cause you to violate Customs laws and incur costly penalties. Please direct any questions to the Customs office nearest you before your departure or upon entry into the United States. If you're uncertain about whether to declare a particular article, always declare it first and then direct your questions to the Customs inspector. If in doubt about an article's value, declare the article at the price actually paid, known as the transaction value. Customs inspectors routinely handle tourist items and are knowledgeable about foreign prices. Moreover, current commercial prices of foreign items are available at all times, so on-the-spot comparisons of these values can be made when you return.

Be especially wary of anyone who asks you to carry an item back to the United States. You are responsible for anything in your possession when you clear Customs. Packages from other individuals have been known to contain contraband or currency, and in such a case, you would be responsible for any penalties that may be assessed.

Play it safe—Declare it All.

YOUR EXEMPTIONS: In clearing U.S. Customs, a traveler is considered either a "returning U.S. resident" or a "nonresident." Generally speaking, if you leave the United States for purposes of traveling, working or studying abroad, and then return to resume residency in the United States, Customs considers you a returning resident. American citizens who reside in American Samoa, Guam, or the U.S. Virgin Islands are also classified as returning U.S. residents. Articles acquired abroad and brought into the United States are subject to applicable duty and Internal Revenue tax, but as a returning resident you are allowed certain exemptions from the payment of duty on items obtained while abroad. U.S. residents living abroad temporarily, however, are entitled to be classified as nonresidents, and thus receive more liberal Customs exemptions, on short visits to the United States, provided they export any foreign-acquired items at the completion of their visit.

Exemptions: $400.00, $600.00, or $1,200.00. Articles totaling $400.00, $600.00, or $1,200.00, depending on your trip destinations, may be entered free of duty, subject to the limitations on alcoholic beverages, cigarettes, and cigars, If: 1. The articles were acquired during your trip for your personal or household use. 2. The articles accompany you at the time of your return to the United States and they are properly declared to U.S. Customs. Articles purchased abroad and shipped to follow at a later date cannot be applied to your $400.00 exemption. This includes purchases made abroad and left for repairs, alterations, or for other reasons. The flat rate of duty does not apply to mailed articles, but Customs will pass mailed articles worth up to $200.00 duty-free. If the package is valued at more than $200.00, duty will be assessed on the entire amount. Duty is assessed when received and cannot be prepaid. 3. You are returning from a stay abroad of at least 48 hours. Example: A resident who leaves United States territory at 1:30 p.m. on June 1st would complete the required 48 hour period at 1:30 p.m. on June 3rd. This time limitation does not apply if you are returning from Mexico or the U.S. Virgin Islands. 4. You have not used the $400.00, $600.00 or $1,200.00 exemption, or any part of it, within the preceding 30 day period. Also, your exemption is not cumulative. If you use a portion of your exemption on entering the United States, you must wait another 30 days before you are entitled to another exemption, other than a $200.00 exemption. 5. Articles are not prohibited or restricted.

$400.00 Exemption: Residents of the U.S. who meet the above conditions are entitled to a $400.00 exemption from paying duty on goods that would otherwise be dutiable. This means that articles acquired abroad with a total value of up to $400.00

will be admitted duty-free as long as they accompany you. Articles you mail home have a different exemption; see the sections on Gifts and Customs Pointers for more information.

Articles beyond the $400.00 duty-free limit may still qualify for duty-free treatment under other exemptions authorities, such as the Generalized System of Preferences, which awards duty-free treatment to many goods from developing countries. Fine art (not handicrafts) and antiques, defined as at least 100 years old, are also duty-free.

This means that a resident could spend more than $400.00 and still not be charged duty when reentering the U.S. For instance, a traveler buys a $300.00 gold bracelet, a $40.00 hat, a $60.00 purse, and a $200.00 unframed painting. Duty would not be charged on these items. The first three items qualify for the $400.00 exemption, and, because fine art is not subject to duty, the traveler can bring in $600.00 worth of goods duty-free. If the painting were framed, however, duty would be charged on the value of the frame.

$1,200.00 Exemption: If you return directly or indirectly from a U.S. insular possession—American Samoa, Guam or the U.S. Virgin Islands—your customs exemption is $1,200.00. You may also bring in 1,000 cigarettes, but only 200 of them may have been acquired elsewhere.

$600.00 Exemption: If you are returning directly from any of the following 24 beneficiary countries, your customs exemption is $600.00:

Antigua & Barbuda	El Salvador	Nicaragua
Aruba	Grenada	Panama
Bahamas	Guyana	Saint Kitts
Barbados	Haiti	and Nevis
Belize	Honduras	Saint Lucia
Costa Rica	Jamaica	Saint Vincent
Dominica	Montserrat	and the
Dominican Republic	Netherlands	Grenadines
British Virgin	Antilles	Trinidad and
Islands		Tobago

If you are returning from any of the three U.S. insular possessions, up to $600.00 worth of the merchandise may have been obtained in any of the beneficiary countries, listed above, or up to $400.00 in any other country. For example, if you travel to the U.S. Virgin Islands and Jamaica and then return home, you would be entitled to bring in $1,200.00 worth of merchandise duty-free. Of this amount, $600.00 worth may have been acquired in Jamaica. In the case of the $600.00 exemption for Caribbean Basin Economic Recovery Act countries, up to $400.00 worth of merchandise may have been acquired in other foreign countries. For instance, if you travel to England and the Bahamas, and then return home, your exemption is $600.00, no more than $400.00 of which may have been acquired in England.

$200.00 Exemption: If you cannot claim the $400.00, $600.00 or $1,200.00 exemption because of the 30-day or 48-hour minimum limitations, you may bring in free of duty up to $200.00 worth of articles for your personal or household use. This is an individual exemption only; it may not be grouped with other family members on a single customs declaration.

Your $200.00 exemption may include any of the following: 50 cigarettes, 10 cigars, 150 milliliters (4 fl. oz.) of alcoholic beverages, or 150 milliliters (4 fl oz) of perfume containing alcohol. If any article brought with you is subject to duty or tax, or if the total value of all dutiable articles exceeds $200.00, no article may be exempted from duty or tax.

Cigars and Cigarettes: Up to 100 cigars and 200 cigarettes (one carton) may be included in your $400.00 exemption. (See other exemption levels for exceptions.) Tobacco products of Cuban origin are generally prohibited. This exemption is available to each person. Cigarettes, however, may be subject to a tax imposed by state and local authorities. For more information on Cuban products, please visit the following Web site: www.ustreas.gov/treasury/services/fac/fac.html.

Liquor: One liter (33.8 fl. oz.) of alcoholic beverages may be included in the $400.00 exemption if: You are at least 21 years of age; It is for your own use or for a gift; It is not in violation of the laws of the state in which you arrive. (See other exemption levels for exceptions.)

Note: Duty on alcoholic beverages is assessed according to alcoholic content; beer and wine will have a lower rate of duty than liqueurs or hard liquor. Also, most states restrict the amount of alcoholic beverages you may import. If the state in which you arrive permits less liquor than you have legally brought into the United States, that state's laws prevail. Information about state restrictions and taxes should be obtained from the state government because laws vary from state to state. Alcoholic beverages beyond the one-liter limitation are subject to duty and Internal Revenue tax. Shipping alcoholic beverages by mail is prohibited by United States postal laws. Alcoholic beverages include wine, beer, and distilled spirits.

GIFTS: Gifts accompanying you are considered to be for your personal use and may be included in your exemption. This includes gifts given to you by others after you return. Gifts intended for business, promotional or other commercial purposes may not be included. **Bona fide gifts** of up to $100.00 in fair retail value may be shipped and received by friends and relatives in the United States free of duty and tax as long as the same person does not receive more than $100.00 in gift shipments in one day. The "day" in reference is the day in which the parcel(s) are received for customs processing. Gifts intended for more than one person may be shipped in a single, consolidated package provided they are individually wrapped and labeled with the recipients' names. A consolidated gift package's outer wrapper should bear the words **consolidated gift package** and should list the recipients' names and the value of each gift. The exemption for gifts is increased to $200.00 if they are shipped from the U.S. Virgin Islands, American Samoa, or Guam. Gifts sent by mail need not be declared when you return to the United States. Perfume containing alcohol and valued at more than $5.00 retail, tobacco products, and alcoholic beverages are excluded from the gift provision. Be sure all gift packages are marked on the outer wrapping: 1) "unsolicited gift," 2) nature of the gift—shoes, sweater, toy truck, etc., and 3) its fair retail value. This will facilitate Customs clearance of your package. If any article imported in a gift parcel is subject to duty and tax, or should any single gift within a consolidated package exceed the bona fide gift allowance, then that gift will be dutiable.

You, as a traveler, cannot send a "gift" to yourself, nor can persons traveling together send "gifts" to each other. Gifts ordered by mail from the United States do not qualify under this duty-free gift provision and are subject to duty. If a parcel is subject to duty, the United States Postal Service will collect it along with any handling charges. Duty cannot be prepaid.

OTHER ARTICLES FREE OF DUTY OR DUTIABLE: Duty preferences are granted to certain developing countries under the Generalized System of Preferences (GSP). Some products that would otherwise be dutiable if imported from any other country have been exempted from duty when imported from GSP countries. For details, obtain the leaflet **GSP & The Traveler** from the nearest Customs office.

The North American Free Trade Agreement (NAFTA) was implemented on 1 January 1994. U.S. residents returning directly or indirectly from Canada or Mexico are eligible for free or reduced duty rates on goods originating, as defined by NAFTA, in either country. Travelers can support a claim of NAFTA origination with either an oral or written statement or with an invoice that contains a valid NAFTA declaration.

Personal belongings taken abroad are entitled to duty-free entry on your return provided they are of U.S. origin. Items such as worn clothing or other American-made belongings may be sent home by mail before you return and receive free entry as long as they have not been altered or repaired while abroad. These packages should be marked "American Goods Returned." When a claim of United States origin is made, marking on the article to so indicate facilitates Customs processing.

Foreign-made personal articles taken abroad are dutiable each time they are brought into our country unless you have acceptable proof of prior possession. Documents that fully describe the article, like bills of sale, insurance policies, jeweler's or other appraisals, or purchase receipts may be considered reasonable proof of prior possession. Items like watches, cameras, tape recorders, or other articles that can be readily identified by serial numbers or permanently affixed markings may be taken to the Customs office nearest you and registered before your departure. You'll get a Certificate of Registration (CF 4457) that will expedite free entry of these items when you return. Keep the certificate, since it remains valid for any future trips as long as the information on it is legible. The Customs officer must actually see the item(s) you wish to register, so it cannot be done by phone, nor can blank forms be given or mailed to you to be filled out at a later time.

Vehicles, boats, and planes taken abroad for non-commercial use may be returned duty-free by proving to the Customs officer that you took them out of the United States. This proof may be a state registration card for an automobile, an FAA certificate for an aircraft, a yacht license or motorboat identification certificate for a pleasure boat, or a Customs certificate of registration (CF-4457) filled out and certified before departure. Repairs performed or accessories acquired abroad for articles taken out of the United States are dutiable and must be declared on your return. **Warning:** Catalytic converter-equipped vehicles (models manufactured in or after 1976) driven outside North America will, in most cases, not meet EPA standards when brought back to the United States.

Household effects and tools of trade or occupation taken out of the United States are duty-free at the time you return if properly declared and entered. All furniture, carpets, paintings, tableware, linens, stereos, and similar household furnishings acquired abroad may be imported free of duty, if: They are not imported for another person or for sale. You have used them abroad for at least one year, or they were available for use in a household in which you resided for one year. **Articles imported in excess** of your Customs exemption will be subject to duty unless the items are entitled to free entry or are prohibited. The Customs inspector will place items with the highest rate of duty under your exemption, and duty will be assessed on the lower-rated items. After deducting your exemptions and the value of any duty-free articles, a flat 10 percent rate of duty will be applied to the next $1,000.00 (fair retail value) of merchandise, except for NAFTA-originating goods. Any dollar amount more than $1,000.00 will be dutiable at the various rates of duty applicable to the articles, as provided for in the Harmonized Tariff schedule. Articles to which the flat 10 percent rate is applied must be for your personal use or for use as gifts. You cannot receive this flat-rate provision more than once every 30 days, excluding the day of your last arrival. The flat rate of duty for articles purchased in the U.S. Virgin Islands, American Samoa, or Guam is five percent, whether the articles accompany you or are shipped.

Payment of duty on articles accompanying you is required at the time of your arrival and may be made by any of the following ways: U.S. currency (foreign currency is not acceptable). Personal check in the exact amount of duty, drawn on a national or state bank or trust company of the United States, made payable to the "U.S. Customs Service." Government checks, money orders or traveler's checks are acceptable as long as they don't exceed the duty owed by more than $50.00. Second endorsement on checks are not acceptable, and identification—passport, driver's license or other picture ID—must be presented. In some locations you may pay duty with credit cards from MasterCard or VISA.

PROHIBITED AND RESTRICTED ARTICLES: Certain articles considered injurious or detrimental to the general welfare of the United States are prohibited entry by law. Among these are: Lottery tickets, narcotics and dangerous drugs, obscene articles and publications, seditious and treasonable materials, hazardous articles (e.g., fireworks, dangerous toys, toxic or poisonous substances) and switchblade knives. Other items must meet special requirements before they can be released. You will be given a receipt for any articles retained by Customs.

Artifacts/Cultural Property: U.S. law prohibits the importation of pre-Columbian monumental and architectural sculpture and murals from certain countries in Central and South America without proper export permits. Federal law and international treaties prohibit the importation of any pieces of cultural property stolen from museums or from religious or secular public monuments.

Automobiles: Automobiles imported into the United States must conform to Environmental Protection Agency emission requirements and Department of Transportation safety, bumper, and theft-prevention standards. Information on importing vehicles can be obtained from the EPA, Attn: 6405J, Washington, D.C. 20460, Tel: C-202-233-9660, and from DOT's National Highway Traffic Safety Administration, www.nhtsa.dot.gov/cars/rules/import>, Office of Vehicle Safety Compliance (NSA-32), Washington, D.C. 20590 or C-1-800-424-9393.

Biological Materials: Biological materials of public health or veterinary importance (disease organisms and vectors for research and educational purposes) require import permits. Write to the Foreign Quarantine Program, U.S. Public Health Service, Centers for Disease Control, Atlanta, GA 30333.

Books, Computer Programs, Cassettes, Video Tapes: Pirated copies of copyrighted articles—that is, unlawfully made articles produced without the authorization of the copyright's owner—are prohibited from importation into the United States. Pirated copies will be seized and destroyed.

Copyright and Trademark-Protected Articles: Customs separates foreign-made products bearing American-registered trademarks into two categories: 1. **counterfeit,** which are illegal products manufactured without the authorization of the company or person who owns the trademark, commonly known as "knock-offs," and 2. **parallel imports**, which are products manufactured under the trademark owner's authorization, but are imported into the U.S. by an unauthorized person or company. Parallel imports are commonly known as "gray-market goods." Returning travelers are allowed an exemption, usually one article of each type bearing a protected trademark.

Ceramic Tableware: Some ceramic tableware sold abroad contains dangerous levels of lead in the glaze that can leach into certain foods and beverages served in them. The FDA recommends that ceramic tableware, especially when purchased in Mexico, China, Hong Kong or India, be tested for lead release on your return or be used for decorative purposes only.

Drug Paraphernalia: The importation, exportation, manufacture, sale, and transportation of drug paraphernalia are prohibited.

Firearms and Ammunition: Firearms and ammunition are subject to restrictions and import permits approved by the Bureau of Alcohol, Tobacco and Firearms (ATF). Applications to import may only be made by or through a licensed importer, dealer, or manufacturer. No import permit is required when it can be demonstrated that the firearm or ammunition were previously taken out of the United States by the same person who is returning with them.

Fish, Wildlife, Hunting Trophies: Fish and wildlife are subject to certain import and export restrictions, prohibitions, permits or certificates, and quarantine requirements. These requirements pertain to: 1. Wild birds, mammals including marine mammals, reptiles, crustaceans, fish, mollusks, and invertebrates. 2. Any part or product, such as skins, feathers, eggs. 3. Products and articles manufactured from wildlife and fish.

Hunting Trophies: If you plan to import a hunting trophy or game, check with the Fish and Wildlife Service first.

Food Products: Bakery items and all cured cheeses are admissible.

Fruits and Vegetables: Most fruits and vegetables are either prohibited from entering the country or require an import permit. Most canned or processed items are admissible.

Meats, Livestock, Poultry: Meats, livestock, poultry, and their by-products are either prohibited or restricted from entering the United States, depending on the animal disease condition in the country of origin. Canned meat is permitted if the inspector can determine that it is commercially canned, cooked in the container, hermetically sealed, and can be kept without refrigeration.

Plants: Plants, cuttings, seeds, unprocessed plant products, and certain endangered species either require an import permit or are prohibited from entering the United States.

Gold: Gold coins, medals, and bullion, formerly prohibited, may be brought into the United States. Gold items originating in or brought from Cuba, Iran, Iraq, Libya and North Korea are prohibited entry.

Medicine/Narcotics: Narcotics and dangerous drugs, including anabolic steroids, are prohibited: A traveler requiring medicines containing habit-forming drugs or narcotics (e.g., cough medicines, diuretics, heart medications, tranquilizers, sleeping pills, antidepressants, stimulants, etc. 1. Have all drugs, medicinal and similar products properly identified; 2. Carry only such quantity as might normally be carried by an individual having that health problem. 3. Have a prescription or written statement from your physician that the medications are being used under a doctor's direction and that they are necessary for your physical well-being while traveling.

Merchandise from Embargoed Countries: The importation of goods from the following countries is generally prohibited under regulations administered by the Office of Foreign Assets Control: Cuba, Iran, Iraq, Libya and North Korea.

Money and Other Monetary Instruments: There is no limit or restriction on the total amount of monetary instruments that may be brought into or taken out of the United States, nor is it illegal to do so. However, if you transport or cause to be transported, including by mail or other means, more than $10,000.00 in monetary instruments on any occasion into or out of the United States, or if you receive more than that amount, you must file a report, Customs Form 4790, with U.S.

Customs (Currency & Foreign Transactions Reporting Act, 31 U.S. C. 1101, et seq). Failure to comply can result in civil, criminal and/or forfeiture penalties.

Pets: There are controls, restrictions, and prohibitions on the entry of animals, birds, turtles, wildlife, and endangered species. 1. **Cats** must be free of evidence of diseases communicable to man when examined at the port of entry. 2. **Dogs** must be free of evidence of diseases communicable to man. Dogs older than three months must be vaccinated against rabies at least 30 days prior to arrival, and a valid rabies vaccination certificate must accompany the animal. 3. **Personally-owned pet birds** may be entered (limit of two if of the psittacine family), but APHIS and Public Health Service requirements must be met, including quarantine at an APHIS facility at specified locations at the owner's expense. Advance reservations are required. **Non-human primates** such as monkeys, apes and similar animals may not be imported.

Textiles: Textiles and clothing that accompany you and that you have acquired abroad for personal use or as gifts are generally not subjected to restrictions on the amount. However, unaccompanied textiles and clothing may be subject to certain quantity restrictions, called quotas.

CUSTOMS POINTERS

Traveling Back and Forth Across Borders. If your travel plans include trips back and forth across the Canadian or Mexican border, don't risk losing your Customs exemption because of the 48-hour rule. If you make a swing-back inquire at the nearest Customs office about these requirements.

Military Space-A Air Opportunities Around the World

This companion book to *Military Space-A Air Basic Training* is designed to help you plan your space-a trip, with contact information for passenger terminals, routes & schedules, and more!

APPENDIX U: Air Mobility Command (AMC) In-Flight Food Service

No matter where you travel throughout the Air Mobility Command (AMC), you will find totally different, greatly improved flight meals. Flight menus have traditionally lacked variety, quality and overall customer appeal. An exciting new in-flight food services program has been developed by the AMC Food Services Branch. The program was established to improve the quality, nutritional content, packaging and presentation of flight meals within AMC.

Improvements to the food service program include the addition of "Healthy Heart" and breakfast menus, the exclusive use of deli meats, fresh fruits and vegetables, pasta salads, fruit cups, two-percent milk, cholesterol-free snacks, and whole wheat bread. "Junk food" items high in fats and sodium, such as candies and cream-filled pastries, are no longer served.

This food service and the in-flight kitchens that produce it are positioned throughout the world. All passengers ordering in-flight meals, even from Space-A terminals in exotic locales, will experience the same high-quality and nutritious food AMC now provides.

Following are some sample menus available on AMC flights. In-flight menu prices are established at the beginning of each fiscal year (1 October) and may vary at different locations.

SANDWICH MEALS $3.00

When selecting your sandwich, please indicate the supplement packages you would like to compliment your meal. Diet soft drinks may be substituted upon request. Menus subject to change due to non-availability.

SANDWICH MENUS
1. Turkey and American Cheese Hoagie
2. Turkey, Ham and Swiss Cheese Hoagie
3. Ham, Roast Beef Hoagie
4. Ham, American Cheese Hoagie
5. Roast Beef, Swiss on Whole Wheat
6. Ham, Corned Beef and American Cheese on Whole Wheat
7. Ham and Swiss Cheese on Rye
8. Turkey, Ham and American Cheese on Whole Wheat
9. Ham and Provolone Cheese on Whole Wheat
10. Corned Beef and Swiss Cheese on Rye
11. Turkey on Whole Wheat*
12. Peanut Butter and Jelly on Whole Wheat*
13. Ham, Roast Beef and American Cheese Kaiser
14. Turkey and Swiss Cheese on Whole Wheat
15. Fried Chicken with Dinner Roll
16. Baked Chicken with Dinner Roll*

*HEALTHY HEART MENUS

STANDARD SUPPLEMENT PACKAGE

A. Fruit Cup
Vegetable Tray
Assorted Veg Bread
Assorted Snack Item
Soft Drink and Juice
Condiments, Flight Pack

B. Fresh Fruit
Italian Veg Past Salad
Raisins
Snack Pack Pudding
Lowfat White Milk & Juice
Condiments, Flight Pack

C. Fresh Fruit
Vegetable Tray
Snack Pack Pudding
Raisins
Soft Drink and Juice
Condiments, Flight Pack

D. Fruit Cup
Italian Veg Pasta Salad
Assorted Snack Item
Assorted Veg Bread
Lowfat White Milk & Juice
Condiments, Flight Pack

SNACK MEALS $1.90

SNACK MENUS

A. Fried or Baked Chicken
Vegetable Tray
Fresh Fruit
Dinner Roll with Margarine
Lowfat Milk
Condiments, Flight Pack

B. Ham and Cheese on
Wheat
Fresh Fruit
Vegetable Tray
Danish
Lowfat Milk
Condiments, Flight Pack

C. Turkey, Ham and Swiss
Cheese on Whole Wheat
Fresh Fruit
Vegetable Tray
Soft Drink
Condiments, Flight Pack

D. Corned Beef, Swiss on Rye
Italian Veg Pasta Salad
Fresh Fruit
Lowfat Milk
Condiments, Flight Pack

E. Roast Beef and Provolone
Hoagie
Italian Veg Pasta Salad
Fresh Fruit
Fruit Juice
Condiments, Flight Pack

HEALTHY HEART MENUS

F. Chef Salad
Diet Dressing, Crackers
Fresh Fruit
Skim Milk
Flight Pack

G. Baked Chicken
Fresh Fruit
Vegetable Tray
Raisins
Vegetable Juice
Flight Pack

H. Turkey and Swiss Cheese
on Whole Wheat
Vegetable Tray
Fresh Fruit
Skim Milk
Condiments, Flight Pack

I. Tuna (unprepared)
Salad Dressing
Wheat Bread
Vegetable Tray
Fresh Fruit
Vegetable Juice
Flight Pack

BREAKFAST MENU $1.50

J. Breakfast Cereal
Fresh Fruit
Danish
Lowfat Milk, Fruit Juice
Yogurt
Flight Pack

K. Ham and Swiss Cheese on
Bagel
Fresh Fruit Danish
Fruit Juice
Condiments, Flight Pack

**NOTE: If Healthy Heart Menus are not available, a hot
TV-Dinner with soft drink, juice or milk and snacks is
$3.00.**

**Meals served to Space-A passengers on commercial
contract flights (Patriot Flights) are standard airline
food and are free.**

*Seasoned Space-A travelers plan ahead and shop for
in-flight snacks at the Exchange or Shoppette!*

APPENDIX V: Major Worldwide Space-A Routes

Most of the major worldwide passenger and cargo routes were established during and immediately after World War II. The routes have remained in full time operation utilizing Military Services organic and contractor aircraft since that time. Major air routes are changed or reoriented when the need to support an area with intra-theater airlift changes, i.e. when the U.S. Forces withdrew from South Vietnam. Also the number and frequency of missions flown on these major routes change as the requirements for inter-theater airlift change.

The missions that are flown on these major worldwide routes are on a scheduled and a non-scheduled basis to meet the operational needs of the Military Services and the Unified and Specified commands overseas. These missions are performed by organic units of the Active USAF, USAFRES, USANG and contractors assigned to the Air Force, Air Mobility Command (AMC).

Missions on these major worldwide routes are largely manned by crews and aircraft that are assigned in the CONUS and fly overseas to one or more countries or U.S. possessions and then return to their home station. There are some theater airlift assets which are stationed overseas and fly local theater missions.

We will identify and explain the details about major routing on which Space-A Air Opportunities are available each month of the year. We have divided these routes into regions of the world where these routes exist. Complete details regarding routing/stations, schedules, days en route and equipment are contained in Military Living's *Military Space-A Air Opportunities Around The World*. Also, you may find a graphic presentation of these data and much more in Military Living's *Military Space-A Air Opportunities Air Route Map*.

NORTH ATLANTIC ROUTE

Missions on this route originate at McGuire AFB, NJ (WRI/KWRI), Baltimore/Washington IAP, MD (BWI/KBWI, Norfolk NAS, VA (NGU/KNGU), Charleston IAP\AFB, SC (CHS/KCHS), Jackson IAP/Allen C. Thompson Field, MS (JAN/KJAN) and are routed direct to Keflavik Airport/Naval Base, IS (KEF/BIKF). These flights continue on to the European mainland at Ramstein AB, DE (RMS/ETAR) and Lajes Field AB (Azores), PT (LGS/LPLA). Most of these flights return to their CONUS bases via Keflavik Airport or Lajes Field AB. There are also missions from McGuire AFB to Thule AB (Greenland), DK (THU/BGTL) and return. Most of these routes require 2 to 3 days of flying and en-route time using heavy lift (C-005A/C, KC-10A, C-17A, KC-135A-R, C-141A/B) Air Force and contractor (DC010, B757, L1011, etc) aircraft.

MIDDLE ATLANTIC ROUTE

This is the most densely traveled route in the Air Mobility Command System (AMC). Missions on this route originate at Westover ARB, MA (CEF/KCEF), Stewart IAP/ANGB, NY (SWF/KSWF), McGuire AFB, NJ (WRI/KWRI), Baltimore/Washington IAP, MD (BWI/KBWI), Wright-Patterson AFB, OH (FFO/KFFO), Dover AFB, DE (DOV/KDOV), Charleston AFB/IAP, SC (CHS/KCHS), Wm B. Hartsfield Atlanta IAP, GA (ATL/KATL), and Jackson IAP/Allen C. Thompson Field (Jackson), MS (JAN/KJAN). Most of the originating stations stage through the primary East Coast stations of McGuire AFB, Baltimore/Washington IAP, Andrews AFB, Dover AFB, Norfolk NAS and Charleston AFB/IAP. Staging means that flights which originate at inland and West Coast stations stop for crew rest, cargo and passengers at these primary (staging) East Coast stations for approximately 3 to 15 hours depending upon the mission requirements. These flights continue on to the Primary Middle Atlantic Stations in Europe: Lajes Field AB, PT (LGS/LPLA), RAF Mildenhall, GB (MHZ/EGUN), Rota NS, ES (RTA/LERT), Ramstein AB, DE (RMS/ETAR), and Rhein-Main AB, DE (FRF/EDDF). Many of these flights continue into the Mediterranean area and the Middle East before they turn around and return to CONUS through the Primary European Middle Atlantic Stations and to their assigned (home) stations. These complete missions require two to seven or more days of flying and en-route time, utilizing Air Force and commercial heavy lift aircraft.

SOUTH ATLANTIC ROUTE

Missions on this route originate at many of the same stations as the Middle Atlantic Route. The primary originating stations on the East Coast of CONUS are Dover AFB, DE (DOV/KDOV), McGuire AFB, NJ (WRI/KWRI), Baltimore/Washington IAP, MD (BWI/KBWI), Norfolk NAS, VA (NGU/KNGU), and Charleston AFB/IAP, SC (CHS). One flight originate on the West Coast at Travis AFB, CA (SUU/KSUU). These missions fly through the Primary Middle Atlantic (Staging) Stations to the Primary European Stations (as listed above in the Middle Atlantic Route) before continuing on to their mission stations in the Mediterranean and Middle East. These stations west to east are Lajes Field AB (Azores), PT, (LGS/LPLA), Rota NS, ES (RTA/LERT), Aviano AB, IT (AVB/LIPA), Capodichino Airport (Naples), IT (NAP/LIRN), Sigonella Airport (Sicily), IT (SIZ/LICZ), Cairo IAP, EG, (CAI/HECA), Incirlik Airport (Adana), TR (ADA/LTAG) (turnaround point), Bahrain IAP/NSA, BH (BAH/OBBI) (turnaround point), Kuwait IAP, KW (KWI/OKBK), Prince Sultan AB, SA (EKJ/OEKJ) (turnaround point), (limited entry to SA), OAFB Thumrait, OM (TTH/OOTH), Al Dhafra Airfield, AE (DHF/OMAM) (limited entry), Al Fujayrah IAP, AE (FJR/OMFJ), and Diego Garcia Atoll, GB (NKW/FJDG) (turnaround point, and NO ACCESS

TO SPACE-A PASSENGERS). Most of these flights turn around and return through the Primary Middle Atlantic Stations in Europe and then continue on to the East Coast of CONUS and their home stations. These complete missions require two to nine days or more of flying and en-route time, utilizing Air Force and commercial heavy lift aircraft.

ATLANTIC THEATER ROUTE

The missions in the Atlantic Theater originate at Ramstein AB, DE (RMS/ETAR). These missions are accomplished by theater assigned aircraft and crews. The missions from Ramstein AB fly to the following destinations and return to Ramstein AB: Aviano AB, IT (AVB/LIPA), Capodichino APT (Naples), IT (NAP/LIRN), Olbia Costa Smeralda (Sardinia), IT (OLB/LIEO), Sigonella NAS/APT (Sicily), IT (SIZ/LICZ), GAFB Araxos, GR (GPA/LGRX), RAFB Akrotiri, CY, (AKT/LCRA), Ataturk/Yesilkoy Airport (Istanbul), TR (IST/LTBA), Izmir AS, TR (IGL/LTBL), Incirlik Airport (Adana), TR (ADA/LTAG), (turnaround), Esenboga Airport (Ankara), TR (ESB/LTAC), Souda Bay HAFC (Crete), GR (CHQ/LGSA), Cairo IAP, EG (CAI/HECA), (turnaround) Ben Gurion IAP, IL (TLV/LLBG), (turnaround) Prince Sultan AB, SA (EKJ/OEKJ), (turnaround), King Abdullah AB, JO (AMM/OJAF), (turnaround), Bahrain IAP, BH (BAH/OBBI), (turnaround), OAFB Thumrait, OM (TTH/OOTH), (turnaround), and RAF Mildenhall, GB (MHZ/EGUN) (turnaround). There are numerous missions flown on the routes each month.

ATLANTIC/AFRICA ROUTE

Missions on this route originate at Charleston AFB/IAP, SC (CHS/KCHS). Stations visited from west to east are Dakar Yoff Airport, SE (DKR/GOOY), N'Djamena IAP, TD (NDJ/FTTJ), Yaounde/Nsimalen IAP, CM (NSI/FKYS), Jomo Kenyatta IAP, KE (NBO/HKJK), (turnaround) Waterkloof AB, ZA (LMB/FAWK), Ascension AUX AF, GB (ASI/FHAW), Alexander Hamilton APT (St Croix), VI (STX/TISX) and return to Charleston AFB, SC. These flights turnaround in West Africa and return to CONUS and their home stations. As a footnote to African travel, most stations on this route require that U.S. personnel, including Space-A passengers, notify the Office of the U.S. Defense Attache (ODA) of their arrival and plans for travel in the country.

CARIBBEAN, CENTRAL AND SOUTH AMERICA ROUTES

There are many missions which cover the Caribbean area, Central America area and South America area. However, similar to the European area these three areas are interconnected in terms of missions. Please note that the destinations in South America are south of the equator and thus have reverse seasons from North America.

CARIBBEAN ROUTE

Missions on the Caribbean route originate at the following stations: Minneapolis-St Paul IAP/ARS, MN (MSP/KMSP), Niagara Falls IAP/ARS, NY (IAG/KIAG), General Mitchell IAP/ARS, WI (MKE/FMKE), McGuire AFB, NJ (WRI/KWRI), Peterson AFB, CO (COS/KCOS), Wright-Patterson AFB, OH (FFO/KFFO), Memphis IAP/ANGB, TN (MEM/KMEM), Norfolk NAS, VA (NGU/KNGU), Pope AFB, NC (POB/KPOB), Charleston AFB/IAP, SC (CHS/KCHS), Dyess AFB, TX (DYS/KDYS), Jackson IAP/Allen C. Thompson Field, MS (JAN/KJAN) and Patrick AFB, FL (COF/KCOF). From these originating stations there are missions to: Roosevelt Roads NAS, PR (NRR/TJNR), Alexander Hamilton Airport, VI (STX/TISX), Grantley Adams IAP (Bridgetown), BB (BGI/TBPB), Port-au-Prince IAP, HT (PAP/MTPP), San Isidro AB, DO (SDQ/MDSI), Guantanamo Bay NAS, CU (NBW/MUGM), Norman Manley IAP, JM (KIN/MKPG), V.C. Bird IAP, AG (SJH/TAPA), Piarco APT (Port-of-Spain), TT (POS/TTPP), Ascension Auxiliary AF, GB (ASI/FHAW). Most of the above flights stage through Norfolk NAS, VA and return through Norfolk NAS en route to their originating (home) stations.

CENTRAL AMERICA ROUTE

Missions on the Central America route originate at the following stations: Wright-Patterson AFB, OH (FFO/KFFO), Jackson IAP/Allen C. Thompson Field, MS (JAN/KJAN) and Maxwell AFB, AL (MXF/KMXF). From these originating stations there are missions to: Belize IAP, BZ (BZE/MZBZ), La Aurora APT (Guatemala City), GT (GUA/MGGT), El Salvador IAP, SV (SAL/MSLP), Toncontin IAP, HN (TGU/MHTG), Augusto C Sandino IAP (Managua), NI (MGA/MNMG), and Juan Santamaria IAP (San Jose), CR (SJO/MROC).

SOUTH AMERICA ROUTE

Missions on the South America route originate at the following stations: Wright-Patterson AFB, OH (FFO/KFFO), Memphis IAP/ANGB, TN (MEM/KMEM), Jackson IAP/Allen C. Thompson Field, MS (JAN/KJAN) and March ARB, CA (RIV/KRIV). From these originating stations missions fly to: Simon Bolivar IAP (Carasco), VE (MIQ/SEGU), Johan A Pengel IAP (Paramaribo), SR (PBM/SMJP), El Dorado IAP (Bogota), CO (BOG/SKBO), Mariscal Sucre Apt (Quito), EC (UIO/SEQU), Jorge Chavez IAP (Lima), PE (LIM/SPIM), Arturo Merino Benitez IAP (Santiago), CH (SCL/SCEL), JF Kennedy IAP (La Paz), BO (LPB/SLLP), Viru Viru IAP (Santa Cruz), BO (VIU/SLVR), Silvio Pettirossi IAP (Asuncion), PY (ASU/SGAS) Brasilia Airport, BR (BSB/SBBR), Rio De Janeiro IAP, BR (RIO/SBGL), Carrasco IAP (Montevideo), UY (MVD/SUMU), and Ezeiza IAP (Buenos Aires), AR (BUE/SAEZ). These missions are known as the "Capitol Run" because of the capital cities in South America which they serve.

NORTH PACIFIC ROUTE

Missions on the North Pacific route originate at the following stations: Elmendorf AFB, AK (EDF/PAED). Travis AFB, CA (SUU/KSUU), Los Angeles IAP, CA (LAX/KLAX), March ARB, CA (RIV/KRIV), and Charleston IAP/AFB, SC (CHS/KCHS). From these originating stations missions fly to: McChord AFB, WA (TCM/KTCM), Seattle/Tacoma IAP, WA (SEA/KSEA), Elmendorf AFB, AK (EDF/PAED), Eielson AFB, AK (EIL/PAEI), King Salmon APT, AK (AKN/PAKN), Eareckson AS, AK (SYA/PASY), Yokota AB, JP (OKO/RJTY), Misawa AB, JP (MSJ/RJSM), Iwakuni MCAS, JP (IWA/RJOI), Osan AB, KR (OSN/RKSO), Kadena AB, JP (DNA/RODN), RSAF Paya Lebar (Singapore), SG (QPG/WSAP), Diego Garcia Atoll, GB (NKW/FJDG), Andersen AFB, GU (UAM/PGUA). These missions turnaround at Osan AB, Yokota AB and Kadena AB and return through Alaska to their home stations.

CENTRAL PACIFIC ROUTE

Missions on the Central Pacific route originate at the following stations: McChord AFB, WA (TCM/KTCM), Travis AFB, CA (SUU), March ARB, CA (RIV/KRIV) and Hickam AFB, HI (HIK/PHIK). From these originating stations missions fly to: Hickam AFB, HI (HIK/PHIK), Wake IS AAF, WK (AWK/PWAK), Bucholz AAF/KMR (Kwajalein Atoll), KA (KWA/PKWA), Johnson Atoll, JO (JON/PJON), Andersen AFB, GU (UAM/PGUA), Yokota AB, JP (OKO/RJTY), Kadena AB, JP (DNA/PGUA), Osan AB, KR (OSN/RKSO), RSAF Paya Lebar (Singapore), SG (QPG/WSAP), Diego Garcia Atoll, GB (NKW/FJDG). Most of these missions transient through Hickam AFB, HI and Andersen AFB, GU turnaround at Yokota AB and Osan AB and return through Hickam AFB and Travis AFB en route their home stations. This route is very rich in flights each month of the year. Yokota AB is the business station in the AMC system.

PACIFIC THEATER ROUTE

These missions, like the European Theater Route, originate outside the CONUS in the overseas theater. Missions on the Pacific Theater Route originate at the following station: Yokota AB, JP (OKO/RJTY). From these originating stations missions fly to: Halim Perdanakusum, ID (HLP/WIIH), Fukuoka IAP/Itazuke AB, JP (FUK/RJFF), Misawa AB, JP (MSJ/RJSM), Kadena AB, JP (DNA/RODN), Kunsan AB, KR (KUZ/RKJK), RSAF Paya Lebar (Singapore), SG (SGP/WSAP), Changi IAP (Singapore), SG (SIN/WSSS), Diego Garcia Atoll, GB (NKW/FJDG), Al Fujayrah IAP, AE (FJR/OMFJ), Iwakuni MCAS, JP (IWA/RJOI), Don Muang Airport (Bangkok) TH, (BKK/VTBD), U-Tapao RTN, TH (UTP/VTBU), Andersen AFB, GU (UAM/PGUA), Hickam AFB, HI (HIK/PHIK), Travis AFB, CA (SUU/KSUU), Osan AB, KR (OSN/RKSO), and Kimhae IAP/AB, KR (KHE/RKPK).

SOUTH PACIFIC ROUTE

These missions originate at: McChord AFB, WA (TCM/KTCM)
The missions fly the following routes, over a seven day period
including en-route stops: (first & third Friday): McChord AFB,
WA (TCM/KTCM), Travis AFB, CA (SUU/KSUU), Hickam AFB,
HI (HIK/PHIK), Pago Pago IAP, AS (PPG/NSTU), RAAFB
Richmond, AU (RDM/YSRI), Alice Springs APT, AU
(ASP/YBAS), RAAFB Richmond, AU, Pago Pago IAP, AS,
Hickam AFB, HI,Travis AFB, CA, McChord AFB, WA.
(Sunday, over a seven day period): McChord AFB, WA, Travis
AFB, CA, Hickam AFB, HI, Andersen AFB, GU, RAAFB
Richmond, AU, Andersen AFB, GU, Hickam AFB, HI, McChord
AFB, WA.
(First & third Sunday over an eight day period): McChord AFB,
WA, Travis AFB, CA, Hickam AFB, HI, Andersen AFB, GU,
RAAFB Richmond, AU, Christchurch IAP, NZ, Pago Pago IAP,
AS, Hickam AFB, HI, McChord AFB, WA.

APPENDIX W: Passenger Bill of Rights

The U.S. Air Force, Air Mobility Command (AMC) has recently
(1996-97) developed the Passenger Bill of Rights listed below.
This notice is posted in passenger lounges at AMC installations.

- Courteous Service

- Accurate Information

- Maximum Opportunity to Travel, Compatible with
  Mission Requirements

- Safe Flight

- Clean Comfortable Facilities

- Transportation to and from Aircraft

- Your Baggage - Right Place, On Time, Undamaged

APPENDIX X: State, Possession and Country Abbreviations

State Abbreviations

AK-Alaska
AL-Alabama
AR-Arkansas
AZ-Arizona
CA-California
CO-Colorado
CT-Connecticut
DC-District of Columbia
DE-Delaware
FL-Florida
GA-Georgia
HI-Hawaii
IA-Iowa
ID-Idaho
IL-Illinois
IN-Indiana
KS-Kansas
KY-Kentucky
LA-Louisiana
MA-Massachusetts
MD-Maryland
ME-Maine
MI-Michigan
MN-Minnesota
MO-Missouri
MS-Mississippi

MT-Montana
NE-Nebraska
NC-North Carolina
ND-North Dakota
NH-New Hampshire
NJ-New Jersey
NM-New Mexico
NY-New York
NV-Nevada
OH-Ohio
OK-Oklahoma
OR-Oregon
PA-Pennsylvania
RI-Rhode Island
SC-South Carolina
SD-South Dakota
TN-Tennessee
TX-Texas
UT-Utah
VA-Virginia
VT-Vermont
WA-Washington
WI-Wisconsin
WV-West Virginia
WY-Wyoming

Possession Abbreviations

AS-American Samoa
GU-Guam
JO-Johnston Atoll
KA-Kwajalein Atoll

MW-Midway Island
PR-Puerto Rico
VI-US Virgin Islands
WK-Wake Island

Country Abbreviations

Foreign Country two-letter abbreviations are taken from ISO 3166, prepared by the International Organization for Standardization.

AE-United Arab Emirates
AG-Antigua
AN-Netherlands Antilles
AR-Argentina
AU-Australia
BB-Barbados
BE-Belgium
BH-Bahrain
BM-Bermuda
BO-Bolivia
BR-Brazil
BS-Bahamas
BZ-Belize
CA-Canada
CL-Chile
CM-Cameroon
CO-Columbia
CR-Costa Rica
CU-Cuba
CY-Cyprus
DE-Germany
DJ-Djibouti
DK-Denmark
DO-Dominican Republic
EC-Ecuador
EG-Arab Republic of Egypt
ES-Spain
ET-Ethiopia
FJ-Fiji
FM-Federated States of
Micronesia
FR-France
GB-United Kingdom
GL-Greenland
GR-Greece
GT-Guatemala
GY-Guyana
HK-Hong Kong
HN-Honduras
HR-Croatia
HT-Haiti
ID-Indonesia
IE-Ireland
IL-Israel
IS-Iceland
IT-Italy

JM-Jamaica
JO-Jordan
JP-Japan
KE-Kenya
KR-Republic of Korea
KW-Kuwait
KY-Cayman Islands
LR-Liberia
MH-Marshall Islands
MK-Macedonia
MP-Northern Marianas,
Commonwealth of
MY-Malaysia
NE-Niger
NI-Nicaragua
NL-Netherlands
NO-Norway
NZ-New Zealand
OM-Oman
PA-Republic of Panama
PE-Peru
PH-Republic of the
Philippines
PT-Portugal
PW-Republic of Palau
PY-Paraguay
SA-Saudi Arabia
SD-Sudan
SG-Singapore
SH-Ascension Island
SN-Senegal
SO-Somalia
SR-Suriname
SV-El Salvador
TD-Chad
TH-Thailand
TR-Turkey
TT-Trinidad and Tobago
US-United States
UY-Uruguay
VE-Venezuela
ZA-South Africa
ZR-Democratic Republic
of the Congo

APPENDIX Y: General Abbreviations Used in this Book

AAA-American Automobile Association

AB-Air Base

AFB-Air Force Base

AMC-Air Mobility Command

APOD-Aerial Port of Debarkation

APOE-Aerial Port of Embarkation

APT-Airport

AS-Air Station

BEQ-Bachelor Enlisted Quarters

BOQ-Bachelor Officers' Quarters

BX-Base Exchange

CAT-Category

CONUS-Continental United States

DoD-Department of Defense

DoDD-Department of Defense Directive

DoDDS-Department of Defense Dependent Schools

DoT-Department of Transportation

DV-Distinguished Visitor

EML-Environmental Morale Leave

FAA-Federal Aviation Administration

FEML-Funded Environmental Morale Leave

IAP-International Airport

ICAO-International Civil Aviation Organization

ID-Identification

LI-Location Identifier

LST-Local Standard Time

MAC-Military Airlift Command

MEDEVAC-Medical Evacuation

MWR-Morale, Welfare and Recreation

MCI-Military Customs Inspector

NAF-Naval Air Facility

NAS-Naval Air Station

NB-Naval Base

NCO-Noncommissioned Officer

NOAA-National Oceanic and Atmospheric Administration

OCONUS-Outside Continental United States

PCS-Permanent Change of Station

PHS-Public Health Service

PX-Post Exchange

RAF-Royal Air Force

RAAF-Royal Australian Air Force

ROTC-Reserve Officers' Training Corps

RSAF-Royal Singapore Air Force

SAC-Strategic Air Command

SATO-Scheduled Airline Ticket Offices

SOFA-Status of Forces Agreement

TAD-Temporary Attached Duty

TDY-Temporary Duty

TML-Temporary Military Lodging

USA-United States Army

USAF-United States Air Force

USCG-United States Coast Guard

USMC-United States Marine Corps

USN-United States Navy

USPHS-United States Public Health Service

USPS-United States Postal Service

VIP-Very Important Person

APPENDIX Z: Status of Space-Available Travel for 100 Percent Disabled Veterans and Widow/ers

Statement on Transportation Policy by the Office of the Assistant Deputy Under Secretary of Defense for Logistics regarding space-available travel for 100 Percent Disabled Veterans

The Department of Defense (DoD) greatly values the contributions of every veteran, especially those who have sacrificed their health in the service of their country. However, the primary purpose of the Department of Defense (DoD) space-available travel program is to provide active duty service members a respite from the rigors of military service. This travel privilege is becoming increasingly critical to our active duty personnel, who are experiencing more frequent family separations due to the DoD's high operational tempo. The privilege is extended to retired members at a lower priority, in recognition of the fact that they may still be recalled to active duty, and as a reward for their many years of military service. The underlying criteria for extending the travel privilege to other categories of passengers is their support to the mission being performed by active duty military personnel, and to the enhancement of active duty Service members' quality of life. In either case, veterans who are not on active duty or retired are not authorized space-available travel. The reference to paragraph 8.1 in Air Force Instruction 36-3026 deals with pay entitlements and does not pertain to space-available privileges. Categories of eligible space-available travelers are defined in DoD Regulation 4515.13-R, Air Transportation Eligibility, and contrary to your statement, the space-available privilege has never been specifically extended to 100 percent disabled veterans.

The Department receives numerous requests to extend space-available travel to additional categories of people. The entire space-available program, including seats on aircraft and air terminal functions necessary to support travel, is resource constrained. If the privilege were extended to the over 164,000 totally disabled veterans or other categories of personnel, the increases in numbers of people seeking space-available travel could overtax present resources and diminish the limited benefit currently available to active duty personnel. Already those currently authorized space-available travel are often disillusioned by the contrast between the promise of space-available travel as a benefit of military service, and the reality of the arduous conditions often encountered when they use the system.

Statement on Transportation Policy by the Office of the Assistant Deputy Under Secretary of Defense for Logistics Regarding Space-Available Travel for Widow/ers

Space-available travel is a privilege which accrues to active duty military members as an avenue of respite from the rigors of military duty. Although travel is available to other categories of travelers at a lower priority, the principle objective of the privilege is the morale and welfare of those currently serving on active duty.

The entire space-available program, including both seats on aircraft and air terminal functions necessary to support travel, is resource constrained. Extending space-available travel privileges to the over 314,000 widows of military veterans could overtax present resources and diminish the limited benefit currently available to active duty personnel and their families.

Already, those currently authorized space-available travel are often disillusioned by the contrast between the promise of space-available travel as a benefit of military service and the reality of the arduous conditions often encountered when they use the system. Any increase in the number of eligible people who seek space-available travel would impact the DoD's ability to effectively accomplish airlift mission support activities. To expand this list would not be prudent in today's resource constrained environment, considering the heavy operational demands that are being placed on our air mobility forces.

The DoD receives numerous requests to extend space-available travel to additional categories of people, including Service-connected disabled veterans, Federal civil service employees, and Peace Corps volunteers. In each case, our review of present and future air travel requirements has precluded the Department from expanding the privilege. As a matter of DoD policy, the space-available travel privilege has not been extended to persons or groups beyond those currently authorized. This policy is primarily based on mission requirements and resource constraints.

While the Department recognizes and appreciates the contributions of widows of military veterans, the space-available travel privilege cannot be extended to them for the above reasons. I regret I cannot provide a more positive response to your request.

Visit Military Living online at
www.militaryliving.com

Where the fun begins! Visit www.militaryliving.com to get the latest news on our various travel publications. Our web pages contain numerous links which give the military member and family ideas for travel vacations that are affordable and fun.

Within **www.militaryliving.com** be sure and click on the following buttons:

Military SpaceA Travel - Hops. Here you will find links and forms needed for the Space-A process. Over twenty military air terminals web sites are reachable through this section.

Temporary Military Lodging gives information on our popular world-wide guide to military lodging of all Services. Also, one can make a reservation at Armed Forces Recreation Centers (AFRCs) on our links page.

Military RV/Camping contains information on RV travel and camping and trip reports from readers. Many U.S. military RV/camping parks are included on the links at this part of our web site.

Military Medical Care is a new, popular area that is just getting underway. Learn the latest news on military medicine and get involved in your own healthcare through the various links.

Two areas which are of interest to anyone who has ever served in the Vietnam War are **The Vietnam Connection** and **Vietnam Light**, an in-progress written memoir about Military Living's publisher's life in Vietnam as a military family member and the unusual happenings having a family in a war zone.

The area that gets the most "hits" is **Tootie Talks**, a column written by none other than Miss Tootie Two, a military dependent dog. Here military pets can talk to each other and share travel information on going around the world as a military dependent pet.

To keep up on Military Living's latest publications and what's happening in military recreation around the world, all you have to remember is

www.militaryliving.com

AFTERWORD

CONGRATULATIONS

You have just graduated from Space-A Air Basic Training!

What was "Greek" to many of us is now old hat. You can travel by Space-A with confidence as far as understanding how the system works. Now it is time to move on to our more advanced Space-A air travel publications.

There are many reasons that military and their families love to travel Space-A on U.S. military aircraft, and this seems like a good time to tell you about some of the things that military travelers love about traveling Space-A. It's a fact . . . they simply adore the opportunity to fly free on U.S. military aircraft to points all over the world.

Their love for Space-A travel is not always about money saved . . . even though that is mighty sweet in any language. Our subscribers have told us that they love to travel Space-A because of the camaraderie. Nowhere in the world can you get on an aircraft and immediately have a sense of oneness with the other passengers and crew.

The Germans have a word for it that describes Space-A air travel perfectly. That word is gemütlichkeit which means "comfortableness, friendliness, informality, coziness, good-naturedness, easygoing nature, and pleasant."

More often than not, Space-A passengers will have already bonded with other travelers in the air passenger terminal as they anxiously await those wonderful words that they have been manifested on a departing flight.

If they aren't so lucky and are stuck at the terminal, they like the idea that their newfound friends will get together with them and check out possibilities at other military air terminals if any are within a reasonable driving distance. If it looks good, they think nothing of renting a car or taking a shuttle together to the other air terminal . . . and sometimes back to their original departure point if the expected flights do not work out for the group!

Rank rarely raises its head at times like these. We have had reports of friendship growing out of flying Space-A together between officers and enlisted. We have also heard about "good Samaritans" taking fellow military, especially the younger ones, under their wing and helping them get wherever they needed to go. We have even heard of people sharing rooms when only one was left in a military temporary lodging facility!

Next, they have told us they love the security they feel in flying with the Air Mobility Command or on other military flights. Despite the news you may have heard about tactical aircraft being involved in accidents, the military transport aircraft have an exceptional safety record.

On top of that, the military has checks and balances in place to secure their operations at military air terminals. It is nice flying with someone you know . . . another military member. Passengers don't mind the extra security precautions; they appreciate them.

The opportunity to fly free virtually worldwide attracts many Space-A buffs. We are constantly amused when we talk with our readers about their desires to go to Timbuktu . . . they have an insatiable curiosity for travel. They love the adventure of Space-A travel. We've learned of some travelers taking both winter and spring clothing with them and opting for any flight to serendipity land. Exciting? You bet!

Some find it hard to believe that they cannot fly on AMC all the way around the world. When we explain that Space-A passengers not assigned to Diego Garcia cannot fly to or through that location, they sometimes find this very disappointing. That makes them get their thinking caps out and figure out how they might still accomplish this dream of flying with the military around the world. Some might even have made that dream come true, but no one has sent us a report on it if they did. Roy has researched this matter and told them how they can get Space-A almost anywhere around the world, but they need a civilian flight connecting two points between the middle and far east to make this dream possible.

The crews- Space-A travelers seem to have an immediate love connection with the flight crews from the pilots right down to the loadmasters. And why not? Most are young and are still not jaded after years of service that can give one the attitude "been there . . . done that." Many have a good listening ear when they are not too busy and love to hear their passengers talk about their days in WWII, Korea, Vietnam or Desert Storm.

In all these years, we have never received a single complaint about an AMC or other military aircraft crew member! This is why we try to encourage our Space-A travelers to bend with the wind should everything not go their way.

Where else in the world will anyone give you a free flight? If you cannot be flexible, then our advice is to stay home. An appreciative heart and a big smile plus a little courtesy will benefit you mightily when flying Space-A or, for that matter, in all aspects of life.

The Air Mobility Command has made many changes for the better in the last thirty years. When we first started writing about Space-A air travel, a potential passenger would have to show for each and every flight. There were no advance waiting lists. If you were in the terminal, had placed your name on that day's list and a seat was available, you flew. If not, you packed up and went back home or to your hotel and waited for the next opportunity.

A world of changes have been made over these years to benefit the military Space-A air passenger. These include being able to sign up without being at the terminal by sending a letter, FAX or e-mail. This gives those living far away from the military air passenger terminals a much fairer shake in getting a seat on a military aircraft.

We know that Space-A travelers love the system. We also know that we love the travelers. They are the most optimistic and interesting people in the world. Though Roy and I do not fly Space-A because of a conflict of interest, we travel with you vicariously as you fly off with Uncle Sam.

I do not know of any other opportunity in the world such as the one that military and their families enjoy with military Space-A air travel. On behalf of all of our readers, I'd like to send this valentine to all those who make this bennie possible.

Thank you USAF AMC and aviation units of the Navy, Marine Corps, Army and U.S. Coast Guard! Thank you all for sharing your flights with military personnel, active and retired, Guard and Reserve and even for families being able to travel on flights going to and returning from overseas! You are to be commended for boosting military morale and adding a lot to the equation that each military member must consider when deciding whether or not to stay in the military service of their country.

Congratulations- you are now ready to enjoy one of the military's biggest morale boosters, Space-A travel.

Ann Crawford, Publisher

Space-A Basic Training Notes

....

Space-A Basic Training Notes

••

Space-A Basic Training Notes

....

ORDER COUPON FOR UNITED STATES MILITARY ID CARD HOLDERS

Military Living Publications
P.O. Box 2347, Falls Church, VA 22042-0347
TEL: (703) 237-0203 FAX: (703) 237-2233

Fill in the blanks, and mail or fax to (703)237-2233. Or if you prefer, write or call us. We are sorry, we do not accept orders to overseas addresses which are not U.S. Military Post Offices. If you have a civilian overseas address please contact http://www.amazon.com to order.

R&R Travel News® The worldwide travel newsletter. 6 issues per year. ISSN-0740-5073 1 yr/$18.00 - 2 yrs/$28.00 - 3 yrs/$38.00 - 5 yrs/$57.00 (Shipped by standard rate). A first-class mail subscription sent in a sealed envelope is $6 per year extra to US & APO addresses. QTY_____

Military Space-A Air Basic Training
ISBN-0-914862-89-8   Item # 23   Price $15.75

Military Space-A Air Opportunities Around the World
NOW AVAILABLE! Published March 2000
ISBN-0-914862-87-1   Item # 31   Price $21.25   QTY_____

Temporary Military Lodging Around the World
ISBN-0-914862-72-3   Item # 26   Price $18.75   QTY_____

Military RV, Camping & Outdoor Recreation Around the World
ISBN-0-914862-74X   Item # 27   Price $16.75   QTY_____

U.S. Forces Travel Guide to U.S. Military Installations (New as of 11/99)
ISBN-0-914862-81-2   Item # 30   Price $16.25   QTY_____

U.S Forces Travel Guide to Overseas U.S Military Installations
ISBN-0-914862-43-X   Item # 25   Price $18.25   QTY_____

United States Military Road Atlas
ISBN-0-914862-83-9   Item # 21   Price $20.25   QTY_____

U.S. Military Installation Road Map. (Folded)
ISBN-0-914862-80-4   Item # 14   Price $8.65   QTY_____
(1 unfolded laminated wall map - hard tube) 14z Price $19.95   QTY_____
(2 unfolded laminated wall maps - hard tube) Price $35.40   QTY_____

European U.S. Military Road Atlas Plus Near East Areas
ISBN-0-914862-73-1   Item # 29   Price $24.25   QTY_____

Assignment Washington Military Road Atlas
ISBN-0-914862-68-5   Item # 6   Price $12.25   QTY_____

COLLECTOR'S ITEM! *Desert Shield Commemorative Maps*
(1 folded wall map) ISBN-0-914862-27-8 Price $8.20   QTY_____
(2 unfolded wall maps in hard tube) Item # 15 Price $19.00   QTY_____

Alaska & Washington States - (Folded Map)
ISBN-0-924862-75-8   Item # 28A   Price $8.15   QTY_____

California State Military Road Map - (Folded)
ISBN-0-914862-76-6   Item # 28B   Price $8.15   QTY_____

Florida State & Puerto Rico - (Folded Map)
ISBN-0-914862-77-4   Item # 28C   Price $8.15   QTY_____

Georgia, North & South Carolina States (Folded Map)
ISBN-0-914862-78-2   Item # 28D   Price $8.15   QTY_____

Hawaii State & Guam - (Folded Map)
ISBN-0-914862-79-0   Item # 28E $8.15   QTY_____

Virginia, Maryland & Delaware States and D.C. - (Folded Map)
ISBN-0-914862-80-4   Item # 28F   Price $8.15   QTY_____

(continued on other side)

(continued from other side)

New Jersey & Pennsylvania States and New York City - (Folded Map)
ISBN-0-914862-81.2   Item # 28G   Price $8.15   QTY_____

Texas State Military Road Map - (Folded Map)
ISBN-0-914862-82.0   Item # 28H   Price $8.15   QTY_____

Any Military State Wall Map
(Unfolded Laminated, mix and match)   Price 1@$19.45_____   2@$33.40_____

Virginia Addresses add 4.5% sales tax (Books, Maps, & Atlases only) $_____

ALL ORDERS SHIPPED BY 1ST CLASS MAIL   **TOTAL** $_____ ____
(except the R&R Report $6/yr extra)

(Please supply name and address info below.)

*Above Mail order prices are for non- APO/FPO addresses within the United States.
APO/FPO addresses must add $4.00 per order for insurance and return receipt.
Shipments to Canadian addresses must add an additional $2.50 per item ordered for
additional postage, shipping, insurance and processing. Sorry, no billing.

We're as close as your telephone. Save time by using our Telephone Ordering
Service. Or see our web site **www.militaryliving.com** for ordering info. We assume
no responsibility for the security of credit card numbers sent over the Net.
We recommend you call us at:
703-237-0203 (Voice Mail after hours) or FAX 703-237-2233
and order today! Sorry, no collect calls. Or fill out and mail the order coupon below.
We are sorry, we do not accept orders to overseas addresses which are not U.S.
Military Post Offices. If you have a civilian overseas address please contact
http://www.amazon.com to order.

NAME:_____

STREET:_____

CITY/STATE/ZIP:_____

PHONE:(_____)_____ SIGNATURE:_____

RANK (or rank of sponsor):_____ Branch Of Service:_____
Active Duty:_____Retired:_____Widow/er:_____
100% Disabled Veteran:_____Guard:_____Reservist:_____Other:_____

Visa   MasterCard   AmerExpress   Discover   (circle)

Credit Card #_____

Expiration Date:_____ Signature of Card Holder: _____

Mail check/money order to:

Military Living Publications
P.O. Box 2347
Falls Church, VA 22042-0347

Phone (703) 237-0203
Fax (703) 237-2233

Prices are subject to change.
Please check here if we may ship and bill the difference. _____

Save $$$s by purchasing any of our books, maps, and atlases at your military
Exchange.